Classics and Film
A Reader

Translated and edited by

Stephen Russell

Department of Classics
McMaster University

Copyright © 2013 by Stephen Russell
All rights reserved. This book or any portion thereof may not be reproduced or used in any manner whatsoever without the express written permission of the publisher.

Printed in Canada.

First Printing, 2013

Dept. of Classics
McMaster University
L8S 4M2

Contents

CHAPTER 1
   Hesiod
      Works and Days 1
      The Theogony 5

CHAPTER 2
   Aeschylus
      Prometheus Bound 18

CHAPTER 3
   Apollodorus
      The Story of Jason and Medea 32
   Euripides
      Medea 37

CHAPTER 4
   Sophocles
      Ajax 55

CHAPTER 5
   Tacitus
      The Story of Messalina 74
   Suetonius
      Caligula 80
   Plutarch
      The Demise of Antony and Cleopatra 83
   Tacitus
      Some Stories about Nero 93

CHAPTER 6
   Apollodorus
      The Cursed House of Atreus 103
   Euripides
      Electra 106

Chapter 7
Herodotus
The Battle of Thermopylae 127

Chapter 8
Sophocles
Oedipus the King 134

Chapter 9
Plautus
Pseudolus 156

Chapter 10
Euripides
The Cyclops 191

Chapter 11
Publius Annius Florus
On Spartactus 207

Chapter 12
Apollodorus
Perseus and Bellerophon 209
Hyginus
The Story of Hercules 212
Apollodorus
The Return of Odysseus 215

Chapter 13
Virgil
The Fall of Troy 219

Chapter 1
Hesiod

The Story: Hesiod lived roughly at the same time as Homer and is famous for two poems. I have translated the first part of his *Works and Days* here, which is an instructive poem about the seasons and farming, and its opening sections talk about Prometheus, Pandora, and the five ages of man. *The Theogony* immediately follows and is translated here in its entirety – it tells the story of the origin of the Greek gods.

WORKS AND DAYS

Invocation

O Muses of the sacred spring Pieria who give glory through song, come here and tell of Zeus your father and sing his praise. Through him mortal men are renowned or unknown, sung or unsung alike, just as great Zeus wills. For easily he makes men strong, and easily he makes the strong man low; easily he humbles the proud and raises the obscure, and easily he straightens the crooked and shoots down the proud, Zeus who thunders from above and who lives on high.

O Muses, please attend here with your eyes and ears, and make judgments that just and moral. And as for me, I'd like to tell you a few true things to you, my brother Perses.

Two Kinds of Trouble

So, after all, it looks like there is not just one kind of trouble alone, but all over the earth there are two. As for the one, a man would praise her when he came to understand her; but the other is blameworthy: and they are completely different in nature. For one favours evil war and battle, since she is cruel. No man loves her, but, through the will of the immortal gods, men honour harsh Eris. But the other kind of trouble was born first. She was the daughter of black Night and Cronus' son who sits above and lives in the sky – they set down her in the roots of the earth, and she is far kinder to men. She stirs up even the shiftless to work, for a man grows eager to work when he considers his neighbour, a rich man who hurries to plough and plant and put his house in good order; and neighbour competes with his neighbour as he hurries after wealth. This trouble is good for men. And the potter is angry with the potter, and the craftsman with the craftsman, and the beggar is jealous of the beggar, and the singer of the singer.

Now Perses, set these things in your heart, and don't let that trouble that delights in mischief keep you from work, while you spend all your time listening to the debates in the market and the courthouse. A person should have little concern with arguments and courts if he doesn't have a year's supply of food already stored up, even the grain from Demeter that comes from the ground.

When you have got plenty of that, then once again you can start arguing and fighting over other people's money and goods. But you won't have a second chance with me. No, let's settle our dispute right here with the best kind of judgment – an honest one from Zeus. Our inheritance was all divided up, but then you seized the greater share and carried it off, greatly playing up to those bribe-swallowing lords who love to judge cases like these. Those damn fools! They don't know the half from the whole, nor do they know what great advantage there is in grass and hay.

Why Life is Hard: Prometheus and Pandora

The gods keep the way to make a living hidden from mortal men. Or else you would easily do enough work in a day to supply you for a full year even without working; soon would you put away your plough and rake over the smoke, and all the fields worked by your oxen and sturdy mule would go to ruin. But Zeus in the anger of his heart hid how to make a living from mortal men, because the crafty Prometheus deceived and tricked him; therefore he planned sorrow and trouble for men - he hid fire. But that the noble son of Iapetus stole it again for mankind right from under Zeus' nose, hiding the flame in a hollow fennel-stalk, so that thundering Zeus did not see it. But afterwards Zeus the cloud-gatherer said to Prometheus in anger:

"Son of Iapetus, you are truly clever! No doubt you're glad that you have outwitted me and stolen fire from me. But this will turn out to be a great plague for you yourself and for mankind. I will give men an evil thing in exchange for the stolen fire – an evil that they may love while they embrace their own destruction."

Thus spoke the father of men and gods, and he laughed out loud. And he ordered famous Hephaestus to hurry and mix earth with water and to put a human voice in it, and some strength as well – and to make the shape like that of a sweet and lovely virgin, and a face just like an immortal goddesses. And he ordered Athena to teach her needlework and weaving; and golden Aphrodite to pour grace upon her head and cruel longing and cares that weaken and weary the limbs. And he ordered the guide Hermes, the slayer of Argus, to put a shameless mind and a deceitful nature inside her.

Thus were his orders. And they obeyed the lord Zeus, son of Cronus. Immediately the famous lame god Hephaestus moulded clay in the likeness of a modest virgin, just as the son of Cronus wanted. And the bright-eyed goddess Athena dressed her up and clothed her, and the divine Graces and queenly Persuasion put necklaces of gold on her, and the rich-haired Hours crowned her head with spring flowers. And Pallas Athena completed her form with all manners of finery. And then the messenger guide, the slayer of Argus, placed within her heart lies and crafty words and a deceitful nature, just as loud thundering Zeus wanted. And then the herald of the gods put speech in her, and he called this woman Pandora, because everyone who lived on Olympus each gave a gift – and she would be a real plague for mankind.

But when he had finished the irresistible and hopeless trap, the father Zeus then sent glorious Hermes, Argus-slayer and swift messenger of the gods, to take her to Epimetheus as a present. And Epimetheus didn't recall what Prometheus had said to him, telling him to never accept gifts from Olympian Zeus, but to send them back for fear that they might prove to be something harmful to mortals. But Epimetheus accepted the gift, and afterwards, when the evil thing was already his, he then remembered and thought about what his brother Prometheus had told him.

For before this the human race lived on earth far away and free from pains and hard work and heavy sickness that the Fates bring to men – for in misery men grow old quickly. But the woman Pandora took the great lid off the jar with her hands and she scattered all the miseries that bring sorrow and trouble to men. Only Hope remained there in the unbreakable great jar, stuck under the rim, and did not fly out at the door. For Pandora put the lid back on the jar before it could fly out – and all this happened according to the will of Aegis-holding Zeus who gathers the clouds. But the rest of the things that were in the jar escaped – and those countless plagues and horrors now wander among men, for the earth and the sea are full of evils. Diseases wander about as they please and they come upon men continually day and night, silently bringing trouble to mortals, for wise Zeus took away speech from them. So is there no way to escape the will of Zeus.

Or if you want, I will sum up another tale for you, and say it well and skillfully. And do be sure to put this deep in your heart — that the gods and mortal men sprang from one source and go back a long way together.

The Five Ages of Man

First the immortal gods who live on Olympus made a golden race of mortals who lived in the time of Cronus when he was king in the sky. And this race of mortals lived like gods without sorrow in their hearts, they lived free from work and grief, and miserable old age didn't visit them. But with legs and arms never failing they made merry with feasting and they were beyond the reach of all evils. When they died, it was as though they were overcome with sleep, and they had all good things. For the land bore fruit for them all on its own, and there was plenty of it. They lived in ease and peace on their lands and had many good things — with plenty of flocks, they were loved by the blessed gods.

But after earth had covered this generation, they became holy and pure spirits who live on the earth - they are kind and deliver men from harm; they are the guardians of mortal men, for they roam everywhere over the earth, covered in mist, and they keep watch over justice, repay criminal acts, and the give out wealth, for this is the royal honour they have received.

Then those gods who live on Olympus made a second generation that was a silver race and less noble than the first. It wasn't like the golden race either in body or in spirit. A child would be brought up at his good mother's side for a hundred years, an utter simpleton, playing childishly in his own home. But when they were full-grown and finally came to full age, they didn't live very long, and it was very painful at that, because of their foolishness. For they could not keep from harming and hurting each other, and they wouldn't serve the immortals, nor would they make sacrifices on the holy altars of the blessed gods as men should do wherever they live. Then Zeus the son of Cronus was angry and did away with them, because they would not give honour to the blessed gods who live on Olympus.

But when earth had covered over this second generation as well – they are called blessed spirits of the underworld by men, and, although they second to the first in status, they still have honour – Zeus the father made a third generation of mortal men, a bronze race this time, sprung up from ash-trees, the tree from which we make spears. And this race was in no way equal to the silver age, but was terrible, heavy, and strong. All they loved were war and violence. They ate no bread, and so didn't till the soil. They had hard hearts and untamable spirits – they were frightful men. Their strength was great, and indomitable arms grew from their shoulders on their strong limbs. Their armour was made of bronze, and their houses were bronze, and their tools were bronze – there was no black iron. These men were finally destroyed by their own hands, and thus they went down to the dark and cold house of Hades, and they left no names behind. As amazing as they were, black Death seized them, and they left the bright light of the sun.

But when the earth had covered this generation also, Zeus the son of Cronus made yet another race, the fourth, to live off the fruitful earth. This race was nobler and more righteous, a god-like and race of heroes who are called demi-gods throughout the boundless earth, the race right before our own. Forbidding war and dreadful battle destroyed them, some in the land of Cadmus at seven-gated Thebes when they fought for the flocks of Oedipus, and some, when it had brought them in ships over the great sea gulf to Troy for the sake of rich-haired Helen – there death's end enshrouded a part of them. But father Zeus the son of Cronus gave a life and an abode apart from men, and he settled them at the ends of earth. And they live, untouched by sorrow, in the islands of the blessed along the shore of deep swirling Ocean, happy heroes for whom the grain-giving earth bears honey-sweet fruit that ripens three times a year. They live far from the immortal gods, and Cronus rules over them; for the father of men and gods released him from his bonds. And he still has among these the honour and glory he deserves.

And again far-seeing Zeus made yet another generation of men, the fifth race of men to live on the bounteous earth. I wish that I had nothing to do with this fifth generation of men, but that either I had died before or been born after it. Because this is a race of iron, and a day doesn't go by that a man doesn't have toil and sorrow, and at night he is worn down by pains - and the gods send us all these pains and sorrows. But there is still some good that is mixed in with their evil, and Zeus will destroy this race of mortal men as well when they come to have grey hair on the temples at their birth. The fathers won't get along with their children, nor will the children get along with their fathers, nor guest with their host, nor friend with friend – nor will brother be dear to brother as they used to be. Men will dishonour their parents when they grow old, and they will curse at them and give them a hard time, unholy monsters who show no fear of the gods, never giving a thought to paying them back for all their parents did to nurture and raise them. Men will start following their own form of justice, and might will be their right, and one man will sack the city of another.

There will be no respect given to the man who keeps his oath or to the just or to the good. But men will instead praise the evil-doer and the actions that he does with violence. Strength will be right and devotion will no longer exist. And the wicked will hurt the worthy man, speaking lies and slander against him, and he will swear an oath on top of those lies. Envy, so foul-mouthed and delighting in evil, with its scowling face, will be everyone's constant companion.

And then Aidos (Shame) and Nemesis, with their sweet forms wrapped in white robes, will leave the wide-pathed earth and abandon mankind to join the company of the immortal gods in Olympus, and bitter sorrows will be left for mortal men, and there will be no help against evil.

Translated from the Greek by Stephen Russell, PhD

THE THEOGONY

Invocation to the Muses (lines 1-115)

With the Heliconian Muses, who hold the great and holy mountain Helicon, let us begin to sing, and let us dance on soft feet about the deep-blue spring and the altar of the almighty son of Cronos.

And, when the Muses have washed their tender skin in Permessus or in the Horse Spring or Olmeius, they make their fair, lovely dances upon the summit of Helicon and move with quick feet. From there they rise up and go abroad by night, covered in a thick mist, and they utter their song with their lovely voice, praising Zeus the aegis-holder, and his lady Hera of Argos, who walks on golden sandals, and the daughter of Zeus, the aegis-holder bright-eyed Athena, and Phoebus Apollo, and Artemis who takes joy in arrows, and Poseidon the earth-holder who shakes the earth, and revered Themis and quick-glancing Aphrodite, and Hebe with the crown of gold, and fair Dione, Leto, Iapetus, and Cronos the crafty planner, Eos and great Helios and glowing Selene, Gaia too, and great Oceanus, and dark Night, and the holy race of all the other immortals that live forever.

And one day they taught Hesiod the glorious song while he was tending his lambs under holy Helicon, and the goddesses first said this word to me – the Muses of Olympus, daughters of Zeus who holds the aegis:

"Shepherds of the wilderness, mere stomachs, shameful creatures, we know how to speak many lies as if they were true; but we also know, when we want, how to speak things that are true."

Thus sang the beautiful-voiced daughters of great Zeus, and they picked out and gave me a stick, a branch of sturdy laurel, a marvelous thing, and they breathed into me a divine voice to celebrate things that are going to be and things that have already happened; and they told me to sing about the race of the blessed gods that live forever, but that I should always sing of them, the Muses, both first and last.

But why all this talk about oak trees or stones?

Come then, let's start with the Muses who brighten the great spirit of their father Zeus in Olympus with their songs, singing what is, what will be, and what has been, blending it all together with their agreeable voice. Their sweet sound flows weariless from their lips, and the thundering halls and house of their father Zeus is filled with joy and laughter at the lily-like voice of the goddesses while it spread abroad, and the peaks of snowy Olympus resound, and the homes of the immortals hear their sweet strain.

And they utter their immortal voice, from the start they celebrate in song the holy race of the gods that Gaia and wide Ouranus bore, and the gods sprung out of these, the givers of good things. Then, second, the goddesses sing about Zeus, the father of gods and men, as they begin and end their song, how much he is the most excellent among the gods and mightiest of all. And then they sing the race of men and the powerful Giants, and the heart of Zeus in Olympus is cheered by these, the Olympian Muses, daughters of Zeus the aegis-holder.

They were born on Pieria when Mnemosyne, who reigns over the hills of Eleuther, joined with their father Zeus, the son of Cronos – they were born to be help in forgetting troubles and sorrow. Nine nights wise Zeus passed with her, entering her holy bed that was far off from the other immortals. But when a year went by and the seasons changed as the moon waned, and many days had passed by, she finally bore nine daughters – all of one mind, whose hearts are filled with song and spirits are free from care – she bore them just a little way from the top peak of snowy Olympus.

There are their bright dancing grounds and beautiful homes, and next to them the Graces and Desire live joyously. Everything is in bloom. And these Muses, uttering through their lips their lovely voice, celebrate the laws and the good ways of the gods, uttering their enchanting voice. Then they went to Olympus, delighting in their sweet voice, with their heavenly song, and the dark earth resounded about them as they chanted, and a lovely sound rose up beneath their feet as they went to their father. And he was ruling in heaven, holding the lightning and flashing thunderbolt in his hand; he overcame his father Cronos by force, and he gave out laws for the gods and he assigned them their rights and privileges.

These things, then, are what the Muses sang who live on Olympus, the nine daughters born from great Zeus:

Clio, Euterpe, Thalia, Melpomene, Terpsichore, Erato, Polyhymnia, Ourania, and Calliope, who is the most important of them all, for she keeps company with the holy earthly princes and kings.

When the daughters of great Zeus honour a prince who comes from the gods, and view his birth, they pour out sweet dew upon his tongue, and from his lips flow gracious words. All the people look toward him while he settles their disagreements with fair judgments: and he speaks true and will soon make a wise end to even great quarrels. Therefore there are princes who are wise in heart, because when the people are being misguided in their assembly, the princes set the matter right again with ease, persuading each side with their gentle words. And when the prince comes to a meeting, they greet him like a god and show him with reverence, and he is the most noticeable among the crowd - such is the holy gift from the Muses to men.

For it is through the Muses and far-shooting Apollo that there are singers and harpers upon the earth; but princes come from Zeus, and happy is the man whom the Muses love – the speech from his mouth flows sweetly. If a man has sorrow and grief in his newly-troubled soul, and if he lives in fear because his heart is distressed, yet when a singer, the servant of the Muses, chants the glorious deeds of men of old or the blessed gods who live on Olympus, at once the man forgets his pains and he doesn't remember his sorrows at all; but the gifts of the goddesses soon turn him away from these troubles.

Farewell, children of Zeus! Grant me a lovely song and allow me to celebrate the holy race of the immortal gods who are eternal, those that were born from Gaia and starry Ouranus, and from gloomy Night, and the ones that the salty Ocean bore. Tell how the first gods and earth came to be, and the rivers, and the endless sea with its wild surge, and the gleaming stars, and the wide heaven above, and the gods who were born from them, givers of good things, and how they divided their wealth, and how they shared their honours among themselves, and also how they first took deep-ridged Olympus. Tell me these things from the start, O you Olympian Muses, and tell me which of them first came to be.

The First Gods (116-136)

At the start there was only Chaos, but next came Gaia, wide-bosomed Earth, the ever-firm foundation of all, those immortals who hold the peaks of snowy Olympus; and Tartarus, dark in the depths of the wide-pathed Earth; and Eros – Love - who is the loveliest of all the immortal gods, who makes the limbs of men go weak and masters their minds and subdues their wills.

From Chaos were born Erebus and black Night; and from Night were born Aether and Day, whom she conceived and bore from her sweet love and intercourse with Erebus.

And Gaia's first child was starry Ouranus, the Heaven, the same size as she was, and made to cover her on every side, and to be an ever-sure place for the blessed gods to live. And she bore the Mountains in their long ranges, the graceful haunts of the goddess-Nymphs who live among the valleys of the hills. She also bore the empty deep Sea with his raging swell, without the sweet union of love. But later she slept with Ouranus and bore Ocean with its deep currents.

And she also bore Coeus, Crius, Hyperion, Iapetus, Theia, Rhea, Themis, Mnemosyne and gold-crowned Phoebe and lovely Tethys.

The Castration of Ouranus (137-187)

After them was born Cronus the crafty deceiver, the youngest and most terrible of her children, and the boy hated his lusty father.

And Gaia also bore the Cyclopes, with their hearts of stone, Brontes, Steropes, and stubborn-hearted Arges, who gave the thunder to Zeus and made the thunderbolt. In every other respect they were like the gods, but one eye alone was placed in the middle of their foreheads. And they were called Cyclopes (Orb-eyed) because they had a single one-orbed eye that was placed in their foreheads. They were immensely strong and mighty, and they knew their craft well.

And there were three other sons born to Gaia and Ouranus, great and hulking creatures that defy description – Cottus, Briareos and Gyes – presumptuous and outrageous children. A hundred arms sprang out from their shoulders – they were grotesque in appearance and not to be approached, for each had fifty heads that grew upon their stumpy necks and the strength of these monsters was irresistible. For of all the children that were born from Gaia and Ouranus, these three were the most terrible, and they were hated by their own father right from the start.

And Ouranus used to stuff all his children back into the hollows of Gaia as soon as each of them was born, and would not allow them to come up into the light – and Ouranus was pleased with this awful act of evil that he was doing. But the vast Gaia groaned within, feeling the pressure of all those inside of her, and she came up with a plan, a really cunning and wicked trick. She made a new mineral – the element of grey flint – and from this flint she created the shape of a huge sickle, and she told her plan to her dear sons. And she spoke, cheering her sons on to action, while she was angered in her dear heart:

"My children, born from your criminal father, listen to me and obey me. We need to punish your despicable father for what he has done to us. After all, he is the one who started all of these shameful acts."

Thus she spoke to her children. But they were all seized by fear, and none of them uttered a word. But great Cronus, who was tricky and whose mind worked in strange ways, took courage and answered his dear mother:

"Mother, I will try to pull off this deed, for I have nothing but hatred for our father – he doesn't even deserve that name. After all, he is the one who started all of these shameful acts."

Thus spoke Cronus, and vast Gaia rejoiced greatly in her heart, and she hid young Cronus in an ambush, and put the jagged sickle in his hands, and went over the whole plot with him.

And then Ouranus came, bringing Night with him and looking for love, and he settled himself on Gaia and spread himself completely upon her.

Then from his place of ambush the son Cronus reached out with his left hand and in his right he took the great long sickle with its jagged teeth, and swiftly chopped off his own father's genitals and he tossed them far behind him. And they didn't fall from his hand without a result, for all the Earth took in all the bloody drops that gushed forth, and as the seasons went by she bore the strong Erinyes (Furies) and the great Giants with their gleaming arms, holding their long spears in their hands, and the tree-nymphs whom they call Meliae all over the boundless Earth.

The Birth of Aphrodite (188-210)

And so soon as he had cut off the genitals with the knife made of flint and tossed them from the land and into the restless sea, they were swept away and floated there a long time. And white foam was spread about from the immortal flesh, and in this foam there grew a maiden. The first place she approached was holy Cythera, and from there she next floated to the island of Cyprus – and when she was there she came to the shore an awesome and lovely goddess, and grass grew up about her beneath her shapely feet.

Both gods and men call her Aphrodite, since she was formed and nourished in foam. She is also called rich-crowned Cytherea because she reached Cythera, and Cyprogenes because she was born on the shore of Cyprus, and Philommedes because she loves the organs involved in sex. And with her came Eros, and beautiful Desire was with her at her birth from the start and also when she went into the assembly of the immortal gods. From the beginning, she has had this honour among both the immortal gods and mortals – she takes care of sweet-talk of virgins, the smiles and deceits of lovers, and all the sweet delights and pleasures of sex and love.

But great Ouranus used to call the sons he produced Titans, which was meant in reproach, for he said that their deed was presumptuous and titanic ("strained") – it was a fearful deed, and he said that they would surely pay a penalty for it later.

The Other Early Gods (211-412)

And Night bore hateful Doom and black Fate and Death, and she bore Sleep and the tribe of Dreams. And again the murky goddess Night, although she slept with no-one, bore Blame and painful Grief, and she bore the Hesperides who guard the rich, golden apples and the fruit-bearing trees beyond glorious Ocean. She also bore the Destinies and ruthless avenging Fates – Clotho, Lachesis, and Atropos – who give men at their birth both evil and good to have, and they pursue the transgressions of both men and gods; and these goddesses never cease from their dreadful anger until they punish the sinner with a severe penalty. And deadly Night also bore Nemesis to afflict mortal men, and after her she bore Deception and Friendship and hateful Old Age and hard-hearted Strife.

But hateful Strife bore painful Toil and Forgetfulness and Famine and tearful Sorrows, Battles and Fights, Murders, Manslaughters, Quarrels, Lying Words, Disputes, Lawlessness and Ruin, all of one nature, and Oath, who most troubles men upon earth when anyone willingly swears a false oath.

And Sea produced Nereus, the eldest of his children, who is true and tells no lies – and men call him the Old Man because he is trusty and gentle and does not forget what is right, but thinks just and kind thoughts. And the Sea mated with Gaia and produced great Thaumas and proud Phorcys, and fair-cheeked Ceto and Eurybia, who has a stubborn heart within her.

And from Nereus and rich-haired Doris, the daughter of Ocean the perfect river, many children were born, all of whom were divinely beautiful: Ploto, Eucrante, Sao, and Amphitrite, and Eudora, and Thetis, Galene and Glauce, Cymothoe, Speo, Thoe and lovely Halie, and Pasithea, and Erato, and rosy-armed Eunice, and gracious Melite, and Eulimene, and Agave, Doto, Proto, Pherusa, and Dynamene, and Nisaea, and Actaea, and Protomedea, Doris, Panopea, and comely Galatea, and lovely Hippothoe, and rosy-armed Hipponoe, and Cymodoce, who with Cymatolege and Amphitrite easily calms the winds and waves upon the misty sea, and Cymo, and Eione, and rich-crowned Alimede, and Glauconome, so fond of laughter, and Pontoporea, Leagore, Euagore, and Laomedeia, and Polynoe, and Autonoe, and Lysianassa, and Euarne, so lovely and with her perfect features, and charming-figured Psamathe and divine Menippe, Neso, Eupompe, Themisto, Pronoe, and Nemertes, who has the nature of her deathless father. These fifty daughters sprang from faultless Nereus, and they were all skilled in their excellent crafts.

And Thaumas married Electra, the daughter of deep-flowing Ocean, and she bore him swift Iris and the long-haired Harpies, Aello ("Storm-swift") and Ocypete ("Swift-flier"), who on their swift wings keep pace with the blasts of the winds and the birds; for as quick as time they dart along on their missions.

And Ceto bore to Phorcys the fair-cheeked Graiae, the sisters who were grey from their birth. And both the immortal gods and the men who walk on the earth call them Graiae – Pemphredo in her robes and saffron-robed Enyo. And she bore the Gorgons who live beyond glorious Ocean on the frontier of Night close to the clear-voiced Hesperides. These Gorgons were Sthenno, Euryale, and Medusa, who suffered a horrible fate: Medusa was mortal, but her two sisters were immortal and did not grow old. The dark-haired one, Poseidon, slept with her in a soft meadow amid spring flowers. And when Perseus cut off her head, there sprang forth great Chrysaor and the horse Pegasus who has this name because he was born near the springs ("pegae") of Ocean; and Chrysaor has his name because he held a golden blade ("aor") in his hands. Now Pegasus flew away and left the earth, the mother of flocks, and came to the immortal gods: and he lives in the house of Zeus and brings the thunder and lightning to wise Zeus.

But Chrysaor was joined in love to Callirhoe, the daughter of glorious Ocean, and produced the three-headed Geryones. Mighty Heracles slew Geryones in sea-encircled Erythea next to his wandering oxen on that day when he drove the broad-faced oxen to holy Tiryns, and had crossed the ford of Ocean and killed Orthus and Eurytion the herdsman in that hazy stead out beyond glorious Ocean.

And in a hollow cave she bore another monster, irresistible, in no way like mortal men or to the immortal gods, the divine and fierce Echidna, who is half a nymph with glancing eyes and fair cheeks, and half again a huge snake, great and awful, with speckled skin, eating raw flesh beneath the secret parts of the holy earth. And there she has a cave deep down under a hollow rock far from the immortal gods and mortal men. There the gods gave her a glorious house to live in: and she keeps guard there in Arima beneath the earth, grim Echidna, a nymph who does not die nor grows old in all her days.

Men say that the terrible Typhaon, outrageous and lawless, was joined in love to this Echidna, the maid with glancing eyes. So she conceived and brought forth fierce offspring; first she bore Orthus, the hound of Geryones. And then again she bore a second, a monster that baffles description and that cannot be overcome – Cerberus, who eats raw flesh, the bronzed-voiced hound of Hades, fifty-headed, relentless and strong. And again she bore a third, the evil-minded Hydra of Lerna, whom the goddess white-armed Hera nourished, since she was angry beyond measure with the mighty Heracles. And Heracles, the son of Zeus, from the house of Amphitryon, together with warlike Iolaus, destroyed this Hydra with the unpitying sword through the plans and strategies of Athena.

She, Echidna, was also the mother of Chimaera, who breathed raging fire, a creature that was fearful, great, swift-footed and strong, who had three heads - a green-eyed lion in the front, a serpent in the rear, and a goat in her middle – and she breathed forth a fearful blast of blazing fire. Pegasus and noble Bellerophon killed this Chimaera.

Echidna mated with Orthus and brought forth the deadly Sphinx, which destroyed the people of Cadmus (in Thebes), and they produced the Nemean lion, which Hera, the good wife of Zeus, brought up and to roam and haunt the hills of Nemea, and to be a plague on men. There the lion preyed upon the tribes of Hera's own people and had power over Tretus of Nemea and Apesas - but the strength of strong Heracles overcame him in the end.

And Ceto was joined in love to Phorcys and bore her youngest, the awful snake who guards the apples all of gold in the secret places of the dark earth at its great bounds, and is the last offspring of Ceto and Phorcys.

And Tethys bore to Ocean circling rivers: Nilus, and Alpheus, and deep-swirling Eridanus, Strymon, and Meander, and the fair stream of Ister, and Phasis, and Rhesus, and the silver Achelous, Nessus, and Rhodius, Haliacmon, and Heptaporus, Granicus, and Aesepus, and holy Simois, and Peneus, and Hermus, and lovely Caicus, and great Sangarius, Ladon, Parthenius, Euenus, Ardescus, and divine Scamander.

Also she brought forth a holy company of daughters who work with the lord Apollo and the Rivers to make boys into men (for Zeus gave them this charge). They were Peitho, and Admete, and Ianthe, and Electra, and Doris, and Prymno, and divinely beautiful Urania, Hippo, Clymene, Rhodea, and Callirrhoe, Zeuxo and Clytie, and Idyia, and Pasithoe, Plexaura, and Galaxaura, and lovely Dione, Melobosis and Thoe and fair Polydora, lovely Cerceis, and soft-eyed Plouto, Perseis, Ianeira, Acaste, Xanthe, the fair Petraea, Menestho, and Europa, Metis, and Eurynome, and saffron-wearing Telesto, Chryseis and Asia and charming Calypso, Eudora, and Tyche, Amphirho, and Ocyrhoe, and Styx who is the most important of them all. These are the oldest daughters that sprang from Ocean and Tethys, but there are many others besides. For there are three thousand neat-ankled daughters of Ocean who are dispersed far and wide, and in every place alike they protect the earth and the deep waters, divine offspring. And there are just as many other rivers, babbling as they flow, who are the sons of Ocean that queenly Tethys bore, but it is hard for a mortal man to tell all their names - but people know the rivers by which they live.

And Theia was mastered by Hyperion in love and bore great Helios (the Sun) and clear Selene (the Moon) and Eos (the Dawn), who shines upon all that are on earth and upon the immortal gods who live in the wide heaven.

And Eurybia, the bright goddess, was joined in love with Crius and bore great Astraeus, and Pallas, and Perses, who was preeminent among all men in wisdom. And Eos bore to Astraeus the mighty winds, bright Zephyrus, and on-rushing Boreas, and Notus, after the goddess mated in love with a god. And after these the earthly-born goddess bore the star Eosphorus (the Dawn-star) and the other gleaming stars that crown the sky.

And Styx, the daughter of Ocean, was joined with Pallas and bore Zelus (Emulation) and beautiful Nike (Victory) in the house. She also brought forth Cratos (Strength) and Bia (Force) – wonderful children. These children have no house apart from Zeus, nor any dwelling nor path except where the god leads them, and they live forever with loud-thundering Zeus. For this was how

Styx, the immortal daughter of Ocean, made her decision on that fateful day when the Olympian Lord of Lightning called all the immortal gods to great Olympus, and said that whoever of the gods would fight with him against the Titans, he would not deprive them of their rights, but each should have the office which they had before among the immortal gods. And he declared that whoever was without office under Cronus before then he would give them rights and honours, as was only just. So immortal Styx was the first to come to Olympus with her children, which was the idea of her dear father. And Zeus honoured her and gave her very great gifts, and he made her what the gods swear their great oaths by, and he decreed that her children would live forever with him. And what he promised to all of them, he absolutely did - but he himself has the power and rules.

And Phoebe came to the desired embrace of Coeus, then the goddess through the love of the god conceived and brought forth dark-gowned Leto, always mild, kind to men and to the immortal gods, mild from the beginning, the most gentle in all Olympus. Also she bore auspicious Asteria, whom Perses once led to his great house to be called his dear wife.

Hecate (413-455)

And Phoebe conceived and bore Hecate whom Zeus, the son of Cronos, honoured above all and gave her splendid gifts – he gave her a share of the earth and the barren sea. She received the honour also in starry heaven, and is highly esteemed by the immortal gods. For even now, whenever any man on earth offers rich sacrifices and prays according to ancestral rites, he calls upon Hecate and he is greatly blessed if the goddess receives his prayers favourably – and riches will come to him, for she has the power to do this.

For as many as were born of Earth and Ocean amongst all these she has her due portion. Neither did the son of Cronus violate her nor did he take away anything from all that she had from the former Titan gods. But she keeps, just as the division was at the first from the beginning, privilege both in the earth, and in the heaven, and in the sea. Also, the goddess receives no less honour because she is an only child, but she receives much more still, for Zeus honours her. She greatly helps and advances whomever she wants; she sits by worshipful kings in judgment, and in the assembly whomever she wants is made important among the people. And when men arm themselves for devastating war, then the goddess is at hand to give victory and grant glory readily to whomever she wishes. She is also good when men contend at the games, for there too the goddess is with them and helps them. And the triumphant victor wins a beautiful prize for his might and strength, and brings glory to his parents. And she is good at standing by horsemen, whomever she favours. And those who work in the dark grey sea pray to Hecate and the Earth-Shaker, and the goddess easily sends a glorious catch their way, or just as easily she takes it away from sight, if she so wishes. She is good, along with Hermes, at increasing the stock in a pen. The droves of cattle and wide herds of goats and flocks of fleecy sheep, if she wants, she increases them from a few, or she makes many become less. Although she is her mother's only child, she is honoured amongst all the immortal gods. And the son of Cronus, Zeus, made her a nurse of the young who from that day on saw with their eyes the light of all-seeing Dawn. So from the beginning she is a nurse of the young, and these are Hecate's honours.

The Birth of the Olympians (456-506)

Later Cronus forced himself upon Rhea and she bore splendid children: Hestia, Demeter, and gold-sandaled Hera, and strong Hades, pitiless in his heart, who lives under the earth, and the loud-crashing Earth-Shaker, Poseidon, and wise Zeus, the father of gods and men, by whose thunder the wide world trembles.

Great Cronus swallowed all of these as each of came forth from the womb to his mother's knees with the intent that no other of the proud sons of Ouranus would hold the title of king among the immortal gods. For he learned from Gaia and starry Ouranus that he was destined to be overthrown by his own son, strong though he was, through the scheming of great Zeus. Well, Cronus wasn't blind – he kept a sharp watch and then swallowed down his children. And Rhea was filled with unbearable grief. When she was about to bear Zeus, the father of gods and men, she asked her own dear parents, Gaia and starry Ouranus, to devise some plan with her so that the birth of her dear child might be concealed, and so that she could make devious Cronus pay the penalty for what he did to his own father and also for the children whom he had swallowed down.

And they readily heard and obeyed their dear daughter, and they told her all that was fated to happen to Cronus the king and his strong-hearted son. So they sent her to Lyctus, to the rich land of Crete, when she was ready to bear great Zeus, the youngest of her children. Vast Gaia received him from Rhea to nourish and to bring up in the wide land of Crete. Gaia carried him swiftly through the black night and first came to Lyctus, and she took him in her arms and hid him in a remote cave beneath the secret places of the holy earth on thick-wooded Mount Aegeum. But then she wrapped up a great stone in clothes intended for newborns and she gave it to Cronus, the mighty ruling son of Ouranus, the earlier king of the gods. Then Cronus took it in his hands and thrust it down into his belly – the poor fool. He had no idea that a stone had replaced his son, and that his son was left behind, unconquered and untroubled as a child, who would soon to overcome him by force and might and drive him from his honours, after which he himself would rule over the immortal gods.

After that, the strength and glorious limbs of the prince increased quickly, and as the years rolled on, great devious Cronus was tricked by the Gaia's clever suggestions, and he vomited up his offspring, defeated by the tricks and power of his own son, and he vomited up first the stone that he had swallowed last. And Zeus took the stone and he set it in the ground at Pytho under the hollows of Parnassus, to be a sign and wonder for mortal men for times to come. And he freed his uncles, the brothers of his father, the Cyclopes, from their deadly bonds – these were the sons of Ouranus whom his father in his foolishness had bound in chains. And they remembered his kindness and were grateful to him, and they gave him thunder and the glowing thunderbolt and lightening: for before that, huge Gaia had kept these hidden. Trusting in these he rules over mortals and immortals.

Prometheus (507-572)

Now Iapetus took as his wife Clymene with her pretty-ankles, the daughter of Ocean, and he brought her to his bed. And she bore him a stout-hearted son, Atlas. She also bore him glorious Menoetius and clever Prometheus, who was full of various tricks, and scatter-brained Epimetheus, who from the start was trouble to all men who eat bread, for he was the one who first took from Zeus the woman, the maiden whom he had formed.

But Menoetius was contemptible and shameful, and so far-seeing Zeus struck him with a thunderbolt and sent him down to Erebus because of his mad presumption and excessive pride. And Atlas, bent over and toiling hard, holds up the wide sky with his untiring head and arms, standing at the ends of the earth before the shrill-voiced Hesperides; for this part that wise Zeus had assigned to him.

And Zeus tied up Prometheus with unbreakable bonds, painful chains, and drove a shaft through his middle, and set a long-winged eagle on him, which that kept eating away at his liver. At night his liver would grow as much again as the long-winged bird devoured during the day before. Heracles, the mighty son of pretty-ankled Alcmene, killed that bird, and he delivered the son of Iapetus from the cruel plague, and released him from his miserable affliction. But this was not done without the will of Olympian Zeus who rules the skies – he allowed this so that the glory of the Theban-born Heracles might become even greater than it had been over the bounteous earth before this.

Thus Zeus valued and honoured his famous son. And this brought an end to the anger felt for Prometheus because Prometheus had tried to match wits with the mighty son of Cronus. This dispute started when the gods and men were in negotiations at Mecone. Prometheus, ever cheerful, cut up a great ox and placed portions before them, trying to trip up the mind of Zeus. For Zeus he laid out flesh and innards that were rich in fat, setting this on the hide of the ox and covered with its belly. But before the others he set out the animals' white bones that he skillfully dressed up and covered with shining fat. Then the father of gods and men said to him:

"Son of Iapetus, most glorious of all lords, how unevenly you have divided the portions!'

Thus Zeus sneered, with his everlasting wisdom, rebuking him. But tricky Prometheus answered him, smiling softly and not forgetting his devious trick:

"Zeus, most glorious and greatest of the eternal gods, take whichever of these portions your heart desires."

So he said, thinking he had tricked the god. But Zeus, whose wisdom is everlasting, perceived the trick, and in his heart he began to plan for trouble against mortals, which was about to be fulfilled. With both hands he took up the gleaming fat and was angry at heart, and rage came to his spirit when he saw the white ox-bones so skillfully laid out. And because of this the tribes of men on earth burn white bones to the immortal gods upon smoking altars. But Zeus who drives the clouds was greatly angered and he said to Prometheus:

"Son of Iapetus, if you're not the cleverest of them all! So, sir, you still haven't forgotten your cunning arts, have you?"

Thus spoke Zeus in anger, whose wisdom is everlasting. And from that time onward he always remembered the trick, and he would not give the power of unwearying fire to the race of mortal men who live on the earth. But the noble son of Iapetus outwitted him and stole the far-seen gleam of unwearying fire in a hollowed out stalk of fennel. And Zeus who thunders on high was angered when he saw the distant gleam of fire among mankind, and rightaway he gave them trouble to pay for the stolen fire.

Pandora (573-617)

The very famous lame god, Hephaestus, out of earth made the likeness of a shy virgin just as Zeus asked him to do. And the bright-eyed goddess Athena dressed her all up with silvery clothes, and with her hands she draped a veil down from her head, which was a wonder to see; and she, Pallas Athena, placed lovely garlands around her head, flowers from new-grown herbs. Also she placed upon her head a crown of gold that the very famous lame god made himself and shaped with his own hands to please his father Zeus. On this crown was an intricate design, which was wonderful to see – for of the many creatures that come from the land and the sea, he put most of them upon it, wonderful things, and it sighed with beauty, and you could almost hear the animals' voices – and great beauty shone out from it.

He made this beautiful evil to balance the good, then he brought her out and led her off to the other gods and men, delighting in the finery that the bright-eyed daughter of a mighty father had given her. And wonder took hold of the immortal gods and mortal men when they saw that she was sheer deception, irresistible to men.

For from her comes the race of women and female species - from her come the deadly race and the tribe of women who live among mortal men to their great misfortune, at home with wealth but not with poverty. It's the same as with bees in their overhanging hives who feed the lazy drones – whose nature is to do mischief. The bees work every day until the sun goes down, busy all day making the white honeycombs, while the drones stay at home, inside the hollowed hives, and stuffing the work of others into their own bellies. That's just how Zeus who thunders on high made women to be an evil for mortal men, with a nature to do evil.

And he gave them a second evil to offset the good they had: whoever avoids marriage and the sorrows that women cause, and will not marry, he reaches deadly old age without any son to support him, and although he has no lack of livelihood while he is alive, when he is dead his relatives divide his possessions among themselves. Then again, as for the man who chooses marriage and takes a good wife that suited to his mind, evil continually contends with good; but if he marries the abusive kind, pain will be in his spirit and in his mind, an incurable evil. Whoever happens to have mischievous children lives always with unending grief in his spirit and heart; and this evil cannot be healed.

It is not possible to deceive or go beyond the will of Zeus; for not even the son of Iapetus, kindly Prometheus, escaped his heavy anger. He knows many things and is clever, but Zeus out of necessity confined him with unbreakable bonds.

The Titanomachy – Clash of the Titans (618-725)

But when their father Ouranus first became angry in his heart with Obriareus and his brothers Cottus and Gyes, he bound them up in cruel bonds, because he was jealous of their arrogant maleness and their good-looks and great size. And he made them live beneath the wide-pathed earth, where they were afflicted, being sent to live under the ground, at the great borders and the ends of the earth, suffering in bitter anguish for a long time and with great grief in their hearts.

But the son of Cronus and the other immortal gods whom rich-haired Rhea bore from her union with Cronus, brought them up again to the light at the advice of Gaia. For she herself recounted all things fully to the gods – how they would gain victory and a glorious honour with these gods. For the Titan gods and as many as sprang from Cronus had long been fighting against one another in a bitter war that was filled with heart-grieving toil – the proud Titans fought from lofty Othyrs, and from Olympus fought the gods, the givers of good, whom rich-haired Rhea bore in union with Cronos. So they battled one another with bitter anger continually for ten full years, with never a truce, and the hard strife had no close or end for either side, and the result of the war hung evenly balanced. But when the Zeus had provided those three [Obriareus and his brothers Cottus and Gyes] with all they needed of nectar and ambrosia, food that the gods themselves eat, and when their proud spirit revived within them all after they had fed on nectar and delicious ambrosia, then the father of men and gods addressed them:

"Hear me, glorious children of Gaia and Ouranus, so that I may say what my heart within me tells me. For a long time now the Titan gods and we who are born from Cronus have fought one another every day to gain victory and gain dominance over the other. But I ask you to show your great might and invincible strength, and face the Titans in bitter conflict. Remember our friendly kindness to you, and from what sufferings you are brought back to the light above, from your cruel bondage and that dungeon under misty gloom – through my will and contrivance."

Thus spoke Zeus, and blameless Cottus answered him again: "Divine one, you speak that which we know well. We already know that your wisdom and thoughts and understanding are supreme, and that you became a defender of the immortal ones from the cold light of war. And through your contrivance we have come back again from the murky gloom and from our merciless bonds, and from the suffering that we didn't look for, O lord, son of Cronus. And so now with our minds fixed and bent on preserving your power we will aid your rule in this horrible conflict and will fight against the Titans in the crushing battle."

Thus Cottus spoke: and the gods, givers of good things, applauded when they heard his words, and their spirit longed for war even more than before, and all of them, both male and female, joined in hated battle that day: the Titan gods, and all that were born from Cronus, together with those dreaded, mighty ones of overwhelming strength whom Zeus brought up to the light from Erebus beneath the earth. A hundred arms sprang from the shoulders of all three of them alike, and each had fifty heads growing upon his shoulders and stumpy neck. They stood against the Titans in the line of battle, holding huge rocks in their strong hands. And on the other side the Titans strengthened their ranks expectantly, and both sides at once showed the work of their hands and their might. The boundless sea shrieked and roared terrible, and the earth crashed loudly. The vast sky groaned and trembled, and lofty Olympus shook from its very foundation under the onslaught of these immortal gods. And a heavy quaking reached dark Tartarus, and the deep sound of their feet in the fearful onset and of their hard missiles. So then they launched their harmful shafts upon one another, and the cries of both armies reached to the starry heavens, and they met together with a great battle-cry.

Then Zeus no longer held back his might and strength. His heart was filled with fury and he showed forth all his power. From the sky and from Olympus he came right-away, hurling his lightning – the bolts flew thick and fast from his strong hand, thunder and lightning were everywhere, whirling an awesome flame. The life-giving earth crashed around everywhere in burning, and the immense forests crackled loudly with fire. The whole lands were seething, as were the streams of Ocean and the barren sea. The blast of heat surrounded the earthborn Titans, and the flame rose as far as the bright upper airs. The flashing rays of the thunderbolts and lightning blinded the eyes of the Titans even though they were strong. The heat was so astounding that it engulfed Chaos. And the sight of it all and its sound made it seem even as if the earth and the wide heaven above had come together – for such a mighty crash would have arisen if the earth were being hurled to ruin, and if the heaven from on high were crushing the earth: there was so great a crash while the gods were meeting together in battle. And the winds brought with them rumbling earthquakes and dust storms, thunder and lightning and the flashing thunderbolt, which are the weapons of great Zeus – and they carried with them the shouting and the cries of war into both sides of the battle. A horrible uproar of terrible strife arose: mighty deeds were shown and the battle remained undecided.

But the battle eventually turned. Before then, they fought with one another continually in the cruel war. But then Cottus and Briareos and Gyes, hungry as they were for war, made a comeback in the front lines of battle. They launched three hundred rocks from their strong hands, one upon another, and the stones they hurled overshadowed the Titans, and they buried them beneath the wide-pathed earth and bound them in harsh chains when they had defeated them with their strength, and in spite of all their great spirit and daring, as far beneath the earth down to misty Tartarus, which is as fat under the earth as the sky is above.

Tartarus (726-825)

A bronze anvil falling down from heaven nine nights and days would reach the earth on the tenth: and again, a bronze anvil falling from earth nine nights and days would reach Tartarus on the tenth. A fence of bronze runs around it, and Night in a triple line flows all around it, while above grow the roots of the earth and the barren sea.

The Titan gods are hidden there, under a misty gloom, by the will of Zeus who drives the clouds. They are in a soggy place where the ends of the great earth are. And they may not leave; for Poseidon fixed gates of bronze upon it, and a wall runs all around it on every side. There Gyes and Cottus and great-hearted Obriareus live, the trusty guards of Zeus who holds the aegis.

And there, all in their order, are the sources and ends of gloomy earth and misty Tartarus and the barren sea and starry heaven, loathsome and grim, which even the gods hate and abhor. The wide-gaping hole is immense – and if once a man were within the gates, he would not reach the floor until a whole year had reached its end, but cruel wind upon wind would carry him this way and that. And this marvel is terrible even to the immortal gods.

There stands the awful home of black Night wrapped in dark clouds. In front of it the son of Iapetus stands immovably upholding the wide heaven upon his head and untiring hands, where Night and Day draw near and greet one another as they pass the great threshold of bronze - and while the one is about to go down into the house, the other comes out at the door. And the house never holds them both inside together, but one is always out of the house passing over the earth, while the other stays at home and waits until the time for her journeying to arrive; and one of them holds all-seeing light for them on earth, but the other holds in her arms Sleep, who is the brother of Death – this is evil Night, wrapped in her fog and mist.

And there the children of dark Night have their dwellings, Sleep and Death – awful gods. The glowing Sun never looks upon them with his beams, neither as he goes up into heaven, nor as he comes down from the heaven. And one of them – Sleep – roams peacefully over the earth and the sea's broad back and is kind toward men. But the other one – Death – has a heart of iron, and his spirit within him is as pitiless as unfeeling iron: whenever he has seized a man he holds onto him, and he is hateful even to the immortal gods.

There, in front of that, stand the echoing halls of the god of the underworld, strong Hades, and of dreaded Persephone. A frightful and pitiless hound guards the house in front and he has a cruel trick. When someone enters he flatters and fawns them, wagging his tail and dropping both his ears, but this hound doesn't let them go out back again, but keeps watch and devours anyone he catches going out of the gates of strong Hades and dreaded Persephone.

And there lives the goddess who is loathed by the immortal gods, terrible Styx, the oldest daughter of back-flowing Ocean. She lives apart from the gods in her glorious house covered over with great rocks and propped up to heaven all round with silver columns. Rarely does the daughter of Thaumas, swift-footed Iris, come to her with a message over the sea's wide back.

But whenever strife and quarrel arise among the immortal gods, and when any of them who live in the house of Olympus tells a lie, then Zeus sends Iris to bring the great oath of the gods from far away in a golden jug, the famous cold water of Styx that trickles down from a high rock. Far under the wide-pathed earth a branch of Ocean flows through the dark night out of the holy stream, and a tenth part of his water is allotted to her. With nine silver-swirling streams he winds about the earth and the sea's wide back, and then return to Ocean's seawater. But the tenth flows out from a rock, a great trouble to the gods. For whoever of the immortal gods that hold the peaks of snowy Olympus pours a libation of this water of hers and breaks an oath, that god must lie breathless until a full year is completed, and never comes near to taste ambrosia and nectar, but lies spiritless and voiceless on a blanketed bed, and a heavy trance overshadows him.

But when he has spent this long year in his sickness, another and a harder trial follows after the first. For nine years he is cut off from the eternal gods and never joins their councils or their feasts – nine full years. But in the tenth year he comes again to join the assemblies of the immortal gods who live in the house of Olympus. Such an oath, then, did the gods appoint the eternal and primeval water of Styx to be – and it spouts through a rugged and forbidding place.

And there, all in their order, are the sources and ends of the dark earth and misty Tartarus and the barren sea and starry heaven, loathsome and chilly, which even the gods abhor and hate. And there are shining gates and an immoveable bronze threshold that has unending roots and is firmly fixed - it is grown out of itself. And beyond, away from all the gods, live the Titans, beyond gloomy Chaos. But the glorious allies of thundering Zeus have their houses upon the foundations of Ocean – Cottus and Gyes; but Briareos, for all his bravery, the deep-roaring Earth-Shaker Poseidon made his son-in-law, giving him his daughter Cymopoleia to wed.

Typhoeus (826-885)

But when Zeus had driven the Titans from heaven, Gaia who was pregnant by Tartarus thanks to the aid of golden Aphrodite, bore her youngest child Typhoeus, a god whose hands were just like engines of war. Strength was with his hands in all that he did and his feet were strong and untiring. From his shoulders grew a hundred heads of a snake, a frightful dragon, with dark, flickering tongues, and from his eyes in his marvelous heads fire flashed forth, and fire burned from each of his heads as it glared. And there were voices in all of his dreadful heads, which uttered all kinds of unspeakable sounds, for at one time they made sounds that the gods understood, but at another time, the noise of a bull bellowed loudly in proud and ungovernable fury, and at another time, they made the sound of a lion, unrestrained and shameless; and at another, they made sounds like the whelps of puppies, wonderful to hear; and again, at another time, he would hiss, so that the high mountains re-echoed in return.

And truly a thing beyond help would have taken place on that day, and Typhoeus would have come to rule over both mortals and immortals, if the father of men and gods had not been quick to perceive and notice what was happening. But Zeus thundered hard and mightily, and the earth all around and the wide heaven above resounded terribly, as did the sea and Ocean's streams and Tartarus below. Great Olympus trembled beneath the divine feet of the king as he rose and Gaia groaned below.

And through the two of them – Zeus and Typhoeus – heat took hold of the dark-blue sea: through the thunder and lightning and the scorching winds and blazing thunderbolt of Zeus, and through the fire from the monster. The whole earth seethed, along with the sky and the sea. And the long waves raged and pounded along the beaches round and about at the clash of the immortal gods, and there was an endless shaking. Hades trembled where he rules over the dead below, as did the Titans under Tartarus who live there with Cronus, because of the unending clamour and the frightful strife.

So when Zeus reached the peak of his anger, he raised up his might and seized his weapons, the thunder and lightning and bright thunderbolt, then he leaped from Olympus and struck Typhoeus, and burned all the marvelous heads of the monster. But when Zeus defeated him and lashed him with strokes, Typhoeus was then hurled down, an injured wreck, so that the huge earth groaned. And flame shot forth from the thunder-stricken lord spread throughout the dim and rugged valleys of the mountain, when he was struck. A great part of huge earth was scorched by the terrible vapour and melted just as tin melts when it's heated by the skill of men in crucibles – or just as iron, which is the hardest substance of all, which is softened by glowing fire in mountain valleys and melts in the divine earth through the strength and work of Hephaestus. Just so, then, the earth melted in the glow of the blazing fire. And in the bitterness of his anger Zeus cast Typhoeus into wide Tartarus.

And from Typhoeus come boisterous winds that blow damp and cold, except for Notus and Boreas and clear Zephyrus. These winds are god-sent blessings to men and are kind. But the other winds blow fitfully upon the seas. Some rush upon the misty sea and cause great devastation among men due to their evil and raging blasts that go in every direction and vary with the season, scattering ships and destroying sailors. And men who meet these winds on the sea have no help against the damage. Other winds blow over the boundless, flowering earth and ruin the fair fields of men who live below, filling them with dust, cruel uproar, and disaster.

The Rule of Zeus (886-969)

But when the blessed gods had finished their work and settled by force their struggle for honours with the Titans, they pressed far-seeing Olympian Zeus to reign and to rule over them, at Gaia's suggestion. So he divided and dealt out their respective privileges and rights among them.

Zeus, now king of the gods, made Metis his wife first, and she was wisest among gods and mortal men. But when she was about to bring forth the goddess bright-eyed Athena, Zeus craftily deceived her with cunning words and put her in his own belly, as Gaia and starry Ouranus advised. For they told him to do so, so that no other god would hold power over the eternal gods other than Zeus. For they said that very wise children were destined to be born from Metis ("cunning intelligence"). First the maiden bright-eyed Athena, equal to her father in strength and in wise understanding; but afterwards she was going to bear a son of overbearing spirit and an arrogant heart, who would be king of gods and men. But Zeus put Metis into his own belly first, so that the goddess might devise with him both good and evil.

Next Zeus married bright Themis who bore the Horae (Hours), and Eunomia (Order), Dike (Justice), and blooming Eirene (Peace), who take care of the works of mortal men, and the Moirai (Fates), to whom wise Zeus gave the greatest honour: Clotho, and Lachesis, and Atropos, who assign to mortal men the evil and the good that they have.

And Eurynome, the beautiful daughter of Ocean, bore to Zeus the three fair-cheeked Charites (Graces) – Aglaea, and Euphrosyne, and lovely Thaleia – from whose eyes as they glance flows love that melts the limbs with desire, and their glance beneath their brows is beautiful.

Also Zeus came to the bed of all-nourishing Demeter, and she bore white-armed Persephone, whom Hades carried off from her mother; but wise Zeus gave her away to him.

And he loved Mnemosyne with her beautiful hair – and from her the nine gold-crowned Muses were born, who delight in feasts and the pleasures of song.

And Leto was joined in love with Zeus who holds the aegis, and she bore Apollo and Artemis delighting in arrows, children lovelier than all those of Ouranus.

Finally, Zeus made Hera his blossoming wife: and she was joined in love with the king of gods and men, and brought forth Hebe and Ares and Eileithyia.

But from his own head Zeus himself gave birth to bright-eyed Athena, the awful, strife-stirring, battle-leading, untiring queen, who delights in fights and wars and battles. But Hera was furious at her husband and so without making love to Zeus she bore glorious Hephaestus, who is more skilled in crafts than all the other sons of Ouranus.

And from Amphitrite and the loud-roaring Earth-Shaker Poseidon that great, wide-ruling Triton was born – and he owns the depths of the sea, living with his dear mother and the lord his father in their golden house, an awesome god.

Also Aphrodite, with shield-piercing Ares, bore Panic and Fear, awesome gods who drive the closed ranks of men into disorder with numbing war, with the help of Ares, the sacker of towns. And she also bore Harmonia, whom the high-spirited Cadmus made his wife.

And Maia, the daughter of Atlas, bore to Zeus glorious Hermes, the herald of the immortal gods, for she went up into his holy bed.

And Cadmus' daughter Semele was joined with Zeus in love and bore him a splendid son, laughing Dionysus – a mortal woman having an immortal son. But now they both are gods.

And Alcmene was joined in love with Zeus who drives the clouds and she bore mighty Heracles.

And Hephaestus, the famous lame god, married blossoming Aglaia, the youngest of the Graces, and he made her his wife.

And golden-haired Dionysus made blonde-haired Ariadne, the daughter of Minos, his blossoming wife:

The Theogony 17

thion. And to Cephalus she bore a splendid son, strong Phaethon, a man in the image of the gods, whom, when he was a young boy in the tender bloom of his glorious youth and filled with childish thoughts, laughter-loving Aphrodite seized and caught up and made him a keeper of her shrine by night, a divine spirit.

And Jason, the son of Aeson, by the will of the gods led away from Aeetes, the heaven-nurtured king, his daughter Medea. Jason did this after he had finished the many hard labours that the great king, overbearing Pelias, that outrageous and presumptuous doer of violence, put upon him. But when the son of Aeson finished these labours, he came to Iolcus after long drudgery, bringing the dancing-eyed girl with him on his swift ship, and he made her his wife. And she slept with Jason, shepherd of his people, and she bore him a son Medeus, whom the centaur Chiron, the son of Philyra, brought up in the mountains. And the will of great Zeus was fulfilled.

But of the daughters of Nereus, the Old man of the Sea, the fair goddess Psamathe was loved by Aeacus, thanks to golden Aphrodite, and she bore Phocus. And the silver-sandaled goddess Thetis slept with Peleus and brought forth lion-hearted Achilles, the destroyer of men.

And Cythereia, Aphrodite, with her beautiful crown was joined in sweet love with the hero Anchises and she bore Aeneas on the peaks of Ida with its many wooded valleys.

And Circe the daughter of Helios, Hyperion's son, loved unwavering Odysseus and she bore Agrius and Latinus, who were faultless and strong. Also she brought forth Telegonus thanks to golden Aphrodite. And they ruled over the famous Tyrenians, in a very far off part of the holy islands. And the bright goddess Calypso was joined in sweet love to Odysseus, and she bore him Nausithous and Nausinous.

These are the immortal goddesses who slept with mortal men and bore them children who were just like gods.

But now, sweet-voiced Muses of Olympus, daughters of Zeus who holds the aegis, sing of of women...

Translated from the Greek by Stephen Russell, PhD

Chapter 2
Aeschylus
PROMETHEUS BOUND

The Story: The essence of the Prometheus narrative is found in Hesiod's *Theogony* and his *Works and Days*. However, there are two other aspects to this play that are illuminated by brief references to their accepted myths. In the first segment, Hyginus tells the story of how Io was raped by Zeus and then transformed into a cow. In the second, Apollodorus discusses how Prometheus eventually warns both Zeus and Poseidon not to have a child with the sea-nymph Thetis, since her son will be greater than his father. Both excerpts are immediately below, followed by Aeschylus' play.

Hyginus [151]: Jupiter [Zeus] was in love with Io and so he raped her. He transformed her into the shape of a cow to prevent his wife Juno [Hera] from recognizing her. When Juno found out what was going on, she sent Argus, whose entire body was covered with flickering eyes, to keep watch over her. But Mercury [Hermes] was given orders by Jupiter to kill Argus, and he did so. However, Juno drove fear into Io's heart and compelled her, in constant terror, to throw herself into the sea that is now called Ionian. From there Io swam to Scythia, and this is how the area received the name Bosporus ("cow's crossing"). Then she went to Egypt, where she gave birth to Epaphus. When Jupiter found out that Io had endured so many troubles on account of his own behavior, he returned her once again to her proper form, and he made her a goddess among the Egyptians, where she is now known as Isis.

Apollodorus – *The Library* [3.13.5]: Later Peleus married Thetis, a sea-nymph who was the daughter of Nereus. Zeus and Poseidon had been rivals for Thetis' hand in marriage, but when Themis prophesied that the son born to Thetis would be more powerful than his father, they withdrew from her. But some say that when Zeus was set on having intercourse with Thetis, Prometheus declared that the son she would bear from this union would become the new king of heaven, replacing Zeus. Others say that Thetis was unwilling to have intercourse with Zeus because she had been brought up by Hera, and they add that this made Zeus so angry that he decided to marry her to a mortal – Peleus. [The child became Achilles.]

Characters

Might
Force (mute)
Hephaestus
Prometheus

Oceanus
Io, daughter of Inachus
Hermes
Chorus (daughters of Oceanus)

The Scene: A bare crag in the Caucasus Mountains, in the upper part of Scythia.

Enter Might and Force, leading captive Prometheus, and followed by Hephaestus

MIGHT: We have come here to the edge of the earth, desolate Scythia, so that you, Hephaestus, might obey the Father's command and spike this criminal to the high craggy rocks in unbreakable chains. For it was your possession – in fact, your pride – all consuming fire, which he pilfered to give to mortal men. Now he must pay a penalty to the gods, learn to respect the rule of Zeus, and abandon his love of mankind.

HEPHAESTUS: Might and Force, the whims of Zeus could find no more suited enactors than the two of you, but I do not relish the idea of lashing a near relation – a fellow god – to a chill rock on this unforgiving cliff. Even so, I am compelled to find the will, for clearly we ignore at our peril any task given us by father Zeus.

Deep-contemplating son of Themis who gives good counsel – yes, you Prometheus – I wish it no more than you do, yet I am about to nail you up and leave you in this desolate place, so far away from your beloved mankind. Here you will not hear their voices, or see their rude shapes. Instead you will be so scorched by the fire of the sun that your skin will blacken. You'll welcome night with her cool cloak made of stars, but the sun will return each morning, the deep burden of your torture always there to wear you down. For the one who could make it stop has yet to be born.

This is what the love of mankind wins you. For, though a god, you did not properly fear the anger of the gods, and gave mortals honours beyond the bounds of Zeus's law. For that you must stand guard on this miserable rock, bolt upright, never sleeping, never bending your knees, doomed to groan endlessly – but groans will not free you. Zeus, you see, rarely responds to prayers, for every callow ruler is harsh when their rule is still new.

MIGHT: Come now, what are you waiting for? Why waste pity on the god all other gods hate? After all, it was your fire he stole, just to give it away.

HEPHAESTUS: Our kinship still has meaning for me, as does our friendship.

MIGHT: That's all very well, but is it enough to tempt you to turn a deaf ear to the express will of Zeus? Are you really so brave?

HEPHAESTUS: Might, always so pitiless...

MIGHT: Sing no sad songs for this one, it will do neither of you the least bit of good.

HEPHAESTUS: Wretched skill, how I despise you just now.

MIGHT: What for? Your skill isn't to blame for his troubles.

HEPHAESTUS: No, I just wish that this were someone else's task.

MIGHT: Every gift carries its own burden, save that of ruling the gods and heaven. No one is entirely free but Zeus.

HEPHAESTUS: I know – and I know my duty.

MIGHT: Then hurry up and bind the chain around him lest father Zeus see you malingering.

HEPHAESTUS: Give me the chains...

MIGHT: Put them on his wrists, and give them a ringing blow with the hammer. Strike hard and nail him firmly to the stone!

HEPHAESTUS: I'm doing it...

Might: Strike again! Make sure it's tight! Let it echo! He's a clever one, and most likely of all of us to be able to find his way out of a situation as hopeless as this one.

Hephaestus: Look you, his arm is fixed in place and cannot budge.

Might: Nail the other just as securely. He needs to learn that for all his cleverness he is not as wise as Zeus.

Hephaestus: No one but Prometheus himself could justly hold it against me...

Might: Now drive the firm edge of the wedge through his chest with all force.

Hephaestus: Forgive me, Prometheus...

Might: Feeling sorry for him again? Tears for the enemies of Zeus? Take care, lest some day soon you have cause to feel sorry for yourself.

Hephaestus: This is a sight that wounds the eye.

Might: I see only an upstart getting just what he deserves. Come, now, through the bonds about his sides...

Hephaestus: I know! I have no choice but to do this, you needn't keep urging me!

Might: But I will keep on, and prodding you as well! Go low and lash his legs in firmly!

Hephaestus: There. The task is done. His legs are fastened. That didn't take so long, now, did it?

Might: Now spike the chains down with all your skill, for our employer is most exacting...

Hephaestus: Your wit is as subtle as your looks.

Might: Malleability is your nature, so don't mock me for my hard one.

Hephaestus: Let us be gone from here, he is inescapably bound now.

Might: Good. Well, Prometheus, let's see you get up to your impious tricks now. You stole privilege from the gods and gave it to creatures of a day, but can they aid you? Forethought? Clearly the gods erred in naming you that, or you wouldn't be here.

Exit Might, Force, and Hephaestus

Prometheus: Lights of the night, swift-winged winds, spring fed rivers, bright laughing waves – Earth, mother of all – and the all-seeing eye that is the sun: I call upon the whole company to witness what I suffer at the hands of other gods. See the wearisome torture with which I am eroded ten thousand years, this mean-spirited shackle that the latest leader of the blessed ones has devised for me. Why, you ask? I should groan for current sorrows, and for sorrows yet to come, and cry to heaven to know whether there will be a time when Zeus will release me from this suffering.

But I already know, for I have already seen all that will be, and clearly. No affliction held in store for me catches me unforeseen. So all that remains is to bear the fate given me as lightly as I can. For I know better than any other to pit my meager strength against that of Necessity.

I cannot moan about my fate, therefore, yet cannot be silent about it either. I bestowed great privilege on mortal man, found out the secret source of fire, and stored it in a stalk of fennel. Since that time it has precipitated their every artifice and skill, and proved the means to ever accumulating greatness.

That was the offence for which I am chained beneath the open sky.

Ah, what is that sound, what is the scent that approaches? For I no longer see clearly. Is it divine, or mortal, or a mixture of both? Has it come to the end of the earth to witness my misery? What does it want? You find here a god in chains, the enemy of Zeus, hated by all the gods of the new court, because I loved mankind too much.

What is that? Is it the rustle of wings I hear? The air is whispering and for the first time I am uncertain and so afraid!

Enter the Chorus, the winged daughters of Ocean

Chorus: Don't be afraid, we are but friends come to your mountain. It was hard, but we finally persuaded our father to let us visit, for the clangor of the hammer on your bronze shackle rang all the way down to the depths of our cavern and shook us from our shameful reticence. We didn't even bother to put on our sandals, but came straight away on swift wings.

PROMETHEUS: O children of abundant Tethys and of Ocean, who encircles the world with his restless stream, look upon the chains that keep me ever at my unenviable watch.

CHORUS: We look, Prometheus, and a mist of tears fills our eyes to find you wasted away in shameful bonds upon these cliffs. The current masters of Olympus are yet new, as are the laws of Zeus, and His ruling seems arbitrary, for what was great before Him He has Himself brought low.

PROMETHEUS: I wish that He had hidden me beneath the earth, lower than Hades who plays host to the dead. Yes, down as far as endless Tartarus, where no other god nor any living thing could gloat over my misfortune. For as I hang here now, I am the plaything of the winds, for my enemies to laugh at while I suffer.

CHORUS: Who among the gods has so hard a heart as to find amusement in this, excepting perhaps Zeus? He is malevolent and inflexible, and stores up slights. He subdued the children of Ouranus, and will not be satisfied with less than all, lest someone, by some good trick, should take from Him the crown that was so difficult to capture.

PROMETHEUS: In fact there will be a day when He will wish me to inform Him of a plot by which He stands to lose the throne. He will find me as inflexible as Himself, and be able neither to charm me to tell what I know with sweet persuasion, nor beat me down with threats.

CHORUS: Your bold heart resists the punishment inflicted on you, but your tongue is too free. We are agonized by the spectacle of your misfortune, and deeply troubled besides to wonder when you are fated to reach the end of them. For the ways of Zeus are written in stone and cannot be softened by persuasion. These are His ways, for He is the son of Time.

PROMETHEUS: I am well acquainted with both His cruelty and His stubborn 'justice'. All the same, His will – that will not bend – will break against what I know comes. Hard as He is right now, He will come to me meek as a lamb and eager to have me with Him. Oh, one day He will come.

CHORUS: Please, Prometheus, tell us the charges Zeus laid against you. What reason had He to treat you so dishonourably? Please teach us, if it will not add to your suffering.

PROMETHEUS: Speaking of it uncaps a well of bitterness, but even if I keep silent the still waters remain. Either way is misery.

When the gods first began their angry war, and god fought against god, each took a side – some eager to drive old Cronus from His throne, others adamant that Zeus should never be king.

Guided by my foreknowledge, I attempted to counsel those rough Titans, the sons of Ouranus and Gaia, but they would have none of it, for in their pathetic ignorance they thought to win easily by main force. My mother, Themis – sometimes confusingly called Earth, though she has many names – had told me that the fates would not allow the contest to be decided by strength, but rather by cleverness, but when I told the Titans they would not hear it.

After that I thought it best that mother and I both go over to Zeus's side. Nor did He have cause to regret our coming, for it is due to my advice the cavernous gloom of Tartarus now hides old Cronus and all his allies safely from the world.

That was the favour I did tyrant Zeus, and this the way He repays me. It is the disease inherent in the tyrannical nature, that the usurper does not trust his friends.

But you inquire as to the current charge.

Directly He had taken His father's throne, Zeus apportioned privileges and powers to the various gods, but to the children of men He paid no mind, as it was His intention to wipe them out and make a new race in their place.

None opposed the plan but me, and that is how I come to be chained to this rock. I felt more sorrow for men than pity for myself, and now I am become a spectacle that shames His name and status.

CHORUS: Whoever did not sympathize with you must be made of stone, and if we had but known what distressing sight awaited us we should not have come.

PROMETHEUS: Yes, my gifts to humanity have made me an object of pity in the eyes of my friends.

CHORUS: Gifts? Did you give them more than one?

PROMETHEUS: Yes. I relieved them also of the terror of death.

CHORUS: Did you discover a cure for the mortal sickness, then?

PROMETHEUS: No, I merely arranged for hope to live within them, so the fear of death need not be with them all throughout their lives.

CHORUS: That was great kindness to bestow on creatures of a day. So these, then, were the crimes for which Zeus...

PROMETHEUS: ...tortures me, yes.

CHORUS: And is there no set end to your sufferings?

PROMETHEUS: None but the day it suits Him to release me.

CHORUS: But what would compel Him to do so? Do you not see that, having given it all away, there is no hope left for you? It gives us no pleasure to point it out, so let us turn to happier matters and seek some way of extricating you from this situation.

PROMETHEUS: It's easy for someone outside to give advice and reproach, but all that you have said is known to me – I knew exactly where I was bound when I crossed the line, and simply grumble to the open cliffs, this lonely mountain top, to pass the time – out of sight and out of mind.

Therefore, do not prick yourselves on my account. Alight and hear what is fated, see the whole design as I was shown it, and have a foretaste of my Necessary woe. For I precede you on a track we all are on, and the sorrow that lights at one time upon one will later visit the others.

CHORUS: Prometheus, our ears open, and with a light foot we leave the holy path of the birds to set foot on this jagged rock, for we wish to hear the story to the end.

Enter Oceanus, astride a monstrous winged creature

OCEANUS: I have journeyed long to visit you, Prometheus, past all boundaries, carried where my thoughts direct me – for my heart aches for you. Perhaps it is our near relation that causes me such exquisite unease, but, aside from that, there is no other that I esteem above you, and I intend to prove it. Tell me how I may help, and you will find you have no better friend than loyal Ocean.

PROMETHEUS: Who is this I see before me? Have you come to gape, appalled, at my wondrous and undignified display? How is it you are so far inland from the coast in this land of iron, away from the water named for you and your cavern kingdom beneath the waves?

Did you come to feast your eyes on my suffering and sip some sweet pity? Take a good look, I'm quite a sight – this is what becomes of the friends of Zeus, even the one who facilitated His tyranny.

OCEANUS: I see you, Prometheus, and I have some advice that you would do well to take, clever though you are. Know yourself and learn new ways, for He who now rules among the gods is also new. If you will persist in such cutting talk, you may rely that Zeus will soon hear of it, though the throne is far away, for He hears like the young do, too. And the pain you suffer now will be made to seem like child's play.

My poor friend, cease this pointless tirade and look instead for a way out. Perhaps this is old news, but let me remind you that you are already reaping the reward for that sharp tongue of yours, which spoke too plainly and above its station. Yet even now you are not humbled! But if you would just learn from me, you wouldn't keep struggling against immovable stone. He is king now, answerable to no one. The order of things has changed and you cannot win.

Now I go to see if I can do anything to gain your release. Do try to hold your tongue while I am gone. For all your wisdom, don't you see that it can only bring you pain?

Prometheus: I envy you that stand so clear of blame, who dared everything that I did. Just let it be, and don't worry about me. Try as you may you won't persuade Him, and you may incur His wrath for having come here.

Oceanus: You always were infallible in your advice to others, but absolutely hopeless when it comes to knowing your own best interest. Don't forbid me to see Him on your behalf, for I am confident He will grant me this favour and free you from these chains.

Prometheus: I do thank you, my friend, for your loyalty and industry, but all is as it must be. Steer clear of harm, as I have no desire to burden you with a share of my misfortune. For I now know what it is to be like brother Atlas, who stands in the west supporting heaven and earth upon his shoulders. I feel, too, how fierce Typhon feels. Do you know, I saw him, and actually pitied that hundred-headed dweller of the Cilician caves? He, too, stood opposed to all the gods, hissing fiercely as his eyes shone forth his intention to topple the regime of Zeus. Now he lies helpless, hard by the narrows, mangled beneath the full weight of Mount Aetna. High above him on the peak, where Hephaestus works his molten ore, a river of fire will one day erupt and consume the level fields of Sicily and all their produce – the boiling anger of Typhon spit out, a fiery, unapproachable torrent, though Zeus' lightning made of him mere ashes.

But you know all of this, you don't need me to tutor you. Look to your own interest as best you know how, for I intend to drain this cup myself.

Oceanus: Don't you know, brother, that a few well-chosen words can soften a hard heart?

Prometheus: Yes, and the wrong ones can make it harder. Leave it alone.

Oceanus: I am trying to help you! What is the worst that could happen – or do your far-seeing eyes spy disaster for me if I make the attempt?

Prometheus: I see only a simple nature wasted on a futile effort.

Oceanus: Simple nature? I won't bristle at that, since it is an advantage to the wise to be thought foolish.

Prometheus: I tell you, anything you might do can only make my situation worse.

Oceanus: ...It seems your words speed me homeward again.

Prometheus: Yes, Oceanus, for the most you could hope to gain by defending me is the enmity of the Omnipotent, and in that regard you would do well to be cautious.

Oceanus: Your plight illustrates that lesson rather vividly.

Prometheus: Then off you go, and see that you remember what you have learned from my example.

Oceanus: You needn't keep telling me to leave... Anyway, you see how my friend here fans the wind-road with his wings, for he is impatient for his own stall, longing to be at home...

Exit Oceanus

Chorus:

We weep, Prometheus, to see you in this pitiable condition, our red eyes welling up ceaselessly and washing our cheeks in frustration at this act of tyranny: Zeus, exerting His cruel will, enforcing His self-made laws, showing His arrogance and conceit toward the former gods.

The wide earth laments your fall and the subjugation of your generation. All the mortals in holy Asia share your hopeless sorrow: those who live in the land of Colchis, women fearless in battle; the enemy in Scythia, up north on the banks of Lake Maeotis, the edge of the world; the flower of Arabia's men in arms; and those who guard the craggy fortress of the Caucasian mountains, frightening fighters, crying for battle, holding forth their sharpened spears – they all mourn for you.

Before this we had seen but one god tortured, in unbreakable bonds: Titan Atlas, whose might exceeded all, and who now bends his back and groans to support the earth and heaven.

The very waves of the sea sob as they crest and fall; the Deep cries out, lamenting you; Dark Hades, the black abyss rumbles in misery below; and the sacred flowing rivers all mutter ceaselessly their pity for you.

Prometheus: Do not think that I am silent out of pride. I admit to disappointment, despite myself, at being thus misused, for was I not the one who elevated these new gods and gave them their privileges and honours – facilitated what had to be?

But what use is there in telling you what you already know? Hear instead about the miserable condition of mankind when I found them mindless, and how I gave them reason. I do not tell you this to reproach humanity in any way, but to show you why I did what I did.

They had eyes, but could not see. They had ears, but could not hear. They were like shapes that lived within a dream, dragging themselves purposelessly through their short existences. They did not know how to make brick houses to face the warm day, nor how to build with wood, but lived beneath the earth like swarming ants, in sunless caves. They did not recognize the signs of approaching winter – no, nor planting spring or fruitful summer – on which they could depend, but were always taken by surprise, until with my gift I taught them to count the calendar of the stars. Yes, Numbers as well, the lever of all sciences, and Letters, the mother of the Muses' art, creator of History. Thanks to me they harnessed beasts and make them submit to collar, pack-saddle and plough, so they might substitute for man in hardest toil, and also pull the carriage. And, then came the carriages that wander on the sea...

These are the clever things for which mankind can thank me, and yet, wisdom will not spare me this affliction.

Chorus: Grief and humiliation have muddled your mind, Prometheus, leaving you a physician who cannot heal himself.

Prometheus: Medicine: that's another one of mine. Formerly when mankind became sick, they must get better on their own or simply waste away, until my gift allowed them to mix remedies to ward off sickness and disorder, and have a longer life. Now they even seek to model me and see the future, striving to judge which of their dreams are most likely to become true, reading significance in ominous sounds that formerly baffled interpretation and strange encounters along the road. In the flights of taloned birds, and in the entrails of those animals that crawl, they see omens, and by these strive to please the gods.

So, yes, you could say it was I who set mankind on the shadowy road of prophecy, making flaming signs that had before been invisible. But who among the gods has a better claim to having introduced them to hidden blessings beneath the earth – bronze, silver, iron, and gold? No one, if he is honest.

In short, every art of mankind comes via Prometheus.

Chorus: How can you aid men beyond all measure, and yet be so careless of your own misfortune? If you were but free of these chains you would be the equal of Zeus.

Prometheus: The Future, ever perfecting, says it is my place to be chained to this rock, pricked by ten thousand pangs before release. As ever, all of my art – my so-called 'trickiness' – is in service to Necessity, against which I do not struggle. Indeed, the opposite.

Chorus: But who determines necessity?

Prometheus: The tripled Fates and tripled Furies, who in concert see all, judge all, and leave no loopholes.

Chorus: Is even Zeus subject to their dictates, then?

Prometheus: Even He cannot slip Fate.

Chorus: But what is fated for Zeus other than eternal rule?

Prometheus: You cannot know that yet, so please don't ask me.

Chorus: Is it some deep secret you must keep hidden?

Prometheus: It is merely the wrong time. By my silence I'll set myself free.

Chorus:

May Zeus, who runs the universe, never use His power to victimize us. May we never be tardy with the holy sacrifice of oxen by our father Oceanus's shore, nor ever offend by our speech: may we keep these rules in mind, and never grow forgetful.

It is a sweet thing to live an endless, cheerful life – to feed an immortal heart with festivity and pleasantry – but a shiver of some foreboding grips us when we see you lashed up there because you did not tremble at the name of Zeus. Your mind was your own, and following a path only you could see you sacrificed yourself – for creatures of a day, Prometheus. A favour that cannot be returned! Tell us, friend, what good is that? What aid can mayflies offer to one eternal? With all the keenness of your vision how is it you do not see their impossible frailty, no more substantial than a dream – a few short breaths and gone. Prisoners of Time, helpless and blind, the plans of mortal men will never supersede the laws of endless Zeus.

This is what we see when we look on your pained face, Prometheus, and a song rises to our lips, so very different from the one we sang you and our sister Hesione to your bridal bed and bath.

Enter horned Io, driven to madness and intermittently lowing (i.e. mooing) like a cow

Io: What land is this? What people are these? Who is it that I see bound upon that rocky crag? What crime has he committed? Oh, tell me to what part of the world my wanderings have finally brought me. O, Io, Io, so low, low...

There it is again, the gadfly, stinging! Keep it away from me, keep it away! I see him everywhere – Argus the herdsman, with his ten thousand eyes! Dead now, but even so he watches me from the depths of the underworld, driving me, famished, from place to place. His shepherd's pipe hums incessantly in my ear, how it drones and drones, low, low...

And where has my wandering course brought me now? O son of Cronus, O Zeus, what fault did you find in me that compelled you to fit me with this yoke of misery? Why torture me with madness, why drive a poor girl to frenzy?

Devour me with flames, bury me in the earth, feed me to the monsters of the deep – but don't ignore my prayer, O Zeus! I have had enough exercise, for pity's sake just let me rest.

Prometheus: Surely this is the daughter of Inachus I hear, whose beauty was so great that even Zeus was smitten. Hera has driven you a long way from home.

Io: How is it you know my father? Who are you that you can call this poor creature by her right name and know of the disease that the gods sent me, that plagues and stings me, pricking me with its goad so that I am always moving, frenzied and hungry and so terribly low, low... Who has ever suffered as I do, the victim of a jealous god?

Please tell me what remedy there might be for my sickness, if you know it! Tell me!

Prometheus: I will tell you what you want to know, without riddles, since we are fellows in suffering. You are looking at Prometheus, who gave fire to man.

Io: Poor sad Prometheus! You proved yourself a blessing to all mankind – why are you punished this way?

Prometheus: I prefer not to dwell on it.

Io: Please?

Prometheus: Ask what you will. I will not refuse you.

Io: Who nailed you to this cliff?

Prometheus: Zeus, though Hephaestus swung the hammer.

Io: What was the offence that merited this punishment?

Prometheus: Fire, as I said – nothing more than that.

Io: God of foresight, what do you see in store for me?

Prometheus: It is better not to know the future.

Io: Please don't hide my fate from me...

Prometheus: I am not merely being difficult, here, child...

Io: Then why don't you speak?

Prometheus: ...I simply wish to avoid breaking your spirit.

Io: Please be less kind to me if it will make you more forthcoming.

Prometheus: ...Then, as you are so determined...

Chorus: Prometheus – if we might first ask about her strange affliction?

Prometheus: Io, would you care to indulge these lovely spirits here? After all, they are sisters of Inachus – therefore your aunts – and it is actually worthwhile lamenting one's fate in the hearing of such exalted and sympathetic listeners as these.

Io: None have better reason than I to doubt that one can refuse a god anything He desires, and yet looking at you, shackled to this desolate place, I feel I can trust you. Of course they will hear from me everything it is in my power to tell, yet even as I begin to speak I feel the bitterness well up in me, fed by the storm that was set on me by god, which destroyed my beauty.

Even as a girl I was plagued by visions in the night, haunting my virgin bedroom, whispering, "Lovely child, so greatly blessed, why are you still a virgin when you could be married to the Highest? Zeus is inflamed with passion, eager to join with you in love. Do not refuse the embrace of god: go to the meadows in Lerna, deep within the grass, to the place where your father's cattle graze, so that Zeus' longing might be satisfied."

I was visited by dreams like these night after night, until desperation drove me to tell my father, Inachus. He sent embassies to the oracles at Delphi and Dodona on my behalf, asking if there might be some word or action from him that might be pleasing to the god, but the pronouncements with which they returned were darkly incomprehensible.

But one day an unambiguous utterance finally arrived, instructing my father in no uncertain terms to drive me out of my home and country, to roam the far limits of the world. If he did not obey, Zeus would send down a fiery thunderbolt to wipe out the entire human race.

And so, having no choice, Inachus obeyed the oracle of Loxian Apollo, sending me out and shutting his doors against me even as both of us sobbed uncontrollably – compelled by Zeus' crooked command. Immediately outside the gates my mind and body were changed, distorted. These horns appeared as you can see them, and the gadfly, with its sharp sting that will not let me be, set me running in frenzied leaps beside the Cerchnean River and Lerna's spring, so sweet to drink, but I am never allowed to quench my thirst. For a time the earth-born herdsman Argus, whose anger knows no limits, also followed my tracks with his hundred eyes, until sudden death overtook him. For this I have cause to envy him, for still driven by that heaven-sent scourge, I continue to lurch, harassed, ungainly, from place to place.

That is my story. If you know what the future holds for me, please do not spare me out of pity, for to my thinking there is no greater evil than a lie born of kindness.

Chorus: Oh! We never thought to hear such shameful words! Such unimaginable suffering, so grievous to look at. Oh, terrible Fate, we shudder to contemplate what has befallen Io!

Prometheus: Wait until you know what is still to come for her.

Chorus: Please, tell us how her story ends! For, to the sick unto death, there must be a kind of comfort in knowing exactly what pain awaits.

Prometheus: Hear, then, what this poor child must yet endure at the hands of Hera. Listen close, daughter of Inachus, and lodge my words within your heart so that despite the confusion of the goad you know and will remember the end of your wandering – and your goal.

From this desolate place you will walk toward the rising sun, over fields no plough has ever touched, toward the nomads of Scythia, who dwell in wicker houses perched on wagons. A well-armed people, they have the bow for striking from long distances, and you should give them a wide berth, passing quickly through their country and only letting your feet touch land where the sea, roaring, breaks upon it.

On your left will be the Chalybes, who work with iron – you must beware of them, also, as they are fierce, and strangers do well to avoid them. When you come to the aptly named river Hubris, do not attempt to cross, for it is not a stream that easily allows it, but trace it back to its source in the highest of the Caucasus mountains, whence the river tumbles from its peaks. You cross those peaks, neighbours to the stars, and take the road southward until you reach the land of the Amazons, who hate men. It has not yet occurred to them to go from there and settle in Themiscyra on the banks of the Thermodon, where

Salmydessos, the rocky jawbone of the sea, loves to gulp down sailors, so they will be only too glad to direct you on your way.

Then you come to the isthmus of Cimmeria: steel your soul to cross the channel of Maeotis there and forever after mankind will memorialize you in its name – Bosporus – the cow's-crossing, where you left the mainland of Europa for Asia.

Now, girls, how does Zeus strike you? Was it just that He should try to lie with this defenceless child, who was mortal, and so bring down this wandering curse upon her? Poor Io, what an unsuitable husband you have found. And all that I have just told you is but the beginning...

Io: O, Io, brought so low, low...

Prometheus: More lowing? You must save some tears, child, for when you hear the rest.

Chorus: Is there still more to tell?

Prometheus: Alas, a sea's portion of tears.

Io: What, then, is the good of living? Why should I not hurl myself from this rugged crag and die at once rather than suffer to the end of my days?

Prometheus: I envy you the choice, as there can no end to my immortal suffering until the day Zeus is pulled down from His throne.

Io: What? Will that day come?

Prometheus: You would like to see it?

Io: How could I not, as it is on His account I suffer?

Prometheus: Then you will want to refrain from dashing yourself upon the rocks.

Io: But who will overthrow Him?

Prometheus: He will do it Himself, with His own shortsightedness.

Io: How? Please tell me, if by letting me know it you will not prevent it coming to pass!

Prometheus: Marriage will be His undoing, just as it was for His predecessors.

Io: To goddess or mortal?

Prometheus: That I cannot tell.

Io: But it will be because of this new wife that He forfeits His throne?

Prometheus: Yes, for she will bear a child greater than the Father.

Io: And is it not possible for Him to avoid the fate that is in store for Him?

Prometheus: Only if it were in His nature to release me from these chains.

Io: But who will set you free if Zeus is against it?

Prometheus: One of your descendants, in fact.

Io: A child of mine will one day free you?

Prometheus: Thirteen generations on from you.

Io: That is so many tomorrows that imagination fails me and vision becomes quite dark.

Prometheus: Then perhaps it would be better to forego this business of the one who will end my troubles and return to the tale of your own.

Chorus: Tell her what she needs to know, Prometheus, but please don't deny us the conclusion of your story.

Prometheus: Well, then, since you are so eager to hear it... But first things first, Io: the remainder of your sad travels.

Once you cross the channel that divides Europa from Asia you will turn toward plains burnt and scorched by the sun, and walk the edge of the surging sea until you arrive at Cisthene. The daughters of Phorcys live there – old women, three in number, in the shape of swans, who share one eye in common and a single tooth as well, and only come out in the brief period when moon and sun, in changing places, both vacate the sky.

Nearby these are their winged sisters, who also number three, the Gorgons, who bind up their hair with snakes and hate mortals. In fact, no mortal can look upon them and live, so be careful.

Watch too for the Gryphons, sharp-toothed hounds of Zeus who have no bark, and the Arimaspian Cyclopes, who ride horseback and live beside the golden stream of Plouto. It is best to keep your distance from these.

At last you will come to a distant land and a dark race of men who live near the waters of the sun, where the Aethiops flows. Travel the banks of the river until you reach a waterfall where, from the Bybline Mountains, the Nile pours forth its sweet stream into the three-angled land of the Nile. And there, Io, the Fates have said you will find your home and a place for your descendants.

If any of this confuses, say so and I will phrase it more clearly, for I have more leisure than I want at present.

Chorus: Is that it? Is it our turn now? You promised, remember...

Prometheus: Yes, now she has heard the end of her travels – though not quite the end of her story. But before I tell it, and she leaves us, I would have her know it is not merely a story, and that she does not listen in vain. As proof I now detail your future past, Io, which I foresaw long before you took your first step – but to avoid tedium I begin just prior to your arrival here, with your entry onto the Molossian plains, on the sharp ridge that encircles Dodona, where you found the oracular seat of Thesprotian Zeus, and that marvel beyond belief, the talking oaks. They greeted you clearly, as the inevitable wife of god. Does the sting of that ring true? Then, hurried along by the gadfly, you ran up against the gulf of Rhea, and though driven back along your tracks by a great storm, that inlet will evermore, in memory of you, be called the Ionian Sea. These are proofs that my eyes see a good deal further over the horizon than others' do, in both directions...

And now the conclusion of Io's tale.

A far city called Canopus lies at the end of the Nile. There it is that Zeus will finally restore your senses and reverse your transformation with the long-delayed caress of His hand, on account of which your dark-skinned son will be called Epaphus – "touch-born". And Epaphus will gather the fruit of all the land watered by the Nile.

Five generations on, fifty young women of your blood will return at long last to Argos, not of their own free will, but fleeing impious marriage to their relations. These improper suitors, hearts aflutter with passion, will pursue like hawks that chase the doves, but God, because His law forbids it, will not allow them the enjoyment of their brides. Rather, Pelasgian soil will be their marriage bed, for in the middle of the night each wife will dip her two-edged sword in the blood of her husband. Would that such a love would come to my nemeses...

But one among these girls, charmed by love, will take the other of two evil names and choose to be called coward rather than murderer, and bear a race of kings in Argos. That is a longer story, and it is enough to say that one child of her breed will be a man brave, bold, and daring with the bow. He it is will deliver me from my chains.

This is the prophecy my mother, ancient Themis, gave me.

Io: Oh... I feel it creeping up on me again, the madness that takes away my mind, burning me up, the stings of the gadfly pushing me forward, heart pounding in terror against my ribs, eyeballs beginning to roll wildly in my head. I lose the mastery of my... of my... tongue, words muddling as they clash against the darkness that engulfs me. Am I making sense? I feel so very low... low...

Exit Io, lowing

Chorus:

It was a wise man who said it is the best thing by far to marry according to one's own station. Let none who work with their hands aspire to marry those who are wealthy or above them in birth.

Never, never, never, O majestic Fates, may you ever see us approach the bed of Zeus: may we never have husbands sprung from among the gods, for we shudder to see sad virgin Io ravaged and ruined, and her mind set wandering thanks to vindictive Hera.

In a marriage between equals there is no cause to fear, and so we pray that the mighty gods never cast amorous, inescapable eyes on us. For that is a fight that none may win, and a source only of misery – surely we would not know what to do to escape the snares of Zeus.

PROMETHEUS: For all His pride, one day Zeus will be humble. He proposes a marriage that will deprive Him of His throne, and by which He will be erased – consigned to oblivion. Thus is brought about the final curse of Titan Cronus, uttered when He was driven from the very same throne, against the son who usurped Him.

No other but me, among all the gods, could tell how to avoid this disaster, for I'm the only one who knows how it will happen. So let Him sit, trusting peacefully in His heavenly thunder and fiery bolt. None of it can preserve Him from dishonour, for without realizing He devises an adversary against Himself, a monster He cannot defeat, with a weapon far more powerful than His incessant thundering – and ultimately more will hear it. That amazing child will shiver the trident of Poseidon that curses sea and land.

And Zeus will learn how different is the life of a ruler to a slave.

CHORUS: But surely this is wishful thinking?

PROMETHEUS: It is my wish – but still it will happen.

CHORUS: Then we really must expect the advent of one who will topple Zeus?

PROMETHEUS: Oh yes – and Zeus will suffer much worse in oblivion than I do now.

CHORUS: How is it you dare say things like that?

PROMETHEUS: What reason have I to fear when I am not fated to die?

CHORUS: Even so, He might still inflict pain worse than you now suffer.

PROMETHEUS: I expect it.

CHORUS: Those who worship Necessity are wise.

PROMETHEUS: Meanwhile you must worship, pray to and adore whichever god serves as your king. But I care nothing for Zeus: He won't be king much longer.

But here is Zeus' lackey now, no doubt with a message for me...

Enter Hermes

HERMES: So clever, so crafty, so tricky, and yet so bitter – bitter beyond reason, for one who committed a crime against all gods in giving honours to creatures of a day. Fire-thief, I have a message for you.

My Father orders you to deliver up all that you know of the marriage you incessantly brag about that will supposedly oust Him from power. Come, out with it, and no riddles. Don't make me come here a second time, Prometheus: these chains should be proof enough that Zeus will not soften His anger toward you.

PROMETHEUS: Such a pompous speech is most apt from the lips of the young servant of a young god. You still really believe that the lofty estate you now enjoy will always be as it is today. But haven't I seen two previous regimes thrown from off of those very heights?

And the third, who is king right now – I will live to see Him fall, as well – and of all three His fall will be the fastest, the furthest, and most shameful.

Do you really think to see me kneel trembling before these upstart gods of yours? No. Now run along, for you'll learn nothing from me.

HERMES: That is the kind of pride that landed you here.

PROMETHEUS: Perhaps, but I assure you I'd sooner have this misfortune than change places with you.

HERMES: I suppose it's better to be servant to this rock than the most trusted messenger of Zeus!

PROMETHEUS: Well said: just the proper amount of hubris.

HERMES: If I didn't know better I would think you actually enjoy your martyrdom!

PROMETHEUS: Enjoy? Hardly. I would wish this on my enemies, and see you chained here instead.

HERMES: ...So you blame even me?

PROMETHEUS: I blame all of the gods whom I installed, and have shown their gratitude thus.

HERMES: Your words prove you mad!

PROMETHEUS: If it is mad to hate your persecutors.

HERMES: You are so arrogant I shudder to think how you would behave if things were actually well with you!

PROMETHEUS: *Jesus...*

HERMES: This is a word that is unknown to Zeus.

PROMETHEUS: Well, time teaches all things, eventually.

HERMES: Yet, old as you are, you haven't yet learned to act wisely.

PROMETHEUS: True, perhaps, or I would not bother trading words with a lackey like you.

HERMES: So you refuse to answer?

PROMETHEUS: What favour do I owe Him?

HERMES: You mock me as if I'm a child!

PROMETHEUS: Yet you are no wiser than a child if you think that I should tell you anything at all. Be clear on this: there is no form of torture, no machine that Zeus can devise, that would compel me to answer Him until He has released me from these chains. Let Him fling His bolts and throw the world around me into turmoil with white-winged snowflakes and deep-resounding thunder from beneath the earth – He will not learn from me the name of the one who is fated to end His tyranny on high Olympus.

HERMES: Think hard, Prometheus, as to whether this is in your best interest.

PROMETHEUS: I've thought it over, for a very long time. I will not be moved.

HERMES: Poor fool! Bend before you break!

PROMETHEUS: Persuade the waves. I am no poor girl to be stung and driven mad by Zeus, only to lay in the end with the one who did it to me.

HERMES: ...I have said too much, to too little effect. I know that you won't be moved by my prayers. Like a new colt, with the bit only just clenched in its teeth, you struggle against the reins. You are too strong, yet weaker than you know, and only half-smart. He is weakest of all who stubbornly stands, not yet aware of just what it is he faces.

Just think of the storm, the triple wave that will rise up to batter you to pieces if you don't listen to me – there can be no escape for you.

First, my father will shatter this jagged cliff to flinders with His thunder and lightning, and hide your mangled body in the depths among the rocks. You'll wait there a tedious long time before ever you see the light of day again.

And when you do the only companion there to greet you will be a winged hound of Zeus, a red eagle to tear great divots of flesh from you – a most unwanted dinner guest who will visit every day to nibble on your liver.

Nor should you expect an end to this unless some other god appears to take your tortures upon himself – and is willing to descend to dark Hades and the shadowy depths of Tartarus to do it.

So keep all this in mind and make your decision. This is no empty boast – the mouth of Zeus does not know how to lie: every word that comes from His tongue He makes truth. Act not in haste, repent not at leisure.

CHORUS: It seems to us that Hermes speaks wisely. He wants you to put aside your will to avoid inevitable pain. Listen to him. It makes no sense that someone so wise should invite certain doom.

PROMETHEUS: I knew the message he was bringing before he came.

Suffering is the price I pay to be righteous.

So let that forked curl of lightning lash down upon me, let the air itself be up-ended with claps of thunder, let the winds scourge the world entire and the earth shake to its foundations – yes, to her very root – in the face of this coming storm. Let the stars mix into the sea, and let that lord of yours lift my body up on high and smash it down into Tartarus, where blackly swirl the waters of Necessity. He can do as he likes, He will never kill me.

Hermes: Is there any part of your speech that is not mad? Is there no space at all within your frenzy that might accommodate sense?

Well then, it is time for all of you who are able to leave this place to do so, quickly as you can. You don't want to be here when the thunder comes...

Chorus: Oh please don't say that! Give us some other instruction we might follow without shame! How can you ask us to behave so badly? We'll stay here and endure with him whatever comes, for he has taught us to hate traitors and treachery...

Hermes: Remember my warning when you are trapped by the ruin and destruction all around you, and curse neither fate nor fortune, nor dare say that Zeus brought this disaster upon you unawares. Blame only yourselves when you are beyond all hope of rescue.

Exit Hermes

Prometheus: The time for talk is past. In truth the earth begins to shake, and from its depths the thunder starts to roar. Fiery flames of lightning flash forth, revealing whirling clouds filled with... dust.

The blasting winds coil about one another in a fury, the earth and sea now one. Here is the storm foretold, and on time.

O holy mother of mine, divine Themis, O sky that circles about and brings the common light to everyone – watch me now. Watch how I suffer.

Translated from the Greek by Stephen Russell, PhD
English by Jonathan Allen and Stephen Russell

Chapter 3
Apollodorus

The Story of Jason and Medea

The Story: The play *Medea* takes place at the very end of Jason and Medea's marriage. To understand why Medea feels as angry as she does, it's important to know more about the details of their story: how Jason sailed to Medea's land of Colchis aboard the Argo, how they fell in love, and how she helped him along the way. The mythographer Apollodorus provides a good summary of this narrative at the end of book one in his *Library*.

[1.9.16] Aeson, the son of Cretheus, had a son with Polymede, the daughter of Autolycus, whom they named Jason. Now Jason lived in Iolcus, where Pelias was king after his father Cretheus. But when Pelias consulted the oracle concerning the kingdom, the god warned him to beware of the man who had one sandal. At first the king didn't understand the oracle, but afterwards he came to understand it - for when he was offering a sacrifice to Poseidon at the sea, he sent for Jason along with many others to participate in the sacrifice.

Now Jason loved farming and therefore he lived in the country, but he hurried to the sacrifice, and in crossing the Anaurus river he lost a sandal in the stream and came up with only one. When Pelias saw him, he remembered the oracle, and going up to Jason asked him, if he were the king, what he would do if he had received an oracle that he would be murdered by one of the citizens. In response, whether by pure chance or as a result of Hera's anger (who wanted Medea to be a curse on Pelias, because he had failed to honour the goddess), Jason answered: "I would order him to go bring back the Golden Fleece." As soon as Pelias heard this reply, he ordered Jason to go out and bring back the fleece. Now this Golden Fleece was at Colchis in a grove that was sacred to Ares, where it was hanging on an oak tree and guarded by a dragon that never slept.

When he was sent to get the fleece, Jason asked for the help of Argus, the son of Phrixus. And Argus, following Athena's advice, built a ship that had fifty oars, and it was named Argo after its builder. And to the prow of the ship Athena fitted a piece of wood that came from the oak of Dodona, and this oak had the power of speech. When the ship was built, Jason asked the oracle, and the god told him that he could sail off once he had brought together the noblest men in Greece.

And the men who gathered for the journey of the Argo were as follows: Tiphys, the son of Hagnias, who steered the ship; Orpheus, the son of Oeagrus; Zetes and Calais, the sons of Boreas; Castor and Polydeuces, the sons of Zeus; Telamon and Peleus, the sons of Aeacus; Hercules, the son of Zeus; Theseus, the son of Aegeus; Idas and Lynceus, the sons of Aphareus; Amphiaraus, the son of Oicles; Caeneus, the son of Coronus; Palaemon, the son of Hephaestus or of Aetolus; Cepheus, the son of Aleus; Laertes, the son of Arcisius; Autolycus, the son of Hermes; Atalanta, the daughter of Schoeneus; Menoetius, the son of Actor; Actor, the son of Hippasus; Admetus, the son of Pheres; Acastus, the son of Pelias; Eurytus, the son of Hermes; Meleager, the son of Oeneus; Ancaeus, the son of Lycurgus; Euphemus, the son of Poseidon; Poeas, the son of Thaumacus; Butes, the son of Teleon; Phanus and Staphylus, the sons of Dionysus; Erginus, the son of Poseidon; Periclymenus, the son of Neleus; Augeas, the son of Helios (the Sun); Iphiclus, the son of Thestius; Argus, the son of Phrixus; Euryalus, the son of Mecisteus; Peneleos, the son of Hippalmus; Leitus, the son of Alector; Iphitus, the son of Naubolus; Ascalaphus and Ialmenus, the sons of Ares; Asterius, the son of Cometes; and Polyphemus, the son of Elatus.

[1.9.17] These men set out to sea with Jason in command and they touched shore at the idland of Lemnos. At that time it happened that there were no men at all in Lemnos and the island was ruled by a queen, Hypsipyle, who was the daughter of Thoas. The reason for the lack of men was this: the women of Lemnos did not honour Aphrodite, and so she afflicted them with a foul smell; therefore their husbands took captive women from the neighboring cities of Thrace and slept with them instead. Because they were dishonored in this way, the women of Lemnos murdered their fathers and husbands – but Hypsipyle alone saved her father Thoas by hiding him. So the Argonauts arrived at Lemnos, which was at that time ruled by women, and they had intercourse with the women, and Hypsipyle slept with Jason and bore him two sons – Euneus and Nebrophonus.

[1.9.18] After Lemnos the Argonauta visited the land of the Doliones, who were ruled by Cyzicus. He received them kindly. But when they were sailing away at night they met contrary winds, lost their way, and without realizing it they soon landed once again among the Doliones. However, the Doliones mistook them for a Pelasgian army (for they were under constant attack from the Pelasgians), and so they joined battle with them at night, with each side in mutual ignorance of the other. The Argonauts killed many of their opponents, including Cyzicus. But at daybreak, when they realized what they had done, they mourned and cut off their hair and gave Cyzicus a lavish burial, and after the funeral they sailed away and touched shore at Mysia.

[1.9.19] There, in Mysia, they abandoned Hercules and Polyphemus. For Hylas, the son of Thiodamasand the lover of Hercules, had been sent to get water but was snatched away by nymphs on account of his beauty. But Polyphemus heard him cry out and, drawing his sword, he set out after him in the belief that Hylas was being carried off by robbers. When he came across Hercules, he told him what had happened – and while the two were looking for Hylas, the Argo put out to sea. So Polyphemus founded a city, Cius, in Mysia and he ruled there as king. But Hercules returned to Argos. However, Herodorus says that Hercules did not sail at all at that time, but served as a slave at the court of Omphale. And Pherecydes says that Hercules was left behind at Aphetai in Thessaly, because the Argo said with a human voice that she could not bear his weight. But Demaratus has also recorded that Hercules sailed to Colchis, and the historian Dionysios even claims that Hercules was the leader of the Argonauts.

[1.9.20] They left Mysia for to the land of the Bebryces, which was ruled by King Amycus, who was the son of Poseidon and a Bithynian nymph. A feisty and determined man, he forced strangers who landed there to box with him, and in that way he brought about their deaths. So he went up to the Argo on this occasion as usual, and he challenged the best man of the crew to a boxing match. Polydeuces took him up on this boxing challenge and killed him with a blow from his elbow. When the Bebryces rushed forward to attack Polydeuces, the Greek heroes quickly grabbed their arms and killed many of them as they fled in the Argo.

[1.9.21] After they left Mysia a second time they eventually came to land at Salmydessus in Thrace, where Phineus lived, who was a seer who had lost the use of both eyes. Some say that he was a son of Agenor, but others say that he was a son of Poseidon. And some accounts allege that he was blinded by the gods for predicting the future to the human race; some say that he was blinded by Boreas and the Argonauts because he had blinded his own sons at the instigation of their stepmother; and some say it was done by Poseidon, because he revealed to the children of Phrixus how they could sail from Colchis to Greece.

The gods also sent the Harpies against Phineus. These were winged female creatures, and when a table was set out in front of Phineus, these harpies flew down from the sky and snatched up most of the food, and what little they left stank so strongly that nobody could touch it. When the Argonauts wanted to ask him about their voyage, he said that he would advise them on it if they would rid him of the Harpies. So the Argonauts set a table of food beside him, and the Harpies suddenly swooped down with a shriek and snatched away the food. When Zetes and Calais, the sons of Boreas,who had wings themselves, saw this, they drew their swords and pursued the Harpies through the air.

Now it was fated that the Harpies would die at the hands of the sons of Boreas, and that the sons of Boreas would die if they could not catch those they were chasing. So they chased the Harpies, and one of flying-women fell into the Tigres river in the Peloponnese, the river that is now called Harpys after her. This Harpy was called Nicothoe, but others called her Aellopus. As for the other Harpy, called Ocypete or, according to some, Ocythoe (but Hesiod calls her Ocypode) – she fled along the Propontis until she came to the Echinadian Islands, which are now called Strophades after her – for when she came to them she turned in her flight on reaching them ("estraphe") and when she was at the shore she fell down due to exhaustion along with her pursuer. But Apollonius in the Argonautica says that the Harpies were pursued as far as the Strophades Islands but that they suffered no harm, because they swore an oath that they would not stop persecuting Phineus.

[1.9.22] When he was liberated from the Harpies, Phineus told the Argonauts the best course to take on their voyage, and he advised them about the Clashing Rocks, which lay ahead of them in the sea. These were huge cliffs, that were forced to clash together by the power of the winds – and when this happened they closed the sea passage and crushed everything that was between them. These rocks were surrounded by thick mist, and their crash was tremendously loud – and it was impossible even for birds to pass between them. So Phineus told them to let a dove fly between the rocks, and if they saw the bird pass through safely, then they could sail through the narrows with confidence. But if they saw the bird die, then they shouldn't try to force a passage. When they heard this advice, they put out to sea, and when they got closer to the rocks they let a dove fly from the front of the ship, and as she flew only the tip of her was snipped off as the rocks clashed together. So they waited until the rocks had drawn back apart, with hard rowing and the help of Hera, they passed through the Clashing Rocks, although the very back of the ship was cut off as they made their way through. From this point onward, the Clashing Rocks stood still – because it was fated that as soon as a ship made it through, the rocks would come to a complete rest.

[1.9.23] The Argonauts now arrived among the Mariandynians, and King Lycus received them kindly there. It was there that Idmon the seer died from a wound inflicted by a boar; and Tiphys died there as well, and so Ancaeus took over and steered the ship.

And they sailed past the Thermodon River and the Caucasus mountains, then they finally arrived at the Phasis river, which is in the land of Colchis. When the ship was brought into port, Jason went to Aeetes, and he explained to the king what Palias has told him to do and then he asked if the king would give him the Golden Fleece.

In turn Aeetes promised that he would hand it over to Jason if he could tame two bronze-footed bulls all on his own. These were two wild bulls, of enormous size, that he owned and were a gift from Hephaestus. They had bronze feet and breathed out fire from their mouths.

Aeetes ordered him to yoke these creatures and to sow some dragon's teeth; for he had received from Athena half of the dragon's teeth that Cadmus used for sowing in Thebes. While Jason thought about how he could master and yoke the bulls, Medea fell in love with him. Now Medea was a witch and the daughter of Aeetes and Idyia, who was the daughter of Ocean. She was afraid that Jason might be killed by the bulls and so, while keeping it a secret from her father, she promised to help him to yoke the bulls and get the fleece, if he in turn would promise to marry her and would take her with him on the voyage back to Greece. When Jason swore an oath that he would do so, she then gave him a potion and told him to rub it all over his shield, spear, and body just before he was about to yoke the bulls – for she said that, after he had been anointed with it, for a single day he couldn't be harmed by fire or iron. And she told him that, after the teeth were sown in the ground, then armed men would spring up from the ground against him. And she said that when he saw a group of these armed men, he should then throw a stone into their midst from a distance, which would cause them to fight among themselves – and then he should kill them.

When Jason heard Medea's instructions, he then anointed himself with the drug, and when he arrived at the grove with the temple he looked for the bulls – and although they charged him while they breathed out fire, he managed to subdue and yoke them. And after he had sowed the teeth of the dragon, armed men sprang up from the ground; and where Jason saw several of them together, he threw a stone into their midst, and when they fought each other he drew near and killed them. But even though the bulls were yoked, Aeetes did not give him the fleece; for the king wanted to burn down the Argo and kill its crew. But before he could do so, Medea brought Jason to the fleece at night, and she lulled the dragon that guarded it to sleep by means of her drugs. Then she grabbed hold of the fleece and made her way with Jason back to the Argo. She was also accompanied by her brother Absyrtus. And that same night the Argonauts put out to sea with them.

[1.9.24] When Aeetes discovered what Medea had dared to do, he set off in pursuit of the Argo; but when she saw that her father was getting closer to them, Medea murdered her brother, cut him up limb from limb, and threw his pieces into the sea. Aeetes gathered the child's limbs, and so this stopped his pursuit. He turned back after having buried the rescued limbs of his child – and he called the place where he buried the limbs Tomi ("cutting"). But he sent out many of the Colchians to search for the Argo, threatening, if they didn't bring Medea back to him, that they would suffer the punishment that she herself deserved. So the ships separated and pursued the search in different areas.

When the Argonauts were already sailing past the Eridanus river, Zeus sent a furious storm upon them and drove them off their course, because he was angry about the murder of Absyrtus. And as they were sailing past the Absyrtides Islands, the ship spoke to them, saying that the anger of Zeus would not end unless they went to Ausonia and were purified by Circe for the murder of Absyrtus. So when they had sailed past the Ligurian and Celtic nations and had voyaged through the Sardinian Sea, they went past Tyrrhenia and came to Aeaea, where they came before Circe as supplicants and were purified by her.

[1.9.25] And as they sailed past the Sirens, Orpheus sang a song to counter the one offered by the Sirens. Butes alone swam off to the Sirens, but Aphrodite carried him away and settled him in Lilybaeum.

After the Sirens, the ship encountered Charybdis and Scylla and the Wandering Rocks, above which a great flame and smoke were seen rising. But Thetis, along with the Nereids, steered the ship through them, in response to a summons from Hera.

After they passed by the Island of Thrinacia, where the cattle of the Sun are, they came to Corcyra, the island of the Phaeacians, where Alcinous was king. But when the Colchians could not find the ship, some of them settled at the Ceraunian Mountains, while some travelled to Illyria and colonized the Absyrtides islands. But some of the Colchians did come to the Phaeacians, and when they discovered that the Argo was there, they demanded that Alcinous surrender Medea to them. He answered that if she had already slept with Jason, then he would let her stay with him, but that if she were still a virgin he would send her away to her father. However, Arete, the wife of Alcinous, took the initiative by marrying Medea to Jason. Therefore the Colchians settled down among the Phaeacians while the Argonauts put out to sea with Medea.

[1.9.26] As they were sailing along at night they encountered a violent storm, and so Apollo took up a position on the Melantian ridges and shot an arrow down into the sea, which caused the area to become lit up. The light allowed them to notice an island close at hand, and when they set anchor there they named it Anaphe, because it had appeared to them ("anaphanenai") unexpectedly. So they raised an altar to Radiant Apollo, and after they made a sacrifice they then settled down for a feast. And there were twelve handmaids there, whom Arete had given to Medea – they joked merrily with the heroes – so from this it is still the custom for the women to make jokes at the sacrifice.

After setting out from Anaphe, they were prevented from touching the shore of Crete by Talos. Some say that Talos was a man who belonged to the race of bronze men, while others say that he was given to Minos by Hephaestus. He was a man made of bronze, but some say that he was a bull. He had a single vein extending from his neck to his ankles, and a bronze nail was rammed home at the end of the vein. This Talos kept guard by running round the island three times every day - and so when he saw the Argo coming near to the shore, he pelted it with stones as he was accustomed to do. But Medea tricked him and caused his death. Some say that she drove him mad with her drugs, or, as others say, she promised to make him immortal and then drew out the nail, which caused him to die when all of the ichor gushed out of him. But there are some who say that Poeas shot him dead in the ankle with an arrow.

After remaining there for a single night they next came to shore in the island of Aegina to get water. When they were there, a contest developed among them as they were fetching the water. From that island they sailed between Euboea and Locris and finally came to Iolcus, having completed the whole journey in four months.

[1.9.27] Now Pelias, thinking that the Argonauts would never return, would have killed Aeson; but Aeson asked if he could be allowed to take his own life, and so while he was offering a sacrifice he drank freely of the bull's blood and died. And Jason's mother cursed Pelias and hanged herself, leaving behind an infant son Promachus. But Pelias killed even this son whom she had left behind.

When he returned Jason gave back the fleece, but he wanted revenge for all the wrongs that had been done to him so he waited for the appropriate time. For the moment he sailed with the other Argonauts to the Isthmus and dedicated the ship to Poseidon, but afterward he asked Medea to come up with a way that he could punish Pelias. So she went to the palace of Pelias and persuaded his daughters to chop their father into small pieces and boil him, promising that she would make him young again with her drugs and potions. And to win their confidence she cut up a ram and made it into a lamb by boiling it. So the daughters of Pelias believed her, chopped up their father and boiled him. But Acastus, the son of Pelias, buried his father with the help of the inhabitants of Iolcus, and he expelled Jason and Medea from Iolcus.

[1.9.28] They went to Corinth, and lived there happily for ten years, until Creon, the king of Corinth, offered his daughter Glauce to Jason, who married her and divorced Medea. But Medea invoked the gods by whom Jason had sworn, and after often reproaching him for his ingratitude she sent the bride a robe covered in poison. When Glauce put this robe on, she was consumed by a raging fire along with her father, who tried to come to her rescue.

But Medea killed Mermerus and Pheres, the children she had with Jason, and from the Sun she received a chariot drawn by winged dragons, which she used to fly to Athens. Another account suggests that on her flight she left behind her children, who were still infants, setting them as suppliants on the altar of Hera Acaria - but the Corinthians forced them away from the altar and then inflicted fatal injuries upon them.

Medea went to Athens, and there she married Aegeus and bore him a son, Medus. Afterward, however, she made a plot against Theseus, and so was driven out as a fugitive from Athens along with her son. But Medus conquered many barbarians and called the whole country under his control Media – and he died while marching out against the Indians. And Medea returned to Colchis without being recognized, and when she discovered that her father Aeetes had been deposed by his brother Perses, she killed Perses and restored the kingdom to her father.

Translated from the Greek by Stephen Russell, PhD

Euripides
MEDEA

The Story: Jason led his ship the Argo to Medea's homeland of Colchis to obtain the Golden Fleece. When he was there, the king's daughter Medea, a witch, fell in love with Jason and helped him steal the Fleece. She also killed her young brother in an effort to convince her father to stop chasing them as they fled.

On the return voyage to Greece, Medea assisted the Argonauts greatly, and Jason and Medea married and had two young boys. When they arrived back in Greece she helped Jason's aged father become young again as well as tricked the daughters of Jason's enemy Pelias into killing their father.

They eventually settle in Corinth as guests of King Creon. But Jason has grown tired of Medea and is planning to leave her so that he can marry Creon's daughter.

This play is the story of what Medea does when she finds out that Jason has betrayed her – this is the story of Medea's revenge.

Characters

Nurse (of Medea and the children)
Tutor (of the children)
Medea
Chorus (women of Corinth)
Creon, King of Corinth
Jason
Aegeus, King of Athens
Messenger
Children (of Medea and Jason)

Scene: Corinth. Medea's house is in the background.

Enter the Nurse

NURSE: If only the Argo had never sailed between the clashing rocks into the harbour of Colchis, or the pines of Mt. Pelion never been felled, nor fit to the hands of the heroes that Pelias sent to fetch the Golden Fleece. For then my mistress, mad from love, would not have sailed for Iolcus, nor persuaded the daughters of Pelias to murder their father, and having assisted Jason in every way possible to please the citizens of this Corinthian land, come to exile with him and the children.

To my mind, the greatest good is when a wife doesn't contend with her husband. But now she hates everything and sickens even toward those most dear to her. For Jason has betrayed his children and my mistress, and now shares the royal marriage bed with the daughter of Creon, ruler of this land. Dishonored, Medea cries, "What of the oaths? The right hand given as a sign of the greatest trust?" She calls on the gods to witness her mistreatment, will not eat, but gives her wracked body over to pain and constant tears. Neither lifting her head nor her eyes from the ground, she ignores the advice of friends, who are unintelligible as stones or the sea to her. She is so quiet, only turning her snow-white neck at times to wail for her father, for her home, which she betrayed for the man who now dishonors her. Now the poor woman learns how important it is not to be cut off from your homeland.

Now she despises even her own children, takes no pleasure in seeing them, and I fear she plots some fresh evil, for her's is a dangerous spirit and will not allow mistreatment. I know her, and dread that she might twist a sharpened blade through her chest, or kill the king, his daughter, as well as he who married her, before contriving some even greater calamity. She terrifies me, for I know that no one who trifles with her long sings a song of victory.

Enter the Children with the Tutor

But look, here come the boys, back from play. They know nothing of their mother's troubles. Young minds cannot conceive of such pain.

Tutor: Hail, fellow toiler, why are you standing here all alone, muttering to yourself? Isn't your mistress missing you?

Nurse: Well, Tutor, when things go wrong for their master, a good servant suffers in equal measure, and my suffering is so great I had to leave that oppressive house awhile to cry my mistress' troubles to the earth and sky.

Tutor: What, has the poor woman not ceased wailing yet?

Nurse: It must be nice to be so situated as to be able to ignore it. No, her pains are just in the beginning stages: they haven't even reached middle-age.

Tutor: Poor fool – if I can speak thus about my mistress – for she can know nothing of the latest!

Nurse: What now, old man? Now is hardly the time to grow a tight lip.

Tutor: I shouldn't have spoken...

Nurse: For pity's sake, don't leave a fellow subject in the dark. I can keep a secret.

Tutor: Well, we just now passed by the place where the old men play dice – you know, near the spring – and, pretending not to listen, I overheard someone say that Creon, the king, is about to order these children and their mother exiled from this land. I don't know how good his information is, but it's bad news for you and me if it is so.

Nurse: But would Jason allow this to happen to his children, even if he is fighting with their mother?

Tutor: Old marriage ties are forsaken for new: that man is not a friend of this house.

Nurse: Great. A fresh disaster, and we're still reeling from the last one.

Tutor: Keep it to yourself: now is not the time for her to hear it.

Nurse: There children, do you see what kind of father you have? Far be it from me to pass judgment on my master, but the way he treats his loved ones...

Tutor: And what man is blameless in that regard? So a father prefers his new bride to his children: are you only just now figuring out that every man loves himself above all others? And that some love truly, while others truly love only gain...

Nurse: Go inside, children: everything will be fine. And you, keep them as far as possible from their mother. Such a look she gave them just now, like a bull preparing to charge. She won't let go of this anger – I am sure of it – until she spends it on someone. I only hope it's an enemy rather than her friends.

Medea (from inside the house): My life has turned to shit! It hurts.... It hurts... so much. I can't live through it...

Nurse: There! Mind your nurse, little ones. Your mother is hurt and angry. Hurry inside now, and steer clear: beware her fierce temper and the savage hate in her tortured mind. Inside now, quick as you can!

The Children and the Tutor enter the house

It's clear that her groans are just the distant rumblings of a grief that will presently darken into a storm of fury. What will that terrible pride not do when stung with such injury?

MEDEA (STILL INSIDE): I've done and suffered such terrible things, things worth cursing. Oh cursed children of a hated mother – you should die along with your father! Curse this house! Curse our home!

NURSE: Oh, this is agony! Why tar the children with their father's sin? O my lovely boys, I am sick with the fear of what you may suffer! The moods of royalty are fierce – they are so used to ruling over everyone and everything, except their own ungovernable tempers.

Far better, I think, to live down among equals. I, at any rate, hope to grow old safely, on modest means, moderation and modesty being by far the best way for mortals to live. Excess is no boon to mortals and a god's anger is drawn like lightning to an over-proud house.

Enter the Chorus (of Corinthian women)

CHORUS: We're here because we keep hearing the cries of that poor woman from Colchis. Is she still so overwrought? Speak, old woman! For her wailing is plainly audible even over the double-gated walls of the city, and the sufferings of her house disturb us now because she is a friend of ours.

NURSE: This house is no more. All is in ruin. He is now held in his royal marriage while she wastes her life away alone in her room and cannot be soothed by the words of her friends.

MEDEA (STILL INSIDE): Oh, bastard, Jason! Oh Zeus, oh land, oh heaven, take pity and strike me dead! What's the point in living? Let me take my ease in death and leave this hateful existence behind.

CHORUS:
Do you hear oh Zeus and land and heaven? Do you hear the miserable song the poor woman sings?

Why is your desire for Death's bed, foolish woman? Would you hurry to his arms? Don't pray for that!

Though your husband occupies another marriage bed, do not eat out your heart.

Zeus will seek justice on your behalf. Don't waste away grieving for your bed-mate.

MEDEA (STILL INSIDE): Oh mighty goddess Justice and lady Artemis, do you see what I suffer, who bound my husband with great oaths? I long to see him and his bride – their whole house along with them – crushed to smithereens, for the wrong they inflict on me! O father, o city of my birth, from which I was shamefully spirited away! I killed my own brother for you and you do this to me?

NURSE: Do you hear her? How she prays to Justice and to Zeus, protector of oaths? My mistress's anger will never die away without leaving some mark.

CHORUS:
If only she would meet with us and listen!

If only she'd let go of her rage. I hope my heart will never exclude my friends.

(to the Nurse)

Go and bring her out here quickly! Say her friends have come to visit.

Hurry before she harms those inside, for this grief is explosive.

NURSE: Fine, but I doubt she will be persuaded. I'll do as you ask, though she glares like a lioness with new cubs whenever one of us approaches her. But people are perennially foolish: though men invented songs, poetry, and music to please the ears at festivals, feasts, and dinners, no mortal ever yet found a way to alleviate with mere talk the sort of human misery that brings death and disaster and overthrows houses. It would be worth your breath if woes were curable with clever words. What profit is there in singing loud and long even when the banquet is plentiful? Surely the feast is pleasure enough.

CHORUS: We come because we heard her calling. We heard her mournful prayers to Justice, protector of oaths, the very goddess who drove her across the sea, and we have come even if the goddess will not.

Enter Medea

MEDEA: Women of Corinth, I have come outside lest you get the wrong idea of me. Some earn a bad reputation simply by never leaving the house. And though it is unjust when, though they have never been harmed by her, new neighbors hate the stranger before they know anything of her character, by the same token, a foreigner must also try to fit into his new city, and I wouldn't praise the man who is stand-offish and by his own churlishness deservedly brings upon himself the scorn of the citizenry.

A sudden blow has fallen upon me and destroyed my life. I am ruined and, having let go all my joy of life, my friends, I want to die. For I now know well that he who was my world has been revealed the worst of men.

Of all creatures who live and breathe, women are the most pathetic. First we spend ourselves to buy a husband, and then we make him master of our bodies. The second part is by far the worst. Our whole fate lies in whether we take a good husband or an evil one, for divorce brings bad reputation, yet not so bad a one as not marrying at all. Every woman, therefore, must strive to be a wife, and try to be a prophet. It is worse still for a foreign wife transported among the unfamiliar customs of a faithless husband. How can she win? If by luck we manage to make all of this work out well for us, and our husband stays, and refrains from laying on too hard with the whip hand, then we'll have a "good life." And if not, it's better we were dead.

A man, irritated at the people in his home, is free to go outside, and in that way put an end to the misery that he's feeling. He goes to see a friend. But women, we stay here – we stay home. They say that women live free from danger, safe at home while they go into battle with swords. They are idiots – I would sooner go into battle three times than give birth once!

Even so, our situations are not the same, wives of Corinth. This is your city: your fathers are here, your friends are here. I am abandoned. I have no city; my husband insults me; I was carried off as plunder from a foreign land, and I have no mother, no brother, nor any relatives I can turn to in my misery.

And so I will ask you now for one small favor: if I tell you how I fix to punish my husband for what he is doing to me – along with his new bride and father-in-law – I ask you to keep silent! In many things a woman is often a fearful coward – in battle perhaps, handling swords – but once wronged in her bed, in her marriage, no heart is more deadly.

CHORUS: Yes: punish your husband, Medea, as you should – little wonder you are in pain. But Creon approaches, with some new message....

Enter Creon

CREON: You! The one so dour and dead-set against her husband: I order you to flee this land and take your brats with you! Do not dally, for I have come to see you off myself and will not return home again until you have been escorted beyond the borders of the land I rule.

MEDEA: Alas, I am destroyed, for my enemies cast me out, and there is no harbor left to me. Nevertheless I will ask: Creon, why do this to me?

CREON: Because I am afraid of you. There's no need to keep it secret: I fear you will do some incredible evil to my daughter. It's hardly unreasonable, is it? You are clever and notoriously well-versed in doing evil, and you are in pain. I have heard that you boast of planning something terrible for the bride-groom, the bride, and me. So I will protect against disaster before it happens. I would rather feel your hatred now, woman, than be soft-hearted and regret it later.

MEDEA: This isn't the first time, Creon, that my reputation has done me harm. No one with sense should ever allow their child to become more than acceptably clever, for thoughtfulness is often mistaken for indolence, or worse yet, feared as unnatural, inspiring hatred and jealousy. For if you bring some new wisdom to fools, they either can't see it, or consider you something special, a danger to those who were previously thought wise, and a threat to the city.

And that is just what has happened to me. But I am not so terribly wise, Creon. You, afraid of me? What can I, a mere woman, do? Don't turn away from me, I beg you, for I don't have it in me to harm a king. After all, what wrong have you done me? You gave your daughter in marriage to the one whom your heart pointed to you, and if I hate my husband, you, I know, have acted wisely. Let the marriage happen

– and good luck to you all. But, please, let me remain in this land, and though I have been treated badly, I will remain silent, since I am wise enough, at least, to know when I am beaten.

CREON: Well, these are calm and soothing words, and I now trust you less than I did before. For a woman who is quick to anger, just like a man, is easier to ward off than one who is clever and can hold her tongue.

So you have to go, immediately – not another word! The matter is settled, and there is no scheme you could devise that will allow you to remain here with us, for you are my enemy.

MEDEA: Please, I beg you, on my knees and in the name of your newly-married daughter!

CREON: You waste your breath – you won't persuade me to change my mind.

MEDEA: You'll drive me out, and not even hear my entreaties?

CREON: I will not love you more than I love my own family!

MEDEA: O my dear home, my dear Colchis, how dearly I remember you now!

CREON: You might have thought of it before: after my children my homeland is by far the dearest thing in life to me.

MEDEA: Oh you bastards, the desires of men are such a terrible evil!

CREON: Now, be fair: try to see it from my point of view.

MEDEA: O Zeus, do not let the man who's done these things get away with them!

CREON: Just begone from here, madwoman, and cease to be a trouble to me.

MEDEA: But I have troubles, too! Will no one help?

CREON: You'll soon be helped outside the city gates by my attendants!

MEDEA: *(grabbing Creon by the knees)* Creon, I beg you, don't do this!

CREON: You are making a spectacle of yourself to no purpose, woman.

MEDEA: I will go into exile! I do not ask you for a pardon.

CREON: Then why won't you let go of my hand?

MEDEA: One day – please allow me to stay just one more day to plan where I might go find refuge for my children, since their father won't be bothered to plan for their future. Have pity on them at least! You are a father yourself! My worry isn't for me, but for my children, innocent victims of cruel misfortune!

CREON: I am not tyrannical by nature, woman, yet I fear I make a mistake when I say to you: you have your day. But I warn you: if the rising sun finds you or your children within my kingdom tomorrow, then you must die. This is my final decree – it will not be changed. So stay, if you must, but one day only. You won't be given the opportunity to do the terrible things I fear.

Exit Creon

CHORUS: *(to Medea)* Poor woman, with all your pains and sorrows: where will you go? What protector of refugees, what house or what land will you find? What god has made things so horrible for you, Medea, leading you into this sea of troubles?

MEDEA: All is lost, who could deny that, but don't imagine it so for me alone. There are still pains awaiting the newlyweds, and no small ones, either, for the father of the bride.

Come, do you really think that I would have crawled for that man a moment ago if I were not up to something? That I'd debase myself in such a way or touched him with my hands? The fool might have thwarted me neatly, but instead he has allowed me one day to make three deaths.

I have so many methods at my disposal, dear friends, that I don't know which to choose. Perhaps I brighten the bridal chamber with fire, silently sneaking in to burn them in their beds. But, then, if I were caught, my death would bring pleasure to my enemies. No. A more direct approach is better, where I can use talent and kill them with poison.

So then, let's suppose them dead. What city will then take me in? What foreign land will have me? There's no one. Still, patience, think on it, see if some place of refuge opens to me and, if it should, I'll commit my murders slyly. But if subtlety should prove impossible, I will grab a sword and, even if I die in the act, kill them myself with sheer force and daring. For never – and I swear by the goddess I worship most of all and whom I have chosen as my accomplice, Hecate, who lives in the dark and secret places of my home – no one breaks my heart and laughs about it afterward.

I'll make the newlyweds wish they'd never met, and Corinth will rue the day it exiled Medea.

Come then, woman, bring all your skill for plotting to bear and move into the shadows. You know what you must do: now is the test of your mettle, so focus on what they do to you, the daughter of a noble father and the granddaughter of the sun-god Helios. ....

(*to the* **Chorus**) And are we not women, reputed altogether useless when there's good to be done, but none more clever when crafting evil?

CHORUS:

The waters of sacred rivers flow backward, Justice, and thus the world, upended. The plans of men are deceitful, pledges made in the name of the gods proved lies, but now the story will change and second-class lives be afforded honour! Respect will come at last to the female race! No longer will we be slandered.

Songs of of our faithlessness by singers born long ago will cease being sung. Apollo, god of music, does not allow us the gift of song or we'd long since have sung our retort, a song against the world of men, for a true history would say as much against men as it would say in favour of women.

Medea, you sailed from your father's home, passed through those clapping rocks in the sea to dwell in a foreign land, but lost to you now is the harbour of your husband, poor thing – and now this country drives you out, an exile, dishonoured.

The honour of promises, the grace of oaths, is dead: respect and reverence no longer reside in great Greece – it has misted up into the sky – for Medea has no father's home in which to shelter from her troubles, and another queen rules her bed.

Enter Jason

JASON: This is not the first time I've seen rage lead to irremediable evil. You could have remained in this city and in this house, if only you had accepted the decisions of your masters with some humility, but by virtue of your vitriolic tongue you've lost this city forever.

It is a matter of complete indifference to me if you go around trying to convince anyone who will listen that Jason is the most evil man alive. But as to what you've been saying about the rulers – well, consider yourself lucky that you're merely exiled! I have repeatedly mediated with them on your behalf: I wanted you to stay. But you will persist in your slander of the royal family. And so you must go.

Through it all, I have never forgotten my loved ones, and I am here now, woman, so you and the children do not leave without money or means. For exile brings its own troubles. And even if you hate me, I could never think badly toward you.

MEDEA: You crawling maggot! You lying, worthless bastard! So you've come at last, you, the enemy of the gods, and of me, and of the whole human race? It's no mere arrogance that you have the temerity to come to me whom you have destroyed and find it in yourself to look me in the eye. No, it is illness, the worst of all diseases in men: an inability to feel shame.

But it is good that you are here; it gives me the opportunity to lance the boil in my soul by speaking my piece.

Let's begin at the beginning, when I saved you, just as every man who sailed with you on the Argo knows that I saved you. I saved you when you were sent to tame the fire-breathing bulls with a harness and had to sow the deadly seeds. And that serpent, the one who never slept and guarded the Golden Fleece with its twisting coils: I killed it and lit your way to safety.

I betrayed my father and my house, and came with you to Iolcus, filled more with passion than wisdom. I killed Pelias, gave him the most painful of deaths – at the hands of his own daughters. I destroyed his entire house, and in return, asshole, you betray me and take a new bride, despite your children, without whom your desire for this new marriage would perhaps be forgivable.

But henceforth the trust that people place in vows and oaths is dead. I don't know if you think the old gods no longer rule, or you've convinced yourself that new laws have been established for mankind, but you know full well that you have broken your oath to me. To hell with this right hand of mine, which you so often held; to hell with these knees of mine – tickled by you, serpent – my faith in you has been my downfall.

But, let's chat like old friends – what good your friendship has ever done me I don't know, but still, by all means, let us shoot the fucking breeze. For nothing you can possibly say will lighten the blackening of your name. But do advise me, husband: tell me where I should go. Perhaps I should return to my father's home and my own country? Oh, except I betrayed it for you. Or perhaps I should go to the poor daughters of Pelias? They'll be so pleased to welcome his murderer into their home.

That's how things stand for me now: I'm hated by those dearest to me, and even the strangers who might have succored me have become my enemies – all my bridges have been burnt, on your account. Still, as thanks, you've made me appear the luckiest of women in the eyes of these Greek ladies you see before you, for what a paragon you have turned out to be. What does it matter, therefore, if I am made an exile, driven out, friendless, alone but for your children? That will make a fine advertisement for the new bridegroom, that his children and the wife who saved him should be reduced to wandering the world as beggars!

O Zeus, you made it so simple to distinguish real gold from fake: why can't a woman as easily bite a man to tell a good one from a bad?

Chorus: Rage wounds deep when love becomes hate.

Jason: It seems I must not be a poor speaker, but like a skilled sailor use the upmost edges of the sail that I might weather your stormy tongue, woman. But as you build up the great service you've done me, I say that it was Aphrodite alone of all the gods and men who made my voyage successful and saw me here safe. You do have a clever mind, but simply cannot wrap it around the fact that it was Eros who forced you to save me with his sure arrows. But why split hairs – you did help me, it's true. However, in saving me you gained much more than you gave me: listen.

First of all, instead of a barbarian land you now live in Greece and you know justice and the use of laws that do now come with force. All the Greeks could see that you are wise so you have become famous – but if you lived far away at the ends of the earth, nobody would have heard of you. As for me, I wouldn't want to have gold in my house or to be able to sing more sweetly than Orpheus if I couldn't develop some level of fame.

But enough about me: you're the one who started this debate. As for the infamy you shower on me for my upcoming nuptials, allow me to demonstrate how clever I've been in the matter, and how long-sighted, and then you'll see what a friend I've been both to you and my children. Wait – hear me out! When I came to Corinth from the country of Iolcus, I dragged with me many seemingly insoluble difficulties: what more miraculous cure for all this could I, an exile, find than to marry the daughter of the king? It isn't – as you complain – that I was somehow overcome with lust for this new bride of mine, or that I had some great desire to sire more children with her. The children I had were just fine.

No, the real reason was – listen – so that we might live decently and without privation, because I know too well that a friend in need is a friend to avoid. I wanted to raise our children in a manner befitting my background and family, and by producing brothers for your sons I planned to put them all on an equal footing and bind the family together, that we would prosper.

Think: what need have I of more children? But the ones I have now will profit by the existence of the ones soon to come. Am I wrong? You would see it my way, if you weren't blinded by rage at having to vacate the marriage bed.

Women always think life is perfect if everything goes well in the bedroom, and when your romantic life is suffering you become enemies even to those nearest and dearest to you. By Zeus, there should be some other way for mortals to reproduce: if there were no female race there wouldn't be such misery for men.

Chorus: A very pretty justification you have made for yourself, Jason, but it seems to us – though you may not wish to hear it – that it does not change the fact of your betrayal.

Medea: Perhaps it's just me, but I think a smooth talker merits even greater punishment for his dangerous belief that rhetoric somehow justifies any evil he might choose to commit. He talks so sweetly he even convinces himself, and then what injustice will he not stoop to? But he is not so clever, really.

You can end your little show now, for the final word is this: if you owed me nothing you would have talked to me first and persuaded me your new marriage was the thing to do, and not kept it secret from your loved ones.

Jason: Oh, I can see it all now. And I suppose you'd be happy with such a speech, when even now you can't hold back your acid tongue?

Medea: That's not what stopped you: your status was suffering because you were set to grow old tied to a barbarian wife.

Jason: I have told you, it was never about the woman: I wanted to sire royal brothers for my children and thereby keep everyone safe.

Medea: I have no desire for a 'happy' life that blasts my heart.

Jason: Then change your desire and be wise as your reputation, Medea. Hope and pray that you never have to do a good thing that looks like evil, and stop feeling sorry for yourself when you're actually quite lucky.

Medea: Go on, then, hero – keep speaking to me as if I were feeble-minded – since you have somewhere to go afterward and someone waiting for you there; as for me, I am alone and about to be a wanderer.

Jason: You brought it upon yourself – don't blame anyone else!

Medea: Am I set to marry someone else, then?

Jason: No, you merely threatened the royal family.

Medea: And I intend to be a curse on your house as well!

Jason: Stop – I'm not going to waste any more breath on this. If you want money, tell me now. I'm prepared to be generous, and also to write letters to foreigners who might aid you. Woman, you'd be a fool not to accept these things. Let go your anger.

Medea: I desire neither your magnanimity nor your friends. I want nothing from you. The gifts of an evil man have no value.

Jason: Fine. I call upon the gods to witness that I was ready and eager to help both you and the children, but you belligerently pushed me away so as to suffer all the more.

Medea: Go! Run back to your new bride! You must be overwhelmed with desire, having been away from her for so long now! Go and have your marriage! But – with the help of the gods – you may yet find that you've taken sorrow into your bed.

Exit Jason

Chorus:

When desire comes on men untempered it does them no credit, but when Aphrodite comes softly, there is no goddess so fair. Please, o goddess, never fire at us your golden arrows, unerringly aimed and tipped with your desire, but let Wisdom, most noble of gods, befriend us, and prevent those troubling shafts ever deranging us with lust for adultery, and preserve us from anger, or strife. Grant us cool contemplation in choosing our mates so that we might build marriage beds rather than battlefields. For battlefields are the proper place for arrows.

O fatherland, our home, grant we may never go into exile, adrift in a life of helpless suffering. Before that let us be laid low, for in death there is nothing worse than the loss of one's native land. We have seen it and have no need to be told twice: no city, no friend, will pity you nor share your burden. Let the man die without laurels who does not honour his friends or open his heart. He will never be a friend of mine!

Enter Aegeus

AEGEUS: Medea, how good to see you!

MEDEA: Why, it's lovely to see you as well, wise Aegeus, son of Pandion. How do you come to be passing through Corinth?

AEGEUS: Just passing through, on my way back from the oracle at Delphi.

MEDEA: Why should you have traveled to the center of the world where Apollo gives his prophecies?

AEGEUS: I wanted to know how I might become a father.

MEDEA: Heavens, no children yet?

AEGEUS: No, still childless, by some cruel twist of fate.

MEDEA: Are you married?

AEGEUS: Yes, I have a wife.

MEDEA: What did Apollo tell you?

AEGEUS: Words too clever for a man like me to understand.

MEDEA: Is it permissible for me to know the answer the god gave you?

AEGEUS: Of course: I could use a clever mind like yours.

MEDEA: What did he say, then?

AEGEUS: He said "not to uncork the wine-skin's spout...."

MEDEA: Until you do what, or come to what place?

AEGEUS: "Until I come to the home of my father once again."

MEDEA: Then why come to Corinth?

AEGEUS: Pittheus lives here. You know, the king of Troezen.

MEDEA: Yes, the son of Pelops, and he is most wise, or so they say.

AEGEUS: I thought to discuss the oracle with him.

MEDEA: Good idea – by all accounts he sounds the ideal man for the job.

AEGEUS: And the dearest to me of all my friends in arms.

MEDEA: Well, I hope you find what you're looking for.

AEGEUS: But...your eyes – have you been crying, my dear?

MEDEA: Aegeus, my husband is the worst man living.

AEGEUS: What's this now? Please, tell me what's troubling you.

MEDEA: Jason has wronged me without cause.

AEGEUS: What on earth has he done?

MEDEA: He has taken another woman as his wife.

AEGEUS: Surely he wouldn't do so shameful a thing?

MEDEA: Oh, he's done it. His old loves are now dishonored.

AEGEUS: Did he fall in love, or did you start to hate your marriage-bed?

MEDEA: Oh, he's very much in love – traitor to his family –

AEGEUS: So then let him go if he's so great an ass.

MEDEA: – He's very much in love with the idea of marrying into a royal family.

AEGEUS: But who has given them his daughter? Please finish your story.

MEDEA: Creon, who rules the land of Corinth.

AEGEUS: Then it's understandable that you should be upset, woman.

MEDEA: Yes. I'm ruined. I'm even being kicked out of this city.

AEGEUS: Who by? Here is an all new disaster!

MEDEA: Creon exiled me from Corinth himself.

AEGEUS: And Jason let it happen? I don't approve of that at all!

MEDEA: He says he doesn't approve, either, yet he does nothing to oppose it. I beg you, Aegeus, holding you by your knees – I am your servant and suppliant – for pity's sake don't watch me forced into lonely exile, but let me come into your country and take me into your home!

If you do this for me, then with the help of the gods your desire for children may come true, and you will die a happy man. You don't know how great a treasure you've uncovered this day, for I can arrange it that you'll be able to have children. I know the drugs that can make it happen.

AEGEUS: Of the many reasons I am happy to do you this favour, first among them is that it would be the will of the gods. And, then, the children whose birth you've predicted for me – for in that matter I am completely at a loss.

So this is how I see it: I cannot smuggle you out of this land, but if you can make it as far as my country, I will take you in and never give you over to anyone. But you'll have to get there on your own, for I would be blameless in the eyes of my friends and neighbours.

MEDEA: That seems reasonable, and if you just offer some pledge or oath to me I'll be well pleased.

AEGEUS: You don't trust me? Is my word not enough?

MEDEA: Oh, I trust you, I do. But both the houses of Pelias and Creon are my enemies, and if you are bound by an oath I am guaranteed you will not give me up if they try to drag me out of your land. You might be tempted to listen to their entreaties, for they have both riches and royal power, and you thus might back out of a mere promise that is not sealed with an oath to the gods.

AEGEUS: There's a great deal of foresight in your words. Yes, if you wish, I'd be happy to give you an oath. In fact, it will be a safety net for me, since I can hold it out to your enemies as a pretext for protecting you. So, there it is: name your gods!

MEDEA: I ask you to swear by the Earth, by Helios – the Sun – the father of my father, and every other god in addition to those ones.

AEGEUS: But to what, exactly, am I contracting? Name it.

MEDEA: Never to drive me out of your land, nor as long as you live to let someone else drag me.

AEGEUS: I swear by the Earth, by the bright light of Helios, and by all the gods, to do exactly as you demand.

MEDEA: That's enough – and what do you agree to suffer if you don't abide by your oath?

AEGEUS: The kinds of things that happen to evil men.

MEDEA: Good then, it's settled. Have a safe journey and I will see you soon – after I have done what I need to do and got what I want.

CHORUS (TO AEGEUS): May Hermes, lord and guide, son of Maia, bring you home, and may you quickly accomplish your purpose, since in our judgment you are a noble man, Aegeus.

Exit Aegeus

MEDEA: O Zeus and the Justice of Zeus and light of the sun! Now, my friends, sweet victory over my enemies will be mine. Now I have hope. This man has provided an answer to my greatest problem – safe harbour – and after my plot has been carried out I shall turn sail directly to him and the town and city of Pallas Athena.

Now let me tell you all that I have in mind. But you won't find it pleasant.

I'll send one of my servants to Jason to beg him back to see me face-to-face. When he comes I'll mollify him, tell him I see everything now and understand why he has done what he has done, that he thought it through carefully to the end and did only what was best for us all when he betrayed me.

Then I'll ask him to let my children stay here, not because I wish to leave them to be mocked by my enemies in an enemy land, but rather so that I may kill their step-mother by guile.

I'll send them off with gifts for the bride in their little hands – a finely-woven dress and a golden crown – begging that they not be sent into exile. And when she wears the dress and touches it to her skin, she will die horribly, as will anyone who tries to comfort her, for I will have treated dress and crown with deadly poison.

But let us not speak of this any further, for it leads inevitably to the deed that must be done next: I will have to kill my children. No-one will stop me from doing this and no-one will take them from me.

Then, when I have destroyed the entire house of Jason, I will leave this land, in flight from the charge of murdering my children and having dared to do the most unspeakable deeds. For, my friends, I will not allow my enemies to laugh at me. No, that will never happen.

There it is, then – what reason is there anymore for me to live? I have neither a country nor a home, nor a refuge from my own troubles. I erred fatally in leaving behind the house of my father and trusting the word of a Greek man. But he will receive his just reward very soon now, with the help of the gods.

He'll never see the children he had of me again after today, nor will he have new ones with his new bride. And I will not be remembered as a weak woman, but a terrible woman, who was as good a friend as she was hateful an enemy. The lives of such people have the greatest fame.

Chorus: Now that you have told us what you have in mind, and though we sincerely wish to help you, we also want to keep the laws of men, and so we beg you now: put an end to your scheme.

Medea: No, this is as it must be. I understand your horror, but you would understand me better if all that has happened to me had been done to you.

Chorus: But, woman, how can you kill your own children?

Medea: Because it is the thing that will hurt my husband most.

Chorus: But you'll live to regret it, and be the sorriest of women.

Medea: But I will live with it. Such talk is a waste of time: now the deed. (To the Nurse) Go now and bring Jason to me, for you're the one I trust the most, but tell him nothing of what I have in store, since you are a woman and care for me.

Chorus:

The Athenians have long been happy children of the blessed gods who sprung from a sacred, never conquered land, fed on the most glorious wisdom, gracefully stepping through the brightest of skies where it is said that the nine Muses Gave birth to golden-haired Harmony.

A song is sung of how Aphrodite took water from the clear streams of Cephisus and breathed upon the land the gentle sweet breezes, and how, as she always wears a fragrant garland of roses in her hair, the Desires accompany her as the companions of Wisdom, inspiring all forms of virtue.

How then will this city of sacred rivers and streams, the city that gives safe protection to friends, welcome you, the killer of children, the unholy one? Think of what it means to stab your children, think of what manner of murder you intend to commit! We beg at your knees, by all that is holy: do not kill your children!

Where will you find the resolve, either of heart or of hand, to inflict horror, pain and destruction on your own babies? How will you look on their faces and see there their coming deaths without sobbing? And when they fall down begging before you, surely you will be unable to wash your hands in their blood.

Enter Jason

Jason: I've come as you've asked, though you abuse me. So tell me, woman, what can I do for you now?

Medea: Jason, please forgive me for all of the things I said before. Surely you can't have forgotten my moods; we have shared so many loving memories together. I have been thinking about everything I said to you and finally I realize that I'm such a stupid woman! Why do I allow my temper to make me curse those who only have my best interests at heart? Why cast myself as an enemy to the rulers of this land and to my husband, who is only doing what is best for us all by marrying the daughter of the king and producing royal brothers for our children? Should I not just let go of my anger? What's wrong with me? Haven't the gods given enough gifts to me already? Don't I already have children? Don't I know that we've been exiled and that we need friends right now?

I see now that I have been very foolish, that my anger was foolish, and that I should listen to good advice. Now I am on your side – I agree that you have made a wise decision and marry for the benefit of us all. I should have been helping you all along with your plans, bringing all my considerable will to bear to make these plans happen. I should have been standing by the bed and counseling you how best to make love to your new bride. But we women are what we are – I won't say bad. Still, what's the sense in you avenging my stupidity with evil? Forgive me – I was foolish, but now I have had a change of heart.

Children, come out of the house, embrace your father and talk to him for me!

Enter the Children

Put aside your hurt feelings, as your mother has, and let us all be friends again. We've made peace; all anger is gone. Take our hands – there.

Oh, but the future looms large! Will our children have the opportunity to stretch out their own arms like this after a long life? I fear I'm about to start crying again, children: at last I have ended this long fight with your father. Comes, let me wet your tender cheeks with my tears.

Chorus: Tears are welling up in our eyes, too – dare we hope that things go for the better now and not for the worse?

Jason: What you have just said cheers me, woman, and if I am honest I can't really blame you for what you said before. It's normal for a woman to get angry when her husband brings a new wife into the home. But now your heart has seen the wisdom in what I have done, as any sensible woman would have, in time.

As for you, my boys, your father hasn't been asleep, but I have come up with a plan that will make you safe, if the gods are kind, and I think that, with your future brothers, you'll live to be the leading citizens of Corinth. You two just worry about growing up strong, and your father and whichever of the gods is on our side will take care of the rest, and one day you'll triumph your father's enemies.

But you, Medea, why do you turn away? Are you crying? Aren't you happy with what I just said?

Medea: Oh, it's nothing, really – I'm just thinking about the children.

Jason: But why? I'm going to see that they are well provided for.

Medea: I know you will. Women are women: we cry a lot.

Jason: Of course – but so many tears?

Medea: It's just that I gave birth to these children, and when you expressed the hope that they would live long and healthy lives I was filled with sadness, wondering if it could happen...

But as to the reasons I asked you to come to me. I realize now that my exile is the best solution for all concerned: I won't be in your way or a worry to those who rule this country, for I have made myself an enemy to them. I go willingly. But so that your children can be raised by the hand of their father, you should ask Creon that they be allowed to stay here with you.

Jason: I don't know if I can convince him, but I will try.

Medea: Push your wife to ask her father.

Jason: That is a good idea – she's a woman, after all, so I should be able to persuade her.

Medea: Yes, if she's a woman like the rest of us, she'll be easy to sway. In fact, I'll help you in this. I'll send the children to her carrying the most beautiful gifts the world has ever seen, a finely-woven dress and a golden crown – I'll get a servant to bring them here quickly – and she'll be doubly happy, having won you – the best of all men – as a bed-mate, and because she'll wear the garments that Helios, the Sun-god, father of my father, once gave to his children.

Boys, take these wedding gifts into your hands and convey them to the lucky bride – how could she resist them?

JASON: But why give away your lovely things? You need them more than she does. Do you think a royal princess has any need of either gold or dresses? Don't throw them away, for if this woman sees me at all, surely she'll value me much more than money.

MEDEA: I won't hear a word of it. They do say that gifts can persuade even the gods, and gold is certainly worth more to mortals than words. She has good fortune, the gods look on her and make her even better off, she is young, is a princess – and to save my children from exile I'd give my own life, let alone gold.

Go, children, to that wealthy house, and bow down before your new mother, the woman who now rules me. Ask her to spare you exile, give her these gifts, and be sure that she takes them from you with her own hands – this part is important.

Go now, quick as you can – do a good job for mother and bring back the good news she has been longing to hear!

Exit Jason, the Tutor, and the Children

CHORUS:
No longer is there any hope for the children's lives: they are gone, already murdered. The bride will accept the golden crown, her own destruction, and on her golden hair she will settle the gift of Death with her very own hands. The unholy beauty of the dress will persuade her to wear it, but she will be dressed as bride for the dead below.

And you, poor man, are both a new husband and curse to the royal family: you have no idea that you are bringing about the destruction of your sons and new wife. Foolish man! Prepare to learn just how far you've wandered from the life you planned!

We also mourn your grief, poor mother of children you will murder because their father broke the marriage law and took another woman into your bed.

Enter the Tutor with the Children

TUTOR: Ma'am, your sons have been spared exile. The royal bride was happy to take the gifts from them, and now there's peace between her and your children.

But what's this? Why the long face when everything is going to plan? Why do you turn your face away? Aren't you happy to hear my news?

MEDEA: O gods!.....

TUTOR: Your reaction doesn't match what I just told you.

MEDEA: Gods!....

TUTOR: Surely I have not brought you bad news without realizing? Was I wrong to think this what you wanted?

MEDEA: You've brought the message I wanted to hear – I can't blame you.

TUTOR: But then why is your gaze fixed upon the ground and why are you crying?

MEDEA: I have to weep like this, old man, for after much planning the gods and I have brought about this wicked thing.

TUTOR: Don't worry, mistress: one day you'll return here, with the children's help.

MEDEA: There can be no coming back for me, old man, or for certain others.

TUTOR: You know, you're not the only woman ever to have been separated from her children. Neither divine wrath nor divine suffering are for you. As you are human, you should bear your troubles lightly.

MEDEA: Yes, yes – that's exactly what I'll do. But you go inside now and give the children whatever they need to get them through the day.

Exit Tutor

Oh my lovely boys, you have a city and a home now, and you can always live here, deprived of your mother, left behind in her misery.

I'll go away into another land where I will miss seeing you prosper, and will not be there to make the plans for your weddings, or prepare your brides, or raise your wedding torches.

O gods, my willfulness has made me so miserable! My dears, raising you was a waste of time – a waste to wear myself down with the effort – and so too were wasted the harsh labour pains that I endured in your births. Silly me: once I put such great hopes in you, that you would care for me when I am old and bury me when I die, the envy of everyone.

Now that sweet future is gone from me. Ripped apart from the two of you I'll lead a life of hardship and pain, and you, you will never see your dear mother again, after you leave for your new life.

Why are you looking at me like that, my children? Why are you smiling this final smile?

Oh gods, what will I do? O women, looking into the bright eyes of my children my courage leaves.

I cannot do this thing – I can't. I need to forget my old plan – I'll take them with me from this place. Why on earth would I harm them to harm their father when it would make me suffer twice as much as him? No, I can't...

I can't let my enemies laugh at me. I must do this thing. I can't be a weak woman, and allow loving thoughts to creep into my head.

Go into the house now, my loves: mother will be with you presently. But he for whom it is not right to attend my sacrifice – Jason – let him remain outside our home until it is done. My hand does not shake, and I will not weaken.

Gods help me... Don't let yourself do this, Medea – listen to what your heart is telling you and let them be, poor girl: spare your children! If you take them with you to Athens, to live there with you, they will make you happy.

What is this drivel? I swear by the avenging demons in Hades below that sooner than see my babes mocked by my enemies I will see them die – and since they must die, it by my hand, because I am the one who gave birth to them.

IN ANY CASE, THE DEED IS DONE: the princess is doomed. Already the crown is on her head and the dress upon her body, which is dying – this I know for fact – and since I am about to set out on the cruelest of roads, and send my children out another, more painful still, I must speak to them one more time.

Boys, each of you give your right hand to mother so that she may kiss it. Oh your dear hands, your lips and mouths so dear to me, both of you born looking so noble and beautiful, may you forever be happy, though it must happen over there. For your father destroyed your chances of happiness here.

Oh the sweet touch of my children, your soft skin and sweet breath! You must go in – go, inside the house! I can't look at you anymore! So overwhelmed am I by the darkness that surrounds me.

Exit the Children

I am aware that what I am about to do is evil, but my anger toward Jason is so intense that it forms all my plans, and it is just this species of anger which will always cause the greatest harm to those who live and die.

CHORUS:

Often we, too, have embraced dark thoughts, and seen greater troubles than woman should endure – but we always found a way through it. For women also have a Muse who travels with us and makes us wise. Though perhaps she does not speak to all of us, and perhaps only one in a great many heeds all that the Muse says. That lucky women is barren, and much happier than parents, for the childless know neither the pleasure nor the pains children bring, miss not the former nor suffer the latter.

But those in whose homes sweet children are born and raised are worn down by constant worry. First they fret about how to feed and raise them well, and then how to leave them some savings, never knowing for sure if the recipients of all their toil will turn out to have been worthy.

But the very worst possibility, and the one from which none of us can be secure, is the danger that even if we raise them well and our children come of age – no matter how good they are – some god will snap his fingers and Death will hurry them off to Hades before you go yourself. How can it be right that, on top of all that we endure for our children's sake, the gods could add this most intolerable pain?

MEDEA: Well, ladies, it seems forever that I have been watching and waiting to find out what has happened at the palace. And finally I see one of Jason's servants coming in this direction. His angry breathing suggests he has bad news.

Enter the Messenger

MESSENGER: O Medea, you've done something horrible. You've broken the law, and now you must flee. Run for your life, in whatever way you can, ship or chariot!

MEDEA: And why, pray tell, would I need to flee?

MESSENGER: The princess has died, along with her father, thanks to your skill with poison.

MEDEA: O that is excellent news! Thank you, my friend: from this point forward you are always welcome in my home!

MESSENGER: What are you saying? Are you mad, woman? You've destroyed the royal family and you rejoice?

MEDEA: I'll be happy to answer any questions you wish to put to me, but first things first: how did they die? And hold nothing back, for you'll give me double the amount of pleasure if they went screaming.

MESSENGER: When your two children arrived with their father at the rooms of the new bride, those of us servants who pitied your troubles were delighted by the news going around that you and your husband had stopped fighting and were friends again.

One of us kissed the children's hands, another their blonde hair, and I myself, out of joy, followed them in to their meeting with the new bride. My mistress, whom we now pity instead of you, at first saw only Jason, but when she noticed the children she was upset and turned away in anger. Your husband, however, tried to calm her by saying to her: "Please don't despise my dear ones. Please, don't be angry: turn your head this way again. Consider the loved ones of your husband as if they are your own, and take these gifts and ask your father not to send my children into exile. Do it for me, please."

Well, when she saw the dress, she couldn't resist: she capitulated completely to her husband's wishes, and before the boys and their father had gone too far away from the palace she had slipped the garment on, placed the golden crown atop her head, and skipped lightly about the house, thrilled with the gifts, checking herself in the mirror again and again to be sure they were properly on.

What happened next was horrible to see. Suddenly she paled and trembled and stumbled sideways, her limbs and body shaking, and just managed to fall into her chair rather than the ground.

One of the old maidservants, thinking the girl had had the good fortune to be struck by a frenzy sent from Eros, hooted joyfully, but as soon as she saw the white foam on the girl's lips – eyes rolling in her head, blood fleeing her face – then the cry was changed to a shriek. Directly another servant ran to her father and another ran to the bridegroom to tell him what was happening. The whole house was filled with the sound of people running.

A good racer might have had time to complete the final sprint to the finish line before the poor girl broke her silence, opened her eyes wide, and let forth a terrible groan. For she was doubly assaulted, the golden crown sitting on her head emitting a torrent of devouring fire, and that beautiful dress, the gift of your children, eating away at her delicate flesh.

She sprang from her chair all on fire, shaking her head this way and that, trying to throw the crown, but its gold binding held fast and when she shook her hair the flames rose up twice as powerful as before.

She fell to the floor consumed, unrecognizable to anyone but a parent. From the top of her head the blood was flowing down mixed together with fire, and the flesh fell away from her bones just as the pitch flows down the pine – she was ripped apart by the invisible power of your poison. It was so horrible, I tell you, we were all too afraid to touch her body, when her father, poor man, unaware of the the miseries she had just endured, burst into the room and immediately gathered her corpse to him. As he kissed her he said, "My poor child, what god has murdered and taken you from me, I wish that I could die along with you, my daughter!"

But when he wanted to lift his old body from hers, he found himself attached to her fine dress as surely as the ivy clings to walls. It was a terrible struggle. He tried to get to his knees, but her body held him fast, and when he violently recoiled his old flesh ripped away from his bones. And finally the poor old man died – how could he survive?

They are there still, father and daughter, side by side, dead corpses, a disaster that would make anyone cry.

As to how this affects you, why speculate: you are certain to find out presently. I have long thought that our lives are but shadows, and I'm afraid that those who appear clever – those crafters of words – will bring upon themselves greater punishments along with their greater rewards. For one mortal can never truly be happier than another: one may appear luckier or be richer, but these things have a way of evening out.

Chorus: It certainly seems that some just god has decided to fasten many disasters to Jason today. O poor daughter of Creon, how we feel for you, gone into the halls of Hades a new bride, who made the mistake of marrying Jason.

Medea: Ladies, my mind is set for the deed – to slay the children with speed and then flee this land. I cannot delay, it would only give my enemies a chance to harm them with less gentle hands. So there it is: they have to die to be protected, and I must be the one to kill them, since I am their loving mother.

Come my heart, arm yourself! Why hesitate when evil is inevitable? Come on! O my bloody hand, take the sword, take it and hurry toward the miserable final consequence of all life!

Don't you dare falter! Don't you dare remember that they are your own flesh, or how dear they are to you, or how you bore them! For this short period forget that they are yours. You can weep forever, afterward.

Chorus:

O bright light of Helios, look down on this cursed woman before she lays murderous hands on her children. They are born of your golden race! They are your grandchildren! Is the blood of your blood to be spilled on account of something a mortal has done? It will happen unless you, o divinely-inspired light, drive this maddened Fury from her house!

The pains you suffered in giving birth will be wasted, Medea! The time spent raising them till now will have been wasted time! You who threaded the unfriendly strait and the clashing rocks! O poor woman, why is your mind so filled with anger that one murder follows so quick upon another? Murder within a family is a stain on us all, and vengeance pursues the perpetrator – sorrows delivered to your door by the gods themselves!

The Children (from inside): Help us! Help!

Chorus: Do you hear the babes shouting? O terrible and cursed woman!

First Child (from inside): What should we do? Where can any flee to evade the blades of home?

Second Child (from inside): Brother, we are done for!

Chorus: Should we enter? Surely we should intervene...

First Child (from inside): In the name of the gods, help us, someone!

Second Child (from inside): She is killing us!

Chorus:

O you evil woman, she must be made of stone or iron who would wield the scythe that harvests the children she raised.

We've only heard of one woman before this who raised her hand against her own: Ino, driven mad by the gods when the wife of Zeus banished her to wander. The poor woman flung herself into the sea and died along with her two children. What, I ask you, could be more horrible than that? Only her survival. O the many pains of love that women feel. They've brought so much evil to mankind!

Enter Jason

JASON: Hey you women who are standing in front of this house! Is the bitch inside, or already gone? She would have to go beneath the earth or sprout wings and fly to Heaven to escape what she has done in this place! Did she suppose that she could murder the rulers of the land and flee the palace without punishment? But it is the children I fear for. She will die badly at the hands of those she has injured still among the living, but I will save my sons despite them.

CHORUS: O you poor man, you don't know how wrong you are, or you'd never have come here.

JASON: What? Does she mean to kill me, too, then?

CHORUS: Your children are dead: their mother has murdered them.

JASON: O my gods – what are you saying? Then she has killed me, after all.

CHORUS: There is nothing you can do now.

JASON: But where? Are they in the house?

CHORUS: If you open the doors, you'll see the bodies.

JASON: Servants, I order you to unlock these doors! Open them so that I can see my boys, and pay her in kind!

Enter Medea from above on a chariot drawn by winged dragons

In the chariot with Medea are the bodies of the Children

MEDEA: Why break down the doors, searching for bodies and the one who killed them? Here I am: if you want something, just say it – if you dare – but you will never lay a hand on me, for just look at the chariot that my grandfather Helios loaned me to protect me from my enemies.

JASON: Hateful cunt, in one fell swoop you have become the enemy of me, the gods, and the whole human race. What evil is in you that you would thrust a sword into your own children simply to make me childless – and still dare show your face to the day? I would see you dead!

Finally I understand you. I didn't when I brought you out of your barbarian land and led you to civilisation, a bitch who betrayed her father and the land that produced and raised you. The gods have cursed me when by rights they should be cursing you, who killed your own brother before stepping lightly aboard the beautiful Argo.

That was when you learned to kill – with the death of your brother. And then you had my children, and killed them, too, when our marriage was over. No Greek woman would ever have dared do something like this, and yet I chose you over any of them to be my wife, in return for which you've taken back everything you ever gave me, leaving nothing but bitter ruin and hate. You're no woman but a lioness, an animal, more monstrous than Scylla with her many heads. But I won't dent you with ten thousand insults: your inhumanity makes you invulnerable!

Away with you, then, child killer – murderess! It's my fate now to mourn: I'll never enjoy my new bride nor ever look upon my children again – I have lost them all.

MEDEA: I would answer your charges point for point if father Zeus didn't already know all that I sacrificed for you, and how you treated me in return. You were never going to mock our bed and then lead a pleasant life laughing at me. Nor were the princess and her father, the one who made this marriage for you, going to send me into exile unanswered.

So call me lioness, or monster who lives in the caves and eats passers-by. I did what I had to: returned pain for pain.

JASON: But you feel it, too: you share in this grief!

MEDEA: Understand this: my pain is less knowing you will never smile again at the thought of me.

JASON: O children, what an evil mother you had!

MEDEA: O children, you died of your father's sickness.

JASON: But it wasn't my hand that killed them!

MEDEA: That's right, it was your arrogance!

JASON: Do you really think it right to kill them because of a marriage?

MEDEA: Do you really think there is anything more important to a woman?

JASON: Well, it would be fine for a sane woman – but you find everything to be a disaster.

MEDEA: Whatever. Your children are dead: you didn't feel for me, but this you can hardly help but feel.

JASON: But they will live, I hope, as spirits that haunt you.

MEDEA: The gods know which of us struck the first blow.

JASON: Yes, and they know that your soul is evil!

MEDEA: Vomit your bile, your piteous, canine whining!

JASON: I loathe the sound of you! It will be good for us to finally be finished with each other!

MEDEA: Will it? Then tell me how, because I want that, too!

JASON: Just let me bury the bodies of my children so I can mourn them!

MEDEA: No, that will never happen, since I am going to bury them myself in Hera's shrine up on the cliff. That way none of my enemies will dare insult them by tearing up their graves – you see, I'm always thinking – and up there I'll establish a holy festival and feast, and bring in rituals as an eternal memorial to unholy murder.

Myself, I am going to the land of Athens, where I will live with king Aegeus, the son of Pandion. As for you, since you are so loathsome and small, it is fitting that your death will be bitter and pathetic as well, struck on the head by a piece of the Argo – a fitting conclusion to our marriage.

JASON: I only pray that the Fury that punishes child-murderers, and the goddess Justice as well, join forces to destroy you!

MEDEA: And what god will heed your prayer – oath-breaker – betrayer?

JASON: And you think they will answer you, polluted with child murder?

MEDEA: Go bury your whore!

JASON: I'll go to her now – alone and childless.

MEDEA: Your sadness is only beginning – it will ripen as you age!

JASON: O my dear children!

MEDEA: Dear to their mother, not to you!

JASON: She who killed them!

MEDEA: To cause you pain!

JASON: All that I have lost, if I could just once more hold and kiss the faces of my sons!

MEDEA: Now you want to talk to them, now you want to hold them, when before you tossed them away.

JASON: In the name of the gods, please let me touch them!

MEDEA: No, there's no chance of that - save your breath.

JASON: Zeus, do you hear how I am rejected and how I am treated by this hateful, polluted, child-killing bitch?

But though you allowed it to happen I will weep and call on all the gods to witness: it would have been better for me if they had never been born than to live to see them murdered.

Medea flies away in her chariot, taking the bodies of the Children with her

CHORUS:

Zeus and the court of Olympians sometimes rule in ways that may surprise us. Often we don't get the verdict we anticipate. But whatever happens is their will, so that must be what happened here...

Translated by Stephen Russell, PhD
English by Jonathan Allen and Stephen Russell

Chapter 4
Sophocles
Ajax

The Story: In the waning days of the Trojan War, the great hero Achilles is killed, and there is a fight over who will get his arms. The mighty Ajax, "second best of the Greeks," believes that he deserves to take the arms, but after a vote they are instead awarded to Odysseus. Ajax is enraged by this decision, which he sees as an insult to his name. This play is the story of how Ajax responds – it is the story of a fallen hero and his descent into madness.

Apollodorus covers the outline of this story in his *Epitome*:

[E.5.5] The death of Achilles filled the army with gloom and dismay, and they buried him with Patroclus in the White Island in the Black Sea, mixing the bones of the two together. It is said that after his death Achilles now lives with his wife Medea in the Islands of the Blessed. And the Greeks held games in his honour, at which Eumelus won the chariot-race, Diomedes the footrace, Ajax won for throwing the discus, and Teucer won for archery.

[E.5.6] When the arms of Achilles were offered as a prize to the bravest, Ajax and Odysseus came forward to enter their names. The judges were the Trojans or, according to some, they were the Greek allies, and Odysseus was picked as the winner. Ajax was so overwhelmed by anger that he planned a night attack on the army; but Athena drove him mad, and she turned him, sword in hand, against the cattle, and in his frenzy he slaughtered all the cattle along with their herdsmen, mistaking them for Greeks.

[E.5.7] But after Ajax came back to his senses he also killed himself. And Agamemnon ordered that his body could not be burned, and so Ajax is the only man of all those who fell at Troy who lies buried in a coffin. His grave is at Rhoeteum.

Ajax

Characters

Athena
Odysseus
Ajax
Chorus (sailors for Salamis)
Tecmessa, the wife of Ajax
Teucer, the brother of Ajax
Eurysakes, the son of Ajax
Messenger
Menelaus
Agamemnon
Guards (of Ajax)

Scene: Outside of Ajax's hut, on the coast of Troy.

Enter Athena, who stands to the side, and Odysseus

ATHENA: Odysseus, son of Laertes, as ever I am beside you as you creep about in search of an edge over your enemies, yet it is confusing to find you here by the sea, in the camp of an ally – Ajax, who holds the last position in the battle lines, guarding the rear of your own troops. You've followed his traces in the sand unerringly like a Spartan tracking hound, and yes – no need to steal a peek – the man you seek is inside that hut, his head and sword hand dripping sweat from the recent slaughter. But tell me why we are here, so I might advise you.

ODYSSEUS: Dearest Athena, nearest to me of all the gods, though I cannot see you I hear your voice clearly. You are not mistaken: I have been following the trail left by an enemy, and now I see it is Ajax the shield-bearer, and no other. Last night he committed a terrible act of treason against us. If it was him. Nothing is certain, surely we can hope... There is still confusion in the matter, so I took it upon myself to find out the culprit personally...

This morning it was discovered that someone had killed the herd of our looted cattle, and with them the guards we posted. Everyone says that man in there is the guilty party. A witness told me he saw Ajax running off alone through the field with his sword dripping blood. Immediately I picked up the trail and... and I am confused. What goes on here? As ever, your arrival is timely, Athena. Your hand has always guided me surely...

ATHENA: Yes, I have long walked beside you, eager companion on your long road.

ODYSSEUS: Dear goddess, am I doing the right thing in coming here?

ATHENA: O yes – this is the man you seek.

ODYSSEUS: What could have inspired him to this frenzy?

ATHENA: He was upset at the loss of the arms of Achilles – to you.

ODYSSEUS: But why, then, attack the herd?

ATHENA: His intent was to murder you and your men.

ODYSSEUS: His Greek brothers in arms?

ATHENA: Yes, and he would have done it if I hadn't intervened.

ODYSSEUS: How did he dare do such a thing? How did he think he'd get away with it?

ATHENA: At night, in secret.

ODYSSEUS: How close did he come?

ATHENA: Very nearly all the way: the gates of Menelaus and Agamemnon.

ODYSSEUS: And what prevented him?

ATHENA: It was me, of course. I diverted his rage toward the spot where the army's stolen cattle and undivided booty were stored, and there he cleaved the spines of the horned beasts on all sides of him, thinking that now, with his bare sword, he was slaughtering the sons of Atreus, Menelaus and Agamemnon, now cutting down one of the other commanders. Yes, I encouraged the man to wander deeper into his own madness, and laid this snare for him.

Once he'd had his fill of killing, he bound up what few cattle remained alive and, still thinking them men, brought the flock back to his own tent, where he tortures them yet. Come, witness his plain madness, and tell the others what you've seen. Have courage.

You in there! Yes, you, Ajax, with all your enemies in chains! I call on you to come outside!

ODYSSEUS: What are you doing? Don't call him out!

ATHENA: Oh, do be quiet: stop acting like such a coward.

ODYSSEUS: For pity's sake, just let him stay inside!

ATHENA: Why? What are you afraid of? Is he not just a man, after all?

ODYSSEUS: Yes, of course, but the hatred he must have borne for me... must still bear...

ATHENA: But isn't laughter sweetest when it's at our enemy's expense?

ODYSSEUS: It's enough for me that he stays inside.

ATHENA: Are you superstitious about gazing on the face of madness, then?

ODYSSEUS: If he were in his right mind, then you know I would face him.

ATHENA: But he could not see you if you stood before him.

ODYSSEUS: Why? Has something happened to his eyes?

ATHENA: It will. He will not see you.

ODYSSEUS: If the gods will it, I suppose it must be so.

ATHENA: Good. Now be quiet and stay put.

ODYSSEUS: Fine, but I'd sooner be anywhere else...

ATHENA: Ajax! Must a friend call you twice?

Enter Ajax from the hut

AJAX: Why, Athena, welcome, blessed daughter of Zeus! I'm very glad that you are here so I can honour you with the spoils of my latest hunt.

ATHENA: That is well said, to be sure, but tell me: did you push your sword all the way through the army of the Greeks?

AJAX: Yes, I can certainly brag on that account, I won't deny it.

ATHENA: Did your mighty sword-hand bring low the two sons of Atreus as well, then?

AJAX: Oh, yes, absolutely – never again will they disrespect Ajax!

ATHENA: Dead then, are they?

AJAX: Yes, yes, the ones who robbed me of the glory that was my due are dead as they come.

ATHENA: Good enough, but what of the son of Laertes? Did he escape your wrath?

AJAX: You want to know what happened to your sneaky little pet?

ATHENA: Of course: your great rival, Odysseus.

AJAX: My dear goddess, that is the best part: he sits bound in chains within the hut, since I am not quite ready to let him die just yet.

ATHENA: What do you plan to do with him? What will it gain you?

AJAX: First, I will lash him to the post in the center of my hut...

ATHENA: Yes?

AJAX: ...then I will lash his back to tatters, and then I will kill him.

ATHENA: Surely you will not torture the poor man?

AJAX: Athena, please be content to have your way in all other things: that man will pay the only apt penalty. I will not change my mind.

ATHENA: Well, there it is. If you are so determined to do this thing, then go, set your hand hard to the culmination of all you have planned.

AJAX: I'm off, then! Bless you, dear lady, and I hope you'll always be my ally!

Exit Ajax back into the hut

ATHENA: See, Odysseus, how great is the power of the gods? Was there ever a man that planned more carefully or completely than that one? Or one more skilled at dealing with the ups and downs of his fate?

ODYSSEUS: I can't think of any. And yet I can't help but feel sorry for him, though he is my enemy. He is undone by madness, and I can't look upon him without thinking how easily his fate could be my own, and I finally see that all of us who live are nothing other than ghosts and empty shadows.

ATHENA: Look upon this picture and never say an arrogant word toward the gods, nor think yourself better than another merely because you are stronger or more favoured than they. A single day can bring low all the high things of man. The gods love those who know humility, and hate the wicked.

Exit Odysseus, and Athena disappears

Enter the Chorus

CHORUS:

Son of Telamon, who holds the solid earth and sea-ringed isle of Salamis, we rejoice when you prosper, but when you are backhanded by Zeus, or if an insult from the Greeks should reach your ears, we become fearful as the round-eyed dove.

From the night just ending a great noise rises, bringing disgrace upon us. Word is that you visited the meadow where the horses pasture and with your sword destroyed the captured cattle of the Greek troops, yet to be shared.

Slanderous Odysseus whispers it in every ear, persuasive, for the things he says about you are easy to believe, for those who wish to believe them. He who takes aim at a great man has a large target: it would not be so easy to spread such infamy about specks like us, but envy works against the great, though in war small men soon fall without their leadership. For small men are supported by the great as surely as the great are by the small.

But try telling the small man that: they it is who eagerly raise a clamour against you – and without you at our head we are powerless to defend against them. Out of your line of sight they twitter away like a flock of birds, but just like birds they would surely stop their chatter and fly if you were suddenly to appear, as from the shadow of an eagle overhead.

Was it Artemis, daughter of Zeus – O terrible Rumour, mother of shame! – who loosed you at the troops cattle? Perhaps she felt she wasn't sufficiently thanked for some victory, felt cheated of some glory owed, or didn't receive her portion of a hunt? Or could it be the war-god Ares, offended in some wise on the field of battle, who punishes you with this nightmare scenario? For never, lord Ajax, would your own inclination have tempted you so far astray that you would war on cattle: it must be a sickness sent by the gods! We pray that Zeus and Apollo protect us from this evil Greek speech, but if the great kings are telling lies, and if Odysseus, descendant of Sisyphus, is chief among the liars, do not, lord, do not linger longer in this hut by the sea, for it only fans the flame of their speculation.

Please: up, out of your seat, where you have loitered too long in the lull between battles, banking the flame of destruction until it licks at heaven. The spite of your enemies wastes no time, upon this you may rely: they laugh openly at you, with words like sword blades, cutting us deep.

Enter Tecmessa from the hut

TECMESSA: Friends who sailed on the ship of Ajax, fellow descendants of the earthborn race of Erechtheus, we who are so far away from the house of Telamon, yet love it dearly: cry out! For our mighty, strong-shouldered Ajax has gone down, swamped by a dark storm of sickness.

CHORUS: What burden has the night exchanged for day? Please tell us, daughter of Phrygian Teleutas, since mighty Ajax loves you dearly and holds you his bride, though captured as a prize of war. We know you would not tell us anything but the truth.

TECMESSA: How should I speak the unspeakable? For I'm about to tell you of a misery as painful as death. Last night our great Ajax was struck mad, and has since been actively bringing disgrace upon us all. Look inside the tent and see his victims – more properly sacrifices – still leaking blood, all bearing his unmistakable signature.

CHORUS:

The unbearable picture you have painted of an out of control man is the very same the Greek leaders are spreading, and makes our worst fear real, however heartily we wish to deny it!

How we dread the inevitable outcome, for everyone knows the man must die who with maddened hand struck down cattle and their guardians.

TECMESSA: Oh no! Then it was from there that he led the cattle in chains? Oh horrible! He slaughtered some of them right away, but others he hacked apart bit by bit, chopping randomly at their sides! Then suddenly he fixed on two white-hooved rams, slit the tongue out of one of them before cutting off its head and throwing it away. As for the other, he tied it to a post and horse-whipped it endlessly, cursing it all the while! What more proof could I need that a god had caused him to do these things?

CHORUS:

Now is the time to hide our faces and flee here with all haste - perhaps we might escape by boat, seated among the swift rowers, to wherever the boat will take us. For two kings utter such dire threats against us that we fear death by stoning – for us and for him. We stand to share the punishment of Ajax, who is in the toils of a terrible fate.

TECMESSA: But his madness is over now, as suddenly as it appeared. His anger has ended and he is once again in his right mind, but a new pain has shown itself to him, for what can be worse than when a man looks upon his own misery and realizes he caused it himself?

CHORUS: But this is good news, woman! Madness can be forgiven once it has passed!

TECMESSA: But ask yourselves: which is worse, to rejoice in your friends' destruction, or to share in their pain?

CHORUS: One is as bad as the other!

TECMESSA: Then, now that he is no longer ill, we are doubly troubled.

CHORUS: How so? What do you mean?

TECMESSA: While he was in the throes of madness, at least he enjoyed what he was doing, though for those of us who were in our right minds it was disaster. Now that he is sane again he is afflicted by guilt and shame, and even more desolate than the rest of us – tragedy compounded!

CHORUS: Yes, we see it now. He must indeed have been struck a blow by some god. Otherwise how could his pain be greater now that his sickness is ended?

TECMESSA: Yet that is how it is.

CHORUS: But what set him off? We share this grief, so please tell us everything.

TECMESSA: Very well, as you have an interest in this matter. Last night, when all of the lamps had been put out, he took his double-edged sword and stalked off on his insane mission.

I tried to stop him, saying: "What is it, Ajax? What are you doing? Where do you go when you haven't been called and no messengers ask for you, not even the sound of the war trumpets? Both armies are asleep."

His answer was short and familiar to me: "Keep quiet. It is a woman's place to remain silent. But not Ajax." And he rushed off alone.

All I know of what followed is that he returned dragging bulls, herd dogs and sheep, all lashed together. Some of them he cut off their heads, others he turned upside down and killed by breaking their backs, and some of them he bound and tortured, falling upon the menagerie just as if they were men!

Not long past he ran outside and conversed with some shadow, first damning the sons of Atreus, Agamemnon and Menelaus, then speaking badly of Odysseus, and laughing like hell all the while about the violence he had done defeating them.

But eventually, after he came back inside – with time and difficulty – he returned to his senses, and looking around the slaughterhouse, he struck his head and cried aloud, and threw himself down among the slaughtered beasts, clutching his hair and scratching his face.

And then, for a long time, he sat there, not saying a word. Finally he turned to me and in a threatening tone demanded that I tell him everything that had happened, and what depth of trouble he was in now.

My friends, I was terrified, and told him everything exactly as I had seen and understood it. And as I finished he cried such wracking sobs and moans as I'd never heard from him before. He always told me that crying was for cowards or the weak – in the past his groan was never so shrill, for previously it was the sound of a bellowing bull.

Now brought low by evil fortune, the man sits not eating, not drinking, there in the midst of that carnage. It's clear that he has something terrible in mind – I can see it.

Please go inside – help him, if you can. A man like Ajax can be swayed by the words of his friends.

CHORUS: O Tecmessa, daughter of Teleutas, it's terrible if, as you've told us, the man was driven mad by evil spirits.

AJAX (INSIDE THE HUT): Oh no, oh no...no no no.....

TECMESSA: He is getting worse! Do you not hear him?

AJAX (INSIDE THE HUT): Oh no, oh no...no no no.....

CHORUS: It sounds as if he's still mad, or mad again from the sight of what his sickness has done.

AJAX (INSIDE THE HUT): My son, my son!

TECMESSA: Eurysakes, he's shouting for you! What is he planning? Where are you, son? We are ruined!

AJAX (INSIDE THE HUT): Teucer! I want Teucer! Where is Teucer? Or is he still fighting while I sit here dying?

CHORUS: He sounds more or less coherent. Open the door, and perhaps, when he sees us, he'll feel some compunction regarding our situation.

TECMESSA: The doors are open – see how things stand...

The doors of the hut are opened

AJAX : Oh, my shipmates, my friends, the only ones still loyal to me – look at the waves of blood that lap about my ankles!

CHORUS (TO TECMESSA): Perhaps you were right – we should come back later...

AJAX : Oh, my only friends, you who brought me here, manning the oars – you and you alone can help end my suffering. Come slaughter me amongst the animals, I beg you!

CHORUS: Don't say such things! You can't cure evil with evil, you will only cause more pain.

AJAX: Are you blind? Can't you see the mighty deeds valiant Ajax has wreaked upon his enemies, the defenseless beasts of the field? I am a laughingstock, the shame too great to ever live down.

TECMESSA: Lord Ajax, we beg you –

AJAX: Won't you just leave me alone! You must distance yourself from me. Ahhh....

TECMESSA: In the name of the gods, we beg you, be sensible and listen.

AJAX: If only I hadn't let those bastards slip through my fingers, and made the fields flow with the blood of beasts instead!

CHORUS: What profit is there in desolation over what cannot be changed?

Ajax: Oh, Odysseus, it is you who have done this to me, you affliction, dirtiest rat crawling in the army – how you must be laughing at me now!

Chorus: But, Ajax, everyone laughs or suffers as the gods see fit.

Ajax: If only I could see him now, the devil, though I am done for...

Chorus: Hold your proud tongue! Can't you see that it's talk such as this that has landed us in this situation?

Ajax: O Zeus, father of my ancestors, if first you would allow me to destroy that detested trickster and the two ruling kings with him – then I would gladly kill myself!

Tecmessa: If you are praying for that, then ask too that I die with you, for what would become of me after?

Ajax: O Stygian Hades, you shine a dark, seductive light, a gloom that is so bright for me: take me, take me, gather me in to live with you. For I have lost my right to look on the race of the gods, nor would I take any pleasure from human companionship. Goddess Athena is torturing me to death, and so where can I flee? Is there any bolt hole that would have one such as me? All of my great deeds have been washed away, my friends, vengeance fallen upon me by means of this farcical 'victory' in the midst of which I stand, for which the army will relish my murder with their swords in both hands.

Tecmessa: Terrible that a sane man should say such things as he would never have said before today.

Ajax: O waves raging in the sea, goodbye, and goodbye caves of the coast! You've held me fast a great long time hereabout Troy, but no longer will you hold me alive, let everyone beware and understand!

O river Scamander and your nearby streams, so friendly to the Greeks, you'll never see my like again, I dare boast, or a greater man that the Trojan army has seen come from Greece. Yet now I must do without honour.

Chorus: We can hardly prevent it, but are not sure this is wise talk coming from one who has fallen on such evil times.

Ajax: Ai-ya! Who would have thought that my name – Ai-yax – would so well foretell my misery? For now I can shout "ai-ya" endlessly and it would never be enough.

My own father sacked Troy with Heracles and returned with all glory, in first place of excellence in the army, with most spoils and honours. I, his son, came to this land with no less strength than he, nor did I achieve lesser deeds with my own hands – yet I am disgraced by the Greeks and will die.

But I am sure of one thing: if Achilles was alive and able to decide which man of all of us would be the most worthy to have his arms, none would have received them before me. Yet the sons of Atreus give them to that scheming liar, spitting upon my own great deeds!

If my mind had not been driven off course, causing my eye to miss the mark, I assure you they would not have lived to fix such a crooked judgment against another man – I'd have been the last.

But Athena – fierce, unconquerable daughter of Zeus – knew what I was up to when I set out against them, grabbed hold and tripped me, caused me to stain my hands with the blood of cattle, not men. So they escaped, and now they are laughing. Yet any coward can escape a better man if the gods choose them over him.

What now? Clearly I am hated by the gods and the army of the Greeks as well, not to mention the entire city of Troy and surrounding plains. Do I go home, cross the Aegean alone, leaving my appointed station and the sons of Atreus? And how shall I look my father Telamon in his eye when I arrive? How allow him to see me return without honours when he won such great prizes in victory? I couldn't endure it.

Should I go instead to the walls of Troy and challenge every last Trojan to hand-to-hand combat, proving my worth to the Greeks by dying there fighting on their behalf? That would certainly make the son of Atreus happy – so that cannot happen.

There must be a way to prove to my aged father that his son is no coward. It's shameful for a man to desire long life when evil surrounds him on all sides. What pleasure is gained from a day when all it does is move you that much closer to death? Any man whose heart beats for empty hopes is no man at all in my opinion.

To be noble one must either live well or die well. That is all I have to say.

Chorus: Ajax, no one is saying you speak falsely – your words come direct from your own proud heart – but you must give way, allow your friends to prevail over you in this matter, and drop these dark thoughts.

Tecmessa: My lord Ajax, fate is necessity: I myself was born the daughter of a free man, as rich and as powerful as any in Phrygia – but now I am a slave. In this the will of the gods and your own hand were in accord, and so, since I have come to share your bed, I honour you and want what is best for you. Now I am begging you, in the name of Zeus who rules this house, and of the bed in which we were united: please do not abandon me to the jeers of your enemies by making me their captive! For on the day that you die I will be taken by the Greeks and live out the remainder of my life with the invective of my new Greek masters ringing in my ears: "See the concubine of Ajax, our mightiest suicide: once admired, now she is nothing more than a slave!"

My destiny is my own, but must I carry it and your shame as well? And, too, think of your father, whom you would be abandoning to bitter old age, not to mention your mother who still has many years left and spends each of them praying that you will come home to her alive. And above all, my lord, pity your son, who deprived of your care will grow up despised and abused.

Think of all the sorrow you bequeath to us if you die. There is nothing I can look to other than you. With your own spear you destroyed my home, and another fate took my mother and father to Hades: I have no other country but you, and no currency. You are my life and my salvation.

Please think of me if I have ever afforded you a moment's pleasure. Kindness should beget kindness, should it not? A man who would forget a debt of kindness was never a noble man.

Chorus: Ajax, if you have any pity in your heart, you will hear and praise the words of this woman.

Ajax: She will certainly receive all due praise from me, so long as she listens and does as I command.

Tecmessa: Dearest Ajax, you know I shall obey you in every way.

Ajax: Then bring my son to me now.

Tecmessa: But I sent him away because I was afraid.

Ajax: Of my madness, you mean.

Tecmessa: Afraid you would kill him.

Ajax: That would be in keeping with my fate.

Tecmessa: And I was trying to avert it.

Ajax: Yes, yes, good thinking.

Tecmessa: Then tell me what I can do to help you now?

Ajax: Bring me my son and let me speak to him face-to-face.

Tecmessa: Of course – the servants are protecting him nearby.

Ajax: Then what is keeping him?

Tecmessa: Eurysakes, my son! Your father is calling for you! Whoever is watching over him, it is safe now: bring him here!

Ajax: Are they deaf, or merely slow?

Tecmessa: The guard is bringing him now.

Enter a Guard with Eurysakes

Ajax: Lift him up, any son of mine will scarcely be fazed by the sight of newly-spilled blood. Let him be broken in like a horse, trained in the savagery of his father, so that he might be just like him. My son, I hope you'll be more fortunate than I have been, but in all other things my equal. If so, you'll turn out well.

But just now I envy you your ignorance, because you can have no idea of the troubles that are at hand. Sometimes the sweetest thing in life is to be innocent, for what you do not know can't hurt you. But a time must come when it will be necessary for you to show the enemies of your father what sort of man you are and who raised you.

Until then, enjoy the soft breezes, let your young soul get lost in them, and be a joy to your mother. Neither the Greeks nor anyone else will dare insult you even with me out of the picture, for my brother, Teucer, will be your tireless protector and raise you well, even if he does wander off to hunt his enemies from time to time. You shield-bearing soldiers, my fellow sailors, I command you to share in this task and communicate my command to my brother Teucer that he should lead this boy to my home, to Telemon and my mother, so that he may care for them in their old age and see them gently into the dark regions of the god below.

Tell him that my arms must not be given to the Greeks to dispose of in some contest where a crooked judge can decide the outcome – and they particularly shouldn't be given to he who has destroyed me. Rather, you my son, Eurysakes – your name means "broad shield", do you know it? – you should take my shield. Grip it tightly by its well-stitched handle and carry its impenetrable thickness, made from seven hides, before you. This shield is yours, my son. Direct Teucer that my other arms be buried with me.

But quick now, take the child inside and lock the gates as best you can. No, don't cry in front of the hut – women are so prone to weeping – any good doctor will tell you that a boil that needs it is best lanced quickly.

CHORUS: It is frightening to see you in such haste – your words have too sharp an edge.

TECMESSA: O my lord Ajax, what does your wild heart drive you to now?

AJAX: Do not question me. Control your tongue, woman.

TECMESSA: I beg you in the name of your son and of the gods not to betray us!

AJAX: You weary me! Don't you understand that I no longer serve the gods?

TECMESSA: Blasphemy!

AJAX: Tell it to someone they haven't betrayed!

TECMESSA: Won't you be persuaded?

AJAX: You've said far too much already!

TECMESSA: Only out of terror, my lord!

AJAX: Just shut the gates. Quickly!

TECMESSA: In the name of the gods, soften your heart!

AJAX: You disappoint me if you think, after all this time, that you can teach me to change my character, especially now. You knew who I was when I took you for my wife.

Exit Tecmessa, Eurysakes, and Guard, Ajax following behind

CHORUS:

Famed island of Salamis, caressed by the sea, blessed of the gods, always bright, never fog-bound! For us it's been such a long, miserable time so far away from you. We no longer count the months, and make our beds here worn thin by the passage of time and the sad expectation that one day soon we'll go, not home, but to Hades, the dark destroyer.

Ajax is with us here qnd will not be cured – best friend and protector turned the most formidable of our innumerable enemies! Alas, his spirit shares lodgings with a divine-sent madness. Long ago, Salamis, you sent him forth valiant to glorious war, but now that he feeds his lonely thoughts he is a source only of grief to his friends, while his former feats, excellently achieved, have all fallen away, leaving him friendless in the eyes of the sons of Atreus, miserable as they are.

Doubtless, when his ancient mother hears tell he is sick with disease that routs the mind – cry sorrow! – she must match the piteous plaint of the nightingale or hold the shriek deep within, beat her fists against her breast, and tear out her thin grey hair.

For better hidden away in Hades beneath the earth is the man who suffers from the empty sickness, for though his inheritance from his father's family was better than that of any of the toiling Greeks he no longer has the temper that he grew up with but is become a stranger to himself. Pity his poor father - how sad the madness of his son, which he is yet to know and has no cause to expect, for it is a ruin never known to afflict any in his family before.

Enter Ajax, carrying his sword, followed by Tecmessa

AJAX: Time, being long, eventually sees the springing up of every happenstance, and just as surely sees them buried again. And, too, nothing is immutable: even the most hardened oath and resolute intention can be conquered by time.

Even I, who was once so steely – as unbreakable as iron – for the sake of a woman have softened my words. I pity her for making her a widow and my son an orphan, leaving both in the hands of my enemies.

So I'll go to the bathing place in the meadow by the shore and there wash away the filth and blood that coats me, that I might escape the anger of the goddess. From there I'll go to some out of the way place, and hide my sword, this most hateful of weapons. I'll dig a hole in a place nobody can find, and Night and Hades can keep it safe for me down below.

Ever since I got this sword as a gift from Hector, my worst enemy, I haven't had anything good from the Greeks. The proverb is true, then: the gifts of enemies are not gifts at all and bring no profit.

In future I shall know better how to yield to the gods, and learn to respect the sons of Atreus again. They are the rulers, after all, one ought to bend to their will. Of course one should. Even the most formidable of powers must yield, in time, to authority. Terrible winters piled with snow must give way to fruitful spring, and even eternal night stands aside so that day might light its torch. The blast of the wind puts the raging sea to sleep, and not even all-encompassing Sleep holds forever those it has bound.

Recognizing this, how could I not learn moderation and restraint? I shall learn it, for just now I see that an enemy should be hated only so far if he may later be a friend. Though as to that, there are friends and there are friends, and where some are concerned it is wiser not to put too much stock in the harbour of their friendship, and friends like those should expect a like amount of friendship in return.

But matters at hand will now be well. As for you, woman, pray to the gods that I can put this right.

Exit Tecmessa

And you, my brothers in arms, honour me the same way that she does and, if my brother happens by, ask him to care for us and be loyal to you until my return. I am going where it's necessary for me to travel, but do just as I say and perhaps you may soon hear that, though I am unhappy now, I have been saved.

Exit Ajax

CHORUS:

We tremble with delight! We soar on wings of spiraling joy! O Pan, o Pan, O sea-roaming god, appear to us from Mt. Cyllene's snowy brow, our lord who makes the gods dance, so that in our company you may dance the rapid Mysian and Cnossian steps that you invented! And may lord Apollo, the Delian god, come over the Icarian sea to keep company with us, undisguised, well-disposed to us for all time!

Ares has lifted the coins from off our eyes, letting in again, o Zeus, the white light of a happy day dawning: Ajax has forgot his sorrows and once more performed with full sacrifices the rites of the gods, paying greatest reverence to them and their divine law! Time extinguishes all things and relights them again; now we can truly say nothing is impossible, when, beyond our hopes, Ajax has been translated from anger against the sons of Atreus.

Enter a Messenger

MESSENGER: Dear friends, I must report that Teucer has arrived from the mountains of Mysia. He went directly to the tent of generals in the midst of the camp and was abused on the way by the mass of the Greeks. Surrounding him, they hurled invectives and insults at him, threatening to stone to death the brother of the lunatic who conspired with the enemy. Their swords were in their hands when the elders stepped in and put an end to it.

But where is Ajax? It's important your commander know everything that has happened.

CHORUS: He left a short while ago a changed man, with a whole new outlook.

MESSENGER: Uh-oh. It seems I have been too slow getting here.

CHORUS: What do you mean?

MESSENGER: Teucer instructed me that Ajax must not be allowed to leave his hut before he has a chance to speak with him.

CHORUS: But he's already gone, as we told you, and in good spirits, left to make peace with the gods, his anger set aside.

MESSENGER: It will do him no good if Calchas' prophecy is true.

CHORUS: What now? What do you know about this that we should know?

MESSENGER: The way I heard it, Calchas slipped out of council in order to whisper in Teucer's ear that Ajax must not come out of his tent as long as there is daylight – that is, if he wanted to see him alive again. For the anger of the goddess still drives him, if only for this one day. Or so the prophet said. He also said: "The unwise mighty are brought low by terrible afflictions fit for mortals who have somehow convinced themselves they rank with the gods. On the day he left home, Ajax was given good fatherly advice, but he would not listen: 'Son, strive for victory with your spear, but always win with the help of a god.' But the prideful boy boasted: 'Father, with the gods on his side, anybody might win glory: but it takes a real man to do without them.' And on another occasion, Athena offered him assistance against the Trojans and he told her to go stand near the rest of the Greeks! For where he was standing the line would never break! Thus he incurred the wrath of the goddess. He does not see that he is just a man."

But take heart: if he is still alive today, perhaps you might still save him – with Athena's help. This is what the prophet told Teucer, and Teucer sent me to tell you. But as Calchas is a wise prophet, if you dally, that man is good as dead.

CHORUS: Poor Tecmessa, daughter of an ill-starred family, come hear what this man has to say and cease rejoicing.

Enter Tecmessa and Eurysakes

TECMESSA: What now? Why have you recalled me from my sweet relief?

CHORUS: This fellow brings disturbing news of Ajax.

TECMESSA: O no....well, man, what is it? Surely we've had disaster enough for one day?

MESSENGER: I don't know how things stand for you personally, but as for Ajax, if indeed he is no longer inside...

TECMESSA: He has gone, yes – what are you saying?

MESSENGER: Teucer sends word advising against it.

TECMESSA: But where is Teucer, and why did he say it?

MESSENGER: He'll be here soon, but sent me ahead, for he believes Ajax must die if he leaves the protection of the hut today.

TECMESSA: How do you know all of this?

MESSENGER: From the prophet Calchas.

TECMESSA: No! My friends, please save me from this new disaster! Some of you fetch Teucer here as quickly as possible; the rest go east and west of the harbour and find my husband wherever his black mood has led him! He has deceived me! He cares nothing for what happens to us, my son – what am I to do? One thing is certain: whatever it is, it must happen now, and I'll go as far as my strength will take me. Let's go! Hurry! There is no time for standing about when you're striving to save a man who is in a hurry to die!

CHORUS: We're on our way! The speed of our feet will be exceeded only by the conciseness and brevity with which we explain to you exactly how exceedingly fast we are leaving! Which is to say: fast! Okay, we're off, right................................. now!

Exit Tecmessa, Eurysakes, the Messenger, and the Chorus

Enter Ajax

AJAX: The killer stands where his thrust will cut the deepest, if he has the time for such calculation. This sword was a gift from Hector, the man most hateful to my sight. Now I will ask this hostile Trojan land to hold it for me very firmly, point up, newly sharpened on the iron-eating whetstone, so that it might be kind and give me a quick death.

So. I am ready. This my will. I call on you first, O Zeus, as is right, to help me. It's not a large boon that I ask. Please send some messenger to bring the news to Teucer, so that he will be the one to lift me up after I have fallen on my sword, and not one of my innumerable enemies, who would only use my body as food for dogs and birds.

I also call on Hermes, guide of the underworld, to please put me gently to sleep when with a quick movement the point of the sword is pushed through my ribs.

I call on the everlasting virgins, the holy Furies with their long strides, who always observe all human suffering, so that they may witness how I have been destroyed by the sons of Atreus. Please snatch those evil men away in a manner that's fitting for them. Just as they see me falling a suicide, let them perish at the hands of their closest relations! Come, swift avenging Furies: feed on the whole army! Spare no one!

Helios, the Sun-god, who drives his chariot over the steep heaven, when you see my homeland, pull up a moment and announce my death to my old father and the wretched woman who nursed me. No doubt my mother's cries, when she hears of this, will echo throughout the entire city.

But what's the use in moaning? The deed must be done, and with speed! Death, come visit me... and I shall return the favour...

I greet you Helios, shining light of the present day, for the very last time.

Holy soil of my home island Salamis, foundation of my father's home and hearth; famous Athens, and the people who grew up there with me; and these springs and rivers; and the wide Trojan plains... Farewell O my nurses! This is all that Ajax has to say to you. The rest I shall say to those in Hades below.

Exit Ajax

Enter the Chorus in two parts, from opposite sides

CHORUS A: Trouble upon trouble! Where have we failed to look? No place seems likelier than any other! But listen! Do you hear that?

CHORUS B: That was us over here, your shipmates.

CHORUS A: What news?

CHORUS B: We've searched the entire west side of the harbour.

CHORUS A: And what have you found?

CHORUS B: Trouble and toil, and little else.

CHORUS A: Nor does the man make his presence known anywhere on the eastern side.

CHORUS:
Which of the toiling sons of the sea who spends their time in endless hunting, or the goddesses of Olympus,

or of the flowing rivers of the Bosphorus, might tell us they see that fierce-hearted man approach and from which direction? For we cannot see the stricken man.

Enter Tecmessa and the body of Ajax

TECMESSA: Oh no...oh no....oh no...

CHORUS: Who comes crying out from the woods?

TECMESSA: This is our ruin!

CHORUS: It is Tecmessa, his ill-fated bride, the captive of his spear, lost in grief.

TECMESSA: I am destroyed, friends.

CHORUS: Tell us.

TECMESSA: Here is Ajax newly-slaughtered, sword hidden deep in his own belly.

CHORUS:
Oh no... Our way home... Lord Ajax, you have killed your shipmates along with you. Poor man! And poor woman, too...

TECMESSA: This is how it is – all we can do now is cry.

CHORUS: But how did this happen? By whose hand...?

TECMESSA: By his own hand, this is clear, his sword fixed firmly in the ground to receive him.

CHORUS:
We are ruined. We didn't see, and now you lie covered in your own blood, having died alone and lonely, without the solace of your friends, and we deaf to your cries.

Where shall unbreakable Ajax lie? Ill-omened name...

TECMESSA: He shall not be seen! I've hidden him with my cloak, for none of his friends could bear to look upon him while the blackened blood flows from his nostrils and the gaping wound that he inflicted on himself.

What should I do now? Which of his friends will lift Ajax up? Where is Teucer? If he were to arrive now he'd be just in time to bury his brother.

Oh, Ajax, for a man like you to have such an end. Even your enemies should cry to see it.

CHORUS:
Immovable man - so finally you fulfill your inevitable destiny, bringing a final close to your interminable moaning through both day and night, and your passionate hatred for the sons of Atreus. That was the beginning of our trouble, when competition was declared for the arms of Achilles.

TECMESSA: No... No... No....

CHORUS: It's true and blameless pain that twinges your heart.

TECMESSA: No... No... No....

CHORUS: We understand, you loved him so.

TECMESSA: You understand it – I have to live with it.

CHORUS: ...You're right.

TECMESSA: Next we'll be slaves, my poor, poor son – those are the manner of people who rule us now.

CHORUS: No, surely that would be unthinkable, even for the ruthless sons of Atreus. The gods will prevent them from doing so!

TECMESSA: None of this would have happened if not for the gods!

CHORUS: It is true, they've placed a heavy burden on your shoulders.

TECMESSA: All this is the work of Pallas Athena, terrible daughter of Zeus, to please her dear Odysseus.

CHORUS: No doubt our celebrated hero is enjoying a good laugh at Ajax's maddened suffering... What fun! Ha ha! And chuckling right along with him, the sons of Atreus.

TECMESSA: Let them rejoice at the misfortunes of this man! Though they had no use for him while he was alive, they will certainly regret the loss of his spear. Petty men don't know what they've got until it's gone.

His death, as painful to me as it is sweet to the Greeks, was for Ajax a pleasure: for with this he has deprived them of their victory. How will they laugh when the gods are the ones who killed him, not men?

Let Odysseus enjoy his futile jeering, for Ajax cannot hear it anymore, and only to me is it a source of sorrow!

Enter Teucer

TEUCER: Oh no!

CHORUS: Everyone be still. Hear the voice of Teucer, who cries out at this disaster.

TEUCER: Dearest Ajax! Face of my brother! Have you done as Rumour says you did?

CHORUS: The man is dead, Teucer – we can tell you that.

TEUCER: If this is true, my fate hangs heavy as well.

CHORUS: Since it is so...

TEUCER: Oh no, no brother....

CHORUS: ...you may well lament.

TEUCER: This pain strikes deep.

CHORUS: Yes, it's terrible sharp.

TEUCER: But what of the boy? Where in this Trojan country is his son?

CHORUS: He is alone, beside the huts.

TEUCER: Then bring him to me as quickly as possible, in case one of his enemies should try to snatch him up like the cub of a lion who has strayed too far from its mother. Quickly! All men mock their enemy when he lies at their feet.

Exit Tecmessa

CHORUS: While he was yet alive, Ajax asked that you care for his child, just as you are doing now.

TEUCER: This is the most painful sight these eyes have ever seen. No other road on which I have stepped has caused me as much pain, dearest Ajax, as the one I entered upon when I heard what happened to you. Swift Rumour passed among the Greeks saying you were dead. When I heard it I shuddered, but now I see it with my own eyes the sight of you destroys me. Ay-ax! Ai!

Uncover him so that I may see this evil in its entirety.

Ajax is uncovered

I can hardly bear to look at that proud face with its bitter courage; how many miseries, Ajax, have you invented for me by dying? Where can I go, and to what people, when I failed you so utterly in your time of need?

I'm sure our father will be delighted to see me when I arrive home without you. Of course he will – the man never cracks a smile at good tidings, let alone bad. What will he not say to me? What vile names won't he hang on me, just a bastard born from an enemy's concubine? Coward and weakling at the very least, or worse, betrayer. He'll say I wished control of the family and to rule Salamis. The old tyrant. I expect I'll be sent into exile, reduced by his words to the level of a slave instead of a free man. And that's just the treatment I may expect in the bosom of our family. Here at Troy...

Oh...what should I do now? Drag you off that spike, for a start, I suppose. That Hector is quite the killer: even dead he managed to put his sword in you. Just think of it! Hector, tied to the back of a chariot with your belt and dragged to death; then you, Ajax, end by falling upon Hector's sword. Was this sword not forged by some Fury, that belt not made by Hades? For it's the gods who have caused these things, sure as I'm standing here, and anyone who thinks otherwise can keep it to himself.

CHORUS: Please, don't linger over your eulogy, but consider how we can hide this man in a grave, and what threatens to happen next if you fail to do so. For an enemy is on the horizon, and when he arrives he'll surely lick his lips over our misfortunes, as evil men are wont to do.

TEUCER: Who is it that approaches?

CHORUS: Menelaus, whom we sailed here to help.

TEUCER: Yes. I recognize that cock-walk even at this distance.

Enter Menelaus

Ajax 69

MENELAUS: You! Leave that body where it lies, I command it!

TEUCER: The enormity of that request is so sheer I wonder you even bother making it.

MENELAUS: It is my decision, and that of my brother Agamemnon, who is in charge of the army.

TEUCER: And on just what grounds do you dare make it?

MENELAUS: Because this man has proven a worse enemy than the Trojans – a traitor who plotted to murder the entire army in its sleep! If the gods had not interfered, all of us would be lying dead in his place! Therefore no man will lay Ajax in the grave: instead, he will be food for the birds that fly along this sandy coast. No, don't bother making a show of your fierce anger: we couldn't control him while he was alive, but we shall certainly master him now that he is dead, whether you will it or no, and make an example of him. We take charge of his body now because at no time previous did we even have his ear.

For it is the mark of a low nature when a man of low rank refuses to obey his betters. Anarchy soon reins in a city where transgression carries no fear of reprisal; likewise, regulations governing an army must be seen to have teeth.

Every man must know that, large and powerful though he may be, he stands to lose it all in an unguarded moment. Only when a man always feels the eyes upon him – fear and shame – is he truly safe. And that is why, if any man commits an outrage and gets away with it, the city, however powerful, and however long it has stood, begins to crumble.

Fear is there to protect us, for we mustn't be allowed to think that if we do whatever we will that we won't be punished. And turnabout is fair play: this man fairly brimmed with insolence in life, now it is my turn, and he won't cheat me by dying. So I order you before all those here not to bury him – and if you do, be prepared to join him!

CHORUS: Menelaus, after such a wise speech, do not lower yourself to mistreating the dead.

TEUCER: Men, never again should you be shocked when a low-born man acts badly, if a noble will stoop to uttering so crooked a speech. Let me say it straight: do you really claim ever to have ruled over this man? Did he not sail away from Salamis as his own master to be an ally to the Greeks? By what right were you his commander, and by what authority do you rule the troops that accompanied him from home? You came here as ruler of Sparta, not us. You can lay no more claim to ruling him than he could have claimed to ruling you. In fact, if memory serves, you sailed here under another's orders, not as general of the assembled forces, so tend to your business of ordering about those actually under your command – spout your pompous drivel at them. But as for him, whether you or the other general wish it or no, in spite of your threats, I will bury Ajax.

He didn't join this expedition in order to reclaim your wife, like those poor, overworked fools of yours, nor at the behest of a non-entity like you – he came because of the oath he had made.

Go on, then, clear off, and come back when you've got more heralds, and maybe the general as well. I'll listen no further to a man like you.

CHORUS: These words seem ill-advised. True they may be, but they cut too deep.

MENELAUS: Seems rather sure of himself for a mere archer.

TEUCER: It's not a vulgar skill.

MENELAUS: You'd be better suited to boasting if you carried a shield.

TEUCER: You're pretty well armoured, why don't you try me?

MENELAUS: I wonder: are you as fierce as your tongue?

TEUCER: Outraged justice inspires courage.

MENELAUS: Is it just, then, to honour the man who murdered me?

TEUCER: Murdered? How strange that you should be dead, yet still standing here talking our ears off...

MENELAUS: The gods spared me: so far as Ajax was concerned I was dead at his hand.

TEUCER: Then how do you, of all men, have the audacity to dishonour the gods?

MENELAUS: How dishonour?

TEUCER: You can ask that, when you stand here demanding that the dead go unburied?

MENELAUS: Yes, my enemies – that is the will of the gods!

TEUCER: Did Ajax ever really stand before you as an enemy?

MENELAUS: He hated me, and I hated him – you know this.

TEUCER: Of course he hated you – you rigged the jury against him in the matter of Achilles' armour.

MENELAUS: That was the decision of the vote, not mine.

TEUCER: Ah, but it was you who did the tally.

MENELAUS: ...These words will go hard for you.

TEUCER: I don't think I'll feel more pain than I cause.

MENELAUS: I have only one thing to say to you: this man will not be buried.

TEUCER: And I have only one thing to say in reply: he will.

MENELAUS: I once knew a man with a tongue as bold as yours. He convinced sailors to go to sea when a storm was expected, but soon shut up when the wind and rain blew up: just lay huddled beneath his cloak and made the sailors step around him as they scurried about. Never said a word. I expect it will be the same with you and your big mouth. Never fear, your storm is coming.

TEUCER: I, too, once knew a man, a moron who liked to show up at funerals and harass the mourners, until one day someone who looked a lot like me, with a short temper not unlike my own, looked him dead in the eye and said – let's see if I remember it right – something like: "If you insist on disrespecting the dead I'm going to put an arrow in you." Yes, I see it all quite clearly now, as if it were yesterday, and, in fact, now I recall that the idiot looked exactly like you. Not being too subtle for you, am I?

MENELAUS: That's it, I'm leaving. Why trade insults with fools when it's so much easier simply having them killed.

TEUCER: Good – get lost. It's an even bigger waste of time dignifying your windy words.

Exit Menelaus

CHORUS: Now hard battle is inevitable –
Hurry, Teucer, find a place
To lay your brother down,
A tomb to be remembered by men forever.

Enter Tekmessa and Eurysakes

TEUCER: Here come his wife and son, just in time for the burial rites.

Child, come here – kneel and embrace your sire. Sit in supplication with three locks of hair in your hands – one from me, one from your mother, and one from your own head: the gift of the suppliant.

Should anyone from the army try to pull you away from this body, may he die badly and be himself unburied, an exile from his own country, and may the whole of his family be cut down along with him as I now cut off this lock of my hair.

Hold onto the body with all your might, my boy: protect it, and let no one move you.

And as for you (*to the* Chorus) - stand near and act like men. Support him until I come back – I go to prepare his grave, come what may.

Exit Teucer

CHORUS:

What then will it be, the number of the wandering years which strand us seemingly forever in wide Troy, suffering the endless torment of battle-sufferings, a sad reproach to the Greeks?

I wish that he had gone instead to Heaven, or into Hades that is common to all, whoever it was who first taught the Greeks to war with hateful weapons and share the pain that brings only more pain, in a round! For that was the man who ruined them, and robbed we poor soldiers of garlands and deep draughts of wine, deprived us of the sweet sound of pipes and the pleasure of sound sleep at night. He cut us off from the passion of love, and now we lie uncared for in the morning, hair strung with thick dew to remind us where we've wakened once again, in miserable Troy.

Previously relentless Ajax was our defense against missiles and terror in the night,; but now he is given up to hateful fate what spoils – what treasure now – will be a soldier's portion? We long for the wooded bay of Salamis, our home caressed by waves, that we might sail out and greet holy Athens!

Enter Teucer

Teucer: I am returned in haste because I spotted Agamemnon rushing toward us. It seems that fool, too, has a few choice words for us.

Enter Agamemnon

Agamemnon: You there! I am informed that you've been gaping your stinking trap like you think you can slander my house and survive it! Yes, I'm talking to you, son of that slave-bitch! Doubtless, had you been born of noble woman you'd be speaking even more boldly and walking taller than you do as a nobody standing in defense of his nothing brother.

You say that Menelaus and I came here neither as generals over either you or the Greeks, and that Ajax sailed as his own commander. Pretty talk from a lowborn slave! Who is this paragon that you trumpet so loudly – where did he go, where did he stand that I did not stand myself? Do the Greeks have no other men but him? It was an evil day for us when we decided there would be a tournament for the arms of Achilles, for since then, despite the decision of the judges, Ajax and Teucer have been revealed the sorest of losers.

If such behavior as you counsel were permitted, then no laws would stand upright, for it would mean taking what has rightfully been earned by the just and bestowing it instead on the second-rate. This will never happen. The brawniest man is not necessarily the best: rather, he of sound mind makes the ideal citizen. An ox has the broadest back, but must be whipped down the straight and narrow road. It is this very remedy I prophesy for you, and presently, if you don't listen to reason. This man here is already a ghost and perhaps beyond reach, but you shouldn't forget I can still lay hands upon you.

Be reasonable: behave according to your class, or failing that task a free man with arguing your case, for the nonsensical babble of a barbarian cannot sway me.

Chorus: Please, gentlemen, be reasonable: you will never receive better counsel than that.

Teucer: It amazes me how quickly the memory fades of the debts we owe the dead. Despite the innumerable times you fought beside him, Ajax means nothing to you now, everything he did for you thrown away and lost just as if it never happened.

For you, of all people, to speak such foolish words... Have you somehow forgotten the day you were hemmed in by a shower of spears, while fire wreathed the masts of the ships and Hector leapt among the trenches? Who was it alone that came to your defense? Wasn't it he who you claim never set foot anywhere that you didn't? Did he do this because you ordered him? Did he face Hector in single combat on your order, or was it decided by lot? And was his token the heaviest he could find, that would sink to the bottom of the helmet, or was it the lightest and most eager to spring from the pot? That is the kind of man he was. And I stood beside him, I the slave, born of a barbarian mother.

Fool, how dare you look me in the eye and speak such idiocies. Have you forgotten, too, that your grandfather was old Pelops, a Phrygian barbarian? And that Atreus, your father, served his brother Thyestes the unholy meal of his own children? You are the child of a Cretan mother, who as a girl was caught with a lover and sent by her father to be food for fish. And you dare chide me about my origins? My father, Telamon, received the royal daughter of Laomedon as his bride as due prize for being first in courage and valour in the army by Herakles, son of Alcmene herself. As the son of two equally noble parents, how could I bring shame on my blood, by allowing you to profane my brother, who now lies in such distress?

Be sure of this: if you cast him aside you do the same to his brother, his wife, and his son. Better I should die fighting on behalf of my brother than to do so for that wife of yours – or should I say the wife of your brother?

You would do better to look to your own affairs and leave mine to me – for, if you think to be bold with me and mine, one day soon you'll wish you had been a coward.

Enter Odysseus

CHORUS: Lord Odysseus! You're just in time, if you've come to salvage this situation!

ODYSSEUS: What's all this, then? I could hear you bellowing over this brave warrior's corpse from all the way down the beach.

AGAMEMNON: Yes, well, then did you also hear the disgraceful things his brother has been saying?

ODYSSEUS: It is easy to forgive a man who merely returns an insult.

AGAMEMNON: Of course he is insulted! He has earned it! His actions toward me were shameful!

ODYSSEUS: What harm has he done you?

AGAMEMNON: He defies me, and insists on burying this corpse!

ODYSSEUS: ...Might a friend speak his mind to you, yet remain a friend no less than before?

AGAMEMNON: Of course, Odysseus – speak! I would not show sense otherwise, regarding you as I do my greatest friend of all the Greeks.

ODYSSEUS: Then listen to me. In the name of the gods, do not leave this man unburied. Do not allow hate to rule and compel you to tread all over justice. Ever since I won the arms of Achilles, Ajax loved me least of any man in the army – but even so, never will I deny that he was the best of us who came to Troy, excepting only Achilles himself.

It is not right for him to be dishonoured by you. If you do that, then you do no harm to him, but great damage to the laws of the gods.

AGAMEMNON: Odysseus, do you fight for this man, against me?

ODYSSEUS: Yes, though I did hate him – when it was right to hate him.

AGAMEMNON: Is it any less fitting for you to wipe your feet on him now he is dead?

ODYSSEUS: O son of Atreus, I beg you, do not reduce yourself to taking unfair advantage.

AGAMEMNON: It is not an easy thing for a ruler to follow the law and show pity.

ODYSSEUS: Nor to honour friends who give good advice?

AGAMEMNON: A good man must abide by the will of those in power!

ODYSSEUS: Stop. You would rule better in this case by yielding to your friends.

AGAMEMNON: Remember the kind of man for whom you are attempting to do a favour, Odysseus. Do you forget what he meant to do to all of us?

ODYSSEUS: He was my enemy, it's true – but he was once noble.

AGAMEMNON: What do you suggest? That we honour him?

ODYSSEUS: His excellence moves me far more than hatred does.

AGAMEMNON: The man was unstable.

ODYSSEUS: Yes, and many men who appear stable later turn out duplicitous.

AGAMEMNON: And you think such people should not be made examples?

ODYSSEUS: It's not in me to abide an inflexible nature.

AGAMEMNON: ...You will make us all look like cowards.

ODYSSEUS: On the contrary, you will look like men of justice in the eyes of all the Greeks.

AGAMEMNON: Are you sincerely telling me that I should let this body be buried?

ODYSSEUS: Yes. For every one of us will also one day come to this same end.

AGAMEMNON: The whole world over, every man looks only to his own self-interest... It is short-sighted, Odysseus.

ODYSSEUS: For whom, then, is it more fitting that I should work than myself?

AGAMEMNON: Very well, then – but let it be called your ruling, not mine.

ODYSSEUS: That's fine – if you abide by it, you will still be acting justly.

AGAMEMNON: Just understand this: to you I would give even greater favours than this one, but that man remains the enemy of us all whether he lies here or is stowed underground. Do what you will...

Exit Agamemnon

CHORUS: Odysseus, after this, anyone who says you are not wise is a fool.

ODYSSEUS: And now I announce before you all that, as much as I was once his enemy, now I am Teucer's friend. I wish to aid in burying the dead, taking part in every phase, neglecting none of the things that should be done in honour of the best of men.

TEUCER: Noble Odysseus, I can give you only thanks. You have completely reversed my expectations of you. While he lived you were the most hated of all the Greeks to my brother, yet you alone stood by him after his death. You do not give way to impious laughter at having outlived your enemy, unlike that insane general and his brother. They it is I pray that the father who rules Olympus, and the unforgetting Furies, and Justice, who can do all things, will destroy. But for your part, Odysseus, son of aged Laertes, I cannot allow you to touch his grave, for fear of offending the dead man. But you may take part in all the rest, and if you want to bring along anyone else from the army, we won't mind.

I'll dig the hole myself, but you should know that as far as I am concerned you are a good man.

ODYSSEUS: That's fine. I respect the wishes of the family and withdraw.

Exit Odysseus

TEUCER: Quickly! Too much time has passed already. Some of you dig a hollow trench with your hands, and others erect a tall tripod in the middle of the fire for the sacred bath. And someone go and fetch the armour from his hut that he used to wear beneath his shield.

You boy, Eurysakes, with all your strength, gather your father lovingly to you and help me raise him. Careful – for his body is still warm and may drool black blood.

Come, everyone who claims to be a friend, and bend to your work for the sake of this man, for there was no better man than Ajax, when he was alive. This is what I say.

CHORUS: Mortals can understand many things when they see them. But before he sees them no one can be a prophet of what will be. Man can make laws, but must judge each case on its own merits.

Translated from the Greek by Stephen Russell, PhD
English by Jonathan Allen and Stephen Russell

Chapter 5
Tacitus
THE STORY OF MESSALINA

The Story: Book 11 of Tacitus' *Annals* takes place in 47-48 AD and features the adventures of Messalina, the notorious wife of the emperor Claudius. Much of what Tacitus writes about Messalina should be treated with a great deal of skepticism.

Tacitus, *The Annals*, Book 11

[11.1] Messalina believed that Valerius Asiaticus, who had twice been consul, was one of Poppaea's old lovers. At the same time she was looking greedily at the gardens that Lucullus had begun and that Asiaticus was now decorating greatly, and so she persuaded Suillius to accuse both Asiaticus and Poppaea. Sosibius was with Suillius, who was the tutor to Britannicus, and he was supposed to give Claudius an apparently friendly warning to be mindful of a form of power and wealth that threatened the throne. Asiaticus, he said, had been the ringleader in the murder of an emperor, and at that time was not afraid to face an assembly of the Roman people, to confirm the deed and claim its glory for his own. He was to add that Asiaticus had thus grown famous in the capital, and that his renown had spread widely throughout the provinces, and that he was planning a journey to the armies of Germany. Asiaticus was born in Vienna, he was to say, and he would find it easy to rouse nations allied to his house because he would be supported by numerous and powerful connections there. Claudius made no further inquiry, but sent Crispinus, commander of the Praetorians, to lead troops out in a hurry, as if they were going to put down a revolt. Crispinus found Asiaticus at Baiae, where he covered him with chains, and then quickly led him back to Rome.

[11.2] Asiaticus was not granted a hearing before the Senate. Instead he was heard in the emperor's chamber, in the presence of Messalina. There Suillius accused him of corrupting the troops, of binding them by bribes and indulgences to share in every crime, of adultery with Poppaea, and finally of unmanly vice. It was at this point that Asiaticus finally broke his silence and burst forth with these words: "Why don't you question thy own sons, Suillius; they will attest to my manhood." Then he started to make the case for his own defense. He moved Claudius quite profoundly and he even drew tears from Messalina. However, as she left the chamber to wipe them away, she warned Vitellius not to let this man escape. She then hurried to cause Poppaea's destruction and so hired agents to force her to commit suicide out of her fear of going to prison. Meanwhile Caesar was so oblivious that a few days after that he asked Poppaea's husband Scipio, who was dining with him, why he sat down to table without his wife, and Claudius was told in reply that she had paid her debt to nature.

[11.3] When Claudius began to deliberate on the acquittal of Asiaticus, Vitellius had tears in his eyes as he spoke of his old friendship with the accused, and he mentioned their joint connection to the emperor's mother, Antonia. He then briefly reviewed the services that Asiaticus had performed for the State, his recent campaign in the invasion of Britain, and everything else that seemed likely to win compassion – and he also suggested that Asiaticus should be offered the chance to commit suicide. Claudius answered with a degree of equal mercy.

Some friends tried to persuade Asiaticus to starve himself, which would be a quiet death – but he declined it with thanks. He took his usual exercise, then bathed and dined cheerfully, then he said that he would rather have been killed by the trickery of Tiberius or by the fury of Caligula than by the treachery of a woman and the shameless mouth of Vitellius. After this he opened up his veins, but not till he had inspected his funeral pyre and directed its removal to another spot, lest the smoke should hurt the thick foliage of the trees. His calmness was complete even up to the last.

* * * *

[11.11] It was in the eight hundredth year after the foundation of Rome, that the Secular Games were celebrated – sixty-four years after those of Augustus...

While Claudius sat to watch the games that took place in the Circus, some of the young nobility performed the battle of Troy on horseback. Among those re-enacting the scene was Britannicus, the son of the emperor, and Lucius Domitius Ahenobarus, who would soon afterward receive the surname of Nero and become adopted as heir to the throne. The strong applause that greeted young Nero was later taken to be a portent of his greatness. There was a commonly reported story that snakes had been seen next to his cradle, and that they seemed to guard over him – but this was likely a fable that was invented to match the marvels from other lands. Nero, never one to be overly-modest, had a habit of saying that there was only one snake, at most that had been spotted in his bedroom.

[11.12] Nero's popularity was received from the remembrances of his grandfather Germanicus, of whom he was the only surviving male descendant. And there was a growing sense of pity and the pity for Nero's mother (and Claudius' niece) Agrippina, which was increased by the cruelty of Messalina toward her. Messalina had always acted as if Agrippina were her enemy, and was now even more furious than ever. She was only stopped from making charges and planting informers against Agrippina by a new and almost insane passion that she had developed.

Messalina had grown so frantically in love with Silius, the most handsome young nobleman in Rome, that she forced him to divorce his wife Junia Silana, a high-born lady, so that she could have her lover completely to herself. Silius was aware that their affair was shameful and could easily end in his peril; but to refuse Messalina would have meant sure destruction, and he had some hope of escaping detection. The rewards of the affair were too great, so he consoled himself by ignoring the future and enjoying the present. As for Messalina, she made no attempt to conceal the affair, but she constantly visited his house in the company of a large group of people, clung to him whenever he went out, and showered wealth and honours on him. Finally, as if the title of emperor had already been handed over to Silius, the slaves, the freedmen, and the very furniture of the emperor were seen in the home of the adulterer Silius.

[11.13] Claudius meanwhile, who knew nothing about what his wife was up to, was busy with his functions as censor. In that role he published edicts severely criticizing the lawlessness of the theatre audiences, when they insulted Caius Pomponius (an ex-consul who wrote verses for the stage) and certain ladies of rank. He also introduced a law that restrained the cruel greed of the money-lenders, and he stopped them from lending money to young men that would be repayable on the death of their fathers. He also ordered an aqueduct that would convey into Rome the waters that flow from the Simbruine hills. And he even invented and popularized some new letters to be used in the Roman alphabet, since he said that he had discovered that even the Greek alphabet had been a gradual creation.

* * * *

[11.25]...and now Claudius' blindness to his own domestic affairs came to an end. He was soon forced to take notice of and punish the outrageous behavior of his wife and to punish her for the scandal she caused, only until he himself afterward became passionately inflamed with his own desire for an incestuous marriage.

[11.26] Messalina was by this time growing weary and bored with the ease of her adulteries, so she was rushing headlong into new and strange forms of depravity. At this point Silius, either through some fatal infatuation or because he imagined that, amid the dangers that hung over him, danger itself was the best safety, began to press Messalina to end the concealment of their affair. "We do not," he said, "have to wait for the emperor to grow old.

Anyway, only innocent people can afford to plan carefully. Those who are guilty have to act and act quickly – to save themselves. And we have accomplices who share the same fears as we do. As for myself, I have neither a wife nor a child, and am ready to marry you and adopt Britannicus. You will have the same power as before, and peace of mind as well, if only we can take Claudius by surprise. He may be slow to discover treachery, but he is still quick to anger."

Messalina was not enthusiastic about the idea, not because she had any love for her husband, but rather she was afraid that Silius, after achieving the highest power, might eventually spurn her as an adulteress, and that he might soon see the crime brought about by an emergency at its true value for himself. But she still longed to be called his wife, because that would add to the outrageous infamy – it would be the ultimate source of delight to the reckless. She waited only until Claudius left for Ostia to perform a sacrifice, and then she formally married Silius, observing all the proper rites and ceremonies.

[11.27] I know well that it will seem unbelievable that anyone in the world could have been so foolish to think themselves safe in a city that knows everything and hides nothing – moreover, that these persons were a consul-elect and the emperor's wife; that, on an appointed day, in front of witnesses summoned for that very purpose, that they came together for the purpose of a legitimate marriage; that she listened to the words of the bridegroom's friends, sacrificed to the gods, that they dined with guests, that he covered her with kisses and caresses, and that they passed the night as man and wife. But this is no fantasy that I am recounting here; I am only writing what I have heard and what older men have written down.

[11.28] A shudder went through the imperial courtyard – and it was especially strong among those in power, the men who had much to fear from a revolution. They didn't keep their thoughts in secret any longer but now voiced them openly. "When the actor Mnestor," they said, "was disgracefully throwing himself into the emperor's bed, it was indeed a scandal, but it was a far cry from a threat to the Emperor. Now, however, there's an intelligent and handsome young aristocrat, who is already close to attaining the consulship – and he is preparing himself for a loftier destination. It's quite obvious where this marriage is heading."

When they thought about how slow and apathetic Claudius was, and how devoted he was to his wife, and of the many assassinations that Messalina had ordered, they became completely terrified. At the same time they grew confident in the fact that the emperor could often be persuaded to change opinions and they felt that if they could convince him of the enormity of the charges against Messalina, that she might be condemned and crushed before a trial could even take place. The most important point was to ensure that he would not hear her try to make a defense, and that he would not even hear her out should she even come close enough to make a confession.

[11.29] Callistus (whom I have already mentioned in connection with the assassination of Caligula), Narcissus (who caused the death of Appius Silanus), and Pallas (who was at this time at the height of influence), debated whether they could use secret threats to force Messalina to give up her affair with Silius, while they would pretend to be ignorant of everything else. Then they quickly gave up the idea for fear that they would only be causing their own ruin. Pallas backed out due to cowardice, and Callistus had learned from his experiences in Caligula's reign, that people maintain power through careful rather than vigorous action. Narcissus, however, was determined to continue, but made only one change to his plan – that no-one was to say anything to Messalina in advance to warn her of the charge or the accuser. Then he eagerly waited for an opportunity, and, when the emperor prolonged his stay at Ostia (the port of Rome), Narcissus found two of Claudius' favourite mistresses, and he persuaded them – with gifts and promises and assurances that they would have more power after Messalina's downfall – he convinced them to act as informers.

[11.30] As the next step, Calpurnia (one of the two women) secured a private interview with Claudius and threw herself at his knees, crying out that Messalina was married to Silius. At the same time she asked Cleopatra (the other mistress), who was standing near and waiting for the question, for corroboration. Cleopatra nodded in agreement, and then Calpurnia asked for Narcissus to be brought in. Narcissus begged forgiveness for the past, for having said nothing about Messalina's affairs with her former lovers such as Vettius or Plautius.

Even now, he said, he was not going to make charges of adultery against Messalina, or, even less was he going to demand back from Silius the palace, the slaves, and the other belongings of imperial rank that he had acquired from Claudius' household. No, let Silius enjoy these things, but he must give back Claudius' wife and annul their new marriage. "Do you know," Narcissus asked Claudius "that you are now divorced? The people, the army and the Senate all witnessed her marriage to Silius. You need to act at once, or else new husband Silius will become the master of Rome."

[11.31] Narcissus then summoned all of Claudius' most powerful and closest friends. First he questioned Turranius, superintendent of the corn supply; next, he questioned Lucius Geta, who was Commander of the Praetorian Guard. When they confirmed that the story was true, the whole company loudly argued that the emperor must go to the camp and secure the support of the Praetorians – since he had to think of safety before he thought of vengeance. It is quite established that Claudius was so overwhelmed by terror that he kept on asking whether he was still emperor, and whether Silius was still a subject. Messalina meanwhile, was indulging in unprecedented extravagances. It was mid-Autumn and she was pretending to celebrate the grape-harvest in her house. Grapes were being trampled, the vats were overflowing with juice and wine, and women dressed in animal skins were dancing as if they were frenzied worshippers of Bacchus. Messalina herself, with her hair flowing down, shook the wand of Bacchus – Silius was at her side, crowned with ivy and the shoes of Bacchus, as he moved his head to the lustful chorus around him. It is said that one Vettius Valens climbed a very lofty tree for fun, and when they asked him what he saw, he replied, "A terrible storm over Ostia." There may have been a storm; but perhaps it was just a word dropped by chance that later became a prophecy.

[11.32] Meanwhile rumours and messengers were coming in from all sides, saying that everything was now known to Claudius, and that he was coming, intent on revenge. The newly-married couple went in different directions. Messalina went to the Gardens of Lucullus; Silius went to do business in the forum in order to disguise his fear. The other guests were flying away in every direction when the officers of the Praetorian Guard appeared and put each of them in chains wherever they found them, whether it was in the public streets or in hiding.

Messalina was too upset by this disaster to make any plans, suddenly determined to do something that had often saved her in the past – to meet her husband and let him see her. She also ordered Britannicus and Octavia to hurry to their father and embrace him. She also asked Vibidia, the oldest priestess of the Vestal Virgins, to meet Claudius in the emperor's role at Chief Priest of Vesta and to beg for mercy on her behalf. Meanwhile, with only three companions (so suddenly she found herself alone), she walked from one end of the city to another. Finally she headed off to Ostia and got on a cart that was used to remove garden waste. People did not feel any pity for her, since she was guilty of such hideous crimes.

[11.33] There was just as much alarm for those on the side of the emperor. They couldn't put much trust in Geta, the Commander of the Praetorian Guards, a man who did just as he pleased and didn't seem to care whether it was right or wrong. So Narcissus, acting with the support of those who shared his same fears, declared that the only hope for the emperor's safety was if they could transfer the command of soldiers for that one day to the command of a freed slave – himself, for he offered to take on the responsibility himself. In addition, Narcissus demanded a seat in the same carriage as the emperor while he was riding to Rome, so that Claudius might not be induced by Lucius Vitellius and Largus Caecina to change his mind.

[11.34] It was later reported that the emperor contradicted himself, at one time criticizing the shameful behavior of his wife, at another time falling into remembrances of their mutual love and thoughts of his infant children. At this Vitellius would only shout, "What audacity! What a crime!" Narcissus kept pushing him to explain his ambiguous remarks and tell them what he really wanted, but Vitellius continued to make confusing responses that were open to many interpretations, and Caecina did the same as Vitellius.

And now Messalina herself came into view, and was crying out again and again that Claudius simply had to hear her out – the mother of Octavia and Britannicus. Narcissus shouted her down, railing at her about her affair with Silius and about their marriage. At the same time he tried to distract Claudius' attention by presenting him a document that listed all of her immoral acts. Soon afterward, as Claudius was entering Rome, their children were about to come forward and greet him, but Narcissus ordered them to be swiftly taken away. But Narcissus could not get rid of Vibidia, who demanded in the strongest terms that the wife of the emperor could not be executed without a trial. So Narcissus replied that the emperor would hear Messalina, and that she would have a chance to refute the charge. In the meantime Narcissus said that Vibidia should go attend to her sacred duties.

[11.35] During all of this, Claudius kept a strange silence, and Vitellius looked as if he had no idea what was happening. Everything was under the control of Narcissus. He ordered that the house of the adulterer Silius be opened up and that the emperor should be brought there. First, when they entered the threshold, he pointed out the statue of Silius' father, which a decree of the Senate had directed to be destroyed; next, he pointed out that all the heirlooms of Claudius' family had been taken to the house of Silius to pay him for his disgraceful service.

When the emperor became furious and broke out into violent threats, Narcissus then led him into the camp of the Praetorian Guard, where he had arranged that the soldiers would be assembled. Narcissus gave a few introductory remarks and Claudius spoke to them very briefly – because he was so angry but could barely express it due to his shame. The troops then started suddenly shouting for the offender to be named and punished.

When he was brought onto the platform, Silius didn't try to defend himself or obtain a postponement, but instead he begged for a quick death. Some distinguished Roman knights also showed equal courage and desired a quick death. Of the accomplices, Claudius ordered the death of: Titius Proculus (who had been appointed to be Messalina's personal Guardian by Silius), Vettius Valens (who confessed his guilt), as well as Pompeius Urbicus and Saufellus Trogus. Also put to death were Decius Calpurnianus (commander of the city-watch), Sulpicius Rufus (head of a gladiator school), and Juncus Virgilianus, who was a senator.

[11.36] Mnester alone became a matter for pause. Tearing off his clothes, he insisted that Claudius should look at the whip-marks and scars and remember that Claudius himself had placed him under the command of Messalina. He said that the others were guilty due to money or ambition, he himself had only acted out of necessity. He added that he would have been the first to die if Silius had managed to become emperor. Claudius was touched by his speech and inclined to grant mercy, but his freedmen prevailed on the emperor not to show so much forgiveness to an actor when so many noble citizens had been put to death. They told the emperor that when crimes were as great as this then it didn't matter whether they were voluntary or forced.

Even the defence of Traulus Montanus, a Roman knight, was not allowed, but was rejected. He was an otherwise virtuous but good-looking young man, and he had been summoned and then dismissed within the space of one night by Messalina, who was equally unpredictable in her passions and dislikes. Suillius Caesoninus escaped the death penalty because of his vices (he claimed to have been forced into the position of a woman during the group's sexual escapades) – and Plautius Lateranus also evaded death (due to the distinguished service of his uncle).

[11.37] Messalina was meanwhile in the gardens of Lucullus and struggling for life. She wrote letters that begged for forgiveness and asked for help, as she alternated between hope and fury. So great was her pride and confidence right up to the end. What is more, if her accuser Narcissus hadn't sped on her death, he himself would have likely been destroyed. For Claudius had returned home to an early dinner; then, in softened mood, when the wine had warmed him, he bade someone to go and tell the "poor creature" (this is the word that they say he used) to come see him in the morning so that she could explain herself. When Narcissus heard this, he noticed that Claudius' anger was subsiding and his passion was returning, and so Narcissus feared what would happen if he delayed – and what might be the result of the approaching night and Claudius' renewed conjugal recollections. So Narcissus rushed out and ordered the centurions and the tribunes who were on guard to kill the woman. This, he said, was the wish of the emperor.

Evodus, one of the freedmen, was appointed to watch and complete the task. He hurried ahead of everyone else to the gardens and found Messalina stretched upon the ground, while by her side sat her mother Lepida.

While her daughter was in command Lepida did not have good relations with Messalina, but she now felt pity by her approaching death and urged her not to wait for the executioner. "Life," she said, "is over; all that can be looked for is honour in death." But in Messalina's heart, which was utterly corrupted by recklessness, nothing noble remained. She still continued with her tears and small complaints until the gates were forced open by the rush of the "visitors" – the sternly silent tribune and the freedman both stood there at her side, overwhelming her a stream of abuse that was used for slaves.

[11.38] Then for the first time Messalina understood her fate and put her hand to a sword. In her nervous state she was pressing it ineffectively to her throat and breast, when a blow from the tribune drove it through her. Her body was released to her mother. Claudius was still at the banquet when they told him that Messalina was dead, but they didn't mention to him whether it was by her own or that of someone else. Nor did he ask how she died, but instead he called for the wine and finished his dinner as usual. During the following days Claudius showed no sign of hatred or joy or anger or sadness; in a word, he showed no sign of any human emotion, either when he looked at her triumphant accusers or at her crying children. The Senate helped him in his desire to forget Messalina by making a decree ordering that her name and her statues be removed from all places, public or private. Narcissus was given the quaestorship as a reward, a small detail to the pride of a man who rose in the height of his power above both Pallas and Callistus.

Translated from the Latin by Stephen Russell, PhD
English text by Stephen Russell and Laura Holtebrinck

Suetonius
CALIGULA

The Story: The Roman emperor Gaius Julius Caesar Augustus Germanicus – also known as Caligula (12-41 AD) – is probably the most notorious of all the Julio-Claudian emperors. The historian Suetonius, in his biography of first twelve emperors, devoted one book to the crimes and perversions of Caligula.

22. That's enough about Caligula as emperor; we must now talk about his career as a monster...

23. Because of Marcus Agrippa's humble birth and origins, he didn't want to be thought of or mentioned as his grandson. Indeed he would become very angry if someone included Agrippa's name in a speech or a poem that was about the family of Caesars. Instead he preferred to boast that his mother was born from an incestuous relationship involving Augustus and his daughter Julia.

24. He lived in continual incest with all his sisters, and at a large and crowded banquet he would make them take turns lying beneath him, while his wife reclined above him. Of all his sisters, he is believed to have violated Drusilla when he was still a minor. And it is even said that his grandmother Antonia, who was responsible for their upbringing, once caught both Caligula and Drusilla in bed together. Afterwards, when Drusilla was the wife of the ex-consul Lucius Cassius Longinus, Caligula took her from him and openly treated her as his lawful wife. And when he was ill he made her the heir to his property and the throne. When she died, he declared that there would be a period of public mourning, during which it was a capital offence to laugh, bathe, or dine in the company of one's parents, wife, or children. He was so upset and distraught with grief that he suddenly fled out of the city at night and crossed Campania. He ended up in Syracuse and then hurriedly returned from there without cutting his hair or even shaving his beard. And he never afterward took any oath about matters of the highest moment, even before the assembly of the people or in the presence of the soldiers, unless he swore by the godhead of Drusilla.

25. It is difficult to decide whether he acted more corruptly and immorally in obtaining his wives, or in getting rid of them. At the marriage of Livia Orestilla and Gaius Piso, he attended the ceremony then gave orders for the bride to be taken to his own house. After a few days he divorced her, then two years later he banished her, because he had a suspicion that in the meantime she had returned to her former husband. Some people write that when he was invited to the wedding banquet, Caligula told Piso, who was reclining next to him: "Take your hands off my wife," and he immediately carried her off with him from the party, and the next day issued a proclamation stating that he had found himself a wife in the manner of Romulus and Augustus.

When he heard the story that the grandmother of Lollia Paulina, who was the wife of Gaius Memmius, an ex-consul who was commanding armies, had once been a incredibly beautiful woman, he suddenly ordered Lollia back from the province. Once he had her separated from her husband, he married her, then a short time later he set her to the side, giving the order that she was never again to have intercourse with anyone.

As for Caesonia, although she was neither beautiful nor young, and was already the mother of three daughters by an earlier husband, she was a woman who was obsessed with reckless luxury and lust – and he loved her all the more passionately and faithfully. In fact, he often saw her off in front of the soldiers, having her ride by his side, decked out with a cloak, helmet and shield – and to his friends it is said that he even showed her off naked. He did not honour her with the title of wife until the day she gave birth, announcing on that same day that he had married her and that he was the father of her baby. This child, whom he named Julia Drusilla, he carried to the temples of all the goddesses, and finally he placed her in the lap of the statue of Minerva and entrusted the goddess with the child's nurture and education. And the evidence that convinced him so strongly that she was his daughter was her fierce and savage temper, which was even then so violent that she would try to scratch the faces and eyes of the little children who played with her.

27. The following are special examples of his innate brutal and cruel nature. When it became too expensive to provide cattle that could be used to feed the wild beasts in one of his gladiatorial shows, he instead selected criminals to be devoured and eaten. He looked over the line of prisoners without examining their individual records, but he merely took his place in the middle of a colonnade and he ordered all those "from baldhead to baldhead" to be led away.

There was a man who had made a promise to fight in the arena as a gladiator if the emperor recovered from an illness, and Caligula forced him to keep his word, watching him as he fought with his sword in hand, and he would not let him go until he won his victory, and then only after the man begged him many times over. There was another man who had offered his life for the same reason, but he had hesitated to fulfill the promise and kill himself – so Caligula ordered the man be turned over to his slaves, with orders that they drive him through the streets covered with sacred boughs and wreaths, demanding the fulfillment of his promise, and then they were to finally throw him off the highest cliff they could find.

He caused many men of honorable rank to be disfigured with the marks of branding-irons and then condemned them to the mines, either to build roads or be thrown to the wild beasts; or sometimes he even closed them up in cages on all fours, as if they were animals, or he would even have someone saw them into little bits. Not all these punishments were for serious offences, but some of them were merely for criticizing one of his shows, or for never having sworn by his Genius. He forced parents to attend the executions of their sons, and when one man tried to excuse himself on the grounds of illness, Caligula sent a carriage to pick him up and bring him. He invited another man to join him at dinner immediately after witnessing the death of his son, and he tried to make him laugh and have some fun.

He forced the manager of his gladiatorial shows and beast fights to be beaten with chains in his presence for several consecutive days, and he would not kill him until he was disgusted at the stench of his putrefied brain. He burned a writer of Atellan farces alive in the middle of the arena, because of a humorous line that contained a potential double meaning. When a Roman knight who was about to be thrown to the wild beasts loudly shouted that he was innocent, Caligula had him taken out, had his tongue cut out, and then he had the man put back once again.

32. Even when he was otherwise relaxing and otherwise spending his time in amusements and feasting, his actions and his words were just as cruel. Often, while he was having lunch or enjoying himself, he would often have torture conducted in his presence, and he had a soldier who was particularly skilled at decapitations cut off the heads of those who were brought from prison.

At the dedication of his bridge at Puteoli, he invited a great number of people who were on the shore to come out to him, but suddenly he had them all thrown overboard into the sea. When some of them caught hold of the rudders of the ships, he had them pushed back off into the sea with poles and oars.

At a public banquet in Rome he immediately handed over a slave to the executioners for stealing a strip of silver from the couches, with orders that his hands be cut off and hung in front of him from his neck, and that the slave be then led through the guests, preceded by a sign explaining the reason for his punishment.

Once, when he and a murmillo from the gladiatorial school were fighting with wooden swords, and the murmillo fell down to the ground on purpose, Caligula stabbed him with a real dagger and then ran about with a palm-branch, just as victors do.

Once when he stood by the altar dressed as a popa and a victim was brought up, he raised his mallet on high and slew the cultrarius. At one of his more extravagant banquets he suddenly broke into a fit of laughter, and when the consuls reclining next to him politely asked why he was laughing, he replied: "What else do you think, except that with just a single nod from me both of you could have your throats cut on the spot?"

33. As an example of his humor, he once took his place next to a statue of Jupiter, and asked the tragic actor Apelles which of them was greater, and when the actor hesitated, Caligula had him flayed with whips, praising the quality of the actor's voice while he screamed and while the poor man begged for mercy, saying that the man was delightful even in his groans. And whenever he kissed the neck of his wife or mistress, he would say: "Off comes your beautiful head whenever I give the word." He even used to now and again threaten that he would resort to torture if necessary, to find out from his own dear Caesonia why he loved her so passionately and deeply.

36. He respected neither his own chastity nor that of anyone else. He is said to have had unnatural relations with Marcus Lepidus, the actor Mnester, and a certain number of hostages as well. Valerius Catullus, a young man from a consular family, publicly proclaimed that he had buggered the emperor and worn himself out due to all the sex. To say nothing of his incest with his sisters and his notorious passion for the prostitute Pyrallis, there were barely any women from the noble ranks whom he didn't pursue. His habit was to invite them to dinner with their husbands, and when they passed by the foot of his couch, he would inspect them critically and deliberately, as if he were buying slaves, even putting out his hand and lifting up the face of anyone who looked down in modesty. Then, whenever he felt like it, he would leave the room, sending for the one who pleased him the most. He would return soon afterward with the obvious signs of what had occurred, and he would openly praise or criticize his sexual partner, listing her charms or defects, and commenting on her conduct. To some women he personally sent a divorce notice in the name of their absent husbands, and he gave orders that these notices were to be entered into the public records.

55. Toward those who were his favourites, his behavior seemed to become madness. He used to kiss the actor Mnester, even in the theatre and the middle of the game. And if anyone made even the slightest sound while his Mnestor was dancing, Caligula had him dragged from his seat and he would whip the man himself with his own hand. When a Roman knight created a disturbance, he sent a centurion to tell him to go without delay to Ostia and then carry a message from him to King Ptolemy in Mauretania – and the message said this: "Do nothing good nor bad to the man I have sent you."

He placed some Thracian gladiators in command of his German bodyguard. He reduced the amount of armor for the murmillones [a type of gladiator]. When a certain fellow named Columbus had won a victory, but was slightly wounded, Caligula had the wound rubbed with a poison that he afterward called Columbinum – and this was the name that was found included in his list of poisons.

He was so passionately devoted to the green faction [in the Circus races] that he used to have his dinner in their stables and he often spent the night there. At one of his parties he gave the driver Eutychus two million sesterces in presents. On the day before the games and races, he used to send his soldiers to keep silence in the neighborhood, so they could prevent the horse Incitatus from being disturbed. Aside from a stall made out of marble, a manger made from ivory, purple blankets, and a collar made out of precious stones, Caligula even gave this horse a house, a troop of slaves, and furniture, so that guests he invited in his name might be entertained most elegantly. And it is also said that Caligula planned to make this horse consul.

59. He lived twenty-nine years and ruled for three years, ten months, and eight days.

Translated from the Latin by Stephen Russell, PhD

Plutarch

The Demise of Antony and Cleopatra

The Story: The conflict between Octavian (later to be called Augustus Caesar) and Antony was a turning point in Roman history. In this widely influential account, the historian Plutarch described the demise of Antony and the last days of his romance with Cleopatra, Queen of Egypt.

The Life of Antony

[58] When Caesar heard of the speed and extent of Antony's preparations, he was deeply concerned, for he did not want to be forced to fight the war that summer. He wasn't yet ready to fight a war, and people were upset by the taxes that he imposed. According to his new scheme, citizens were forced to pay one fourth of their income, and freedmen one eighth of their property - and both classes cried out against Caesar, and this led to disturbances and turmoil throughout all Italy.

Many men think that Antony's greatest mistak was his slowness in starting the war. For this delay gave Caesar time to make preparations and put an end to the disturbances among the people back in Rome. For the people were angry while the money was being taken from them, but after it had been taken they then became calm. Moreover, Titius and Plancus, two ex-consuls and friends of Antony, who had strongly opposed to her accompanying the expedition, were treated so badly by Cleopatra that they fled over to Caesar's side, and they told him all about Antony's will, the contents of which they knew.

This will had been placed with the Vestal Virgins, and when Caesar asked for it, they would not give it to him; but they added that if he really wanted to take it, then they told him to just come and take it himself. So he went and took it. At first Caesar read its contents through by himself, making note of the most discreditable and reprehensible sections. And then he called a meeting of the senate and read the contents of the will out loud to them. Most of them were upset that he did this, for they thought it was a strange and awful thing to do in calling a man to account while he is still alive for what he wished to have done after his death. Caesar places most of the emphasis on the clause in the will that related to Antony's burial – for it said that Antony's body, even if he were to die in Rome, should be ceremoniously escorted through the forum and then sent away to Cleopatra in Egypt.

Calvisius, who was a companion of Caesar, also brought forward more charges against Antony regarding his behaviour towards Cleopatra. He said that to please her Antony had given her the entire library from Pergamum, in which there were two hundred thousand volumes; that at a banquet where there were many guests Antony had stood up and rubbed her feet, to fulfill some wager or agreement that they had made; that Antony had agreed to let the Ephesians in his presence salute Cleopatra as their queen; that often, while Antony was seated on his tribunal and hearing the pleas from rulers and kings, he would receive love-letters from her in tablets of onyx or crystal, and he would read them instead of attending to state business; and that once, while Furnius, who was one of the most eloquent and highly regarded orators in Rome, was in the middle of a speech, Cleopatra was carried through the forum on a litter, and Antony, the moment he saw her, sprang up from his tribunal and left the trial, and accompanied Cleopatra's litter on her way with his hand resting on the side of the litter.

[59] However, most of the charges thus brought by Calvisius were thought to be lies.

[60] When Caesar had made sufficient preparations, a vote was passed to wage war against Cleopatra, and to

take away from Antony the authority that he had surrendered to a woman. And Caesar said in addition that Antony had been drugged and was not even master of himself, and that the Romans were carrying on war with Mardion the eunuch, with Potheinus, with Iras, who was Cleopatra's hairdresser, and with Charmion – and that these people were in charge of the most important parts of Antony's government.

[62] However, by this time now Antony was more or less completely an appendage of Cleopatra. This could be seen by the fact that although his land forces were far superior to those of Caesar and he therefore had a definite advantage there, in order to please Cleopatra he wanted the victory to go to his navy, even though he could see that due to lack of a competent naval crew his ships were bringing in from poor Greece any vagrant, mule-driver, harvester, and riff-raff youth that thy could find – and that even then his ships were short of men, and so most of them were underserved and were handled incompetently...

[66] Although the struggle was beginning to start, the ships did not ram or crush one another at all. Antony's ship were too slow, due to their weight, and therefore they were unable to make an effective impact through ramming. Caesar's ships not only avoided a head-on collision with Antony's rough and hard bronze armour ships, but they also weren't so foolish at to try to ram the enemy's ships in the side. For their beaks would easily have been broken off by the impact against Antony's vessels – which were constructed of huge square timbers fastened together with iron.

The fight was therefore like a battle on land; or, to use a better image, like an assault on a walled town. Three or four of Caesar's boats would circle around one of Antony's all at once, and the crews of each boat fought with shields and spears and javelins and flaming missiles; the soldiers of Antony's ships also shot at the enemy using catapults that were mounted on wooden towers.

And now, Agrippa began to extend the left wing with the goal of encircling the enemy, and so Publicola was forced to make an advance against him – but by doing this he was separated from the centre. The boats in the centre fell into confusion and engaged by the enemy ships under Arruntius. Although the sea-battle was still undecided and could have easily gone either way, suddenly Cleopatra's sixty ships were seen raising their sails for flight and making off through the middle of the fighting ships. They had been posted in the back, behind all of the large boats, and they threw these other ships into confusion as they forced their way through. The enemy looked at all of this with amazement, as Cleopatra's ships took advantage of the wind and made for Peloponnese.

Indeed this was the part where Antony made it clear to the whole world that he was ruled neither by the thoughts that of a proper commander nor those of a brave man, nor was he even ruled by his own mind. Someone once made a joke and said that the soul of the lover lives in someone else's body, and this is the way that Antony was dragged along by Cleopatra: as if he had become one body with her and had to go wherever she went. As soon as he saw her ship sailing away Antony forgot everything else and followed her. He betrayed and ran away from the men who were fighting and dying on his behalf, quickly got into a quinquereme, letting only Alexas the Syrian and Scellius to come with him, and he hurried after the woman who had already destroyed him and would merely make his ruin still more complete.

[67] Cleopatra recognized him and so raised a signal of acknowledgement on her ship. Antony came up and was taken on board, but he neither saw nor was seen by her. Instead, he went forward alone to the front of the ship and sat down by himself in silence, holding his head in both hands. But just then Liburnian ships were seen pursuing them from Caesar's fleet; but Antony ordered that the ship be turned to face them, and so stopped them. But he couldn't ward off the ship of Eurycles the Spartan, who attacked vigorously and waved a spear about on the deck as if he were going to hurl it at Antony. Antony was standing at the front of the ship and asked: "Who is this that is pursuing Antony?" The answer was: "I am Eurycles, the son of Lachares, and thanks to Caesar I have the chance right now to revenge my father's death." Lachares had been beheaded by Antony because he was involved in a charge of robbery and piracy. However, Eurycles did not hit Antony's ship, but hit the other one of the two main ships (for there were two of them) with his bronze beak and spun it round and captured that one – along with one of the other ships well, which carried expensive costly equipment that was for household use. When Eurycles was out of the way, Antony resumed his previous pose and he did not move.

He spent three days there by himself at the front of the boat, either because he was angry with Cleopatra, or perhaps he was too ashamed to see her. Then when they finally landed at Taenarum, the women from Cleopatra's company managed to bring them together to talk, and then they persuaded them to eat and sleep together.

In a short time quite a few of their heavy transport ships and some of their friends began to gather about them after the defeat, bringing word that the fleet had been destroyed, but that they thought that the land forces were still intact and together. So Antony sent messengers to Canidius, ordering him to pull back with his army through Macedonia and into Asia as fast as he could. Antony himself was planning to cross over the sea to Africa and Libya from Taenarum. So he selected one of the transport ships that carried coined money and very valuable silver and gold royal treasures, and he gave it to his friends as a present, telling them divide up the treasure and look after their own safety. They refused his gift with tears in their eyes, but he comforted them and spoke to them with kindness and affection, pleading with them to accept the gift. Finally he sent them away, after writing to Theophilus, who was ruling Corinth for him, that he should keep these men safe and hidden until they could make their peace with Caesar. This Theophilus was the father of Hipparchus, who had the greatest influence with Antony, and was the first of Antony's freedmen to defect to Caesar's side, and afterwards he settled in Corinth.

[68] This was the situation with Antony. At Actium his fleet held out for a long time against Caesar's, and only after it had been severely damaged by the high seas did it reluctantly give up the struggle, after nine hours of fighting. At the most five thousand men died, but three hundred ships were captured, as Caesar himself has written. Antony's flight was only known by a few people, and those who first heard the story thought that it was incredible. They could not believe or understand how he could go off and leave nineteen legions of undefeated soldiers and twelve thousand cavalry. After all, they thought, he had so often experienced both kind good and bad fortune and should not be stressed by the reversals of countless wars and battles. Moreover, his soldiers missed him and were hoping that he would soon make his appearance from some quarter or other. Their faith in him was so great that, even after his had become undeniable, they still displayed so much fidelity and bravery that held together for seven days, ignoring the messages that Caesar was sending them. But at last, after their general Canidius ran away one night and abandoned the camp, since they were not without a leader and betrayed by their commanders, they surrendered to their conqueror Caesar.

As a result of this, Caesar next sailed to Athens. After he came to terms with the Greeks, he distributed the grain that was left over after the war among their cities. These cities were in bad straits, because their money, slaves, and farm animals had been stolen. At any rate, my great-grandfather Nicarchus used to talk about how he and all his fellow-citizens were forced to carry a fixed measure of wheat on their shoulders down to the sea at Anticyra, and how whips were used to ensure that they moved at a quick pace. They had carried one such load in this manner, he said, and the second was already measured out, and they were just about to depart with it on their backs, when the news arrived that Antony had been defeated. This news was greeted as the salvation of the city - for Antony's soldiers and commanders immediately took off and fled, and the citizens then divided the grain among themselves.

[69] After Antony landed at Paraetonium on the coast of Libya, he sent Cleopatra ahead into Egypt. He was left with nothing but solitude, and so he wandered about aimlessly with two friends – one a Greek, the rhetorician Aristocrates, and the other a Roman, Lucilius. I've told a story about Lucilius elsewhere, when he was at Philippi and, in order to help Brutus escape, he pretended to be Brutus and surrendered himself to his pursuers. Antony spared his life, and for this reason Lucilius remained a loyal and faithful friend to Antony, and stayed with him up to the bitter end.

When the general to whom he had entrusted his forces in Libya took those forces with him and defected to the enemy, Antony tried to kill himself, but was prevented by his friends and brought to Alexandria. Here he found Cleopatra engaged on a hazardous and great undertaking. The isthmus that separates the Red Sea from the Mediterranean Sea off Egypt and is considered to be the boundary between Asia and Libya – in the part where it is most constricted by the two seas and has the least width – measures about three hundred stades at its narrowest point. It was here that Cleopatra was trying to lift her fleet out of the water and drag the ships across. She wanted to launch them again in the Arabian Gulf, taking a great deal of money and soldiers with them, and then settle them somewhere outside of Egypt, so they could escape the dangers of war and slavery.

But since the Arabians who lived around Petra burned the first ships that were being dragged along, and since Antony still thought that his land forces at Actium were holding together, Cleopatra gave up this plan and decided instead to protect the regular approaches to Egypt instead. And now Antony left the city and the society of his friends, and he moved to Pharos, where he built for himself a house by the sea. Here he lived as an exile from men, and said that he was contentedly imitating the life of Timon. After all, he said, his own experiences were very similar to those of Timon, for he himself had also been wronged and treated with ingratitude by his friends, and therefore he had come to hate and distrust all of mankind.

[70] Timon was an Athenian and he lived during the time of the Peloponnesian War, as we learn from the works of Aristophanes and Plato. In their writings he is presented as grumpy and mean-spirited. But although he avoided and shunned all human interaction, he was glad to see Alcibiades, who was then young and headstrong, and showered kisses upon him. And when Apemantus was amazed at this and asked the reason for it, Timon said he loved young Alcibiades because he knew that this man would eventually be a great pain to Athens. Timon would sometimes admit this Apemantus fellow, and no one else, into his company, since Apemantus was similar to him and tried sometimes to imitate his way of life. In fact once, at a festival, the two men were eating by themselves, and Apemantus said: "Timon, what a fine symposium [dinner] we are having!" "It would be," said Timon, "if you weren't here." We are also told that once, when the Athenians were holding an assembly, he got up onto the speaker's platform, and this was apparently so odd that the crowd became silent with deep anticipation. Then he said: "I have a small building lot, men of Athens, and a fig-tree is growing in it, from which many of my fellow citizens have already hanged themselves. Accordingly, since I intend to build a house there, I wanted to give public notice to that effect, in order that all of you who desire to do so may hang yourselves before the fig-tree is cut down." After he died and was at Halae near the sea, the shore in front of the tomb eroded away, and the water eventually surrounded it and made it completely inaccessible to man. The inscription on the tomb was:

"Here I lie, having brought a miserable life to its final end.

My name is not your business, but I curse you people to a vile death"

He is said to have composed this inscription himself, but the one that was known through general circulation is the one from Callimachus:

"Timon, hater of men, lives here – so walk on by;

Curse me if you like, as long as you keep walking."

[71] These are just a few of the many stories that we hear about Timon. As for Antony, Canidius brought him news of the loss of his forces at Actium in person, and Antony also heard that Herod of Judea, with a number of legions and cohorts, had defected to Caesar's side, and that the other kings in a similar manner were also deserting Antony so that nothing longer remained of his power outside of Egypt.

However, none of these things seemed to greatly disturb him. But, it was as if he was pleased to lay down his hopes, since this meant that he could also lay aside his fears, anxieties, and cares. To this end he left that house of his on the beach, which he called Timoneum, and after he was received back into the palace by Cleopatra, he turned the city to a course of eating, drinking, and displays of generosity. He also inscribed the son of Cleopatra and Caesar among the list of young men who had come of age, and he conferred upon Antyllus, his son with Fulvia, the toga virilis. He celebrated these acts with many days of banquets, parties, and feasts throughout Alexandria. Cleopatra and Antony now dissolved their famous Society of Inimitable Livers, and formed another one instead. This new group was just as devoted to sensuality, indulgence, and extravagance as the other one was, and they called it the Society of Partners in Death. Their friends enrolled themselves as those who would die together, and they passed the time delightfully in a round of hedonistic dinners. Cleopatra was also getting together collections of all sorts of deadly poisons, and she tested whether each of them were painless by giving them to prisoners who were already sentenced of death. But when she saw that the speedy poisons also brought increased pain, while the slower poisons were also the milder ones in terms of pain, she started to test the poisons from wild animals, and watched with her own eyes as these animals were set upon the prisoners. She did this daily, and tried them almost all – in the end she found that the bite of the asp alone induced a sleepy lethargy without any spasms or groans. Instead it left only a gentle perspiration on the face, while the senses were dulled painlessly, and the men resisted all attempts to rouse them and wake them up, just like people who are fast asleep.

[72] At the same time they also sent a delegation to Caesar in Asia, with Cleopatra asking that her children might be able to inherit the realm of Egypt and Antony requesting that he might live as a private citizen in Athens, if Caesar did not want him to stay in Egypt. But because they had so few friends remaining and the distrust that they felt on account of so many defections, they sent the children's tutor, Euphronius, to deliver their message. For Alexas the Laodicean, who had been introduced to Antony in Rome through Timagenes and had more influence with him than any other Greek – and who had also been Cleopatra's most effective instrument against Antony when she wanted to stop him from considerations arising in his mind in favour of Octavia – had been sent to keep Herod the king from defecting. But he remained there with Herod and betrayed Antony – after which he had the audacity to seek a meeting with Caesar, relying on Herod to keep him safe. Herod, however, could not save him, but the traitor was at once arrested and carried in chains back to his own country, where he was put to death by Caesar's orders. Such was the penalty for his treachery that Alexas paid to Antony while Antony was still alive.

[73] Caesar would not listen to the proposals from Antony, but he sent back word to Cleopatra that she would receive all reasonable treatment if she either put Antony to death or threw him out of Egypt. He also sent, as a personal messenger from himself to Cleopatra one of his own freedmen, Thyrsus, a man of considerable intelligence and one who could persuasively convey messages from a young general to a woman who was conceited and astonishingly proud of her own beauty. Thyrsus had longer interviews with Cleopatra than did any of the other delegates, and she treated him with a noticeable amount of respect, so much so that Antony became suspicious of him because he wondered what Thyrsus was up to. In the end Antony grabbed him and had him flogged, and then sent him back to Caesar with a written message stating that Thyrsus had irritated him with his arrogant and self-important manner, at a time when his tempers were at their shortest because of all his troubles. "But if you are upset at what I have done to your freedman," Antony wrote Caesar, "then you now have my freedman Hipparchus. You can hang him up and give him a flogging, and we'll be even." After this, Cleopatra tried to redeem herself in Antony's eyes and get rid of his suspicions by paying excessive amounts of attention to him. She celebrated her own birthday in a modest way that was appropriate for their current circumstances, but she celebrated his birthday with an excess of all kinds of expensive festivities, so that many of those who were invited to the dinner arrived poor and went away rich. Meanwhile Caesar was urged to immediately come home by Agrippa, who frequently wrote him from Rome that matters there greatly needed his presence and attention.

[74] Thus, because Caesar returned to Rome, the war was suspended for the moment. But when the winter was over, Caesar again marched through Syria, and his generals made their way through Libya. When Pelusium fell there was a rumour that Seleucus had surrendered that city with the consent of Cleopatra, and so Cleopatra fought this rumour by allowing Antony to kill the wife and children of Seleucus. By this time she now had built for herself a tomb and monument that were lofty and beautiful, which were erected near the temple of Isis. And in this tomb she placed the most valuable of the royal treasures – gold, silver, emeralds, pearls, ebony, ivory, and cinnamon. In addition to all this, she also placed great quantities of firewood and rope in there, which made Caesar worry about the reason. He was afraid that the woman might become desperate and burn up and destroy all her treasure and wealth, so he kept sending friendly messages that were supposed to keep her hopes up that he was going to treat her well, while at the same time he was advancing on the city with his army.

When Caesar took up position near the hippodrome, Antony advanced against him and fought brilliantly – he routed Caesar's cavalry and pursued them as they retreated to their camp. Then, exalted by his victory, Antony went back into the palace, kissed Cleopatra, and, while still wearing his arms, he presented to her the one of his soldiers who had fought with the greatest distinction. Cleopatra gave the man a golden breastplate and a helmet as a reward for courage. The man took them, of course, but that very night he defected to Caesar.

[75] And now Antony once more sent Caesar a challenge of single combat. But Caesar answered that there were many routes that Antony had to die. Then Antony, realizing that there was no better death for him than that by battle, was determined to attack Caesar by land and sea at the same time. And at dinner, we are told, he ordered his servants to serve him food and wine with a more generous hand than usual – for it was uncertain, he said, whether they would be doing the same thing the next day, or whether they would be serving other masters, while he himself would be lying dead, a lifeless body and a nothing. Then, when he saw that his friends were crying at what he said, he told them that he would not be leading them out into the battle, since what he wanted from this battle was an honourable death for himself rather than safety and victory.

During the middle of the night, it is said, while the city was quiet and depressed through fear and expectation of what was about to happen, suddenly people could hear harmonious sounds from all kinds of instruments, and there was the loud shouting of a crowd, accompanied by cries of Bacchic revelry and satyric dancing, as if a troop of revelers, making a great commotion, was setting out from the city. Their course seemed to lie more or less through the middle of the city and toward the outer gate that faced the enemy, at which point the noise grew to a climax and then died down. Those who were looking for some meaning in this omen thought that the god to whom Antony always most likened and attached himself – Dionysus, Bacchus – was now deserting him.

[76] Early the next morning, Antony positioned his land forces on the hills in front of the city, and he watched his ships as they went out to sea and attacked those of the enemy. Since he expected to see something great accomplished by his navy, he kept his land forces inactive. But the crews of his ships, as soon as they were near to those of Caesar, they saluted Caesar's crews with their oars, and when the other ships saluted them in turn, all of Antony's ships changed sides and all the ships now were united into one fleet and thus sailed directly toward the city. No sooner had Antony seen this than his cavalry also abandoned him and went over to the enemy. After his infantry was defeated he retreated back into the city, crying out that Cleopatra had betrayed him to his enemies when he waged war on them in the first place only for her sake.

Cleopatra was afraid of what he might do in this state of anger and madness, so she fled into her tomb for refuge and let drop-doors fall, which were reinforced by bolts and bars. Then she sent messengers to tell Antony that she was dead. Antony believed the message, and said to himself: "Antony, why are you waiting? Fortune has robbed you of your only reason for living." He made his way to his own chamber and put aside his breastplate after he unfastened it. He said: "O Cleopatra, it's not the loss of you that hurts me so much, for I'll join you soon enough. What hurts is that I claim to be such a great commander but have been found to have less courage than a woman."

Now, Antony had a trusty slave named Eros. Antony had long before entrusted him, in case of need, with the job of killing him – and now he demanded the slave keep his word. So Eros drew his sword and held it up as though he would strike Antony, but then turned his face away and killed himself. And as he fell at his master's feet Antony said: "Well done, Eros! Even though you couldn't do this yourself, you've taught me what I have to do." Then Antony stabbed himself right through the stomach and fell back on his couch. But the wound did not bring a speedy death, since his position on the couch stopped the blood from pouring out of his wound. After he recovered consciousness, he came and asked others if someone would finish him off. But they quickly fled from the room, and he lay there writhing in pain and crying out loud, until the scribe Diomedes came from Cleopatra with orders to bring him to her where she was in the tomb.

[77] When he learned that Cleopatra was alive, Antony eagerly ordered his servants to lift him upright, and he was carried in their arms to the doors of her tomb. Cleopatra, however, refused to open the doors, but appeared at a window, from which she let down ropes and chords. Antony was fastened to these and she drew him up to

her, with the help of the only two women she had allowed into the tomb with her. Those who were there tell us that there was never a sadder and more pitiable sight imaginable. Antony was drawn up, smeared all over with blood and in the midst of death, stretching out his hands to her even as he dangled in the air next to the tomb. The task was not an easy one for the women, and Cleopatra, with the strain showing on her face, could barely pull the rope up, while those below called out encouragement to her and shared her pain.

And when she finally got him inside and laid him down, she tore her clothes in grief over what had happened to him, and beat and tore at her breasts with her hands. She smeared some of his blood all over her face, and called him her master, husband, and imperator. Her sadness for his condition for a while almost made her forget her own troubles. But Antony stopped her from crying and asked for a drink of wine, either because he was thirsty, or he hoped that this would give him a speedier death. When he had drunk the wine, he advised her to take care of her own safety, if she could do so without disgrace, and of all Caesar's companions to put most confidence in Proculeius. He also begged her not to mourn for him in this recent misfortune, but to consider him fortunate and happy for the good things that come his way. After all, he had achieved supreme fame, had won the greatest power, and now had been honourably defeated – a Roman by a Roman.

[78] Antony had just died, when Proculeius arrived on a mission from Caesar. After Antony had stabbed himself and while he was being carried to Cleopatra, Dercetaeus, one of his bodyguards, grabbed Antony's sword, concealed it under his clothes, and slipped out of the building with it. He ran to Caesar and was the first to tell him about Antony's death, showing him the sword that was all smeared with Antony's blood as evidence. When Caesar heard this news, he went back into his tent and wept for a man who had been his brother-in-law, his colleague in office and command, and his partner in many military and political activities. Then he took the letters that had passed between them, called in his friends, and read those letters out loud, showing how reasonably and justly he had written to Antony, and how rude and overbearing Antony had always been in his replies to Caesar. After this he sent Proculeius, asking him to do everything that he could to get Cleopatra into his hands alive. He did this because not only was he worried about the treasures that might be burned in her funeral pyre, but he also thought it would add greatly to the glory of his triumph if he could lead her in the procession back in Rome. But Cleopatra refused to put herself into Proculeius' hands. But she did talk to him after he had come near to the tomb and stationed himself outside at a door that was on the ground level. The door was strongly bolted and covered with bars, but it allowed a clear passage for their voices. The point of their conversation was that Cleopatra asked that her children might be allowed to inherit the kingdom, and Proculeius told her that she didn't need to worry and that she could trust Caesar in everything.

[79] After Proculeius surveyed the place, he brought word back to Caesar of what he had seen, and Gallus was sent to have another conversation with Cleopatra. He went up to the door he purposely prolonged the conversation. Meanwhile Proculeius placed a ladder up against a wall and went in through the window through which the women had taken Antony inside. Then accompanied by two servants he went down at once to the very door at which Cleopatra was standing and listening to Gallus. One of the women who was imprisoned with Cleopatra cried out, "Oh no, poor Cleopatra, they are going to take you alive." When she heard this Cleopatra then turned around, saw Proculeius, and then tried to stab herself with a small dagger that she happened to have in her belt – the kind of dagger that robbers carry. But Proculeius ran up to her quickly, threw his arms about her, and said: "O no Cleopatra, that would be wrong to you and to Caesar. You'd be robbing him of an opportunity to show you great kindness, and you'd be accusing the gentlest of commanders of dishonesty and intransigence." While he was saying this he took away her weapon, and shook out her clothing to see whether she was hiding any poison. There was another person there who was sent from Caesar – one of his freedmen, Epaphroditus – and Caesar had given him orders to do whatever necessary to keep the queen alive, but otherwise to make any concession to her that would make her comfortable and happy.

[80] And now Caesar himself rode into the city, and he was conversing with the philosopher Arius, who was riding on his right side, in order that Arius' profile might at once be raised among the citizens and that he would be admired for this honour shown to him by Caesar. He entered the gymnasium and ascended a tribunal that

was set up there for him. The people there were beside themselves with fear and prostrated themselves before him, but he ordered them to get up, and said that he pardoned all the people in Alexandria for three reasons; first, in memory of Alexander, their founder; second, because he admired the great size and beauty of the city; and third, as a favour to his companion, Arius.

In addition to this honour that Caesar bestowed upon Arius, he also pardoned many other persons at the request of the philosopher. Among these was Philostratus, a man who was more skilled at extemporaneous speaking than any sophist that ever lived, and who improperly represented himself as belonging to the school of the Academy. This is the reason that Caesar hated the man's character and he would not listen to the man's pleas. So Philostratus, with his long white beard and dark robe, would follow behind Arius, always repeating this verse:

"A wise man will save a wise man, if he is a wise man."

When Caesar heard about what Philostratus was doing, he pardoned him, wishing to free Arius from the public's hatred rather than caring much about Philostratus' fear.

[81] As for Antony's children, Antyllus, his son by Fulvia, was betrayed by his tutor Theodorus and was put to death. After the soldiers had cut off the young boy's head, Theodorus stole a very valuable gem that the boy used to wear around his neck and then he sewed it into his own belt. Although the tutor denied the theft, he was convicted of it and crucified. Cleopatra's children were kept under guard along with their attendants, and they were treated quite generously. But Caesarion, who was said to be Cleopatra's son by Julius Caesar, was sent by his mother to go to India via Ethiopa, and she gave him a lot of money and treasure for the journey. But Rhodon, another tutor who was much like Theodorus, persuaded the boy to return, on the grounds that Caesar invited him to take over his kingdom. But while Caesar was debating what to do about this situation, the story is that Arius told him:

"Too many Caesars is not a good thing."

[82] And so Caesarion was put to death by Caesar; but this happened later – after the death of Cleopatra. Many generals and kings asked for Antony's body so that they might give it a proper burial, though, but Caesar would not take it away from Cleopatra, and it was buried by her hands in sumptuous and royal fashion. Caesar allowed her to do whatever she wished for the occasion. But as a result of so much grief and pain (for her breasts were wounded and inflamed by the blows she gave them) she contracted a fever, and she welcomed it as an excuse for abstaining from food and so releasing herself from life without interference. There was a physician, Olympus, among her company of friends, and she told him the truth, and so he became her confidant and he assisted her in speeding up her death, as Olympus himself writes in a history of these events that he published. But Caesar was suspicious, and he used threats and her fears for her children against her. These threats and fears undermined her resolution as if they were engines of war, and finally she surrendered her body to those who wanted to care for it and nourish it.

[83] After a few short days Caesar himself came to talk with her and put her mind at ease. She was lying sadly on a straw mattress, wearing only her tunic, but she sprang up as soon as he entered and threw herself at his feet. Her hair and face were in terrible disarray, her voice trembled, and her eyes were puffy and swollen. The many marks of the cruel blows that she placed upon her breasts were also visible. In a word, her body seemed to be no better off than her mind and spirit. Nevertheless, her famous charm and charisma and the power of her beauty were not altogether extinguished but shone forth through her misery from somewhere inside and made themselves evident in the play of her features. Caesar asked her to lie down on the mattress while he sat down beside her. She began to try to justify her actions, blaming them on necessity and fear of Antony. But Caesar opposed and refuted her on every point, and so she quickly changed her tone and tried to move him to pity with prayers, behaving like one wanted nothing more than to go on living.

And finally she gave him a list that she made of all her treasures and possessions. But when one of her servants, Seleucus, proved conclusively that she was stealing away and hiding some of them, she jumped up, seized him by the hair, and showered blows upon his face. And when Caesar offered a smile and stopped her, she told him: "But Caesar, it just isn't right, is it? It's ok for you to come and talk to me even though I am in such a horrible state, but my slaves are denounce ming for keeping back a little bit of my jewelry. I'm not doing this for myself, you know – I am too messed up for that. But I'm doing this so that I can give some small gifts to Octavia and your Livia, and through them perhaps they will encourage you to be more merciful and gentle with me."

Caesar was pleased with her speech, since he still had the opinion that she wanted to live. Therefore he told her that it would be up to her to look after her valuables, and that in all other ways he would treat her more gloriously than she ever expected. Then he left, thinking that he had deceived her, but it was rather she who had deceived him.

[84] Now, there was a young man of distinction among Caesar's companions, who was named Cornelius Dolabella. This man was quite attracted to Cleopatra and so now, in response to her request, he secretly sent word to her that Caesar himself was preparing to march with his forces through Syria, and had decided to send her and her children away in two days. When Cleopatra heard this, she asked Caesar if she could be allowed to pour libations for Antony. When Caesar granted her request, she had herself carried to Antony's tomb in the company of the women who were usually about her.

She then embraced the urn that held his ashes and said to him: "Dear Antony, I buried you just recently while my hands were still free; now, however, I pour libations for you as a captive, and I am so carefully guarded that I cannot either disfigure my body with blows or tears of lamentation. My body is already that of a slave, and it's closely watched so that it may be preserved and be used to celebrate Caesar's triumph over you. So you shouldn't expect any other honours or libations; these are the last you'll receive from Cleopatra now that she is a slave. In life there was nothing that could come between us, but in death we are likely to change places: you, the Roman, will lie buried here in Egypt, while I, poor me, will lie in Italian soil - and I'll never get more of your land than that portion for my grave. But if indeed there is any might or power in the gods of that country (for the gods of this country have betrayed us), please do not abandon your own wife while she is still alive, and don't allow a triumph to be celebrated over me in my presence. Instead, hide me and bury me here with you, since of all my countless miseries none are as great and dreadful as this short time that I have lived apart from you."

[85] After such laments, she placed a wreath around the urn and kissed it, and then ordered her slaves to prepare her bath. After her bath, she reclined at her couch and ate a sumptuous mid-day meal. And then a man from the country came carrying a basket. When the guards asked him what he was bringing, he opened the basket, took away the leaves, and showed them that the dish inside was full of figs. The guards were amazed at the great size and beauty of the figs, and so the man smiled and asked them to take some. For this reason they weren't suspicious of him and told him that he could enter. After her meal, however, Cleopatra took a tablet upon which she had already written and sealed up and sent it to Caesar. Then, after she sent away all the rest of the company except for her two faithful women, she closed the doors to her chamber.

When Caesar opened the writing-tablet, he found in it a passionate and emotional plea that she could be buried with Antony, and Caesar quickly knew what had happened. At first he was prepared to go himself there and see if he could help, but then he changed his mind and ordered messengers to go quickly and find out what had happened. But the sad event had happened too quickly for them. Caesar's messengers came running and found the guards there still unaware that anything was going on. When they opened the doors they found Cleopatra lying dead on a golden couch, dressed up like a queen, while one of her two servant women, Iras, lay dying at her feet. Her other servant, Charmion, was already weak and could barely stand upright, but she was still trying to arrange the diadem which encircled the queen's forehead. Then one of Caesar's men said to her in anger: "This is a fine deed, Charmion!" She replied: "It is indeed most fine, and is appropriate for a descendant of so many kings." She didn't say another word, but fell there where she was, by the side of the couch.

[86] It is said that the snake was smuggled in with those figs and leaves and that it lay hidden beneath them, for this is what Cleopatra had ordered – so that the snake might fasten itself upon her body without her being

The Demise of Antony and Cleopatra

aware of it. But when she took away some of the figs and saw it, she said: "Here it is, then" – and she uncovered her arm and held it out for the snake to bite. Yet others say that the snake was kept carefully shut up in a water jar, and that while Cleopatra was stirring it up and provoking it with a golden distaff, it suddenly sprang out and fastened itself onto her arm. But no one knows what the truth of the matter is. It was also said that she carried poison around inside a hollow hairpin and that she kept the hairpin hidden in her hair. But there were no marks found on her body, nor any other signs of poison found on her. What is more, there were also no sightings of the snake within her chamber, although some people said that they saw some traces of it near the sea, where the window of the room looked out. And some people also say that Cleopatra's arm was noticed to have two slight and indistinct punctures; and this is the version that Caesar also seems to have believed, because in his triumph he had a picture of Cleopatra carried in the procession, which showed the snake clinging to her. At any rate, these are the various accounts of what happened.

But although Caesar was angry that the woman was dead, he was still impressed by her nobility and he admired her lofty spirit. So he gave orders that her body should be buried with that of Antony in a fashion that was fitting for a queen. He also gave orders that Cleopatra's attendants were also to receive honourable burials. When Cleopatra died she was thirty-nine years old – she had been queen for twenty-two of those years and had shared her power with Antony for more than fourteen of them. Some writers say that Antony was fifty-six years old, while others say fifty-three. The statues of Antony were torn down, but those of Cleopatra were left standing, because one of her friends, Archibius, paid Caesar two thousand talents, in order to prevent them from suffering the same fate as Antony's.

[87] Antony had seven children by his three wives. Antyllus, who was the oldest, was the only one who was put to death by Caesar. The rest were taken in by Octavia and raised along with her own children. Octavia gave Cleopatra, Antony's daughter by Cleopatra, in marriage to Juba, the most accomplished of kings, and Antony, the son of Fulvia and Antony, she raised so high that, while Agrippa held the first place in Caesar's estimation, and the sons of Livia the second, Antony was thought to be and really was third.

With Marcellus Octavia had two daughters and one son, also called Marcellus. Caesar adopted this Marcellus and had him marry his daughter Julia so that he became his son-in law as well. And Caesar gave one of Octavia's daughters to Agrippa. But since Marcellus died very soon after his marriage and it was not easy for Caesar to select from among his other friends a son-in law whom he could trust, Octavia proposed that Agrippa should take Caesar's daughter Julia as his wife, and divorce her own daughter. First she persuaded Caesar, then she won over Agrippa to this idea, whereupon she took back her own daughter and married her to young Antony, while Agrippa married Caesar's daughter Julia.

Antony had two daughters with Octavia, one of whom Domitius Ahenobarbus took as his wife, and the other, Antonia, famous for both her beauty and virtue, was married to Drusus, who was the son of Livia and therefore the stepson of Caesar. From this marriage sprang Germanicus and Claudius; of these children, Claudius later became emperor, and of the children of Germanicus, Gaius (Caligula) ruled for only a few demented years before he was put to death along with his wife and children, while Caligula's sister Agrippina had a son with Ahenobarbus, Lucius Domitius, before she finally became the wife of Claudius Caesar. And Claudius, after he adopted Agrippina's son, gave him the name of Nero Germanicus. This Nero came to the throne in my lifetime. He killed his mother, and by his recklessness and madness he nearly destroyed the Roman Empire. He was the fifth in descent from Antony.

Translated from the Greek by Stephen Russell, PhD
English text by Stephen Russell and Laura Holtebrinck

Tacitus

SOME STORIES ABOUT NERO

The Story: In his *Annals* the historian Tacitus presents Nero, the last Julio-Claudian emperor, in a most unfavourable light. In the following excerpts, he describes how Nero plotted to kill his mother Agrippina, how he was believed to have set fire to Rome so that he could replace it with his own "Neropolis," and how his former advisor and tutor Seneca is forced to commit suicide. The final section deals with another forced suicide – this time that of a fellow named Petronius, who some believe is the same Petronius who wrote *The Satyricon*.

1. The Death of Agripinna (59 AD): Annals 14.1-16

1. With the arrival of the new year, Caius Vipstanus Apronianus and Gaius Fonteius Capito became consuls and this was the time that Nero stopped putting off the crime that he had long been planning. He was in love with Poppaea more and more each day, but as long as his mother Agrippina was still alive, Poppaea didn't see any likelihood that he was going to divorce Octavia and marry her. So she kept nagging him and mocking him in an effort to spur him to action. She said that he was under the thumb of his guardian – that he neither ruled the empire nor himself. "If this wasn't the case," she said, "then why have there been all these delays in our marriage? I guess my looks and my ancestors must not be good enough for you. Or do you doubt that I'll be able to have children? Or do you think that my love isn't sincere?"

She continued: "No! I think that you are simply afraid that, if we were married, I would be honest with you and tell you how the senate is beaten down by your mother and how the public is angered by her egotism and greed. If Agrippina only wants to have daughters-in-law who hate her son, then I might as well marry Otho again. I'd rather go anywhere in the world where I can only hear about the humiliations of the emperor, and where I don't have to see them every day. And so that I don't have to see you in danger, like I am myself." Poppaea backed up her plea with tears and all the kinds of tricks that lovers possess. She won Nero over, and nobody really bothered to fight against her in the matter – for everyone wanted to see Agrippina's rule come to an end. However, no one really believed that Nero's hatred would lead him so far as to kill his own mother.

2. The author Clivius Rufus reports that Agrippina was so obsessed with retaining power that in the middle of the day, at the very time when Nero was starting to become a bit drunk with wine and feasting, she would often appear in front of her intoxicated son all tarted up and ready for incest. The people who were with them noticed the sensual kisses she would give him, and their mutually shared and suggestive caresses – an unspeakable evil. In turn, Seneca thought that the way to ward off the advances of a woman was with another woman, so he called upon the ex-slave Acte to help in the matter. She told him that she was worried about Nero's reputation – and, incidentally, her own safety as well. And her orders were to tell Nero that his mother Agrippina was bragging that she was having sex with her own son, that her stories were gaining a large audience, and that the Roman army wouldn't endure to have an emperor who behaved in such a way.

Still another writer, Fabius Rusticus, says that Nero was the one who so evilly lusted after his mother – and not the other way around – but that his wicked desires were put in check by the work of that same Acte. But most of those who are in the know support first version of the story, as does the tradition. The reason that people are so ready to blame Agrippina is that she may really have been ready to do such a wicked thing – or perhaps it just seemed to everyone that such an act of sexual depravity was perfectly believable in a woman like her. It was, after all, common knowledge that while she was young she illicitly used her sex to seduce Marcus Aemilius Lepidus so that she might gain some leverage of power – and that same level of ambition in her led her to take Pallas as her lover as well. Finally, by marrying her uncle Claudius, she brought her education in sexual decadence and shame to new lows.

3. So Nero did his best to avoid being alone with his mother. When she went away to her gardens or her estates at Tusculum and Antium, he praised her for taking a well-deserved holiday. But he finally became convinced that his mother would be intolerable no matter where she was – so Nero decided that he would have to kill her. His only point of hesitation involved deciding whether he should use poison, or a sword, or some other violent method. At first poison seemed to be the best option – but another death taking place at the emperor's table wouldn't look good, especially after his step-brother Britannicus just recently died that way. At the same time it seemed practically impossible to bribe any of his mother's staff to help in this plot, since her own devious and criminal mind kept her constantly on the lookout for any plots that might be aimed against her. What is more, she had been strengthening herself against poison by taking a number of preventative antidotes.

And nobody could think of a way that they could stab her that would remain secret even after the event took place. Of course there was also the other danger – that the potential killer might not have the nerve to carry out his orders and complete the horrible deed. At this point Anicetus, a former slave who controlled the ships at Misenum, made a rather brilliant suggestion. Anicetus had been a tutor to Nero when the emperor was still a boy – and from that time both he and Agrippina shared a mutual hatred for one another. He explained that they could make a ship that would have one section suddenly break free so that Agrippina would be suddenly thrown into the sea, where she would then drown. Anicetus said, "Nothing offers so many surprises and accidents as the sea does. And besides, if she should happen to die because of a shipwreck, what sort of a lunatic would blame a person for that instead of the winds and the waves? What is more, after she is dead, if it happens this way, then the emperor will still be able to dedicate temples and altars and other such signs of filial piety as signs of respect to his deceased mother.

4. Nero liked this plan. And it also fit nicely in with his plans at that time of year, since he was about to celebrate the festival of Minerva at Baiae. He convinced his mother to join him there and told everyone around him that children have to live with the tempers of their parents and that in the end they have to soothe their spirits. He did all of this so that people might start to have the impression that he and his mother had become reconciled. And he wanted Agrippina to feel the same way as well, of course – for women are especially gullible to accept welcome and happy news.

As she approached, he went down the shore to meet her (she was coming from Antium), and welcomed her with outstretched arms. There they embraced, and he conducted her to Bauli, which was the name of a mansion that was on the road between Cape Misenum and the lake of Baiae. There were some ships already waiting in the water right in front of that mansion, and one of those boats was far more luxurious than the others, which was obviously an attempt to please his mother, since she used to be in the habit of travelling in warships that were manned by members of the imperial navy.

Once she was safely arrived at the mansion, she was then invited out to a banquet back in Baiae. It was to take place this way with the thought that the darkness of night might help provide cover for the crime. But it is said that an informer told Agrippina all about the plot and she was unsure whether she should believe the story. All the same, she decided to be safe and so was conveyed to Baiae by land in her carriage.

The soothing words that Nero gave when she arrived there helped remove her fears. He was very gracious and kind to her, and he even gave her the place of honour right next to himself. The party lasted for quite a long time and they talked about many different things. Nero moved between moments of boyish mirth and serious constraint. When she was getting ready to leave, he walked her out, holding her tightly and giving her all kinds and manner of kisses. He did this either to add one final piece to the ruse, or because this final sight of mother, as she was leaving for her death, was so traumatic for him and his heart to bear.

5. But it seemed that the heavens were determined to reveal the crime that was about to be committed, since the night was quiet, the sea was calm, and the stars above provided a great deal of light. The ship pulled out and began to move on its way back to the mansion at Bauli. Agrippina had brought two attendants along with her. One of them, Crepereius Gallus, stood watching the control of the boat, while the other, Acerronia, sat down next to Agrippina's feet as the two of them relaxed and spoke delightedly about Nero's change of heart and of his mother's soon-to-be restored influence.

Then all of a sudden the signal came and the roof caved in, for it had been loaded up with a number of very heavy lead weights, and Crepereius was crushed and immediately killed. Agrippina and Acerronia were protected and saved by the raised sides of the couch, which just happened to be too strong to yield under the weight. But this was not followed by the breaking up of the boat – for the ship in fact stayed in one piece. Everyone was confused by what was happening, and the people who were in on the plot were slowed by those who weren't. Some of the crew then had the idea of throwing the vessel onto one side so that they could sink the whole ship, but they couldn't organize themselves quickly enough to make this happen. At the same others were working against this attempt to capsize the boat by pushing toward the other side – all of which efforts made the boats descent into the sea a rather mild and gentle one.

However, Acerronia foolishly started shouting that she was Agrippina, and begging everyone around to help her as the emperor's mother. Much to her surprise she was struck dead with poles and oars, and whatever ship's equipment happened to be around. Agrippina, on the other hand, remained silent and thus avoided detection. All the same, although she received a wound in her shoulder, she still managed to swim until she met up with some small boats that brought her to the Lucrine lake, and from there she was brought to her home.

6. It was at this point that she realized that the whole evening had been a set-up – that that invitation to the dinner, the special attention that Nero had paid her, and the collapse of the ship – all of it had all been planned out beforehand. She also reflected that the collapsed roof of the boat seemed a great deal like something that would happen on the stage, and not at all like something that should happen on a boat. And the death of Acerronia, and the wound that she herself had suffered, gave her a moment's pause. Weighing all the options, Agrippina decided that the best way to deal with such a plot was to pretend that it didn't happen. Therefore she told Agerinus, an ex-slave of hers, to visit her son and tell him that thanks to the gods above and her own good fortune she had just survived a serious accident. She also told the messenger to add that, even though Nero must be worried about her health following such an accident, he shouldn't come to visit her just yet. Rather, she needed rest at the moment.

And so, acting as if she felt completely safe, Agrippina took care of her wounds and her body in general. She also demanded that Acerronia's will be found and that her property be sealed up – for in this action no acting was necessary.

7. Meanwhile, Nero was waiting for news about the crime, hoping to hear that the deed had been accomplished. He was surprised and shocked to hear that she had escaped the boating disaster with only a slight wound – after she encountered the kinds of dangers that left no doubt as to how they were caused. Nero all of a sudden became paralyzed all over with fear, believing that his mother was about to shop up at any moment in order to seek her vengeance on him. He thought that she would incite her slaves against him, or that she had the power to call an army together, or perhaps she would run to either the senate or the mob, showing off her wounds and blaming him for the death of her friends. Nero frantically asked about how he could protect himself against this and whether Burrus or Seneca could come up with a plan that might help him – for he had called both of them the moment that he heard that Agrippina was still alive. It's unclear whether they had been involved in the original plot.

For a long time neither Burrus nor Seneca spoke. Perhaps they were worried that Nero might reject their advice, or perhaps they were just aware that this matter had reached such a level that Nero had to strike Agrippina at once or he might face his own demise. Finally Seneca turned to Burrus and asked him whether they needed to turn to the soldiers to commit this murder. He answered that the Guard were loyal to the whole royal household and to the memory of Germanicus, and that they couldn't be expected to kill Agrippina, who was one of Germanicus' children. He added that it would be up to Anicetus to fulfill his promise and complete the deed.

Thus Anicetus didn't hesitate, but he instead took it upon himself to finish the crime. When Nero heard him promise to take care of matters, he shouted that this was the first day of his rule – and that this great gift came to him from the hands of a former slave. "Go right away," said Nero, "and take the kind of men with you who are good at obeying your orders."

When Agerinus, Agrippina's messenger, arrived, Nero played a trick and set the fellow up on false charges. While Agerinus was delivering the message from Agrippina, Nero put a sword down next to the feet of the man and demanded that he be arrested immediately. Nero's goal was to pretend that his mother had made a threat against his life, but that her plot had been detected early, and so she was forced to commit suicide out of shame.

8. The disastrous adventure that happened to Agrippina was becoming more well known, and the common response was to believe that it had only been an accident. The moment people heard about it they ran down to the beach. Some people ran out onto the piers, while others got into the first boats they could find. Other people just walked into the water as far as they were able, where they waved their arms and jumped around a lot. The entire shore was resounding with screams and prayers and the noise of all kinds of people asking questions and nobody having an adequate answer. A great number of people came there with torches and when they finally discovered that Agrippina was safe, they were preparing to wish her well with a show of rejoicing.

But this celebration quickly came to an end when an armed guard that looked altogether menacing came into sight and frightened everyone away. Anicetus made his way to the house where Agrippina was staying and he surrounded it with his soldiers. Then he knocked the gates and doors down, arresting any slave that tried to stand in his way. Finally he came to the door of her bedroom. There were still a few servants who stood here – all of the rest had been frightened away by the invading guards.

There was only a small lamp in the room, and one slave-girl was in there with Agrippina, who was becoming very nervous when she noticed that no messenger – not even Agerinus – was returning from Nero's residence. She also noticed that the shore had suddenly changed – one moment it was quiet and the next it was all kinds of commotion, but the kind that portended the worst kind of disaster. As the slave-girl got up in order to leave, Agrippina shouted: "Are you abandoning me as well?" Then she looked around and saw Anicetus, who walked into the room with a naval captain, Herculeius, and Obaritus, a centurion from the marines – both of whom were standing behind him.

She told them, "If you have come here just to see me, then you can bring back word that I am better. But if you are here to kill me, I know that my son can't be the one who is behind this. He would not order the murder of his mother." The murderers then closed in around her bed. The captain was the first to hit her on the head with his club. Then, when the centurion took out his sword to finish the job, she screamed out "strike me here!" and she pointed to the womb that once bore her son, her murderer. Thus they struck her with many blows and she fell dead.

9. Thus far all of our accounts agree. Some people say that Nero himself inspected the body of his mother after her death and praised her beauty – but other people deny that. Her body was cremated that night on a dining couch, with a very small ceremony. While Nero was in power, the earth where she was burned was neither raised into a mound, nor was it covered over in a decent way – although members of her household later gave her a tomb near to the road to Misenum, near the hilltop where the house of Julius Caesar overlooks the bay below. While she was being cremated, one of her former slaves, Mnestor, stabbed himself to death – either he did this out of love for his mistress Agrippina or he feared that someone else would kill him.

Agrippina had anticipated that she would reach such an end many years prior to this – but the prospect did not deter her. For when she asked the astrologers about her son Nero, they told her that he would one day become emperor and then kill his mother. She said, "Then let him kill her, as long as he becomes emperor."

10. But Nero only understood the horror of the crime he had committed once it was accomplished. For the rest of that night he was silent and in a daze, at times staring straight ahead as if he were paralyzed and at other times jumping to his feet in terror – as if he were waiting for the coming dawn, which he believed was bound to be his last.

2. The Fire in Rome (64 AD): Annals 15.37-44

37. Nero now tried to make it look like Rome was his favourite place to live. He held feast and celebrations out in the public as if the whole city were his private home. But the most extravagant and notorious banquet was the one put on by Tigellinus. I'll give a brief account of it, if only so that I won't have to keep repeating similar examples of extravagance again and again.

The entertainment took place on a raft that was placed in the middle of Agrippa's lake. The guests were placed on the raft and it was towed by other boats, ones that were all shining in gold and ivory. The rowers were all unsavory characters, arranged according to their ages and perversions. Tigellinus had birds and other beasts brought in from far off countries, and he had a number of sea monsters from the ocean. On the shore of the lake some brothels were set up in which various noble and high-ranking ladies were working, and on the opposite side there were naked prostitutes who were posing indecently and offering all manners of gestures.

When darkness came, all the woods and the houses nearby resounded with singing, and lights blazed forth from everywhere. Nero had already been polluted by every kind of vice and lust – natural and unnatural – and it was believed that there wasn't a single abomination that he hadn't tried. But he proved this wrong, for a few days later he lowered himself to marry someone from that disgusting rabble who went by the name Pythagoras. Right in front of witnesses, the emperor decided that he was going to put on the bridal veil and play the part of a woman. There was a dowry, wedding torches, marriage bed – everything was there. In fact everything was exposed for public view – even the kinds of things that would be kept hidden by darkness in a normal marriage.

38. A disaster soon followed. It's uncertain whether it was an accident or it was caused by some criminal act on behalf of the emperor. There are plenty of people who argue for each side. The most terrible and destructive fire that had ever taken place in Rome started up. It began in the Circus Maximus, which is connected to the Palatine and Caelian hills. At first, it broke out in little shops that sell flammable goods, and then it was pushed to become greater by the wind, until finally the blaze grew so large that it swept over the whole of the circus. In this place there were no mansions or temples surrounded by walls that could pose a threat to the fire.

So the fire first swept through the flat areas of the city, then it eventually climbed to the hills, then it returned once again to assault the places down below. It was stronger than any measure taken to try to stop it. The city was at the mercy of the blaze – and its narrow and irregular streets only encouraged the fire and helped spread its progress.

There were terrified and screaming women everywhere – along with the elderly and those who were too young, and some who were saving themselves or others, those who were altruistically helping the disabled and waiting for them: the constant bustle and flight made the scene even more confusing. Often, when people looked behind them, they saw menacing flames leap up to their side and surround them. Or if they escaped and made it as far as a nearby district, they would discover that this area was seized by the fire as well and that even places that they had imagined to be too far off were involved in the same misery.

At last, since they had no idea where they should go and flee, many of them crowded into the streets or flung themselves down into the fields. Some of them, who had lost everything, even their food for that day, could have made it out and escaped, but instead they decided that it would be better to die. And there were others who also died out of love for their relatives, whom they were unable to rescue. And no one dared to stop the fire, because there were a number of menacing gangs that stopped people from doing so. And there were other men who openly threw torches into the fires, and they kept shouting that there was someone who was ordering them to do so. Perhaps they really were following orders, or perhaps they just were looking for a way to steal things more freely.

39. While all this was happening Nero was at Antium, and he only returned to Rome when the fire approached his house – the one he had built to connect the palace on the Palatine with the Gardens of Maecenas. But the fire could not be stopped from destroying the palace, the house, and everything around it. However, to offer relief to the masses of newly homeless people, he threw the Campus Martius open to them as well as the public buildings of Agrippa, and even his own Gardens. Nero also had some temporary structures built to take in and help the needy masses. Supplies of food were brought up from Ostia and the neighbouring towns, and the price of corn was reduced less than a quarter sesterce a pound. These actions, even though they were popular, failed to produce any gratitude from the masses, since a rumour was spreading everywhere that, at the very time when the city was all in flames, the emperor appeared on his private stage and sang about the destruction of Troy, comparing this present disaster with more ancient misfortunes.

40. Finally after five days they were able to put an end to the fire at the bottom of the Esquiline hill, by destroying all the buildings in that vast space so that the violence of the fire was met by clear ground and open sky. But before people had time to let go of their fears, the flames returned once again, with just as much this second time - and the fire especially attacked the more spacious regions of the city. Even though there were fewer deaths and casualties, the destruction that came to the temples of the gods and the porticoes that were devoted to enjoyment brought even more widespread ruin. And this new fire brought even more ill feeling with it because it was reported to have started on Tigellinus' estate in the Aemilian district. This created problems because people started to believe that Nero was trying to burn down Rome so that he could fulfill his ambitions and build a new city that he would call by his own name. Rome is divided into fourteen districts, but only four of them remained unscathed by the fire – three of them were leveled to the ground, while the other seven were reduced to only a few shattered and half-burnt ruins of former homes.

41. It wouldn't be easy to list all of the mansions, apartment buildings, and temples that were destroyed by the fire. Among them were some of the oldest shrines, such as the one dedicated by Servius Tullius to Luna; the great altar and shrine dedicated by Evander to Hercules; the temple to Jupiter the Stayer, which had been dedicated by Romulus; Numa's royal palace; and the sanctuary of Vesta, which held the household gods of the Roman people – all these were burnt.

Among all the things that were lost were the riches that had been acquired by our many victories, various masterpieces of Greek art, and the ancient and genuine historical monuments of our ancient Roman genius. Despite all the beauty and splendour of the restored city, old men will still remember many things that could not be replaced. Some people noticed that the beginning of this conflagration was on the 19th of July, the day on which the Senonian Gauls captured and set fire to Rome. Other people have been pushing the curious story that the two fires were separated by the same number of years (418), months (418), and days (418).

42. In the meantime Nero used the opportunity of his country's destruction to bring profit to himself personally, for he started to build a palace in which the gold and jewels, although amazing enough marvels in and of themselves, paled in comparison to the sight of the fields and the lakes that were a part of that palace. On one side there were woods that were made to look like a forest, and on the other there were open spaces and magnificent views. Severus and Celer, the architect and engineer of the marvel, had the boldness to attempt to create the kinds of things that nature herself would not allow.

But they also frittered away the wealth of the emperor with this foolish endeavor. They were planning to dig a canal wide enough for ships to pass through that would travel all the way from the mouth of the Tiber as far as lake Avernus, all the way through those rocky shores and the mountain passes – a total of 250 kilometers.

The only way to bring water to this canal was from the Pontine marshes, since everywhere else was either too steep or dry. Moreover, even if they could have found a way to cut the canal through the rocky terrain, the labour would have been absolutely unbearable, and there was no logical reason for such a waterway. However, Nero, was eager to attempt the impossible – so he ordered them to start digging their way through the hills next to Avernus, and there are still traces of those failed hopes that are visible to this very day.

43. Meanwhile, in the parts of Rome that were still left unoccupied by his palace, the streets were being rebuilt not in the same manner that they had been after the destruction left by the Gauls, when things were constructed without any rhyme or reason. Rather, the new rows of streets were being constructed with exact measurements, and the streets were broad, the homes were restricted to certain heights, and they were built around courtyards, with colonnades in the front to protect them from potential fires. Nero promised to build these colonnades using his own wealth and to remove all of the debris from the sites before he gave them over to their new owners.

He also offered bonuses, in proportion to each person's rank and level of resources, that people could receive if the homes and blocks were completed before a specific date. He said that all of the waste and garbage was to be dumped in the marshes of Ostia, and he arranged that the ships that had brought up corn by the Tiber should sail down the river bringing piles of this garbage.

The buildings themselves were to be solidly constructed to a specific height, but they were not allowed to contain wooden beams, but they were rather made of stone from Gabii or Alba, since these materials are impervious to fire. And to ensure that the water that some people had illegally diverted and stolen might flow in greater abundance in several places for the public use, officers and guards were appointed, and everyone had to have the tools for fighting a fire in his house. And every building was ordered to be enclosed by its own proper wall, which meant that there could be no semi-detached homes.

Many people welcomed these changes utility, and they also added beauty to the new city. Some people, however, thought that its old arrangement had been more healthier, since the old narrow streets and high roofs offered ample protection against the heat of the sun, while they argued that the new open spaces, unsheltered by any shade, burned with a fiercer heat.

44. Anyway, so much for the precautions of human wisdom. The next thing to mention was the attempts that were made to please and placate the gods. After consulting the sibylline books, prayers were offered to Vulcan, Ceres, and Proserpina. Juno received her share of prayers as well – first by the widows in the Capitol, then on the nearest part of the coast, where water was brought to sprinkle the temple and temple of the goddess. And there were also sacred banquets and nightly vigils celebrated by married women.

But all of these human efforts, all of the lavish gifts offered by the emperor, and the prayers sent toward the gods – none of this could lift the suspicion that this fire had been set under the orders of the emperor. Therefore, to make this rumour die, Nero found scapegoats and placed the guilt on the Christians – and he punished and tortured this group in any way he could, since the rumour was already out there that they were a depraved lot. Christ, from whom the group received its origin, had been executed during the reign of Tiberius at the hands of one of our procurators, Pontius Pilatus. But in spite of this death, which caused a minor setback, which stalled the progress of this deadly superstition for a while, it soon broke out not only in Judaea, which was the first source of the evil, but also even in Rome, where all hideous and shameful things from every part of the world eventually find their centre and become popular.

And so Nero forced every Christian to be arrested. Then, on the information that was received, a great multitude of others were also arrested and convicted, not so much for the fire as for their supposed anti-social tendencies. Their deaths were turned into displays of public mockery. They dressed up in the skins of animals and then torn to pieces by dogs, while some were nailed to crosses and crucified, and others were tuned into human torches and were thus burned in the evening to serve as a source of light after the daylight had departed.

Nero offered his Gardens for the spectacle, and he also gave a display in the Circus, where he himself mingled with the crowd of people or standing high on a chariot while wearing the dress of a charioteer. Thus, although these Christians were criminals who deserved extreme and ruthless punishment, the victims started to receive a certain level of compassion and pity - for people thought that they were being sacrificed to satisfy one man's brutality rather than for the sake of the public good.

3. The Death of Seneca (65 AD): Annals 15.60-64

60. The next one whom Nero killed was Plautius Lateranus, the consul-elect. His murder was so quick that he was not allowed to embrace his children or to have the customary brief choice of his own death. He was dragged off to a place that was reserved for the execution of slaves, and there the hand of the tribune Statius executed him. Through it all Plautius Lateranus kept a determined silence, and he didn't reproach the tribune for being complicit in the plot.

Seneca's death followed right after this one, which served as a special delight to the emperor. Nero had absolutely no proof that Seneca was involved, but he was still happy to use arms against him since poison had clearly failed to do the job. The only piece of evidence that was brought against Seneca was from Natalis – who said that he had been sent to visit the recently ill Seneca and to scold Seneca for refusing to meet with Piso. Natalis told him that friends should be nice to their friends, but Seneca answered that frequent meetings and conversations wouldn't be helpful for either one of them, and that his own life and welfare depended on Piso's.

Gavius Silvanus, a tribune of the Praetorian Guards, was ordered to report all of this to Seneca and to ask him whether he admitted that this was what Natalis and he both said. Either by chance or on purpose Seneca had just returned that day from Campania, and had stopped at a country-house about four miles outside of Rome. So the tribune came there the very next evening, surrounded the house with troops of soldiers, and then delivered the emperor's message to Seneca while he was having dinner with his wife, Pompeia Paulina, and two friends.

61. Seneca replied that Natalis had been sent to him and had complained to him on Piso's behalf because of his refusal to see Piso, after which Seneca excused himself because of his failing health and his need for rest. "I had no reason," he said, "for placing the interest of any private citizen above that of my own safety, and I am not one to give into flattery. No one knows this better than Nero, who has received more frankness than servility from Seneca."

When the tribune reported this answer in the presence of Poppaea and Tigellinus, the emperor's most confidential advisers in his moments of rage, Nero asked whether Seneca was preparing to commit suicide. The tribune asserted that he saw no signs of fear or sadness in his words or in his appearance. So Silvanus was thus ordered to go back and to announce Seneca's death sentence. Fabius Rusticus tells us that Silvanus did not return the same way that he came, but that he made a detour to visit Faenius, the commander of the Guard. He showed and explained the emperor's orders to him, and then asked whether he should obey them. Faenius told him to do as he was ordered, revealing that fatal level of cowardice that was common to them all. For Silvanus himself was actually one of the conspirators, and he was now adding to the crimes that he had united with them to avenge and stop. But he spared himself the pain of delivering the message, but instead sent one of his centurions to Seneca, who would tell Seneca that he had to die.

62. Seneca was altogether unmoved and so asked for tablets on which he could write his will. When the centurion refused, Seneca turned to his friends, and he told them that since he was forbidden to thank them properly, he would leave them the only, but still the noblest, possession that he still had. This gift was the pattern of his life, which, if they remembered it, they would win a name for moral worth and unwavering friendship. At the same time he checked their tears and told them to take courage – sometimes with friendly talk, and sometimes with harsher reproaches. "Where," he asked again and again, "is your philosophy, and where is that dedication and resolve against evil that they had prepared and planned after so many years of study? Was there anyone who didn't know that Nero was cruel? After killing his mother and his brother, it only seemed logical for Nero to kill his guardian and teacher."

63. He obviously spoke these words so that they could be heard by everyone. Then Seneca embraced his wife and, with a softness that was very different from his serious philosophical attitude, he begged her to spare herself the burden of perpetual sadness, and, in remembering their virtuously spent life, he told her to endure the loss of her husband with honourable consolation. She answered that she too had decided to die, and claimed for herself the blow of the executioner. Seneca did not oppose her noble and brave decision. In fact, he loved her so much that he was loath to leave her behind merely to be persecuted.

He told her: "I tried to show you a way to live a life with solace and comfort, but you prefer death and glory. I will not stop you from setting such a noble example. We can die with equal amounts of courage. But yours will be nobler than mine, and it deserves more fame than mine."

Then they each made one cut with the blade and Seneca and his wife each cut the arteries in their arms. But Seneca had a very old body, and it was lean from his frugal lifestyle, so his blood left him only slowly. So he also severed the veins in his ankles and those behind his knees. Worn out by all the cruel pain, and afraid that his pains and agonies might break his wife's spirit – or that he himself might lose his own strength when he looked at her suffering – he persuaded her to go to another bedroom. Even at the last moment his eloquence didn't fail him. For he summoned his secretaries and dictated a great deal to them – most of which has been published for all readers in his own words, so I don't want to paraphrase it.

64. Nero had no personal hatred against Seneca's wife Paulina. And so in order to avoid increasing his reputation for cruelty, he ordered that she not be allowed to kill herself.

So, on instructions from the soldiers, slaves and ex-slaves bandaged up her arms and they stopped the bleeding. She may have even been unconscious. But small-minded people are always ready to think the worst, and some people took another view – that as long as she lived in fear of Nero and his cruelty, she wanted to share the glory of her husband's death, but the idea of life became a better option for her when a new opportunity was given to her. She lived for a few years after that, living honourably and loyally to the memory of her husband, with her skin and limbs so white that revealed how much blood she had lost.

Meanwhile Seneca's death was slow and took a long time to take place. The poison had long been prepared, so Seneca now begged his doctor Statius Annaeus, who was one of his oldest and best friends, to bring it to him. When it was brought to him, Seneca drank it down – but there was no effect. For his limbs were cold and his body was numbed to the effects of the poison. Finally he had himself placed in a bath of hot water. He sprinkled a little of the water on the slaves that were closest to him, telling them it was a libation to Jupiter. Finally he was brought into a bath filled with steam, where the vapours suffocated him. He was cremated without a ceremonial funeral. That was exactly as he instructed in his will – which was written at the height of his wealth, strength, and power.

4. The Death of Petronius (66 AD): Annals 16.18-19

18. Gaius Petronius deserves a brief obituary. His days he passed in sleep, his nights he spent in the business and pleasures of life. Others achieved fame through their energy, but Petronius did so through laziness. But he was not thought of as immoral and a spendthrift, like most of those who squander their wealth, but rather as a man of refined luxury. And indeed people liked the apparent freshness of his unconventional and unselfconscious sayings and doings. But as proconsul of Bithynia and soon afterwards as consul, he showed himself to be a man of vigour and equal to business.

Then falling back into vice, or pretending to fall back into vice, he was chosen by Nero to be one of his few intimate associates, as a critic in matters of taste, for the emperor thought nothing was charming or elegant in luxury unless Petronius had expressed to him his approval of it. Therefore Tigellinus became very jealous, and he looked on Petronius as a rival and even his superior in the science of pleasure. And so he worked on the emperor's cruelty, which dominated every other passion, charging Petronius with having been the friend of Scaevinus, bribing a slave to become informer, robbing him of the means of defence, and hurrying into prison the greater part of Petronius' household.

19. It happened at the time that the emperor was on his way to Campania and that Petronius, after going as far as Cumae, was arrested there. He no longer bore the suspense of fear or of hope. Yet he did not fling away life with abrupt haste, but having made an incision in his veins he then, according to his manner, bound them up while he talked with his friends, not in a serious way or on topics that might win him a name for courage. And he listened to them as they repeated, not thoughts on the immortality of the soul or on the theories of philosophers, but light poetry and playful verses. To some of his slaves he gave the present of freedom, while he gave a beating to others. He dined, indulged himself in sleep, so that his death, though forced on him, might look natural. Even in his will he did not, as many others did in their last moments, flatter Nero or Tigellinus or any other of the men in power. On the contrary, he described the emperor's shameful excesses in full, with the names of his male and female companions and their habits of depravity, and he sent the list under seal to Nero. Then Petronius broke his signet ring, so that it might not be subsequently available for incriminating others.

Translated from the Latin by Stephen Russell, PhD
English text by Stephen Russell and Laura Holtebrinck

Chapter 6
Apollodorus

THE CURSED HOUSE OF ATREUS

The Story: To understand the play *Electra* one needs to know a bit about her family and its long and sad history. In his *Epitome*, the mythographer Apollodorus traces the most important parts of the doomed house of Atreus, the relevant parts of which I have reproduced here.

[E.2.1] Tantalus is punished in Hades by having a stone hanging over him, and he is perpetually in a lake, seeing at his shoulders on either side trees with fruit growing beside the lake on its banks. The water touches his jaws, but when he wants to take a drink of it, the water quickly dries up; and when he wanted to eat from the fruits, the trees with the fruits are lifted by winds as high as the clouds. Some say that he is punished in this manner because he gave away the mysteries and secrets of the gods to men, and some add that it was because he tried to share ambrosia with his friends.

[E.2.3] Pelops, after he was slaughtered and boiled at the banquet of the gods, was more beautiful than ever when he came to life again, and on account of his amazing beauty he became the beloved of Poseidon, who gave him a winged chariot – one that could run across the sea even without getting its axles wet.

[E.2.10] The sons of Pelops were Pittheus, Atreus, Thyestes, and others. Now the wife of Atreus was Aerope, the daughter of Catreus, and she was in love with Atreus' brother Thyestes. And Atreus once promised that he would sacrifice the finest lamb from his flocks to Artemis – but when a golden lamb appeared, they say that he neglected to fulfill his vow to the goddess.

[E.2.11] Instead of sacrificing the lamb to Artemis, Atreus choked the lamb and placed its fleece in a box for safekeeping and then kept it there. But Aerope gave this fleece to Thyestes, by whom she had been seduced. For the Mycenaeans had received an oracle that told them to choose one of the sons of Pelops as their king, and they had sent for Atreus and Thyestes. And when a discussion took place concerning who should become king, Thyestes declared to the assembled crowd that the kingdom should go to the one who could produce the golden fleece, and when Atreus agreed, Thyestes produced the fleece and was made king.

[E.2.12] But Zeus sent Hermes to Atreus and told him to reach an agreement with Thyestes that Atreus should become king if the sun reversed its course. And when Thyestes agreed, the sun went down in the east. Therefore the god was clearly stating that Thyestes didn't deserve the crown, and so Atreus got the kingdom and banished Thyestes.

[E.2.13] But afterwards, when Atreus learned of the adultery, he sent a herald to Thyestes with a proposal of reconciliation. And when he had lured Thyestes by this pretense of friendship, he then slaughtered the sons of his brother – Aglaus, Callileon, and Orchomenus – the children whom Thyestes had with a Naiad nymph. Atreus killed these children as they sat down as suppliants on the altar of Zeus. And then he cut them up limb by limb and boiled them, before he finally served them up to Thyestes without the extremities. And when Thyestes had already swallowed them down, Atreus then showed his brother the extremities of his dead children, and then he expelled Thyestes from the country.

[E.2.14] But seeking a way to get revenge on his brother Atreus, Thyestes asked the oracle what he should do about the matter, and he received an answer that he could gain his revenge if he were to have a son by having intercourse with his own daughter. He did just as the oracle suggested, and with his daughter he produced Aegisthus. And Aegisthus, when he was grown to manhood and learned that he was the son of Thyestes, he then killed Atreus and restored the kingdom to Thyestes.

[E.2.15] But Agamemnon and Menelaus, the sons of Atreus, were taken by their nurse to Polyphides, who was the king of Sicyon. Polyphides in turn sent them to Oeneus, the Aetolian. Not long afterwards Tyndareus brought them back again, and then they expelled Thyestes, making him swear an oath, when he was seeking refuge at the altar of Hera, that he would settle and remain in Cytheria. And they became the sons-in-law of Tyndareus by marrying his daughters: Agamemnon received Clytaemnestra as his wife, after he had killed her husband Tantalus, who was the son of Thyestes, together with their newborn child; and Menelaus received Helen as his wife.

[E.2.16] And Agamemnon became king of the Mycenaeans and married Clytaemnestra, the daughter of Tyndareus, after he killed her former husband Tantalus, son of Thyestes, along with their child. And Agamemnon and Clytaemnestra had a son, Orestes, and three daughters – Chrysothemis, Electra, and Iphigenia. And Menelaus married Helen and ruled over Sparta, since Tyndareus entrusted the kingdom to him.

[E.3.1] Afterward Alexandros/Paris carried off Helen, as some say, because that was the plan of Zeus, in order that his daughter Helen might become famous for having caused a war between Europe and Asia; or, as others have argued, Zeus did this so that the race of the demigods might come to be and become worthy of praise.

[E.3.2] For one of these reasons that I stated Nemesis/Eris/Discordia threw an apple in front of Hera, Athena, and Aphrodite, as a prize to be given to the most beautiful. And so Zeus commanded Hermes to lead them to Alexandros on Ida in order that he would judge of their beauty. And each of them promised to give Alexandros gifts. Hera said that if she were preferred to all other women, then she would give him the power to rule all men; Athena promised him victory in war; and Aphrodite promised him the hand of Helen. And thus he decided in favour of Aphrodite and sailed away to Sparta with ships that were built by Phereclus.

[E.3.3] For nine days Alexandros was entertained by Menelaus; but on the tenth day, Menelaus went away on a journey to Crete to celebrate the funeral of his mother's father Catreus, and that's when Alexandros persuaded Helen to go off with him. And she abandoned her daughter Hermione, who was then nine years old. And she put most of the property and treasures of the house on board, and then she set sail with him by the cover of night.

[E.3.4] But Hera sent a violent storm against them, which forced them to seek safety at Sidon. And fearing that someone might be pursuing him, Alexander delayed for a long time in Phoenicia and Cyprus. But when he thought that there was no longer a chance that he's be pursued, he finally went to Troy with Helen.

[E.3.5] But some say that Hermes, who was following the orders of Zeus, stole Helen and carried her off to Egypt. They say that Hermes gave her to Proteus, the king of the Egyptians, for safekeeping, and they say that Alexandros went back to Troy with a phantom of Helen that was fashioned out of clouds.

[E.3.6] When Menelaus became aware of the abduction of Helen, he came to Agamemnon in Mycenae and begged his brother to gather an army to wage war against Troy and to raise troops in Greece to do so. And Agamemnon sent a herald to each of the kings, reminding them of the oaths that they had all sworn, and warned each of them to consider the safety of his own wife, saying that the insult to Menelaus had been offered equally to the whole of Greece.

[E.3.21] But when after they had sailed away from Argos, they arrived in Aulis for a second time and the fleet was held back here due to lack of wind for sailing. The prophet Calchas said that they could not sail unless the most beautiful of Agamemnon's daughters were offered as a sacrifice to Artemis; for the goddess was angry with Agamemnon, both because, Agamemnon had shot a deer and announced: "Artemis herself could not do it better!" and also because Atreus had not sacrificed the golden lamb to Artemis as he had once promised.

[E.3.22] When he heard this oracle, Agamemnon sent Odysseus and Talthybius to his wife Clytaemnestra and asked for Iphigenia, claiming that he had promised to give her in marriage to Achilles as a reward for his participation in the campaign. So Clytaemnestra sent the young girl to her husband, and Agamemnon brought her to the altar and was just about to sacrifice her, when Artemis carried her off to the Taurians and appointed her to be a priestess of Artemis in this city, substituting a deer for the young girl at the altar. But some say that Artemis made her immortal.

[E.6.23] When Agamemnon returned to Mycenae with Cassandra, he was murdered by Aegisthus and Clytaemnestra; for she gave him a shirt without sleeves and without a neck, and while he was putting it on they struck him down. And Aegisthus became king of Mycenae – and they killed Cassandra as well.

[E.6.24] But Electra, one of Agamemnon's daughters, smuggled away her brother Orestes and gave him to Strophius, the Phocian, to raise and protect. And

Strophius raised Orestes along with his own son Pylades. And when Orestes became a man, he went to the oracle at Delphi and asked the god whether he should take vengeance on the murderers of his father.

[E.6.25] The god told him that he should kill them, so Orestes secretly went to Mycenae along with with Pylades, and he killed both his mother and Aegisthus. And not long afterward, he was struck by madness and pursued by the Furies, so he fled to Athens and was put on trial in the Areopagus. Some say that he was brought to trial by the Furies; some say he was indicted by Tyndareus, or perhaps by Erigone, the daughter of Aegisthus and Clytaemnestra. And when the votes of his trial were even, he was then acquitted.

[E.6.26] When Orestes asked the oracle how he could get rid of his affliction, the god answered that he could get rid of it if he brought back the wooden image that was in the land of the Taurians. Now the Taurians are a part of the Scythian race, and they murder strangers and throw them into the sacred fire. This fire lay in the sanctuary and it rose up from Hades through a certain rock.

[E.6.27] So when Orestes arrived in the land of the Taurians along with Pylades, they were detected, caught, and taken in chains to Thoas, the king, who sent both of them to the priestess. But Orestes was recognized by his sister Iphigenia, who acted as the priestess for the Taurians, and he fled with her, carrying off the wooden statue with him. It was then brought to Athens and is now called the Statue of Tauropolis. But some say that Orestes was driven in a storm to the island of Rhodes, where the statue remained and was dedicated in a defensive wall according to the wishes of the oracle.

[E.6.28] And returning to Mycenae, Orestes united his sister Electra in marriage to Pylades, while he himself married Hermione, the daughter of Menelaus and Helen. Or according to some, he married Erigone, the daughter of Aegisthus and Clyaemnestra, and he became the father of Tisamenus. He was killed by a snake-bite at Oresteum in Arcadia.

[E.6.14] And when Orestes went mad, Neoptolemus, the son of Achilles, carried off Orestes' wife Hermione, who had been promised to him when he was in Troy. And for this reason he was killed by Orestes at Delphi. But some say that Neoptolemus went to Delphi to demand reparations for the death of his father, and that in his anger he stole the votive offerings and set fire to the temple – and for this reason he was killed by Machaereus the Phocian.

Translated from the Greek by Stephen Russell, PhD

Euripides
Electra

The Story: When king Agamemnon of Argos sets sail for the Trojan War, he sacrifices his oldest daughter Iphigenia in order to persuade the goddess Artemis to send him a fair wind. Agamemnon's wife, Clytaemnestra, swears that she will avenge her child and, while her husband is away at war, begins an affair with Aegisthus, the cousin and enemy of her husband.

When Agamemnon returns from the war, Clytaemnestra and Aegisthus kill him while he is in his bath and then seize the throne. Clytaemnestra's young son Orestes is spirited away from the murderers and out of Argos to seek refuge in a neighbouring city. Clytaemnestra's daughter Electra, mourning interminably for her dead father, is forced by Aegisthus to marry a failed noble who ekes out a shabby living on a farm outside the city limits of Argos, and it is there that our story begins...

Characters

    Farmer
    Electra, daughter of Agamemnon
    Orestes, son of Agamemnon
    Pylades, friend of Orestes
    Chorus (of Argive peasant women)
    Old Man
    Aegisthus, a corpse
    Clytaemnestra, wife of Agamemnon and Aegisthus
    Attendants of Clytaemnestra, slave girls from Troy
    Castor and Polydeuces (the Dioscuri – gods)

Scene: A depressing dirt farm on the outskirts of Argos, complete with altar.

Enter the Farmer who, arrested by the sight of the altar, bows guiltily and proceeds to explain himself to the gods.

FARMER: Ancient land of Argos, where the waters of the river Inachus flow: from here King Agamemnon set sail for Troy with a thousand ships of war, and there killed Priam, its ruler, and took control. Returned to Argos, he set the spoils taken from the barbarians upon the towers of our lofty temples. In Troy he found success, but back in the bosom of family his wife Clytaemnestra plotted his demise, abetted by Aegisthus, son of Thyestes. Agamemnon is dead, relinquishing the ancient sceptre of his great-grandfather Tantalus, and Aegisthus is king in this land, which he rules with Clytaemnestra.

As for the children Agamemnon left behind when he sailed for Troy, the boy Orestes was spirited away to Phocis by his father's old tutor before Aegisthus could slay him, and placed in the care of Strophius, who has seen him safely to manhood.

But Electra remained in her father's home, and when she blossomed, suitors came seeking her hand – the leading men of Greece. But Aegisthus feared noble offspring who might be capable of avenging her father, and so kept her locked up and forbade her to marry any of them. Yet even then he dreaded she might secretly bear the child of some noble, and determined to kill her. However, her mother – cruel and savage though she is – saved Electra from that fate, for you see, Agamemnon sacrificing one of her children had justified her killing her husband, and killing one of them herself might just stir up bitter resentment here in Argos...

So Aegisthus worked things this way: he promised gold to whoever killed Orestes, and he gave Electra to me as my wife. My ancestors are from Mycenae, so I bear no shame insofar as the place of my birth, but I lack possessions. Settling her on a lowly man like me, Aegisthus thinks that he'll have fewer reasons to fear reprisal, for a nobler husband than I might rouse the spectre of foul murder from its sleep, and introduce Aegisthus to justice.

As Aphrodite is my witness, though, Electra is untouched. I am not so shameless that I would inflict myself on the daughter of a blessed family when I am unworthy of her. And, also, I prefer to be blameless when my 'brother-in-law', poor Orestes, returns to Argos and sees the unlucky marriage that his sister has made. Anyone who mocks me for never having laid a finger on my virgin bride simply hasn't thought the thing through...

Enter Electra, carrying a water-jug on her head

FARMER: Unhappy woman, why do you insist on working so hard? You were raised to live better than this, so why do you not stop when I ask it?

ELECTRA: O black Night, nurse of the golden stars, beneath which I carry this pitcher to the stream to get water: know that no one forces me, I choose to do this, so that despite my isolation at least the gods can look down and see how thoroughly Aegisthus, in his hubris, has ruined me. Even my mother, deadly daughter of Tyndareus, has cast me out in favour of her new husband, for since she gave him new children my brother and I are robbed of our status in that house.

Husband, I regard you as true a friend as any of the gods, for you have not seen fit to take advantage of my difficulties, as clearly you might, but instead balm my wounds like the most tender of medics – which is just the way I think of you.

So though you don't demand it of me, I share your load to the extent that my strength allows. You have so much to do on the farm, and it is my job to keep the house in order, for when a man comes home from the fields, he likes to find things just so.

FARMER: Well, if that's the way you feel about it, I won't fight you. I suppose, after all, the stream is not so very far from the house. And, for my part of the bargain, at dawn I will take the oxen and begin the planting. None may live without some manner of toil: pray to the gods, but sow your fields, I always say...

Exit both the Farmer and Electra

Enter Orestes and Pylades from the opposite side

ORESTES: Pylades, I regard you as the first and dearest among friends. You alone of those whom I loved have stayed with me, reduced though my circumstances have been by the man who, with the help of my bitch of a mother, killed my father.

I have returned in secret to Argos by way of Apollo's shrine at Delphi, in order that I might fulfill the oracle that I received there and pay the murderers of my father in kind. This night we visited the family tomb, where I offered tears and a lock of hair for my poor father, and over the altar sacrificed a sheep, all unseen, unknown to the tyrants now ruling this land.

We won't set foot inside the city just yet, but linger on the outskirts to seek my sister. They say she is no longer a girl, now married, yet I would make her my partner, in murder, and learn what really goes on within the city walls. So, since dawn is just now lifting her bright white eye, let us move from the thoroughfare and wait our chance. Perhaps some peasant will pass by, and then we might ask directions to my sister's abode.

108   Electra

Here comes one now, with a pitcher of water balanced on her shaved head. Hunker down and listen sharp, Pylades, and perhaps we may hear something pertinent to our mission...

Orestes and Pylades hide

Enter Electra, with the water-jug on her head

ELECTRA (SINGING):

Move your feet, now's the time:
Keep on in sadness: me oh my!

Born to Agamemnon,
Mother Clytaemnestra
– Daughter of Tyndareus –
Call me poor Electra,

For I sing of work and pain,
Lamenting both this hateful life
And Agamemnon dispatched below,
By Aegisthus, and an evil wife.

It feels so good to sing along,
The bitter pleasure of a sad, sad song!
Move your feet, now's the time:
Keep on in sadness: me oh my!

In what far city,
And what strange home,
Brother do you shelter,
Brother do you roam?

For crowned now by a ceramic cistern
Your sad, forlorn, forsaken sister
Dreads and yet anticipates
The next disaster, or next blister.

Come and free her from suspense,
And this desperate life of endless woe:
Avenger find your wandering way
And wander back to old Argos!

Take the pitcher from my head
And lay it down upon the ground,
And I will raise chin to the sky
And make a mournful crying sound

For you, my father, my father, for you,
'Neath earth directing my desolate cry,
Daily unending bitter lamenting
For the dreadful way it was fated you die.

Ever I grieve at the thought of the axe
And its surgical use in the ploy
That descended unexpected when you traveled
Unmolested and home arrived safely from Troy.

She did not receive you with garland or wreath,
Nor ribbon of victory,
But upon you bestowed a double-edged sword:
New husband for her, and for you treachery.

Enter the Chorus

CHORUS:

Child of Agamemnon, we have come to pay a visit. We just had a visitor ourselves, a man from Mycenae, bred on the milk of the mountains, and he told us they proclaim a sacrifice in Argos two days from now. All the girls will pass in procession to the temple of Hera.

ELECTRA:

No, my friends. No beautiful garments or golden necklaces for me, for no such finery could move my sad heart. I won't dance along with the girls of Argos and twinkle my toes. In tears I'll pass my nights, for in tears is the way I spend my days. Look at my filthy hair, the dirty rags I wear: is this fitting attire for the daughter of a king, or suitable tribute from Troy, which surely cannot have forgotten my conquering father?

CHORUS: Great is the goddess! You must borrow from us thick-woven party garb of wool, and gold to decorate it! But do you think that lamentation alone will bring victory over your enemies? Only prayers and reverence for the gods bring about better days.

ELECTRA: Clearly none of the gods is with us or they'd have been watching over my father, murdered all those years ago. All we can do is cry for the dead man and his wandering son somewhere in another country, trudging miserably through empty days, though noble born. And here I languish in the home of a farmer, rotting away up here in the mountains, exiled from my home while mother revels in her murderous marriage with a stranger.

Chorus: Your mother has become just like her sister, Helen – she who is most to blame for so many evils visited upon the Greeks and on your house.

Enter Orestes and Pylades

Electra: What's this? Strangers approach who lay in ambush behind our altar! Fly, women: run down the path and I'll take my refuge in the house!

Orestes: Wait, girl! You need fear no violence from me!

Electra: Apollo save me! I beg you, please sir, do not kill me!

Orestes: There are a good many others I'd kill before you, believe me.

Electra: Keep back! You have no right to lay a finger on me!

Orestes: On the contrary, there is no person yet living that I have a greater right to touch.

Electra: Why do you lie in wait outside my home with sword in hand?

Orestes: Well, if you'd quiet yourself a moment you might find out...

Electra: Well, then, I'm not going anywhere, am I? For I could hardly resist if you should decide to take me against my will...

Orestes: Good gods, woman, I have come with word of your brother!

Electra: Orestes? Is he alive then?

Orestes: Alive and well. I see you prefer your good news first, then.

Electra: You have already given me the best news! But where in the world does he bear his terrible burden of exile?

Orestes: From city to city, calling none of them home.

Electra: Does he eat well? And keep a roof over his head?

Orestes: As far as that goes he is fine, but then again there is more to life than bodily comfort.

Electra: But what word do you bring from him?

Orestes: I bear not a message so much as a mission, to see if you live, and if so, just what manner of existence you lead.

Electra: Well, as to that, just look at me!

Orestes: Yes, you certainly appear eaten away with grief and toil.

Electra: And my beautiful hair has all been shorn away.

Orestes: Separation from your father and brother still preys upon you, then?

Electra: Of course. Who in this life was dearer to me than they are?

Orestes: And do you imagine anyone dearer to your brother than yourself?

Electra: He may love me, but he isn't here, is he?

Orestes: ...Why are you living up here, so far from the city?

Electra: Because I have been given in marriage to an ignominious fate, stranger.

Orestes: Which man of Mycenae is your husband?

Electra: None to whom my father would ever have allowed me to go.

Orestes: Then give me his name so that I may tell your brother.

Electra: This is his house here, where I live quite isolated from the city.

Orestes: Is he a worker then, or a shepherd, that he must reside in a hovel such as this?

Electra: He is a poor man, yet still a noble one, and treats me well.

ORESTES: Well? How does this husband of yours treat you well?

ELECTRA: He has never yet come to my bed.

ORESTES: What, has he made some vow of chastity, then, or are you not good enough for him?

ELECTRA: No, he simply thinks it beneath him, for he thinks me above him.

ORESTES: But he should be over the moon at having made such a marriage!

ELECTRA: And yet he understands that the man who gave me to him had no right.

ORESTES: Ah, I see: he's afraid of what would happen to him should Orestes return...

ELECTRA: That too, but nevertheless he is a good man.

ORESTES: A truly noble man, then, to be esteemed rather than punished?

ELECTRA: Yes, if the one who would esteem him should ever come home.

ORESTES: But what of your mother? Did she approve this marriage?

ELECTRA: Sadly, stranger, it has been my experience that mothers prefer their men to their children.

ORESTES: Just what did Aegisthus have in mind when he shamed you this way?

ELECTRA: I think he hoped a powerless man would give me similarly powerless children who he need not fear.

ORESTES: He thought to deprive you of sons of quality enough to revenge you and father? That was his plan?

ELECTRA: Yes, and I hope, with the passage of time, to make him rue the day he ever thought of it.

ORESTES: Does he know you are still a virgin?

ELECTRA: No, we have kept this to ourselves.

ORESTES: And, uh, these eavesdropping women? They are friends of yours, I trust?

ELECTRA: Oh, they won't tell anyone.

ORESTES: And what should I tell Orestes he must do about all this?

ELECTRA: You need to ask? What a question! Surely he must come home!

ORESTES: And...?

ELECTRA: And do to his enemies what they dared do to our father.

ORESTES: Would you be bold enough to join with him in murdering your own mother?

ELECTRA: Yes, and with the same axe used to kill Father.

ORESTES: Can I tell him this? Are you absolutely certain you're ready to take that step?

ELECTRA: I would die happy.

ORESTES: If only Orestes could hear this...

ELECTRA: Sadly, stranger, I don't think I'd recognize my brother if he stood before me right now.

ORESTES: Well, you were very young when you were separated.

ELECTRA: Yes, and I have only one friend who might still recognize him.

ORESTES: Ah, the one they say took him out of harm's way?

ELECTRA: Yes, our childhood servant, now very old.

ORESTES: And... your father... I trust he found his way into the family tomb?

ELECTRA: The only grave he found was the dusty street in front of our house, where they cast his body like so much garbage!

ORESTES: What! This news is painful even to one who is not part of the family, but do not spare me! Tell me all, so I may take your words, hard as they are, to your brother, who must certainly hear them. Ignorance may be bliss, but it is suitable only for slaves, so educate me, however much it hurts.

CHORUS: Our desire is the same as the stranger's, for living so far away from the city we know little of what happens there.

ELECTRA: If you insist, for we are all friends here, are we not? I will tell you all about the fate that befell our family, and then, stranger, I beg you to relate every word just as you hear it to Orestes, for these are his troubles as well.

First, tell him how you found me, the rags I am forced to wear, penned here like any other animal relegated to this farm. Tell him of the filth that coats my body, and the shack that I have to call home in lieu of the palace. Here I must make my own clothes on the loom like a common slave or go naked and, as you have seen, I am reduced to lugging my own water from the river. Nor am I allowed to attend holy festivals, or take part in dances, and even so, lonely as I am, I keep my distance from the other women, for I am still a virgin, still blush like a girl to think of Castor, my uncle, who was my suitor before he ascended to the ranks of the gods.

In the meantime, my mother sits upon her throne, which is balanced atop all the spoils of Troy, and at her hand cluster the Trojan women my father won when he plundered the city. Clad in robes woven from the wool of Troy's snow-covered Mount Ida and fastened with golden brooches, they are her servants now. And all the while the blood of my father still stains the floor black where he fell, and the man who murdered him gads about town with the reins of the dead man's chariot in one hand and, in the other, the scepter with which our father commanded the army of the Greeks.

Agamemnon's tomb goes without honours, never yet having enjoyed holy libation nor received the green branches of the myrtle. The altar before it has never seen a single offering, though they do say that mother's new husband visits when he's in his cups so that he might dance upon the empty grave, chuck stones and gob upon the marble, asking, "So where is Orestes now, when he should be here protecting his father's tomb?"

So please, stranger, tell Orestes that many people call for him to come home and take his rightful place: I am only their spokesman – my hands, my tongue, my miserable thoughts, my head shaved in mourning – and his father's blood cries out to him to return as well. It would be shameful beyond reason if the son of he who sacked Troy could not find the courage to kill one insignificant man.

CHORUS: Look! Your husband, finished with his work for the day, returns home.

Enter the Farmer

FARMER: What is all this? Who are all these strangers at my door? Why have they come to the gates of my farmhouse? To see me? For it is a shameful thing, I tell you, for a woman to be keeping company with young men.

ELECTRA: Dearest husband, there's no call for suspicion. The truth is that these strangers are here as messengers with news of Orestes! Strangers, please forgive my husband's rudeness, he meant no offense.

FARMER: Then does you brother still walk in the light of the living?

ELECTRA: So they say, and I pray they are not untrustworthy.

FARMER: And does he still think of you?

ELECTRA: I hope so, but what can a man in far off exile do about it?

FARMER: Well then, what news have they brought of Orestes?

ELECTRA: He sent them here to find out my troubles.

FARMER: Well, they can plainly see some of them. Did you tell them about the rest?

ELECTRA: Yes, I left out nothing of my shame.

FARMER: Oh, good. Well, then we might as well invite them in! Please, friends, do step inside, and in return for your good news let us give you what meager hospitality we can. Allow me to get your baggage and spears – no, I insist, any friend of Orestes', after all... We may not have much, but let no one say we're ill-bred.

ORESTES (TO ELECTRA): This is the man who shams marriage with you so as not to disgrace Orestes?

ELECTRA: Yes, he is called husband to the poor woman before you.

ORESTES: You see! It just goes to show, virtue is a tricky thing, isn't it? You just never can tell when it comes to men. It often happens that the sons of the noble turn out worthless, while excellent children regularly spring from the loins of men who are themselves of no perceptible value. I have seen wealthy men with heads full of air and poor men of enormous character. How then can we test to divide the good from the bad? What scale can we use? Not wealth, certainly. Lack of wealth, then? But poverty can drive men to evil out of basic necessity. Perhaps we should judge a man according to his prowess in battle?

This man here is neither great nor noble by the standards of the Greeks, nor does he lay claim to a great family name. He is an ordinary man. Yet we have found him to be truly noble. When will we learn to distinguish nobility by the company a man keeps and the way he behaves? For it is men of this kind who rule our cities best, not to mention our homes, while the well-bred stud, with muscle and no brains, is only good if you want a model for a statue to decorate the park. Even in battle great size is no guarantee of valour – it all boils down to a question of nature and courage.

Well, then, since by a more proper standard this must certainly be a noble house – as is the house of Agamemnon, whose son we represent – let us gladly accept its hospitality. I'd much sooner be welcome in the home of a poor, generous man than one who is merely rich. Still, I cannot help but wish it were your brother returned and leading us inside his reclaimed palace.

But perhaps he will come, for the oracles of Apollo do not err, though men are prone to misinterpreting them.

Exit Orestes and Pylades into the hut

CHORUS: We have a good feeling about this, Electra. Perhaps a change in your fortune slouches toward home even now.

ELECTRA: How could you, husband? You know that the cupboards are bare! Don't you see they're better off than we?

FARMER: Well, what of it? If they are as well-bred as they seem, they will be as content among the humble as they would the wealthy.

ELECTRA: Since it's apparently slipped your mind that we're destitute, you'd best cut along to the home of my father's old tutor. He's lived and tended his flock by the Tanaus river, right at the point where it crosses out of Argos into Sparta, since he was driven from the city. Tell him of our visitors and ask him to fetch along some fit food. He will thank the gods to do it, I am sure, when he hears that the child he once rescued still lives. Of course, the news wouldn't be received nearly so well at the palace...

FARMER: If that is what seems best to you, I'll go, but in the meantime you should hurry inside and see to our guests. A woman can always scratch together a decent meal when she has to, and as a matter of fact there's more than enough in the house to fill these men's bellies for one day, maybe two...

Exit Electra into the hut

It never ceases to amaze me, the stock people place in money. Yes, it allows you to treat guests lavishly, and, too, gold attracts the doctor when you need him, but the price of good, simple food enough for a day isn't so very much, and whether he is rich or poor, a man's stomach holds just about the same amount...

Exit the Farmer

CHORUS:

Famous ships once sailed for Troy, propelled by countless oars, escorted by the dancing sea-nymphs and the dolphin, who loves the flute: he leapt and jumped among the dark-nosed boats as he led Achilles the swift runner and Agamemnon to the banks of the river Simois, near Troy.

It was the sea-nymphs from the banks of the Euboea that bore the heavy golden shield and armour up along Mount Pelion, along the sacred woodland slopes of Mount Ossa, and through the rocks where they kept watch for the horse-man, Chiron. For he had raised Achilles the swift runner, the son of Thetis – herself a nymph – to be a light for Greece and a help to the sons of Atreus. We heard it in the harbour of Nauplia, from a man returned from Troy, that on Achilles' shield were engraved emblems – terrors to the Trojans.

On the outer rim was Perseus flying over the sea with the head of Medusa in his hand, and beside him Hermes, great messenger of Zeus and son of Maia who enjoys the flocks and fields. On the shield's bowl blazed the chariot of the sun, driven by winged horses, and the stars danced in the heavens – the Pleiades, the Hyads. On the helmet were Sphinxes, the human prey they had trapped with their song in their talons. On the bit that covered Achilles' ribs was the clawed Chimaera, breathing fire and running, affrighted at the sight of winged Pegasus. Truly here were scenes that dimmed with fear the eyes of even mighty Hector!

Such was the armour worn by the fearless leader of that legion that evil-minded Helen's base lust decimated, for which the gods in heaven will one day exact just retribution upon her and we will see the red blood jet from her slender neck.

Enter the Old Man

OLD MAN: Where is she? Where is my princess, the daughter of Agamemnon, whom I once raised and love so dearly? How steep is this path up to her house, especially for a withered old man. But when friends call, you must make your way as best you can despite your weak back and weaker knees...

Enter Electra from the hut

O my daughter, there you are! As you asked I've brought you this young lamb, best of my flock, and also flowers for garlands, and cheeses fresh from the churn, and this deliciously odorous vintage, a gift of Dionysus – just a bit at once, mind you, but good to mix with weaker drink. In a moment we will take it to your guests, but first let me dry my eyes on these filthy rags I am reduced to wearing.

ELECTRA: But why are you crying, old man? Not because my situation reopens wounds long since healed, I hope? Or do you still weep after all these years over Orestes' exile and the fate of my father, both of whom you helped raise. Much good though it did you, poor soul...

OLD MAN: I received little enough reward for that, it is true. But there was one thing the bastards could not prevent me doing: I stopped by his tomb on my way here, and wept at the graveside. I poured a small libation for your father from this very wineskin I brought for your guests, and put down some myrtle.

But right on the altar I saw a black-fleeced sheep, with its throat cut and its blood still warm! It was only recently slaughtered! And I also saw trimmed locks of golden hair made as an offering to Agamemnon!

My child, who in the world would have had the courage to pay homage to that tomb? No-one from Argos, surely. Could it somehow have been your brother, come here in secret to pay his respects to your father? Take a close look at this hair – place it beside your own and see if it is not the very same shade...

ELECTRA: Oh, do stop prattling! Surely you don't really think that my brother, if he returned to the land of Aegisthus, would come fearfully and undercover? And what similarity could you hope to find between the locks of a great man trained in rugged games and the cropped tresses of a veritable slave girl like me? There is no match, because it is an impossibility that he could be here. I'm sure you could find a great many people you could match that hair to, old man, even some who aren't blood relations to Orestes.

OLD MAN: Well, then go there and stand in the footprints left about the tomb – see if they match your own!

ELECTRA: Even if there were a footprint left in that rocky ground, what on earth makes you think the foot of brother and sister would be the same size?

OLD MAN: But if your brother has come back to Argos, mightn't there be some scrap of clothing, woven by you and worn by him when I helped him escape, by which you might recognize him?

ELECTRA: I was a child when Orestes fled Argos, and even if I had made some garments for him, they would hardly fit him now... Stop this. Either some stranger or some kind citizen of Argos took pity and left his locks on father's grave, despite the watchful eyes of Aegisthus' spies.

OLD MAN: Yes, mistress. Then introduce me to these guests of yours, if you would, for I should like to ask after your brother.

ELECTRA: They'll be joining us presently.

Enter Orestes and Pylades from the hut

OLD MAN: Well, they look noble enough, but none know better than we how apparently noble people may turn out evil. All the same, greetings to you, strangers.

ORESTES: And to you, old man. Electra, where, or to which of your friends, does this ancient relic belong?

ELECTRA: This is the man who raised my father, stranger.

ORESTES: What's this? The man who spirited your brother away and saved his life?

ELECTRA: The very same – if, indeed, Orestes is still alive.

ORESTES: Why does he peer at me so strangely, as if he's searching for marks on a silver coin?

ELECTRA: For pity's sake, old man! My apologies, stranger: I suspect he is just happy to meet a friend of Orestes, and perhaps hopes to divine an echo of him in you.

ORESTES: Yes, well, Orestes is dear to me... But what is the old man doing now? Why does he circle round me this way?

ELECTRA: I'm wondering that myself – for the gods' sakes, old man, what are you doing?

OLD MAN: O my lady, my daughter Electra, pray to the gods!

ELECTRA: What would you have me pray about, then, something I have or something I lack?

OLD MAN: That you may have the sense to grasp the gift, within your reach at this very moment, that some kind god has sent you!

ELECTRA: Fine! I'm praying, I'm praying, all right? Now will you calm down, old one?

OLD MAN: My dear child, open your eyes and look upon this man!

ELECTRA: Are you out of your mind? I've been looking at him!

OLD MAN: Perhaps I have indeed relinquished my senses, for it seems to me that I see your brother before me!

ELECTRA: How can you make such a cruel jest, and to me of all people!

OLD MAN: I tell you that I see the son of Agamemnon in this man!

ELECTRA: How so? Persuade me!

OLD MAN: The scar that runs along his eyebrow! Orestes once fell and cut open his head, in the yard in front of your father's house, while you and he were chasing a fawn.

ELECTRA: It seems to me I do detect the mark of a fall...?

OLD MAN: Then what are you waiting for? Embrace him!

ELECTRA: Orestes, could it be? Have you returned to me at long last? Come, let me hold you, as I never dared hope I would again have the chance to do!

ORESTES: Nor did I, sister, after all this time!

ELECTRA: I never thought it would happen!

ORESTES: I, too, gave up hope, if only for a while!

ELECTRA: Is it really you, Orestes?

ORESTES: Yes, I am he, your best friend and hunting companion of old. Now if only we can catch up with our new prey... But I am confident we will succeed, for if we fail, and evil were to escape justice for all time, we'd have no choice but to conclude that the gods no longer exist.

CHORUS: Finally the long awaited day has arrived! You have shone out bright and made a beacon of the city, calling home the miserable exile who wandered so far from his ancestral land.

Now a god – a god! – brings about our victory, dear friend. Raise hands, raise voices, send up prayers to the gods so that good fortune accompanies your brother as he sets foot within the city.

ORESTES: Well then, I have had the sweet pleasure of your embrace, sister, and I will repay that warm welcome again and again in years to come. But you, old man, have arrived just in time to advise me: please tell us, what would you recommend as an adequate gift for the man who murdered my father, and my sweet mother who helped him do it? Do I have any friends in Argos? Am I alone, as bereft of allies as I am of means, or is there someone I should meet?

OLD MAN: My child, you have no friends anymore: they left your side when your luck deserted you. It's rare that you find a man who will share your portion both good and bad, and as you are regarded as utterly ruined, with no hope of return, you must take heed of what I tell you now: everything depends on you, and you alone. Your own courage and your good fortune will dictate whether or not you are to take back your city.

ORESTES: Then by night or by day, what approach should I take toward my enemies?

OLD MAN: You'll have to kill them both.

ORESTES: This is the goal and the crown I have set myself, but how can I take this victory?

OLD MAN: You won't do it by going inside the walls, however much you might wish it.

ORESTES: Many watchmen and bodyguards, then?

OLD MAN: Oh, yes, for Aegisthus sleeps badly at night, awaiting your return.

ORESTES: That is a pity – perhaps you might suggest a way I might better attempt to release the poor man from his agony?

OLD MAN: An idea does occur to me.

ORESTES: I hope it's good, and that I am its equal.

OLD MAN: It just so happens that I saw Aegisthus on my way here.

ORESTES: That does sound promising – where?

OLD MAN: He was in the royal pastures, not so very far from these fields.

ORESTES: You interest me strangely. What was he about?

OLD MAN: He appeared to be preparing a feast for the goddess Nymphs.

ORESTES: This offering, was it on behalf of the children he's got or one that's on the way?

OLD MAN: I only know one thing, he was armed only for ox-killing.

ORESTES: How many were in his party?

OLD MAN: Just a couple of palace servants.

ORESTES: Were there any among them who would know me?

OLD MAN: They are all slaves imported from his former household, and as such would never have had occasion to see you.

ORESTES: And how do you think that these household slaves would react if I were to kill him?

OLD MAN: The way slaves typically react in such a situation – which is an advantage to you.

ORESTES: What would be the best way to get close to him?

OLD MAN: Simply let him see you pass while he is the performing his sacrifice –

ORESTES: I take it his fields are right beside the road then?

Old Man: Yes, and when he sees you he'll invite you to join in the feast.

Orestes: He'll find me an unpleasant dinner-guest, gods willing!

Old Man: After that you're on your own.

Orestes: But where is my mother while all of this is happening?

Old Man: In Argos. She will join her husband when it is time for the feast.

Orestes: Why didn't she accompany him?

Old Man: Presumably she dreads the reproachful looks that would be directed at her and wishes to delay them as long as possible.

Orestes: The people are against her, then?

Old Man: The people hate a promiscuous woman.

Orestes: How then will I get at her?

Electra: Leave our mother to me.

Orestes: Fine, but fortune has lent a hand in the murder of Aegisthus; who will aid you in your attempt?

Electra: Our friend here will help out.

Orestes: Right then. How do you propose to kill mother?

Electra: Old man, you will go to Clytaemnestra and tell her I've given birth to a son.

Old Man: And should I say when?

Electra: It's been nine days – that's how long a woman must stay ritually clean after childbirth.

Old Man: But how will this facilitate your project?

Electra: I am confident she'll come as soon as she hears that I am confined to bed.

Old Man: But why? Do you really think she still cares for you, child?

Electra: Yes, I do, and she will be feeling bad about my child's low birth.

Old Man: Perhaps. Then what happens, when she arrives?

Electra: Well, then she dies.

Old Man: Yes, yes, but she makes the journey to the doors of your house, and then…?

Electra: And then she'll only have to go a bit further to get to Hades.

Old Man: …To be allowed to see that I would happily die myself.

Electra: You can't die just yet, old man, you still have to point the way for Orestes.

Old Man: To the place where Aegisthus is sacrificing to the gods…

Electra: Yes, and then take my message to mother.

Old Man: I'll make it sound as if the words were coming right out of your mouth.

Electra: Now it is up to you, Orestes – you have drawn the first lot.

Orestes: I'm ready if my guide is.

Old Man: It will be a pleasure.

Orestes: O Zeus, god of our fathers and defeater of my enemies…

Electra: …have pity on us, for our suffering is worthy of your pity.

Old Man: Yes, pity them, for these children are your descendants.

Orestes: O Hera, you who rule over the altars of Mycenae…

Electra: …help us achieve victory, if you deem our intention just.

Old Man: Yes, grant vengeance to these children for the murder of their father.

Orestes: And you, father, wrongly ensconced below the earth…

ELECTRA: ...and Earth, my queen, on whom I beat my hands...

OLD MAN: ...defend, defend these children, so dearly loved by you.

ORESTES: ... come, father, and bring an army of the dead to fight with us...

ELECTRA: ...the men who helped you lay waste to Troy...

OLD MAN: ...and bring along, besides, all others in Hades who find adultery an offense to the gods.

ORESTES: Do you hear, father, who suffered such horrible things at the hands of my mother?

OLD MAN: Your father hears, believe me. But now it's time to go.

ELECTRA: I know it. Be a man like he was, Orestes, and see to Aegisthus. For if you are taken, then I too am dead, for I will spit my head on a double-edged sword. I retire now to make ready. When I hear happy news, the whole house will ring out in celebration. But if you die things will turn out very differently, that is my word to you.

Exit Orestes, Pylades, and the Old Man

As for you ladies, be prepared to signal the results of this encounter. I will be standing at the ready with sword in hand, either way. Even if I am defeated, they will have to be content to take their vengeance on my corpse.

Exit Electra into the hut

CHORUS:

There is an ancient tale told of a golden lamb, stolen from beneath its tender mother in the hills of Argos – pilfered by Pan, guardian of the fields who plays sweet music with his wondrous reed pipes. A messenger stood on a platform of stones and cried - "Go to the assembly, people of Mycenae, see this marvel, this fearful portent." And choruses cheered on the house of Atreus.

Altars of hammered gold were built and a sacrificial fire burned round the town of Argos. The lotus flute, servant of the Muses, sent up a beauteous melody in praise of Thyestes, for he it was that had secretly wooed the wife of Atreus and with her help carried off the remarkable lamb, and told the people that the golden beast, was at his house, fleece and horn.

It was then that Zeus changed the course of the blazing stars, reversed the shining sun and the gleaming face of dawn, and afflicted the western sky with the heat of his divine flame. The clouds flew northward and the land of Africa dried up, parched, thereafter denied the bounty that Zeus's sweet rain provides.

That, at any rate, is what they say, though we don't give much credence to them - that, to the sorrow of the entire world, the sun turned its back and changed its position in the sky, all to punish one man. But such frightful stories bring profit to men and further worship to the gods. You would have done well to have remembered it, Clytaemnestra, before you killed your husband – you who are a sister of glorious brothers.

Wait! Listen, friends, do you detect shouting? Or have we been tricked by anxiety into hearing things, such as happens when someone claims to hear the thunder from Zeus? No, there it is again! The breath of the wind rising from the city brings a message. Princess, come out of the house! Electra, come quickly!

Enter Electra from the hut

ELECTRA: Friends, what is happening? Have you heard something?

CHORUS: We know only that we heard a sound that contains some manner of death in it.

ELECTRA: I hear it, also, quite far off...

CHORUS: Very far, but growing nearer...

ELECTRA: Is it the people of Argos who groan, or my people?

CHORUS: There is a great welter of voices, all confused...

ELECTRA: What you are saying bodes ill for me. Why do I hesitate to do what is inevitable for me?

118 Electra

CHORUS: Wait! Wait until we know for certain!

ELECTRA: It is over. We are lost. Otherwise where are our messengers?

CHORUS: They will come. It's no small matter to kill a king.

Enter Pylades

PYLADES: Women of Mycenae, I bring the glad tidings that Orestes has triumphed. Aegisthus, killer of Agamemnon, lies dead, praise the gods!

ELECTRA: But who are you? How can I trust that you speak the truth?

PYLADES: What? Don't you recognize me?

ELECTRA: Uh…

PYLADES: I was just here. Pylades? The servant of your brother?

ELECTRA: Oh, yes, dear, dear… uh, servant! Yes, yes, it was only my great fear that prevented me recognizing your face, but I remember you now.

Could you repeat what you just said? Is the hated destroyer of my father finally dead?

PYLADES: Yes, he's dead – it's news so nice I give it to you twice…

ELECTRA: Oh gods, all-seeing Justice, at long last you have come! How did he die? Tell me everything, leave nothing out!

PYLADES: When we set out on our way from this house, we soon came to a wagon-path that led us to the pasture where the new king of Mycenae was. As we approached he was walking about a lush orchard, plucking sprigs of tender myrtle to put in his hair, and when he caught sight of us he called out, "Hello strangers! Who are you and from where do you hail?"

Orestes replied, "We are from Thessaly, and headed for the Alpheus river to offer sacrifices to Zeus."

When he heard this, Aegisthus declared, "But today you stop here and share our feast as our guests, for as it happens I am sacrificing an ox to the Nymphs. In the morning you can be on your way, but for the time being accompany us to the shrine." And, so saying, he took us each by the arm and led us off the road: "I won't take no for an answer."

When we reached the garden he called out, "Someone fetch purifying water, that our guests may join us at the altar."

But Orestes told him, "There is no need, we only just left the pure waters of a flowing stream that we used to purify ourselves. If strangers may join with citizens in the sacrifice, my lord Aegisthus, then we are ready."

They were speaking thusly in the midst of the crowd when the slaves set aside the spears they used to protect their master and set themselves to new duties, some bringing a bowl to catch the blood, others carrying baskets, still others lighting the fire, placing basins round the cauldrons round the base of the fire…

Then your stepfather took up the barley in his hands and threw it upon the altar with the words, "Nymphs of the rocks, bless me so that we may make many sacrifices to you in the future, both me and my wife who is at home, the daughter of Tyndareus. May we continue to fare as we now fare, and our enemies not so well." By which he meant Orestes and you. And as Aegisthus said these things, my master prayed for the exact opposite, though not aloud – that he would regain his family house.

Next Aegisthus took a straight-blade sacrificial knife from the basket, cut some hair from the calf and with his right hand placed it on the fire. Then he cut the throat of the calf as the servants lifted it on their shoulders, and once again he addressed your brother: "I have heard boast that the men of Thessaly are best at butchering bulls and also in breaking horses. Please, stranger, take the knife in your hand and prove whether what they say is true."

Orestes took the Dorian knife in his hands, shrugged his cloak from off his shoulders, and chose me – Pylades – to help him in his task, waving away the slaves offering to assist. Taking hold of the calf's hoof, he skinned the hide faster than a runner can twice lap the horse-track, then opened up its sides.

Aegisthus took the sacred portions of the beast in his hands and examined them. On the liver was no hanging lobe, and the portal-vein and the gall bladder said plainly to him that some evil was imminent. His face darkened so that my master asked what was bothering him?

Aegisthus responded, "I fear some manner of ambush crouched at my door. The greatest enemy of my house, the son of Agamemnon, yet lives."

Orestes said, "How is it you live in fear of one exile when you rule an entire city? Come now, please – won't someone help us feast on the insides of this beast? Fetch me a Phthian knife instead of this Dorian one here, so that I can smash open the breast bone."

When they handed him the requested blade he turned to Aegisthus, who was leaned over, taking up the entrails one by one and examining each in turn, and raising himself on the tips of his toes Orestes struck the king square through the backbone. Aegisthus' body convulsed, twisting and jerking as he shrieked his agony, and he then fell dead in his own grimy blood.

When the servants saw this, they moved quickly for their spears – it was to be an army of men against two. But we, spurred on by courage, stood our ground, and Orestes shouted, "I have not come to this city to oppose my own people, but to exact deserved vengeance on the murderer of my father! I am Orestes, son of Agamemnon! Will you kill me now, you men who used to serve my father?"

When they heard him speak these words, they lowered their spears, and one old man who used to serve his family recognized him. Right-away they put a crown of flowing leaves on your brother's head, and shouted in celebration. And now he's on his way here to give you a gift. It isn't Medusa's head he brings, oh no, but that which belonged to the man you hated, who has now paid a bitter and bloody price for the bloodshed he caused.

Exit Pylades

CHORUS:
Set your feet to dancing, dear girl! Skip like a fawn! Your brother has won the contest for the crown, a far greater glory than any awarded at the Olympics! Come, sing a song of victory, and give us something to dance to!

ELECTRA: O bright light, chariot-mounted fire of the Sun, O Earth and Night on which I gazed so many years past: finally I am free to open my eyes and heart to you again, for the murderer of my happiness is at long last himself dead. Come, friends, let us bring from the house whatever I have kept hidden as adornment for the hair, so that I may wreath the head of my victorious brother when he arrives.

Exit Electra into the hut

CHORUS: That's okay. You dig out your brother's new crown, we'll delight the Muses and keep dancing, for once again our former, beloved rulers will be masters in this country – with justice on their side they have defeated the unjust! Come, let us sing and dance!

Enter Electra from the hut

Enter Orestes and Pylades with the body of Aegisthus

ELECTRA: Orestes, truly you are your father's son! Please accept these twisted garlands that I settle upon your brow with my own hands, for you return home not from some worthless sporting competition, but having dispatched the one who slaughtered our father.

And you, Pylades, my brother's companion in arms, most loyal of men, please accept a wreath from my hand as well, for you carry an equal share of glory in this victory. May both of you be blessed always!

ORESTES: Electra, we must credit the gods first and foremost as the ones responsible for all that has transpired today, and praise them first. Only then should you praise me, as their agent.

I return as the killer of Aegisthus, it is true, but to remove all possible doubt and anxiety from your mind I bring you the body that you may look at it. Set him out for the beasts to gnaw, or impale him high on a stake for the children of the air if it pleases you. Whatever you decide, he who was once your master is now your slave. You might even give him a piece of your mind.

ELECTRA: I... I am too ashamed to speak what is in my heart aloud, and yet, and yet...

ORESTES: Why ashamed? Of what? Tell me your mind, at least, for there's nothing to fear any longer.

ELECTRA: I am fearful of insulting the dead, for fear of repercussions.

ORESTES: No one here would blame you, that is certain.

ELECTRA: Ah, but the city is quick to criticize, and loves slander.

ORESTES: Get if off your chest, sister. We owe the man nothing but bile.

ELECTRA (TO THE CORPSE OF AEGISTHUS): Well, then... where to begin? And where end?

I fantasized for a long time about what I would say to you, Aegisthus, if I no longer had reason to fear you. I went over my speech last thing at night, first thing in the morning, every day. Now I am finally free I no longer feel a burning need to say much of anything, but I will try...

You destroyed us, me and my brother, though we'd never done you any harm. You formed a shameful alliance with our mother to kill our father, the man who commanded the whole Greek army – you, who never went to Troy yourself.

Were you really so fond as to believe that mother would make a faithful wife? Did you somehow fail to notice she was already married when she took up with you? Anyone would think that a man who seduces another man's wife would be in a position to know just what he is getting, but not you, apparently.

Sure enough, your life together was torture, though you presented as if everything were fine to the world outside your house. Because, in the end, you could not ignore the fact that you had made an unholy marriage, and your bride had first hand knowledge that she had married a weak and evil man. As married people do, you helped one another carry your burdens, but, rotten to the core, all that meant was that she got a share of your evil, while you took a share of hers. Zero sum.

All of Argos whispered, "There goes the man who belongs to a woman who doesn't belong to him." It's a disgrace when a woman has all the power in the house, and the children are known in the city by the name of their mother and not their father. For when a man marries a woman of greater status than he, no one pays him any mind – they speak only of her, except to disparage him.

But what marked you as a truly quintessential fool was that you never knew it, because you were wealthy, and thought that was enough. Worldly riches are nothing and fade away: strength of nature, strength of character, is eternal, and determines whether or not we may survive the loss of riches, to live to see riches again. A fool and his money are soon parted, leaving only... a fool.

It would be indelicate for me, as a virgin, to discuss in detail your dealings with women, and decorum dictates I only hint as to my knowledge, but I witnessed disgraceful things in the short time we resided under the same roof. You thought you could get away with it because of your power and your physical charms, but I tell you frankly that your effeminate looks always turned my stomach. Personally, I prefer a man who looks like a man, and plays at war, rather than a boy who plays at dancing.

Enough of this. You have consumed enough of my life and I'll waste no more of it upon you. So go ahead and rot, damn you, never knowing how time has found you out and meted out fit punishment. Be an example to other criminals that they can't outrun Justice, even if they happen to get a good head start: show them what awaits them at the finish line...

CHORUS: He did terrible things, and now has paid a terrible price. Justice may be slow, but it is sure, and inescapable.

ELECTRA: Take his body into the house and hide it in the shadows. I wouldn't want to spoil the surprise when mother comes calling.

Pylades carries the corpse of Aegisthus into the hut

Orestes: On that subject, look who approaches...

Electra: Good. Here she comes. See how regal she looks, in her chariot and fine robes, riding blithely into our trap!

Orestes: Are we really going to do this?

Electra: Surely you feel no pity for her?

Orestes: O god, how can I bring myself to kill the woman who bore me?

Electra: The same way she killed our father!

Orestes: Forgive me, Apollo, but there was much in your pronouncement that seems unwise!

Electra: If Apollo is a fool, what man can then be called wise?

Orestes: He tells me to kill my mother!

Electra: Don't think of it as killing your mother, but avenging your father.

Orestes: That I have already done, and no dishonour could attach to me: now I will be a matricide, when previously I was without stain.

Electra: You'll hardly be unstained if you fail to carry out the instructions of the oracle!

Orestes: I know! But could it be worse? These instructions I've been given are so awful I can't help but wonder if a demon impersonated Apollo?

Electra: A demon? Throned and sitting on the holy altar in Delphi? I think not!

Orestes: But how can this be right?

Electra: Don't be a weakling! Go inside and prepare the same welcome for her that she and Aegisthus gave our father!

Orestes: ...I'll go. But it is an awful place I go to, and a terrible thing I am about to do. If this is the will of the gods, then so be it. But it is a bitter game for children to be playing with their mother...

Exit Orestes into the hut

Enter Clytaemnestra on her carriage, attended by several Trojan slave girls

Chorus: Greetings, O queen of Argos, sister of the Dioscuri, Zeus' sons, Castor and Polydeuces, twin patron gods of sailors who breathe in the fiery heaven between the stars! Revered you are, for your great wealth and blessed life, and on this blessed day may you get the rest of what's coming to you.

Clytaemnestra: Step lightly from the chariot, women of Troy, and help me down. Good day ladies. We gave most of the spoils of Troy to the religious houses, you know, but I decided to keep these, the flowers of Troy, to decorate my home. They are but paltry compensation, and no substitute for Iphigenia, my beloved daughter, but I think them rather nice ornaments all the same.

Electra: Very pretty. I would offer you my hand to assist you from your chariot, but fine as they are I fear that I would be no substitute, considering my reduced circumstances.

Clytaemnestra: They have me, you needn't put yourself out on my account.

Electra: No. After all, I am but prisoner, who like your pet women here has lived to see my home captured.

Clytaemnestra: Well, you can blame your father for that, for he brought it about when he betrayed those who deserved only his deepest love and devotion. It is time you heard the story from someone who knows, child, and I'll tell it gladly, for when bad reputation begins to take hold of a woman, she can become rather bitter about it. I am bitter. I have reason to be. If you will insist on slandering me, daughter, learn the facts first so you can do it right – if you can still find it in your heart to hate me.

When my father bestowed me on your father, it was no part of his plan nor mine that my children should die as a result of it. But your father tricked Iphigenia – your sister – into believing she was going to marry Achilles, lured her from our home and spirited her away to Aulis where his ships were stuck.

And there he stretched her above an altar and slashed her pale white throat. Now, if he had done this to prevent the capture of Argos, or to help our house in some way by sacrificing one child to save the other two, perhaps I could have forgiven him. But my daughter died because Agamemnon's brother Menelaus couldn't control his slut!

Even then I had no notion of killing your father, richly though he deserved it. But then he dared come back from Troy with a raving mad prophetess, and brought her into our bed! He tried to keep two wives beneath the same roof! Now, women can be foolish, too, why deny it? And when a husband desecrates the marriage bed, the woman may very well follow his lead and find a new partner of her own. She is criticized for this, while the man who made it happen receives no blame at all.

Just imagine that it was Menelaus who had been spirited away to Troy as some trophy. Should I then have killed your brother so that I could sail off and save my sister's husband? How would your father have liked that? What would he have done to me?

Yes, I killed him, and I did it in the only way open to me: I turned to his enemies.

Now you can speak if you wish, and tell me why it was wrong for your father to die.

Chorus: There is some justice in what you have said, but it is shameful nonetheless. A sensible woman goes along with her husband in everything, and anyone who thinks differently is beneath contempt.

Electra: Bear in mind, mother, what you just said at the end – you told me that I had the freedom to say exactly what I wanted against you.

Clytaemnestra: Yes, and I say it again, and won't retract it, child.

Electra: And you won't hear me out and hurt me after?

Clytaemnestra: I won't do that. I want to know what you think.

Electra: Fine, then: let's get started. Above all, I really wish that you had more sense, mother. You and your sister Helen are equally beautiful; you are also equally vicious, and wholly unworthy of Castor, your brother. Helen went willingly to her own ruin, and you, mother, destroyed the most noble man in Greece. You claim to have done it for the sake of your lost daughter, but other people don't know you as I do, and I know better. Even before your Iphigenia was sacrificed to free the ships – the very second your husband had set out for war – you were sitting in front of your mirror, preening and fixing your hair. Any woman who goes out of her way to make herself beautiful while her husband is away is a dirty whore: there's simply no need for her to show her pretty face in public unless she's looking for trouble.

I was there with you, mother! I know only too well that you alone, of all the Greek women, were happy as a lark when reports were that things went well for the Trojans, but when the tide turned and it began to look again as if you might have to face Agamemnon, returned from Troy, your mood became black as a stormy sky. It would have been so easy for you to have behaved properly! Agamemnon was not inferior to Aegisthus – you were married to the man that the whole of Greece had chosen as its commander! And seeing that your sister had behaved so disgracefully, this was your great opportunity to prove your virtue and gain your own glory and have it stand out in stark relief, for virtue fairly pops against so black a backdrop as the one Helen provided.

But for a moment let's forget all of that, and tell me one thing: Agamemnon killed your Iphigenia; fine; but tell me, what wrong did I or Orestes ever do you? Are we not your children, too? How is it possible that once you'd killed our father you then proceeded to drive us from his house and used it as a dowry to buy yourself a lover? How is it this new husband of yours is not in exile himself for having sent one of the children you love so very dearly away? Why haven't you killed him in retribution for making my life more painful than my sister's death?

If murder demands another murder in return I should kill you myself on behalf of our father, and then Orestes can kill me for killing you, and we can all be dead together. How would it be any less just than what you have done?

Any man who marries for wealth or status is a fool, for he will find that a humble home and respectable marriage would have been preferable to his great one.

CHORUS: It's always a gamble when one marries a woman. Some marriages are good, others not so much: this I have seen.

CLYTAEMNESTRA: Electra, you always preferred your father to me. I always knew, and I've learned to live with it. And I forgive you for what you have said. For you see, child, I regret the things I have done. You will never know how I suffer for all that I plotted! I allowed the anger that I had for my husband to push me much further than ever I should have!

ELECTRA: The time for mourning is long past: father is dead and nothing can change that. But why don't you seek to bring home your son now, who is wandering around from place-to-place in exile?

CLYTAEMNESTRA: Because I am afraid. They say he is bitterly angry about his father.

ELECTRA: And what of me? How can you stand to see me treated so?

CLYTAEMNESTRA: What can I do? You and Aegisthus are equally prone to anger and equally immoveable!

ELECTRA: The difference between us is that I am in pain! But my anger will eventually cease...

CLYTAEMNESTRA: At which point he'll stop persecuting you, I know he will!

ELECTRA: That would be most magnanimous behaviour on the part of the stranger who lives in my house instead of me.

CLYTAEMNESTRA: You see? There you go again!

ELECTRA: I'll keep silent, then, since I fear him...

CLYTAEMNESTRA: Oh, enough of this circular talk – why did you summon me here, child?

ELECTRA: I think you know that I've given birth. I wanted you to make the appropriate sacrifice on my behalf... the one that is supposed to be made on the baby's tenth night in the air, according to custom. I have no experience of such matters, this being my first child, and don't know the appropriate thing.

CLYTAEMNESTRA: But this is the proper work of the woman who delivered your child.

ELECTRA: I was my own doctor. I gave birth alone.

CLYTAEMNESTRA: What? Is your house so distant from friends and neighbours?

ELECTRA: No one wants people as poor as we are for friends.

CLYTAEMNESTRA: And look at you now. You've just given birth and yet you stand here so filthy and clad in rags. Of course I will sacrifice for the child!

Come, girls, take the chariot and lead the horses to the feed stall. Find me here when adequate time has passed for a sacrifice to the gods, after which I go to meet my husband.

Exit Attendants of Clytaemnestra

ELECTRA: Please, step into our poor home, mother, but take care not to let the soot that covers the walls get on your fine clothes.

... I just know you'll make the appropriate sacrifice to the gods.

Exit Clytaemnestra into the hut

The basket of grain is ready and the sacrificial knife already sharpened – the one that was already used to kill the bull, next to whom you will soon lie, cow, and thereafter you can marry him again in Hades... That is my favour to you, and all I ask in return is that you finally give father the justice he deserves.

Exit Electra into the hut

CHORUS:

The evils are being repaid. The winds of the house's fortune change direction. Then it was our ruler, killed while he bathed: the very foundations groaned in sorrow, the stones on high echoed throughout the palace as the poor man shouted: "Cruel woman, why do you murder me who has finally returned after ten long years to my dear homeland?" Her luckless husband had returned after many years to his high stone walls, built by the hands of the Cyclopes, and she lay in wait for him, the sharp axe in her hands. O poor tormented husband – whatever madness made of that woman a mountain-lioness that prowled your oak-covered home, the tide of justice has finally reversed and now she is repaid for her shameful union.

CLYTAEMNESTRA (FROM INSIDE): My children, in the name of the gods, do not slay your mother!

CHORUS: Do you hear the shouting?

CLYTAEMNESTRA (FROM INSIDE): I am murdered!

CHORUS: We shudder to hear you slaughtered at the hands of your children. God always hands out justice, be it sooner or later. You suffered greatly, but the things you did, hard-hearted woman, were unholy.

Enter Orestes, Electra, and Pylades from the hut

The corpses of Clytaemnestra and Aegisthus can be seen behind them

Here they are, splattered all over with the blood of their mother... Look, there lies their trophy – their act of sacrifice.

There is no house, nor has there ever been, that has endured more suffering than the one that belongs to the family of Tantalus and Atreus.

ORESTES: Gods who see everything men do, look upon these bloody deeds, these bodies lying side by side, struck dead by my hand in payment for the wrongs done me.

ELECTRA: Cry for me, brother, and what I have done. The hatred I bore for our mother burned so strong within me, and this is the sad result...

CHORUS: Cry for the fate of a mother whose unfathomable pain gave birth to unforgiving anger, for all her children brought her such sorrow it would have been better for her if she'd been barren. But she has paid her just debt now for the murder of their father.

ORESTES: Phoebus Apollo, the purity of the justice you directed I obtain remains a mystery to me, but the pain you've given me is crystal clear. Now my destiny will be that of a matricide, doomed once again to wander in exile, far from the land of Greece.

But where can I go? What city will have me, what host will embrace me, the child who slew his own mother?

ELECTRA: And what of my fate? Where will I go, who will ask me to dance, what marriage could I possibly make now?

CHORUS: Their thoughts have shifted just like the wind now that the deed is done. They speak like the pious again, when only moments ago sister egged brother on to dreadful things, dear girl, when he was reluctant.

ORESTES: You all saw her agony, how she revealed to us the pale breasts upon which we were suckled – and I answered by plunging in the blade! Oh god! When she crumpled to the ground all my strength left me, too!

CHORUS: We know this only too well, for how could you not be agonized at the miserable cry of she who gave you birth...

ORESTES: She reached her hand up to my face and cried, "My child, I beg you!" And the sword drooped in my hand...

CHORUS: Poor woman! How could you bear to look at her as she took her final breath?

ORESTES: I didn't look, but covered my eyes with my cloak like a frightened child, and blindly drove the blade through her throat...

ELECTRA: And I urged you to it... I held the sword as surely as you, just not in my hand...

ORESTES: Take it! Take my cloak and cover our mother's limbs! Clean her wounds and close them up!

O mother, you gave birth to your own death!

ELECTRA: Look, mother: we who loved and hated you, cover you lovingly now... bringing a close to this family's great sorrows...

Enter Castor and Polydeuces from the sky above

Chorus: Look! Up in the sky! Over the top of the house something divine comes into view – for human beings don't travel through like that! What could compel gods to make themselves visible to the eyes of men?

Castor: Listen, son of Agamemnon, and see who is calling you! We are the twins of Zeus, brothers of your mother! I am Castor and beside me is Polydeuces, come from calming a storm at sea that was threatening the ships – for we saw from afar the murder of our sister!

Her punishment is just – but it was not just that you be the one to mete it out! Apollo is our lord, so we say nothing against him except that, wise though he is, what he told you to do was not wise, though we have to accept it – what Fate and Zeus ordered you to do.

Give your sister Electra to Pylades to be a wife for his house – and you yourself, Orestes, must leave Argos, never to return. Having killed your mother, the dreadful Furies – beast-faced goddesses – will hound you to and fro across the earth, so get you to Athens and embrace the knees of the sacred statue of Athena you find there. For though the foul creatures hiss round you like terrible serpents, she will keep you from their reach.

In Athens there is a hill dedicated to the war god Ares, where the gods first sat jury in a trial of murder, on account of Ares having killed Halirrothius, the son of Poseidon, ruler of the sea. He'd done it in vengeance for Halirrothius having taken his daughter in impious marriage. From that time onward they have argued cases there, and been commendably honest and scrupulous in their judgment. There it is you must stand your trial for murder.

But I'll call it now and predict that the voting pebbles will come up an even number on each side and deadlock will save you from death. If I know Apollo, he will take the blame for what you did upon himself – with some justification, since he was the one who ordered the matricide. And ever after the law will be that a hung jury means victory for the accused.

The dreadful Furies will shake with grief and rage at the decision, and go down into a crack in the earth alongside the hill of Athena, which will thus become a holy oracle for men to venerate them.

As for you, Orestes, you are tasked with founding a city in Arcadia, close by the streams of Alpheus and the Lycaean sanctuary, and this city will receive its name from you.

As to the body of Aegisthus – it will receive burial here from the citizens of Argos. Clytaemnestra's brother-in-law, Menelaus, has only just returned to Greece after his long journey back from Troy, so he and Helen will bury her. Helen, by the way, has come from the land of Proetus in Egypt. Proteus, you ask? Yes, Proteus! She never went to Troy! Zeus, feeling impish, sent an image of her to Troy and the real Helen to Egypt! So there's that...

So then let Pylades marry your sister Electra, his virgin-wife, and let him take her out of the land of Achaea to his homeland. He can drop Orestes' other brother-in-law, that farmer fellow, off in the land of Phocis, where they will heap riches upon him.

Well, Orestes, it's a long trip, so you might as well get started. Make your way now – on foot, mind – across the narrow isthmus, and from there to that blessed hill in Athens. But don't be too downcast, for when you have fulfilled your latest destiny, you'll then have happiness and rest from your troubles.

Chorus: O sons of Zeus, might we have a word?

Castor: Of course: none of you are defiled by this murder.

Chorus: We were just wondering, if you are gods as well as brothers to the deceased woman, why don't you just speed the process along and refuse the Furies entry to this house?

Castor: Look, everything has happened the way it had to. Fate and necessity, dear ladies, fate and necessity. Well, that and the unwise proclamations of Phoebus Apollo.

Electra: Might I ask a question as well, uncles?

CASTOR: Well... Oh, why not? Let's be honest: we place the blame for this murder entirely at the feet of Apollo, anyway. What is your question, child?

ELECTRA: Just this: what oracle said that I had to murderer my mother?

CASTOR: Your actions have been done as one. Your destinies are shared. The single doom of your house has afflicted you both.

ORESTES: Well, sister, no sooner do I get to see you after so many years apart, than I am again robbed of your love. We are doomed to be apart, it seems.

CASTOR: You just worry about yourself, young Orestes. She'll have a husband and a house. She hasn't suffered so badly and needs no pity, except that she has to leave Argos.

ELECTRA: Oh yes? And what grief is greater than to be forced to leave the land of your birth?

ORESTES: Leaving the land of your birth to be judged by foreigners in the murder of your mother, perhaps?

CASTOR: It won't be so bad: you'll get to see the holy city of Athena, after all.

ELECTRA: O dear brother, hold me tight! Once again the curse of our mother separates us from our family home!

ORESTES: Come to my arms, sister... Sing a lament for me, sometime.

CASTOR: Oh...oh...these words of yours are terrible even for the gods to hear. The gods above still feel pity and pain for the sufferings and toils of mortals.

ORESTES: I'll never see your face again, dear sister...

ELECTRA: And I shall never again feel your presence, or visit your grave...

ORESTES: These are the final words we will ever speak to one another.

ELECTRA: O my city – farewell! And a fond farewell to all of you, my fellow citizens!

ORESTES: My sister, my most loyal love, must you leave so soon?

ELECTRA: I cannot bear to remain, for my eyes well up with tears!

ORESTES: Farewell Pylades. Go forward, and be good to your new wife...

CASTOR: Well, Polydeuces, off they go to be married, like we told them. And if you squint, Orestes, you can just now see the Furies approaching! If I were you I'd hurry for Athens while you can! They have snakes for hands and their skin is black, and they are on track to collect their terrible reward from you...

As for us, we're off to the Sicilian seas! For as you know, we are forbidden to offer safe harbour to the impious or the polluted, and there are some boats out there that require our attention.

So remember: always sail a straight course, and never ship out with those the gods have reason to hunt. It's good advice, nephew, and the most we can do for you.

CHORUS: Farewell. It just goes to show you: the man who does no evil avoids troubles and leads a blessed life.

Exit all

Translated from the Greek by Stephen Russell, PhD
English by Jonathan Allen and Stephen Russell

Chapter 7
Herodotus
THE BATTLE OF THERMOPYLAE

The Story: In 480 BC the forces of Persia, under their king Xerxes, set out to conquer the cities of Greece. One motivation for this invasion was the defeat that the army of Xerxes' father Darius received ten years earlier at the battle of Marathon.

The historian Herodotus chronicles the Persian wars in his *Histories*, and in book seven he talks about how a small group of Spartan troops make a stand against the Persian invaders at Thermopylae. This resistance of theirs has taken on a great deal of significance not only for the Greeks, but also for western thought and imagination.

Herodotus, *The Histories*, Book 7

[7.205] Because Leonidas had two older brothers, Cleomenes and Dorieus, he had no thought of gaining the throne himself. However, when Cleomenes died without a male heir, and since Dorieus had also already died while he was in Sicily, the crown then fell to Leonidas, who was older than Cleombrotus, the youngest son of his mother Anaxandridas. Moreover, Leonidas was married to the daughter of Cleomenes (his brother).

Leonidas had now come to Thermopylae, accompanied by the three hundred men which the law assigned him, whom he had himself chosen from among the citizens, and all of whom were fathers with living sons. On his way there he had taken the troops from Thebes, whose number I have already mentioned, and who were under the command of Leontiades the son of Eurymachus. The reason why he went out of his way to bring troops from Thebes, and to note that it was Thebes only, was that the Thebans were strongly suspected of being sympathetic with and collaborating with the enemy from Persia. Leonidas therefore asked them to come along with him to the war, because he wanted to see whether they would go along with his request for troops, or whether they would openly refuse and avoid supporting the Greek alliance. The Thebans, however, did send troops, although it is clear that their sympathies were with the Persians.

[7.206] Leonidas and his troops were sent by the Spartans in advance of their main army, so that the sight of these Spartans might encourage and inspire the other Greek allies to fight, and prevent them from defecting to and helping the Persians, which they likely would have done if they had seen that Sparta were not taking the lead.

As for the other Spartan troops, first they had to celebrate the festival of Carnea, and this was keeping them from leaving Sparta. Once that festival was over, they intended to quickly join Leonidas with a full army and to leave behind in Sparta a small garrison that could be used for self-defense. The other allies were also planning to act in a similar fashion: because it happened that the Olympic festival was taking place at exactly the same time. Since none of the allies expected that the battle of Thermopylae would be decided so quickly, they were therefore content to merely send only an advanced guard for the time being. At any rate, those were the intentions of the allies.

[7.207] When the Persian army came closer to the entrance of the pass, the Greek forces at Thermopylae became quite afraid and they held a meeting to consider whether they should make a retreat. The Peloponnesians thought that it would be a good idea for the army to fall back as far as the Peloponnese, and from that point guard the Isthmus at Corinth. But Leonidas saw that the Phocians and Locrians were altogether angry about this plan, and so he voted in favour of remaining where they were. He also sent envoys to the other cities and towns to ask for help, since the forces at Thermopylae were too small to make a stand against an army as large as that of the Persians.

[7.208] While this debate was taking place, Xerxes sent a spy on horseback to see how many Greeks there were and to take note of what they were doing. While he was still in Thessaly he had heard that there was a small force led by the Spartans that was guarding the pass. He also heard that the Spartans were under the command of Leonidas, who was a descendant of Hercules. The spy made his way up to the camp and looked about, but he did not see the whole army – because some of the Greeks were out of sight behind the wall that had just been rebuilt and was now carefully guarded. However, he did get a look at those who were stationed on the outside of the wall. At the moment it happened to be that the Spartans were posted outside the wall, and the spy watched these men while some of them were stripped for exercise and others were combing their long hair. The spy found this to be quite amazing, and he took care to add up their number, along with anything else that seemed necessary to know. Then he rode off quietly back to Xerxes. No one set out after him or even tried to pursue him. In fact, it seemed that nobody took the slightest notice of him while he was there.

[7.209] So he returned, and told Xerxes everything that he had seen. Xerxes was confused by this report. He couldn't to understand the truth – that the Spartans were getting themselves ready to either kill or be killed and that they were prepared to do so with all of their strength. Instead Xerxes thought it was laughable that they were engaged in such pursuits as gymnastics and combing their hair. So he sent for Demaratus, the son of Ariston, who had travelled with him on this expedition. When Demaratus arrived, Xerxes told him everything that the spy had told him and then he questioned Demaratus about this news, since he wanted to find out why the Spartans were behaving in such a manner.

Then Demaratus said to Xerxes: "O king, I told you about these men before, just when we were beginning our long march against Greece. At that time you laughed at me when I told you what would happen in this war. What I value most, my lord, is telling the truth in all circumstances, and I have always been forthright with you – so I will say it again and beg that you hear me out. These Spartan men here have come to fight us for this pass at Thermopylae and they are making their preparations for just that. It's the Spartan custom to do their hair just before they risk their lives. But I can assure you that if you can beat these men and the army that waits for you in Sparta, then there is no other people or nation in the world who would dare to take up arms or try to resist you, my lord. For now you will be fighting the finest and noblest city in Greece, and the place that has the bravest men."

Xerxes was unable to believe what Demaratus had just said, so he asked him again how it was possible that such a small group of men could resist his entire army. Demaratus answered: "My lord, if things don't turn out as I have told you, then you should treat me as you would any common liar."

[7.210] But Xerxes was still not persuaded. The king waited four whole days, expecting that the Greeks would eventually run away. When, however, he discovered on the fifth day that they hadn't left, he started to view their actions as stupid impudence, and so he became angry and sent the Medes and Cissians out to meet them, with orders to take back some prisoners alive and then bring them into his presence. The Medes rushed forward and made a charge at the Greeks, but they died in great numbers; others, however, took the places of those who had been killed, and they refused to be beaten off in spite of their terrible losses. It suddenly became clear to all, and especially to the king, that he may have had plenty of men in his army, but he had but very few soldiers and warriors. And so the battle continued for the entire day.

[7.211] Then the Medes eventually withdrew from the fight, since they had been treated so roughly; and their place was taken by the band of Persians under the command of Hydarnes, which the king called his "Immortals." It was confidently believed, as these "Immortals" advanced forward to attack the Greeks, that they would bring the matter to a quick and easy end. But when they faced the Greeks in battle, they did no better than the Medes had done right before them. All of the conditions remained the same – the two armies were fighting in a narrow space, the Persians were using shorter spears than the Greeks were, and so they could in no way take advantage of their superior numbers.

The Spartans fought a memorable battle. They made it very clear that they were the experts in matters of war, and that they in turn were fighting against amateurs. One of the tactics that the Spartans often employed was to turn their backs and pretend that they were making a retreat and were in confusion, at which point the enemy would pursue them with great cries of triumph. However, the Spartans would let the Persians almost catch up to them when they would suddenly turn around and face them, inflicting numerous losses against the Persians. The Spartans also lost men in these encounters, but they weren't many. Finally the Persians realized that their attempts to assault and attack this pass were useless – and that it didn't matter what type of force they sent in or what kinds of tactics they employed. They simply couldn't gain any ground this way – and so they broke off the fighting and withdrew.

[7.212] During these attacks, it is said that Xerxes, who was watching the battle, jumped up three times from the throne on which he was seated, in terror for what was happening to his army.

On the next day the combat started once again, but the Persians had no better luck. The Greeks had so few numbers that the Persians hoped that they would have been so badly wounded that they wouldn't be able to offer much resistance – and so they attacked the Greeks once again. But the Greeks never gave an inch. They were divided up into units according to their cities, and each of them took their turn in the line - all except the Phocians, who had been stationed on the mountain to guard the pathway there. So, when the Persians found that things were no better for them than they had been on the previous day, they once again withdrew.

[7.213] Xerxes was at a loss – he had no idea how to deal with this situation. But just then it happened that he was approached by Ephialtes of Malis, who was the son of Eurydemus. Motivated by the hope of receiving a rich reward from the Persian king, he had come to tell Xerxes about a path that led across and over the mountain to Thermopylae – and by doing this Ephialtes caused the deaths of all the Greeks who had made a stand there.

This Ephialtes later on, because he was afraid of the Spartans, fled to Thessaly. While he was away in exile, the Amphictyons held an assembly at Pylae, a price was set upon his head by the Pylagorae. When some time had passed by, he eventually returned from exile, and went to Anticyra, where he was killed by Athenades, a native of Trachis. Athenades did not kill him for his treachery at Thermopylae, but for another reason that I shall mention in a later part of my history: yet the Spartans still honoured Athenades nonetheless. In any case, Ephialtes did die later on.

[7.214] There is also another story, which I don't believe at all – that Onetas, the son of Phanagoras, who was a native of Carystus, and Corydallus, a man of Anticyra, were actually the people who told Xerxes about the mountain pass and showed it to the Persians. This second story, to me, is very unconvincing. My first reason is that the Pylagorae, who must have had the best means of knowing what the truth was, didn't offer a reward for the heads of Onetas and Corydallus, but instead for that of Ephialtes of Trachis – and they most likely did this after looking into the facts. Moreover, we know that Ephialtes was sent into exile for this very reason. I admit that Onetas might have known about this path through the mountains even though he was not a Malian, especially if he had spent much time in that part of the country. But it was Ephialtes who was the person who actually showed the Persians the way around the mountain by the pathway, so I'll leave his name on the record as the man who is guilty of the deed.

[7.215] Xerxes was very pleased with Ephialtes' offer. He was happy with the terms, and quickly sent off Hydarnes with his troops. They left the Persian camps at evening, just about the time that the lamps are lit. The track was originally made by the Malians who lived in the area, and they later used it to help the people from Thessaly when they needed a path to attack the Phocians, back when the Phocians blocked the pass at Thermopylae with a wall to protect themselves from attack. So the evil uses of this mountain pass had been known for a long time by the Malians.

[7.216] Here is the course of the path: it begins at the Asopus, a stream that flows through the narrow gorge in the hills, runs along the ridge of the mountain (which is called, like the pathway over it, Anopaea), and ends at the city of Alpenus – the first Locrian town as you come from Malis – near the stone called Melampygus and the seats of the Cercopians. At this part it is at its narrowest point.

[7.217] This was the path that the Persians took after they crossed the Asopus. They continued their march throughout the whole night, with the mountains of Oeta on their right, and those of Trachis on their left. At dawn they found themselves at the peak of the pass. The hill was guarded, as I said previously, by a thousand men from Phocis, who were placed there to defend the pathway and at the same time to defend their own country. They had been given the guard of the mountain path, while the other Greeks defended the pass below, because they had volunteered for the service, and had promised Leonidas that they would maintain their post.

[7.218] The ascent of the Persians became known to the Phocians in the following manner: During all the time that they were making their way up the mountain, the Phocians were completely unaware that they were doing this, since the entire mountain was covered with oak trees. But chance had it that there was no wind, and the Persian troops made a great deal of noise as they marched through the branches and leaves. When the Phocians heard these noises, they jumped up to their feet and quickly grabbed their arms.

The Persians soon came into sight and they were surprised, because they did not expect to encounter any troops from the enemy along the way. Hydarnes was frightened by the sight and so he asked Ephialtes where these troops were from, fearing that they might be from Sparta. Ephialtes truthfully told him that they were from Phocis, and so Hydarnes got his men ready to engage in battle against them.

The Phocians came under heavy fire from a shower of Persian arrows, and so they retreated up to the top of the mountain because they thought that they were the exclusive reason for the Persian attack. They were preparing for a greater fight – one to the death – and while they were doing this, the Persians, including Hydarnes and Ephialtes, just ignored them and went down the other side of the mountain as quickly as possible.

[7.219] The Greeks at Thermopylae received the first warning of the death that was coming with the dawn from the seer Megistias, who saw their doom in the victims that he was sacrificing. While it was still dark some deserters also came in and reported that the Persians were circling around behind them. Also, just as day was breaking, the lookouts came running in from the hills to warn them that the Persians were on their way.

The Greeks then held a council of war to debate what they should do, and opinions were divided: some of them said that they must not abandon their positions, while others held the opposite opinion. So when the meeting ended, some of the troops departed and went their way homeward to their various cities; however, some of them resolved to stay in place and stand right by Leonidas to the end.

[7.220] It is said that Leonidas himself sent away the troops who left for their respective home, because he wanted to spare their lives, but that he thought that it would be wrong if either he or his Spartans abandoned the post that they had been especially sent to protect. I am of the opinion that Leonidas made up his mind, gave the order, and dismissed them when he saw that his allies were demoralized and unwilling to face the common danger. Therefore he told them to go home, but he said that honour would not allow him to retreat. He knew that if he stayed, then he would gain glory and Sparta would preserve its prosperity. For at the very start of the war, the Spartans sent an embassy to Delphi to consult the Pythian oracle about what they should do, and they received word that "either Sparta will be destroyed by the barbarians, or one of her kings must die." The prediction was given in hexameter poetry, and it read like this:

> "Here is your fate, O you who live in wide Sparta:
> Either your great and famous town will be destroyed
> By the sons from Perseus, or that will not happen;
> But the land of Sparta will mourn the death
> Of the king from the house of Heracles;
> For neither the strength of lions or bulls will hold him down,
> Try as they might – for he has the power of Zeus.
> Nothing will stop him until he has your king as his prey,
> Or he has your glorious city."

I believe that the Spartans were thinking about this response from the oracle, combined with his desire to win the fame for the Spartans that no other city could share – and this is what caused Leonidas to send those other troops home. I don't think that they volunteered to go home in such a disgraceful manner, or that it was because they were fighting with Leonidas.

[7.221] I have an important piece of evidence that backs up my view on this matter as well. The seer Megistias – the Acarnanian, who is reputed to be from the family of Melampus – was with the army and he predicted the coming disaster when he inspected the entrails of the sacrificial victims. He clearly received orders from Leonidas to go home so that he could avoid the same fate as that of the army. But he refused to leave even though he was ordered to do so. Instead he stayed with the Spartan army, but he did send home his only son, who was present with him on the expedition.

[7.222] So when Leonidas ordered the allies to leave, they did what he said and went home. Everyone left quickly, but only the Thespians and the Thebans stayed behind with the Spartans. The Thebans were held back by Leonidas as hostages, very much against their will. The Thespians, on the other hand, stayed entirely of their own accord, refusing to retreat, and they declared that they would not abandon Leonidas and his men. So they remained with the Spartans and died along with them. Their leader was Demophilus, the son of Diadromes.

[7.223] When the sun came up Xerxes poured out libations, and then he waited until the middle of the morning before he began to make his advance forward. Ephialtes had given him instructions to do this, since the path down the mountain was much more direct and far shorter than the long and winding road that they had travelled up and around the mountain the night before.

So the troops from Xerxes began to move closer, and the Greeks under Leonidas, now aware that they were bound to die, went out further into the wider part of the pass then they had previously done. Before this they had remained rather close to the wall, and had made only brief sorties into the narrows of the pass – but now they were moving much beyond those narrows. Many of the Persians were killed, and the enemy fell in heaps because their commanders stood behind them and whipped them indiscriminately, driving them forward from the back with continual blows. Many of them fell into the sea and drowned there, while an even greater number was trampled to death by their own comrades. It was impossible to count the number of the dead.

The Greeks knew that the enemy was already on its way down the mountain pass and that sure death was inevitable, so they put all their strength and energy and thus fought with fury and desperation, no longer paying any heed to their own safety.

[7.224] By this time most of the Greek spears were broken, and they were forced to kill the Persians with their swords. In the middle of the battle, Leonidas was killed, fighting with the utmost bravery. He died along with many other Spartans whose names I have taken the care to learn because they fought so bravely. In fact, I've learned the names of all three hundred.

At the same time a number of distinguished Persians died as well. Among them were two brothers of Xerxes, Abrocomes and Hyperanthes, sons of Darius by Artanes' daughter Phratagune. Artanes, a son of Hystaspes and the grandson of Arsames, was the brother of king Darius, and when he gave his daughter Phratagune to the king, he also made Darius the heir to all of his possessions, for she was his only child.

[7.225] Thus two brothers of Xerxes fought and died at Thermopylae. And now there was a fierce struggle between the Persians and the Spartans over the body of Leonidas. The Greeks drove the enemy back four times and at last their courage helped them succeed in carrying off his body. The battle with the Persians remained close until Ephialtes arrived with his men. When the Greeks realized that these new troops were at hand, the manner of fighting changed. The Greeks once again withdrew into the narrowest part of the pass, and retreated even behind the wall, where they drew up a position in a single compact body – everyone except the Thebans. They did this on the little hill at the entrance to the pass, where the stone lion stands that was set up in honour of Leonidas.

Here they fought to the very last, using their swords if they still had them, while others resisted with their hands and teeth. They kept fighting until the Persians finally overwhelmed and buried them in a shower of missiles as they advanced from the front over the remnants of the broken wall while the rest surrounded them from all sides.

[7.226] Of all the Spartans who fought nobly and bravely among the whole group of Spartans and Thespians, a Spartan named Dieneces is said to have distinguished himself above all the rest. He made a speech before the Greeks fought the Persians that remains on record. One of the Trachinians told him that the number of Persians was so great that when they shot forth their arrows, there would be so many of them that they would block the sun.

Dieneces was not at all frightened by these words, but he instead made light of the Persian strength, answered "Our friend from Trachis brings us excellent news. If the Persians hide the sun, then we'll have to have our fight in the shade." This same man is reported to have made other sayings of a similar nature, which are still on record.

[7.227] After Dieneces the next bravest Spartans are said to have been two brothers. Their names were Alpheus and Maro and they were the sons of Orsiphantus. There was also a Thespian who gained greater glory than any of his countrymen – he was a man named Dithyrambus, the son of Harmatidas.

[7.228] The dead were buried where they fell; and in their honour – and to pay honour to those who died before Leonidas sent the allies away – an inscription was set up, which said:

"Four thousand here from Pelops' land,
Against three million did once stand."

This statement was in honour of everyone. But the Spartans have their own special epitaph, which reads:

"Go tell the Spartans, you who read,
We took their orders and lie here dead."

There was one for the seer Megistias as well, which reads:

"Here lies Megistias, who died
When the Persian passed Spercheius' tide.
A prophet, yet unwilling to save
Himself, but shared the Spartans' grave."

These inscriptions and their respective pillars, were set up to honour the dead by Amphictyons. But the epitaph that honours Megistias was set up by Simonides, the son of Leoprepes, because of their great friendship.

[7.229] Two of the three hundred Spartans, Aristodemus and Eurytus, are said to have been attacked by an inflammation of the eyes, and because of this they received orders from Leonidas to leave the camp before the battle and so both went to Alpeni to get better. These two men, had they been so inclined, might have agreed to return alive to Sparta; or if they did not want to return, they might have returned to the field of battle and died with their countrymen.

But at the time when both options were open to them, they could not agree and so made opposite decisions. Eurytus no sooner heard that the Persians had come round the mountain than straightway he called for his armour, and when he buckled it on he then ordered his slave to lead him to the place where his friends were fighting. The slave did just that, and then just as quickly turned and fled. But Eurytus threw himself into the thick of the battle and died while fighting there.

Aristodemus, on the other hand, had a weak heart, and so he remained at Alpeni. I think that if Aristodemus had been the only person to have been sick and returned home that way, or if both of them had returned together, then the Spartans wouldn't have been angry. But since there were two men with the very same excuse, and since one of them had died, while the other avoided death, the Spartans could hardly help being furious with Aristodemus.

[7.230] There is another account that some give about how Aristodemus made his way back to Sparta alive. They say that he and another soldier had been sent from the camp to deliver a message, but that he purposely loitered on the road even though he had it in his power to return in time for the battle – and that this was the way that he outlived his comrades. They add that his fellow-messenger came back in time to the battle, where he died with the other Spartans.

[7.231] When Aristodemus returned to Sparta, he was met with reproach and disgrace. It was a disgrace, since no Spartan would give him a light to start his fire, or would even speak a word to him; and reproach, since everyone referred to him as "the coward." However, he managed to make amends for everything at the battle of Plataea.

[7.232] There is another story about one of the three hundred who is said to have survived the battle. This man was named Pantites, and Leonidas, it is said, sent him to Thessaly to deliver a message. When he returned to Sparta after the battle, he is reported to have been met with such disgrace that he hanged himself.

Translated from the Greek by Stephen Russell, PhD
English by Stephen Russell and Laura Holtebrinck

Chapter 8
Sophocles
OEDIPUS THE KING

The Story: There is a plague in the city of Thebes. Its king, Oedipus, once solved the riddle of the Sphinx ["What walks on four legs in the morning, two legs in the afternoon, and three legs in the evening?" – the answer is 'man'], which saved the city and won him the hand in marriage of the recently widowed queen Jocasta. Now Oedipus, this "child of fortune," is determined to discover what is causing the new plague.

Characters

Oedipus, king of Thebes
A Priest of Thebes
Creon, Oedipus' brother-in-law
Chorus (of Theban Elders)
Tiresias, a blind prophet in Thebes
Jocasta, Oedipus' wife
First Messenger
Shepherd
Second Messenger
Silent Characters
A Group of Theban Suppliants
Attendants (to Oedipus)
Servant (to Tiresias)
Attendant (to Jocasta)
Attendants (to Creon)
Antigone and Ismene, daughters of Oedipus

Scene: In front of the palace of Oedipus at Thebes.

A Priest stands facing the crowd of suppliants

Enter Oedipus

OEDIPUS: Children of Thebes, most recent generation of the family of Cadmus, why do you come carrying boughs and wearing crowns of supplication? Why is the city rank with incense and filled with moaning? I prefer not to get my news second-hand, so I come in person to ask who you are – I think you all know me.

You there, old man, I take it you speak for these children? So tell me what it is you fear, or what you want, that you gather here suppliant? It would be a hard-heart indeed that could look upon a people in such obvious distress and not do all in his power to alleviate it...

PRIEST: King Oedipus, look around and you will see only the very young and the very old assembled here, united – by helplessness or infirmity – in our inability to flee the city. I am a priest of Zeus, and these here with me are a deputation of the youth of Thebes. Others are occupying the marketplace, where they sit, clad in the garlands, ranged about the two temples of Pallas Athena there and the sacred shrine where Ismenus made his fire prophecies.

For the city, as you cannot fail to have noticed, is deluged by wave upon wave of disaster, and cannot lift itself from the murderous tide.

Blight afflicts all the buds in the fields and orchards, and disease fells the cattle as they pasture. The city's women are barren! The god of scorched earth, hateful Pestilence who brings plague, lays claim to Thebes, sparing no one as he empties the house of Cadmus into Hades' storehouse.

We do not come to do obeisance to a god, but to plead intervention from the best of men. Your genius for dealing with matters of life and death – and those that perhaps involve gods – is legend since the day you alone proved able to free us of the Sphinx. Further, it is whispered hereabout that some god assisted you. So we beg that you exercise your wisdom, and failing that, your influence, and come to our aid once more. Clearly, no one could be more qualified: you have been saviour of the city before. Don't let the glory of that feat tarnish by failing us now.

You once brought us good fortune and favourable omen – we need you again, as indeed you need us, for it is little benefit to a king that he rule an empty nation.

OEDIPUS: O children, I know why you are here – I knew it before you came. You are hurting, but not more than I, I promise you, for my soul suffers for each of you and the city entire. You did not wake me, for my mind has travelled down many roads in the course of the long night. Know that I settled on a plan before you arrived, which has already been set in motion. Creon, son of Menoeceus, brother of my wife, was dispatched to the Pythian shrine of Apollo in Delphi, to inquire of it by what means I might heal our city.

In fact, I am somewhat surprised that he hasn't yet returned, for he was expected back some time ago. When he does arrive, you may deem me no fit ruler if I fail to do whatever the god pronounces necessary to save us all.

PRIEST: This is wonderful news, not to mention timely, for I am informed by some of my party that Creon is just now arriving...

OEDIPUS: O lord Apollo, send us good news and let it light the way to good fortune...

PRIEST: It must be good news, or Creon would not wear such a thick wreath of laurels round his hair.

OEDIPUS: We'll know momentarily, when he comes within shouting distance.

Enter Creon

Lord Creon, my royal brother, son of Menoeceus, what word have you brought us from the god?

CREON: A good word, milord! A very good word! Though even bad tidings can be considered good fortune if things turn out well in the end.

OEDIPUS: But what is the oracle? The way you speak I hardly know whether to be confident or afraid.

Creon: Perhaps we should speak inside.

Oedipus: Speak it aloud to the crowd, for you'll relieve my mind quickest by relieving theirs.

Creon: Very well. Apollo was very clear: we must drive from this land a pollution that has been nurtured here. We mustn't harbour it any more, but it must be purged.

Oedipus: But how do we achieve this purification? What manner of trouble is it?

Creon: The cure is either exile or killing for killing, for the stain is murder: it is bloodshed that has brought a plague upon Thebes.

Oedipus: And who is this criminal the god has fingered?

Creon: Before your timely arrival in Thebes we had another leader, by the name of Laius.

Oedipus: I've heard tell of him, but never met the man myself.

Creon: He was slain, and the god has told us plainly that we must punish his murderer, whoever he may be.

Oedipus: But where on earth might we find him? Where can we hope to find a trace of this ancient blood crime?

Creon: The god says that the killer is here, in Thebes. He says: "One can only find what one looks for, but what one turns a blind eye to slips the net."

Oedipus: Then tell me: where did Laius die? At home or abroad?

Creon: He was journeying to Delphi, and never returned.

Oedipus: Did any of his companions witness his demise?

Creon: All were killed but one, who fled in blind terror, thereby seeing very little, and subsequently recollecting little of what he had seen.

Oedipus: Any bit of information, however small, could lead to something greater. If we could find even the smallest opening into the matter...

Creon: All the man said was that they met a group of marauders on the road, and that Laius died at the hands of many assailants.

Oedipus: No mere thief would dare lay hands on the king unless he had been well paid by someone with an interest in Thebes.

Creon: That's what we thought at the time.

Oedipus: And what prevented you from finding him out?

Creon: We had rather more pressing problems to deal with then. What with the Sphinx and her riddle, the mystery behind Laius's death was simply set aside.

Oedipus: Well, now I am going to take charge of the inquiry and attempt to shed some light. Apollo is correct to be concerned on behalf of the victim. We have an obligation to the dead, who cannot get justice for themselves. Henceforth consider me at once champion of the dead, my country, and my god, for I won't be doing it merely for the sake of a friend I never met, but in order to purge the land of its grave illness. Besides, anyone who would kill one king might easily set his hand against another, and by avenging Laius, I defend myself.

But away now children, clear the steps – quickly! – and take your branches of supplication with you. Let the business of Thebes resume with my assurance that I will do everything I can to resolve this problem. God will decide whether or not fortune is with us.

Priest: Up children, we have heard what we came for! Let us hope and pray that Phoebus Apollo, who sent us the oracle, will also stop this plague!

Exit everyone

Enter the Chorus

Chorus:

O sweet word of Zeus, please be kind! What is the meaning of the oracle that the prophetess of gold-rich Delphi has pronounced for glorious Thebes? We are down on our knees in terror, O Delian healer, in awe of you and of what your word may now evoke. Will it be something new? Or the return of something from seasons long ago? Tell me, O child of golden Hope, immortal oracle!

First we call on you, daughter of Zeus, immortal Athena. And, too, we beg your sister Artemis, who guards the land and seated on her round throne enjoys renown in the markets of Thebes. We also call on you, Phoebus Apollo of the long reach. Come, all three, protect us from destruction. If ever in times past when destruction loomed over the city it was you who drove the flame away, then please come again!

Oh the countless troubles that bear down on us! Sickness lies heavily on all the people and we can find no way to fight the plague ourselves. No crops grow in our glorious land, no Theban woman suffers the sweet pangs of birth, and everywhere, faster than fire consumed, we wing like birds toward the god who dwells on the coast of the western shore – Hades. **THE CITY IS DYING A PIECEMEAL DEATH:** her children lie beyond pity, carried out of reach with no one to console them. Before the altars wives and grey-haired mothers stand groaning as suppliants to Misery. The hymn to the healing god Apollo rings out, and the sound of lamentation with it. For all of this, Athena, O golden daughter of Zeus, grant us your bright face and your protection.

We pray that fierce Ares, god of war, who batters us incessantly though we have no shield and burns through us unopposed, will turn away from our land. Give him a fair wind to take him back to the great chambers of Amphitrite or the waves of the Thracian sea, for if the long night leaves anything standing in this place, the following day sees it knocked down. Father Zeus, smash the war god, for yours is the thunderbolt: you are the lord of lightning, you the lord of fire.

Lord of light, Apollo, we would dearly love to celebrate the shafts from your golden bow as you stand beside us and rain down the fiery beams of Artemis in our defense.

And finally we call upon Bacchus, god with the golden cap, born in this land, aglow with wine to whom the Maenads cry! Come near with your bright torches of blazing pine and strike at the god whom the other gods hate!

Enter Oedipus

OEDIPUS: In answer to your request, I dare say that if you are ready to follow my instructions to the letter we may yet root out this plague. I say it, however, as one newly acquainted with the crime that caused it, for it took place before my time in Thebes, and I won't get very far along the track of it without the aid of those of you who were here. As a recently minted citizen of Thebes I appeal to those of you who are of long-standing: if any among you knows anything at all that might lead us to the identity of Laius's killer, then I require you to tell me now!

Have no fear that you will draw down wrath upon yourself thereby, for it is my pledge that even if you were in some manner involved, you will leave this land unharmed, having helped save it. Likewise, if you know of any foreign influence, speak now, for I will be very grateful, and pay out great rewards, to any who come forward.

But if I learn that anyone has heard and not heeded my order, either to protect the guilty or himself, I will forbid everyone who lives in this land over which I rule ever to speak to or offer him shelter. He will not be allowed to share in prayers or sacrifices to the gods, nor to sprinkle the water in religious rites, but we will drive him from our homes as one who has polluted us, as the oracle at Delphi revealed. This is how we will stand cheek by jowl with the god, fighting for justice for the former king.

I condemn his murderer, whether it is a lone assassin who has gone undetected or a conspiracy, and I pray that they suffer a miserable fate fit for a worthless man, and the same goes for any who knowingly harbour him.

I command all of you to do these things for my sake, for the sake of the god, and for the sake of the country, which has decayed into a barren and godforsaken wasteland. For even if Apollo had not sent his holy oracle to us, it wasn't right that this terrible act should go so long unpunished, so long unclean. A great man was cut down, and a search should have been made for his killer without Apollo's urging.

But now it happens that I hold the power that he once held, as well as the wife he once married, and if he had not died childless our children would have the same mother. Therefore, I intend to pursue his killers like they had murdered my own father, and go to any lengths necessary to find who has the king's blood on his hands. I do this for old Agenor, for Cadmus, for Polydorus, for Labdacus, and for his son Laius, last son of a great family.

And to any who oppose me in this, I pray that the gods damn you and your crops, and that your women remain barren: in short, that you die by the fate that now afflicts us all, if not something worse. But as for those faithful people of Thebes who are listening to my words: may Justice always protect you and the grace of the gods be with you forever.

Chorus: Since you have placed us under oath, my lord, let us say: we didn't kill him, and don't know who did. But as the one who proclaimed the hunt, Apollo will likely be the one to identify the wrongdoer.

Oedipus: Perhaps, but no man can compel the gods if they are unwilling.

Chorus: Then we might suggest another option...

Oedipus: Of course, and if that should fail suggest a third.

Chorus: It is well known that Tiresias, of all men living, has sight closest to that of Apollo. If you asked the prophet's help...

Oedipus: Creon and I came to the same conclusion, so I sent two men to bring him, though I am starting to wonder what's keeping them.

Chorus: Without his skill we only have old rumour to guide us.

Oedipus: And just what is the rumour? It's important that I consider everything, so tell me every word.

Chorus: It is said that the old king was waylaid on the road.

Oedipus: So I am told: the question is by whom.

Chorus: Whoever it was, if he is capable of fear, he won't be long revealing himself after hearing your curse.

Oedipus: I worry that the man who would dare so impious a deed doesn't fear cursing...

Enter Tiresias, guided by a young servant

Chorus: Here is the one who will find our killer, the divine prophet – the one man among mortals who knows the truth.

Oedipus: O Tiresias, well-versed in wisdom and knowledge, of things explainable and things unspeakable, of earth and the heavens: though you are blind you doubtless see the sickness that ravages this city more clearly than any other citizen, and we hope to find in you a champion, and our salvation.

The messengers will have informed you of Apollo's diagnosis that we will only be released from this plague when the killers of Laius are either dead or in exile. And so, we ask that you help us, with oracles from the birds or any other forms of prophecy at your disposal. Save yourself, save the city, and save me from the infection that healed-over murder has caused. We are in your hands

I tell you, it is the most noble thing a man can do, to serve others with his particular gift.

Tiresias: And what manner of gift is foresight when prophecy profits neither the prophet nor his patron? I knew it of old – I foresaw this day, and tried to avoid this very scene – yet it was fruitless: here I stand, where I would not have come of my own accord.

Oedipus: But why are you despondent?

Tiresias: Please, let me go home. You bear your load and I will bear mine, and heavy as they are we will both be better off for it. I beg you to believe me that it would go easier on us both if only you will give me leave to depart.

Oedipus: But this is unfriendly behaviour toward the city that fostered you, and in this, its hour of need! Would you really cheat us of the future when it is in your power to provide it?

Tiresias: Oedipus, if you could see the irony your words contain, I promise you would not press me for mine.

OEDIPUS: In the name of the gods, if you know something, do not deny your supplicants!

TIRESIAS: You should thank the gods for blessed ignorance, and me that I refuse to increase my burden by sharing it with you.

OEDIPUS: What are these riddles? If you know something you must speak, or betray us all and doom the city!

TIRESIAS: By speaking I would betray you and myself. Why do you insist on harassing an old man who has nothing to say to you?

OEDIPUS: Then you flatly refuse? Donkey, you would move a stone to anger! How can you stand there, tight-lipped and inflexible, totally unmoved by our common plight?

TIRESIAS: You defame me for an implacable nature when all your troubles lie in your own, if you only knew it.

OEDIPUS: Who would not be driven wild to hear that you hold the key to our salvation in hand, but do not love the city enough to give it?

TIRESIAS: What I know will come out in its own time, whether I speak it or not.

OEDIPUS: But if it is inevitable, why will you not tell it?

TIRESIAS: I will say no more, however vicious my silence makes you!

OEDIPUS: Then I must accept your challenge and leave nothing unsaid! For I begin to think that you had some part in the murder, and if you were not blind would have done the deed yourself, or else you would break your silence!

TIRESIAS: So that is how it is to be, then... Very well. Then I must ask you to refrain from speaking to me, or anyone else, from this day forward, and abide by the new law you have proclaimed.

OEDIPUS: What is this insolence? Do you think that you can speak this way to me and not regret it?

TIRESIAS: I go under protection of the truth.

OEDIPUS: And who compelled you to speak this 'truth'? For certainly that was no prophecy!

TIRESIAS: You it was who forced my unwilling tongue.

OEDIPUS: Then perhaps I do you an injustice. Perhaps you had better say it again, plainer, so I might better understand.

TIRESIAS: Surely I was plain enough, or you would not be asking me to compound my treason and dig my grave deeper.

OEDIPUS: No, I didn't quite grasp it: say it again...

TIRESIAS: You are the murderer you seek, you the infection that destroys this land – the source of the curse.

OEDIPUS: Now you have twice slandered the king!

TIRESIAS: Shall I tell more and upset you further?

OEDIPUS: Do as you like, for your words carry less sense than the wind, and harm you more than me.

TIRESIAS: You do not know the corrupting influence you have become for the very good reason that you cannot imagine the depth of your sinning, and with your blood relations.

OEDIPUS: Do you imagine you can speak such filth to me and live?

TIRESIAS: If truth is any shield.

OEDIPUS: Truth has power, to be sure, but you won't enjoy it, as you are apparently as deaf to truth as you are blind.

TIRESIAS: Poor fool, taunting me with the very insults they will soon throw back at you.

OEDIPUS: You see nothing but darkness, and cannot harm me or any other man who sees the light.

TIRESIAS: Fair enough, as far as it goes, but then again it is not me who brings your doom, for surely Apollo needs no aid from old men.

OEDIPUS: Tell me, is this scheme yours alone, or did Creon help devise it?

Tiresias: Creon is not the root of this infection, you are.

Oedipus: Wealth and power inspire as much enmity as admiration, but how profound a hatred Creon must have conceived for me if this crown – which the city bestowed upon me as a gift, unasked for – inspires he whom I have always regarded as my most loyal friend to secretly engineer my ouster. He has arranged an ambush for me with a conniving beggar whose sight is activated only by silver, and to whom the future is as dark as it is to any of us!

Tell me, prophet, how is it that when the Sphinx sang her deadly song in Thebes you had nothing to say? Surely her riddle required the skill of a prophet, so where were you before I happened along and stopped her with no assistance whatever, either from your significant birds or your talkative gods!

And now you seek to drive me out, thinking you'll have more influence standing beside the throne of Creon. But you and your compatriot will live to regret this conspiracy. If you weren't such an old man, I would take my satisfaction out of your hide right now.

Chorus: Surely the prophet speaks in anger, Oedipus, as do you! But there is no time for it – we must fulfill the wish of the god and locate the murderer.

Tiresias: Though you are king and have power over me, in this I am more than your equal word for word. For I am not your slave: I serve the will of Apollo, and I won't be called the cat's paw of Creon.

You see fit to ridicule my sightlessness, yet you cannot see your own evil, nor where you live, nor with whom you share your home. Do you even know who you are? Do you know where you come from?

Until you do, you can have no idea that you are enemy to your nearest and dearest, alive and dead – and, what is worse, that the double-edged curse that emanates across the years from your mother and father, step by ineluctable step, will one day soon drive you from this land. At this moment you have sight but no understanding – later, you will understand, and see only darkness. Will there be any place – perhaps a corner of Mount Cithaeron on the outskirts of Thebes – that will not echo your cries when you learn the truth of the safe harbour you thought you'd made at the end of your "lucky" voyage?

And there are still more surprises in store for you, that will mean the ruin of both you and your children, so go ahead, shovel dirt upon Creon and insult me – I may forgive you – for no man living will ever suffer more cruelly than you.

Oedipus: Why do I stand here and allow this old fraud to inflict himself upon me? To Hades! Distance yourself from me and from my house! Away!

Tiresias: Gladly, for I did not want to come, and did so only under order.

Oedipus: If I had only known what you would bring with you I would never have extended the invitation.

Tiresias: I am who I am. Call me fool, if you like, but your parents thought me wise.

Oedipus: My parents? Wait! Do you know them?

Tiresias: This day you will know them, too, and it will be the end of you.

Oedipus: Why is everything you say a riddle?

Tiresias: I thought you were the best there is at solving riddles...

Oedipus: Have your fun. I'll soon solve your riddle, and you'll wish you'd never posed it.

Tiresias: We have this much in common, then, that our greatest talent is also our ruin.

Oedipus: But where we differ is this: if it saves the city, my own ruin doesn't matter to me.

Tiresias: Then I'll leave you to it. Boy: lead me away.

Oedipus: By all means, take him, for I can deal with him any time, and just now he's nothing but a distraction when matters are pressing.

Tiresias: I go knowing that I have nothing to fear from you, for the power you had to hurt me will not last the night.

But before I go, here's a riddle to test your vaunted skills: the one you seek is believed an immigrant to Thebes, but will soon be revealed a native. The discovery will bring him no pleasure, for he will be forced to wander strange lands whose sights he will not enjoy, will be poor when once he was rich, and will feel his way with a stick as he taps over the hills. He'll be discovered brother and father of the children with whom he lives, to his mother prove both son and husband, and, as to his father, find that he both shares with him a wife and is his killer. Remember what I have said, and if you find me mistaken in any of it, then you may feel free to mock my skill in prophecy.

Exit Tiresias, who is guided out by the young servant

Exit Oedipus, who goes into the palace

CHORUS:

Whose are the bloody hands of which the rock of Delphi Sings? He should fly faster than winged Pegasus, for the son of Zeus hunts him now with fire and lightning, and in his wake come the horrible Furies who never miss.

Now from snow-capped Mount Parnassus comes express instructions that all of us must seek the regicide. Somewhere in the wild forests he hides, ducks into mountain caves, bolts blindly on bleeding feet, trying desperately to outrun prophecies that the earth spits up – but always they spiral around him, implacable.

The soothsayer has brought us terrible trouble. We can't believe him. We can't deny him. We don't know what to say, unable to see the present for the future, with no choice but to trust to fate. Is there a subterranean feud between the Houses of Laius and Polybus to explain an attempted assassination of the public life of Oedipus by implicating him in the death of Laius?

Zeus and Apollo are wise and know the affairs of mortals, but when it comes to man who is the better judge, the mouthpiece of the gods or his fellow man? Never will we pile on as accusers of the king until we see the word of the prophet proven finally, for with our own eyes we all saw his wise handling of the terrible Sphinx. He proved his worth to this city, and so far as we are concerned, until we know otherwise, he can do no wrong.

Enter Creon

CREON: Fellow citizens, I come before you because I have heard that King Oedipus has made an outrageous accusation against me. If, in the midst of our present difficulties, he truly believes I could have taken the opportunity to wrong him – by word or deed – then I don't think I can go on living. If I am to be known as a traitor to my city and its people my shame would be too great.

CHORUS: The king spoke in the heat of the moment.

CREON: And said publicly that I persuaded the prophet to speak lies against him?

CHORUS: Yes, but it was said with little time for consideration.

CREON: But did he believe it? How could he believe it?

CHORUS: We would not presume to know the minds of our rulers. But here he comes: you can ask him.

Enter Oedipus

OEDIPUS: You there! How is it that you dare show your face here? Are you so utterly without shame that you would enter my house, having been proven not only murderer of my predecessor, but revealed to have designs upon my crown?

What possessed you? Did you think me so craven, weak, or feeble-minded that I wouldn't see your fine hand in all of this and move to defend myself? Even if your slander had not been too incredibly ridiculous to be believed, how did you think to succeed without friends, wealth or the popular will behind you? Perhaps you might have done without one or two of these, but all three?

CREON: You should listen very carefully to what I am about to say before you ring down your condemnation upon me.

OEDIPUS: You always were a good speaker, Creon, but you will find me a very poor listener since I've learned that you are my nemesis.

CREON: Please, listen to this thing that I have to say...

OEDIPUS: Please, don't try to convince me you haven't betrayed me.

CREON: If you truly think this rush to judgment is reasonable, you are not the wise man I have always thought you.

OEDIPUS: And if you truly think you can sin against a member of your own family without consequence, then I must question your wisdom as well.

CREON: On the contrary, I agree completely with that principle, and beg you to explain why it is you accuse me.

OEDIPUS: Did you, or did you not, advise me to send for that so-called prophet?

CREON: I did, and I stand by my advice.

OEDIPUS: How long has it been since Laius...?

CREON: Since Laius... what? I don't understand you...

OEDIPUS: Since he vanished – died – disappeared?

CREON: A long time ago.

OEDIPUS: And did your prophet practice his art at that time?

CREON: Yes, he enjoyed much the same exalted reputation as he does today.

OEDIPUS: And did he ever once speak of me?

CREON: Not to the best of my knowledge.

OEDIPUS: And where was your infallible seer and his prophetic accusations when the investigation into Laius's death was ongoing?

CREON: I don't know. And when I don't know, I have sense enough to keep quiet about it until I do.

OEDIPUS: What you do know, and would admit if you were honest...

CREON: What? If I knew anything I would tell it.

OEDIPUS: ... is that if the prophet hadn't spoken to you before he spoke to me he would have come here with a very different report, though no doubt just as false.

CREON: I don't know what he said to you, or the truthfulness of it, not having prepared his speech for him. But perhaps it is my turn to depose you now, in my own defence?

OEDIPUS: Ask. I won't be proved a murderer.

CREON: Why would you think I want you to be? Are you not married to my own sister?

OEDIPUS: Is that a rhetorical question?

CREON: And do you rule this land together, sharing power equally?

OEDIPUS: She gets everything she wants from me.

CREON: And am I not third in line, equal to the two of you?

OEDIPUS: Yes, and for that reason the one who stands to benefit from the disgrace of the other two!

CREON: Not if you look at it from my point of view. First, consider whether anyone would swap sound sleep for constant anxiety merely to obtain a negligible increase in power. I have no desire to be king! I have royal power enough already, with none of the attendant responsibility! I am a pragmatic man, and hardly so foolish as to desire honours that come without benefits. As things stand, everyone fawns over me, and I haven't an enemy in the world: on the contrary, those who desire something from you curry favour with me, because I am their best hope for success. Why would I give all of this up to join some plot against you? A lazy man can be relied upon never to turn traitor, and even if I could be prevailed upon I would certainly never turn against you.

So put me to the test – go to the oracle at Delphi and ask the Pythia if I tell you true. If you prove that I conspired with that prophet, then you will sentence me to death with not one vote but two: yours and my own. But don't condemn me on guesswork, without proof. Bad as it is to see a criminal go free, it is infinitely worse to convict an innocent man. Myself, I would sooner die than throw away a true friend, and in the fullness of time you will know that you had one in me. The passage of time gradually reveals the just man, though he was ruined in a single day.

CHORUS: It is good advice, my lord, for someone not known to be desirous of committing injustice – for those who jump rashly to conclusions are liable to rash action as well.

OEDIPUS: When treason flares like wildfire, one must move quickly to stomp it out. If I sit and watch, the plan will be accomplished, and I destroyed.

CREON: What, then? Will you send me into exile?

OEDIPUS: Hardly – it is unwise to exile conspiracy: one kills it, so it cannot try again.

CREON: I have done nothing to deserve death!

OEDIPUS: You deserved it the moment you proved the depth of your resentment for me.

CREON: Why won't you believe me!

OEDIPUS: Because, for the prophecy to be untrue, you must be a liar.

CREON: You're insane!

OEDIPUS: I know I am no murderer.

CREON: You will be if you do this terrible thing.

OEDIPUS: You are a traitor!

CREON: And if you've gotten it wrong?

OEDIPUS: I have no choice but to rule.

CREON: Not if you rule badly.

OEDIPUS: O, my city! What you are forcing me to do...

CREON: It is not yours alone.

CHORUS: Stop my lords! Jocasta joins us from the house at the critical moment. Let her put an end to this dispute!

Enter Jocasta

JOCASTA: What is this commotion? Aren't you ashamed to waste time on bickering while the country is wrecked? Please, Creon, go home. Don't allow whatever this is to get out of hand...

CREON: Sister, your husband just offered to kill me for the good of the city.

OEDIPUS: He's arranged a coup d'état against the two of us.

CREON: If I have done any of the things with which you charge me, may I live in misery and die under a curse.

JOCASTA: Oedipus, in the name of the gods, I beg you to believe him! He has sworn by the gods! Respect that, for my sake, and the sake of all those assembled here.

CHORUS: My lord, we beg you, be persuaded...

OEDIPUS: In what way?

CHORUS: He has never been a danger in the past, and now he has sworn to the gods: please respect the power of the oath!

OEDIPUS: Do you realise what you ask of me?

CHORUS: We do.

OEDIPUS: Then tell me, what do you advise?

CHORUS: He is your friend. He has made an oath before the gods. You must not defile it with a dubious charge.

OEDIPUS: Do you not see that by exempting Creon from death or exile you condemn me to that fate?

CHORUS: Heaven forbid! In the name of brightest shining Apollo, may we die friendless and forsaken by the gods if that was any part of our intention! But the plague infecting this land eats away at our hearts, too, and this quarrel of yours simply adds to the trouble we have already.

OEDIPUS: So be it. Let him go, even if means death or wandering for me. It is your plea that has convinced me, not his pleading, and wherever he goes from now on my hatred goes with him.

CREON: So your hatred is as strong now when you have set me free as it was when you condemned me. It must be difficult to be you. It should be difficult to be you...

OEDIPUS: Go now, before I change my mind.

CREON: I go, knowing that I would have been very hard done by indeed, by you, if they had not been here to save me...

Exit Creon

CHORUS: Lady, you should accompany him inside – he is very shaken.

JOCASTA: I'll join him when I have found out what happened here.

CHORUS: Certain accusations were made, and hard words spoken.

JOCASTA: On both sides?

CHORUS: Yes.

JOCASTA: What did they say?

CHORUS: I think it in the best interest of the country that we don't repeat it.

OEDIPUS: Do you see what you have done? Despite your normally excellent judgment, you place me in danger by softening my anger.

CHORUS: Lord, I say again that you should know we would go mad if we were ever to turn away from you. You piloted our country safely out of a sea of troubles, gave it a fair wind and prosperity. Now we merely pray that you can do it again.

JOCASTA: My lord, I beg you to tell me what made you so angry?

OEDIPUS: I will tell you, for I trust your judgment, my wife, far more than I do theirs. It was Creon, and the snare he laid for me.

JOCASTA: But tell me plainly how the fight began!

OEDIPUS: He says that I murdered Laius!

JOCASTA: He actually spoke those words?

OEDIPUS: No, he sent in his pet prophet to deliver the news for him!

JOCASTA: A prophet! Is that all? Let me tell you a little something about prophets.

Laius once received an oracle – I won't say that it came from Apollo himself, but from one of his 'servants' – that he would die at the hand of his own son. As a result of this prognostication my son was taken from me when he was not yet three days old. Laius fastened his ankles together and had him left to die of exposure on the mountain. And we know, do we not, that Laius was murdered by foreign brigands at a place where three roads meet?

That's prophets for you, so pay no attention to their prattling. If a god feels the need to tell you something, surely he requires no intermediary, least of all a man...

OEDIPUS: O Jocasta, what you have just said... I am reeling...

JOCASTA: What's wrong, my darling – why are you so pale?

OEDIPUS: Did I just hear you say that Laius was murdered at a triple crossroads?

JOCASTA: That was the story at the time...

OEDIPUS: Where, exactly?

JOCASTA: The place is called Phocis, where the road from Thebes forks, one road going to Delphi and another to Daulis.

OEDIPUS: And... exactly how long ago...?

JOCASTA: Not long before you arrived and became the king of our land.

OEDIPUS: O Zeus, do you conspire against me now?

JOCASTA: But what is this all about, Oedipus? What is it that oppresses you so?

OEDIPUS: Please, just describe Laius to me – what he looked like... how old he was...

JOCASTA: Why, he had a dark complexion, with his hair just going white and... well, he looked somewhat like you, actually.

OEDIPUS: Oh, gods, why me! In my ignorance have I called down curses upon myself?

JOCASTA: What are you saying? The look on your face...

OEDIPUS: I begin to have the terrible notion that the prophet might have the sight after all... I will know one way or the other if you will tell me just one more thing...

JOCASTA: I'll try to do as you ask, but Oedipus, how you do frighten me...

OEDIPUS: Did he travel with a small group, or did he have a large entourage with him, appropriate for a king?

JOCASTA: Altogether there were five of them, including his herald – and the one wagon, which carried Laius.

OEDIPUS: O god, I can see it! Who told you this, woman?

JOCASTA: A slave, the only one to return alive...

OEDIPUS: Is he still here, in our household?

JOCASTA: No. When he came back alone to Thebes, and saw that Laius was dead and you were in power, he begged me to send him out to the fields and pastures. He wanted to be as far away from the city as possible, and so I sent him there, for he was a good slave and I owed him far more than he asked.

OEDIPUS: Could he be brought back here, as quickly as possible?

JOCASTA: Yes, but why?

OEDIPUS: I fear I may have said too much already. I wish to see him.

JOCASTA: And so you shall, but I do think that I deserve to know what worries you so, my lord.

OEDIPUS: I won't keep it from you. After all, who has a better right to hear what I am going through, since it is your story as well?

My father was Polybus of Corinth, and my mother was Merope, a Dorian. I was brought up in Corinth and in the fullness of time became its leading citizen. Then something happened – a curious thing, which made me curious – but perhaps, in hindsight, it would have been preferable had I left it alone...

There was a dinner, and one of the guests had too much to drink. He accused me of not being my father's son. I was incensed, but managed to control myself, and the next day I went to my parents and told them what he had said. They were extremely upset that the man had slandered me so, and made him pay a heavy price for insulting me.

They thought they had done everything necessary to comfort me, and yet the matter continued to prey on my mind, for now the story was circulating about the city. I didn't tell my parents, but on my own departed for the oracle at Delphi and the Pythia there. Apollo sent me away from there feeling very hard done by, because it seemed to me that I hadn't gotten the information I'd asked for, though he told me other things... Terrible things, inevitable horrors in store.

He said that I was destined to sleep with my mother and to father children upon her so polluted that no mortal should ever have to look on them. He also said that I was bound to murder the very man who'd given me life.

When I heard this, obviously it was impossible for me to return to Corinth. Vowing never to set foot there again, and using the stars as a guide, I set a course designed to take me as far from Corinth as I could go, so that the revolting prophecy could never be fulfilled.

In my trek from Corinth I passed through the region where you say your king met his death. And I am going to tell you the truth here, woman. At a place where three roads met – right at the cross-roads – I met with a herald and a man riding in a wagon, and all the rest, just as you described it to me.

When we came abreast, the driver tried to force me from the road and, angered, I struck him. Seeing this, the old man they were escorting waited until he was even with me and clouted me upon the head with his spiked whip, but I repaid him in full. In fact, I took a stick and knocked him backward out of the chariot... and then I killed them. All of them.

...If that stranger had any connection to your Laius – could there be anyone more wretched than I? Any more hated by the gods, since no citizen or stranger may allow me into his home, since no-one may talk to me, and everyone must drive me from their door? I am doubly condemned by curses I brought down upon myself, one many years past, and the other mere minutes ago. I have desecrated the bed of the dead man with the very hands that murdered him. Is it possible that I should be such a criminal? Can it be that I am so utterly unholy and unclean, when my entire life has been dedicated to averting such a fate?

Did I not exile myself from my own country, never to see my loved ones again, in order to frustrate the prophecy and avoid being joined in marriage to my mother and killing Polybus, my father? And now this? Surely everything that's happening to me can only have issued from the cruel imagination of some malicious god? O great gods in the sky, I hope – I pray – please let me vanish from the earth before I see myself so stained and disgraced in the eyes of men.

CHORUS: My lord, all of this is terrible, but until you meet the witness you must cling to hope.

OEDIPUS: Yes, I'll await the herdsman...

JOCASTA: But what will you do when he gets here?

OEDIPUS: If he repeats one peculiarity of his story as you told it to me just now, I will have escaped disaster.

JOCASTA: What was it?

OEDIPUS: You said that he reported Laius and the others attacked by a group of thieves, in which case I couldn't be the killer, for I was alone.

JOCASTA: Well, that's just what he told everyone when he returned here, and he can't very well take back his story now, since the whole city heard it, not just me. And even if he were to change it, it still wouldn't prove that Laius's death was in any way connected to Apollo's oracle, since he couldn't have died at the hand of his own son. That poor baby was already long dead, and that is why I do not believe in prophecy.

OEDIPUS: You're probably right. All the same, send someone to fetch that slave. I'll leave no stone unturned.

JOCASTA: I'll send for him right away, but do come inside now, and I will do my best to soothe your troubled mind.

Exit Oedipus and Jocasta into the palace

CHORUS:
We should all pray that the future always finds us unquestioned in our purity, our words and deeds sanctified by the high laws, conceived in heaven above, whose father is Olympus. Mortal men did not create these laws and time will not erode them. The god is great in these laws, and the god never grows old.
    Hubris gives birth to the tyrant. Hubris, when it overflows and gluts itself on things neither proper nor appropriate, causes man to climb too high and walk off of a cliff and find no foothold in the air. And though we pray that the god does not damp that special strain of ambition that benefits the city, if a man lives arrogantly in word or in deed, oblivious to Justice and irreverent toward the gods, we hope he meets the miserable fate proper to overweening pride. If he takes what is not his, and does not fight impiety, and touches what ought not to be touched – then may that man fail in his ambition, and no shield protect him from the arrows of god. For if evil is rewarded, why would we honour the gods with dances? No longer would we go in reverence to the sacred centre of the earth – Delphi – nor the temple at Abae, nor the one in Olympia, if oracles no longer told the truth. O Zeus, if you are rightly called ruler, do not let this matter slip your attention, for the oracles given to Laius are fading, becoming lost to memory before they are seen to come true, and when the word of Apollo is unclear – half-remembered – then is the power of the gods dying...

Enter Jocasta

JOCASTA: Princes of this land, I think it advisable that we visit the temples with gifts to the gods – garlands and incense – for Oedipus is disordered in his mind, bewildered by stress and grief, and weighing by old prophecies each new tidbit of information that he hears. Previously the most rational of men, now he is wracked with uncertainty, and seemingly at the mercy of whoever is speaking to him at the time. I cannot get through to him.

Thus I make an offering to you, Lycian Apollo, your temple being the closest, that you might bring some resolution – some light out of the darkness. The captain of our ship has been shaken, and when we see it we are afraid.

Enter a Messenger

MESSENGER: Strangers, is this the house of King Oedipus?

CHORUS: It is, stranger, and he is at home. This fair lady is his wife and the mother of his children.

MESSENGER: Well then, may the blessing of the gods always be upon you, as you are the wife of that noble man!

JOCASTA: And upon you, courteous stranger – but tell me, what brings you here?

MESSENGER: I come with good news for you and your family, my lady.

JOCASTA: Indeed? And where do you come from?

MESSENGER: Corinth, with news that will bring you much pleasure, though perhaps a measure of sorrow as well.

JOCASTA: How's that? What manner of news could have the power to do both at once?

MESSENGER: I am told that the people of Corinth are ready to make your man their king.

JOCASTA: How is this possible? Isn't old Polybus still in power?

MESSENGER: No, he is dead and buried.

JOCASTA: Oedipus's father is dead?

MESSENGER: I swear on my life that it's true.

JOCASTA (TO HER ATTENDANT): You, servant, go in at once and inform your master! Prophecies from the gods, indeed! How long did Oedipus avoid his beloved father for fear of killing him, as the oracle predicted, and now the man has died a natural death.

Enter Oedipus

OEDIPUS: What is it, Jocasta?

JOCASTA: Listen to what this man has come to tell you, and then lecture me some more regarding the truth of sacred oracles.

OEDIPUS: Who is he?

JOCASTA: He comes from Corinth with the news that Polybus is dead.

OEDIPUS: Can it be true? Please deliver your message, stranger!

MESSENGER: I thought this part was the bad news, and yet it appears to be occasioning much joy. Yes, yes, you may be sure that the man has passed.

OEDIPUS: Was he overthrown, or was it natural causes?

MESSENGER: It takes very little to guide old bodies to their final bed.

OEDIPUS: So then the poor man died from sickness?

MESSENGER: Yes, combined with old age.

OEDIPUS: Ha-ha! Well, dear wife, what need have we to resort to the oracle at Delphi, or spend our time 'bird watching'? They it was who told me I was doomed to kill my father, but now he sleeps his final sleep, with no help from yours truly – unless it was missing me that killed him! Whatever, Polybus is in Hades now, and he has taken those worthless oracles with him!

JOCASTA: What did I tell you?

OEDIPUS: Yes, you tried to talk sense to me. Fear sent me in a different direction.

JOCASTA: And now, at long last, you can let it go.

OEDIPUS: There is the second part of the prophecy. Should I still be afraid of my mother's bed?

JOCASTA: But why should you be? Don't you see we've just learned that chance rules everything, and that it's impossible to predict the future? The best any of us can do is to live day-by-day, as best we are able, and let the future take care of itself. Forget your mother: I imagine a great many men have been troubled by desire for their mothers, in dreams, but such things mean little to those who know how to bear life easily. You must learn to relax, my darling.

OEDIPUS: What you say is all very well, and if mother were dead, too, I would agree with you, but as long as she still lives – though I know you are right – I also know I will never entirely shake that superstitious fear.

JOCASTA: At the very least, your father's death should bring us some form of ease and comfort.

OEDIPUS: Yes, but as ever, it's the living I fear.

MESSENGER: But who is this woman who frightens you?

OEDIPUS: Her name is Merope, old man – she was Polybus' wife.

MESSENGER: Why on earth should you be afraid of her?

OEDIPUS: On account of a horrible prophecy.

MESSENGER: Can this prophecy be spoken aloud? Or does sacred law forbid others to hear it?

OEDIPUS: I once received an inconvenient oracle from Apollo to the effect that I would sleep with my mother. It's the reason I've lived so far from Corinth all these years, which turned out rather well for me, but, still, it appears to me one of the greatest of joys to be able to look upon the faces of your parents.

MESSENGER: This was the reason you left Corinth?

OEDIPUS: Yes, old man – that and because I didn't want to kill my father.

MESSENGER: Well, then I am happy to be in a position to release you from this fear once and for all.

OEDIPUS: If you could achieve that feat you'd be in line for quite a reward from me, indeed.

MESSENGER: The reward I anticipated in coming here was the benefit I would receive when you come home to Corinth.

OEDIPUS: Then I fear you are doomed to disappointment, for I'll never go to Corinth while either of my parents are there.

MESSENGER: Son, it is very clear to me that you've been grossly misinformed.

OEDIPUS: How so, old man? In the name of the gods, don't keep me in suspense!

MESSENGER: If your parents are the only reason you fled your home...

OEDIPUS: Yes, for fear that the word of Apollo would prove true.

MESSENGER: Then you have no reason to be afraid!

OEDIPUS: But why?

MESSENGER: Because Polybus was not your blood relation!

OEDIPUS: What are you saying? Was Polybus not my father?

MESSENGER: No more than I am!

OEDIPUS: Then why did he call me his son?

MESSENGER: You see, you were a gift, delivered to them by these very hands.

OEDIPUS: Yet still he loved me so greatly!

MESSENGER: Because he could not have children himself.

OEDIPUS: How is it you came to give me to him?

MESSENGER: I found you in a wooded area near Mount Cithaeron, not far from here.

OEDIPUS: What were you doing there?

MESSENGER: I was in charge of a flock of sheep in the foothills.

OEDIPUS: A shepherd then, a wandering servant?

MESSENGER: And also the man who saved your life.

OEDIPUS: And what was my condition when I was found?

MESSENGER: Your own feet will confirm that what I say is true.

OEDIPUS: That ancient affliction of mine?

MESSENGER: Yes, I had to unbind your ankles, which had been pierced through with a pin.

OEDIPUS: I have carried the terrible scar of it from infancy!

MESSENGER: And it was on account of the injury you received the name that you have now, that is to say 'Swollen Foot'.

OEDIPUS: By the gods, who did it to me? My mother? My father?

MESSENGER: I never knew, but the man who gave you to me would perhaps know better.

OEDIPUS: So you didn't find me? Someone gave me to you?

MESSENGER: Yes, another shepherd.

OEDIPUS: Who was he? Do you know his name?

MESSENGER: I believe he was reputed to be one of Laius' men.

OEDIPUS: The former king of this land?

MESSENGER: Yes, the man in question was one of his slaves.

OEDIPUS: Is the man alive? If so, I must talk to him!

MESSENGER (TO THE CHORUS): Those who live here would know better than I.

OEDIPUS: Is there anyone among you who knows anything about the shepherd of whom this man speaks? Have any of you seen him here or in the fields? If so, tell me – it's time that everything was finally brought to light!

CHORUS: It is possible he may be referring to the very man you sent for just now. But perhaps Jocasta here would be in a better position to know.

OEDIPUS: Yes, Jocasta, you know the man we just sent for! Is he the same man that this fellow is talking about?

JOCASTA: Why are you asking about this? Just leave it alone! Chase what he said out of your mind – it's a waste of time, I tell you!

OEDIPUS: But I can't, woman! Not when I'm so close to finding out the truth of my birth!

JOCASTA: I beg you, in the name of the gods, don't do this if you value your life, or mine! Haven't I suffered enough?

OEDIPUS: Why should you worry? Even if it turns out I am the offspring of three generations of slaves, you'll still be noble-born.

JOCASTA: All the same, listen to me, I beg you! Don't do this!

OEDIPUS: I will not be deflected from the truth!

JOCASTA: I ask you for your own good, out of loyalty to you!

OEDIPUS: The things that I thought had been 'best' for me have plagued my life up till now!

JOCASTA: O you poor man – may you never find out who you are!

OEDIPUS: Will no-one fetch that shepherd? Go and bask in your rich and noble birth and let me find out mine!

JOCASTA: O Oedipus, O poor Oedipus – I did what I could... I'll say nothing more...

Exit Jocasta into the palace

CHORUS: What awful pain drives your wife into the house, Oedipus? Doesn't her silence mask some terror?

OEDIPUS: Let the chips fall where they may – I need to know! My good wife is embarrassed at the very possibility of my low-birth, but whatever my true parentage I will always think of myself as the child of Fortune, for she has always been good to me, and I will never disavow her. Fortune is my mother, the seasons my brothers, and it is they who have determined if I am small or if I am great. Lacking a parent like Fortune, perhaps I would be the kind of man who could renounce his search for truth, but that man is not me...

Chorus:

If we can be prophets for a moment, O Mount Cithaeron, we know that tomorrow's moon will praise you as nurse and mother of Oedipus, and we honour you with dancing who grants such favour to our leader. O Apollo, to whom we cry out, may our prayers be pleasing to you!

Who was it that bore you, child? Was it one of the nymphs who slept with Pan? Or some woman with Apollo, who loves to spend time in mountain pastures. Or was it perhaps Hermes, who comes from Cyllene? Or did Dionysus who lives on the mountains receive you as a lucky find from his nymphs with whom so often he dallies?

Oedipus: Though I've never met him, I wager I see off in the distance the shepherd we've been waiting for. He's about the same age as our old messenger from Corinth here, escorted by my servants. But all of you have the advantage of me and should know, as you've seen the man before.

Chorus: Yes, we recognize him, to be sure. He was one of the most trusted servants of Laius' household, though only just a shepherd.

Enter the Shepherd

Oedipus: Stranger from Corinth, is this the man?

Messenger: Yes, it is he.

Oedipus: You there, old man – look at me now and answer true. Did you once belong to Laius?

Shepherd: Yes, I was his slave. But I wasn't purchased – I was born into his house and brought up here.

Oedipus: And what did you do here?

Shepherd: For the greater portion of my life I was with the herds.

Oedipus: Whereabouts in this country did you usually work?

Shepherd: In the vicinity of Mount Cithaeron.

Oedipus: And do you recognize this man? Have you ever had dealings with him?

Shepherd: Not that I can recall.

Messenger: It's not so surprising, my lord Oedipus, but just let me stir up the past and his memory. For I know that he's very familiar with the land around Mount Cithaeron, and he'll surely remember how he and I spent three years in that area. He had two flocks, I had one, and we spent the time together six months at a time, from spring until autumn. Then when winter came I would take my flock back to Corinth and he would take his to Laius' stables.

Is that not so, old friend?

Shepherd: What you say is true... It's just so very long ago...

Messenger: Now, tell me – do you remember giving me a child to take and bring up on my own?

Shepherd: Why on earth are you asking me this question?!

Messenger: Because this man here is that child.

Shepherd: Damn you! Couldn't you keep your trap shut about this?

Oedipus: Don't you hit him, old one! From the sound of things it would appear you are the one that deserves striking.

Shepherd: But, o noblest of masters, what is my crime?

Oedipus: Withholding what you know about the child this man speaks of!

Shepherd: Because he doesn't know what he's talking about! He's wasting your time, milord!

OEDIPUS: If asking nicely won't loosen your tongue, I'm sure pain will...

SHEPHERD: Please, no – by the gods, I'm an old man, please don't torture me!

OEDIPUS: That's it – someone bind his hands behind his back! Quickly!

SHEPHERD: O god, why me? What do you want to know?

OEDIPUS: Did you give this man a child?

SHEPHERD: Yes, I did – and I wish that I had died as soon as I did so.

OEDIPUS: You may yet get your wish, if you don't tell the truth here today.

SHEPHERD: And a worse death is surely in store for me if I do.

OEDIPUS: Do you intend to be difficult, old one?

SHEPHERD: No. I said I gave him the child.

OEDIPUS: Where did it come from? Was the child your own, or someone else's?

SHEPHERD: I got it from someone else.

OEDIPUS: From whom? Whose house?

SHEPHERD: O gods, master, please don't ask me any more.

OEDIPUS: Your life is forfeit if you force me to ask again.

SHEPHERD: It was someone from the house of Laius!

OEDIPUS: A slave? Or was it someone in the family?

SHEPHERD: O god, I've come to the point where to speak may seal my doom!

OEDIPUS: Mine, too – but hearing it is something that I have to do.

SHEPHERD: The child was Laius's, but she who is inside the house could better tell you how it was.

OEDIPUS: Was it she, then, who gave the boy to you?

SHEPHERD: She did, my lord.

OEDIPUS: For what purpose?

SHEPHERD: So that I could destroy it.

OEDIPUS: How could a mother be so cruel?

SHEPHERD: Because she feared a prophecy.

OEDIPUS: What prophecy?

SHEPHERD: The story was that the child would grow up to kill its parents.

OEDIPUS: Then how did you come to give it to this man?

SHEPHERD: My lord, I felt sorry for the child, and I thought the man might take it safely to another country, as he is a foreigner. But it turns out that in saving the infant we only invited hideous calamity...

OEDIPUS: O god! O god! It all becomes clear to me now! O light, let me look on you one last time, for I have been revealed as cursed from my very birth – cursed in my marriage, cursed in my killing!

Exit Oedipus into the palace

Exit the Messenger and the Shepherd

CHORUS:

> O generations of men, our lives amount to little. Does any man, anyone at all, find true contentment, or is it all just a reflection in a pond that too quickly drains away? You are my model, Oedipus - your fortune is the same as ours, your fate, unfortunate Oedipus, to teach us that no man is to be envied.
>
> It was you whose arrow found the mark of success and happiness when you defeated that hook-clawed maiden the Sphinx. You stood like a fortress guarding our country, warding off death. That is why you are called king and receive the greatest honours, ruling mighty Thebes.
>
> But now is there another story sadder than yours – pain so cruel, or ruin so final? Who else has experienced a reversal of fortune so total? Famous Oedi-

pus, the same harbour that sent you forth as a child received you as a husband. How is it that the fields your father plowed remained silent for so long?

All-seeing time has found you out despite all efforts to evade the nets of fate, and judges your marriage not a marriage, for the begetter of the children is one of them. Oh son of Laius, we wish now for your sake that we had never seen you and lament on your behalf, for you restored our lives to us and we are used to speak your name before we sleep.

Enter the Second Messenger

MESSENGER: Honoured elders of the land, what sad acts you will hear of, what horrors you will see, what mourning you will now endure if you are true to the house of Laius. For there is no river great enough to wash away the stain on this house – the horrors it conceals are too great.

CHORUS: We very much doubt that anything could be worse than what we just learned. How do you propose to top it?

MESSENGER: The news that I must impart is that our glorious queen Jocasta is dead.

CHORUS: O, the poor woman – what happened?

MESSENGER: She killed herself. You are to be spared the worst of it, since you were not there to see, but I must tell as best I can how the poor woman suffered.

She came back into the palace in a terrible state, raging, and ran straightaway to the marriage chamber, tearing her hair with both hands. Once inside she slammed shut the doors and shouted out the name of Laius, so long dead, and groaned to recall how they made love – cursed the bed in which she had conceived a double tragedy – the act that caused her to bear a husband of her husband and the accursed children of her own child.

Just how she died we did not see, for at that moment Oedipus burst into the palace shouting so that we were distracted, staring wide-eyed as he rushed about in great agitation demanding a sword and the whereabouts of Jocasta, who rather than wife he called his mother! Some god must have told him, for it wasn't any of us who were standing by, but with an agonizing bellow he rushed the bedroom doors, wrenched the bolts from out their sockets, and charged inside.

And there he found her hanging with the twisted rope around her neck. When he saw her, and with a fearful scream, the poor man untied the knot, and the unhappy woman was lowered to the floor. What we saw him do next is near unspeakable... For tearing out the long golden pins that fastened her robe, he raised them high, and struck them into his own eyes, shrieking as he did so that they would no longer look upon the evil he had done, and in future he would see only in his inward darkness those people he should never have seen, for his cursed eyes had failed to recognize the people he needed most to know. Bellowing such as this he struck his eyes time and time again, until the mess ran upon the cheeks of his face like black rain.

These horrors are not down to one person, but husband and wife, united in their misery. Where once was happiness – and it was happiness – now there is nothing but sadness, ruin, destruction, death, shame, every evil that can be named – not one of them is missing.

CHORUS: Is there no relief at all for the poor man?

MESSENGER: He is begging for someone to open the gates so that all of Thebes might see the patricidal motherfu– I cannot say it! It is unholy! He means to cast himself from out this land, for he would not bring down on this house the curse he proclaimed against the plague-criminal of Thebes before he knew that was himself.

He will need a guide to lean upon, for he is too broken to make his way alone. But you'll see for yourselves: the bolts of the gates now open, and the wretched figure who stands there would inspire pity in his worst enemy.

Enter Oedipus, now blind

CHORUS: Oh, what a terrible thing for anyone to have to see! Has there ever been a more appalling tragedy than this? You poor man, was it madness or some god who guided your hand, for you are unbearable to look at, though we have so many questions and need to understand so many things...

Exit the Messenger

OEDIPUS: I am destroyed... so now, sorrow, where will you lead me? Where will my cries echo next? O my fate, how changed you are!

CHORUS: Changed into something awful, beyond that we can bear to see or hear.

OEDIPUS: Darkness covers me like a hideous cloud – I can't resist it – and again and again I feel the stabbing pain, remembering the deeds I have done!

CHORUS: Is it any wonder?

OEDIPUS: Ah, my friends, I recognize your voices even in the darkness. Do you linger still to comfort the untouchable man, despite the ban your king placed upon him?

CHORUS: Alas, poor friend, what compelled you to destroy your own sight?

OEDIPUS: It was Apollo – yes, it was Apollo, my friends, who has done this to me. But no hand other than my own took my eyes. For what need have I for eyes, when there is nothing in this world I might look upon with pleasure?

CHORUS: We understand and sympathise...

OEDIPUS: What could I ever look upon now and love – what greeting bring pleasure to my ears? Take me away, please, as soon as you can, for I'm utterly lost – cursed – the mortal most despised by the gods!

CHORUS: Now that your thoughts are bitter as your fate, how we wish we had never known you, for it is too painful.

OEDIPUS: O damn the man who took the cruel shackles from my feet and saved me from death... What he did was no kindness, for it would have been better had I died back then and never become a burden to my friends.

CHORUS: Perhaps it would have been best...

OEDIPUS: Now Oedipus is the new name for infamy.

CHORUS: It seems as though one would be better off dead than blind and living.

OEDIPUS: Don't tell me what I would better have done, for how could I bear to lay eyes upon my father in Hades, or my poor mother, having done things to both of them for which I ought to be hanged? Could I ever again look at my children with these eyes, born as they were? Nor could I view the city, its wall, its towers, the statues of the gods and its temples, for I robbed myself of all of these things the moment I proclaimed my new law casting out the impious one – for I could not exempt myself!

Now that I have admitted the stain that covers me, could I ever look on my people again without shame? Never! In fact, if I could have devised a way to cut off the sounds from my ears without consigning myself to Hades, then I wouldn't have hesitated to close this broken body off from this world of pain and hurt entirely, blind and deaf.

O Mt. Cithaeron, why ever did you reject me? Why didn't you take and then kill me at once?

O Polybus and Corinth and the house that I used to call my father's! How wonderfully you cared for me, and hid my secret sickness, so that only now am I revealed evil, and born of evil ancestors!

O the three roads, and the hidden clearing in the forest in which those three roads met, paths that drank my father's blood, offered up to you by my own hands – do you remember the deeds you saw me perform?

O marriage, marriage – you were the cause of my birth, and the cause of my destruction. You produced fathers who were brothers, children born of incest, a bride both wife and mother to her husband – all things that are considered foul in this world.

But since it is unseemly to speak of vileness, I beg you: hide me abroad, somewhere far away from here, or failing that kill me, throw me in the sea – either way, conceal my corruption from the eyes of innocent men. Come closer – don't be afraid – no man will endure these pains other than me.

Enter Creon

CHORUS: Here is Creon, whose duty it is as sole remaining ruler of this land to make that decision.

OEDIPUS: O god, what can I say to him? Why would he listen? For I've behaved so abominably toward him.

CREON: Oedipus, I come neither to mock nor to reproach you for past wrongs, but if you have so little shame you would stand in the sight of men, at least show some respect for the sun, and conceal from Helios a corruption so great that neither earth nor rain nor light should touch it. Take him inside the house at once! It is only fit that relatives bear witness to the evils of relatives.

OEDIPUS: In the name of the gods, since against my expectation you've come in noble spirit to a man who treated you so badly, I beg a favour of you, for your sake and not my own.

CREON: What is it you ask of me?

OEDIPUS: Cast me out of this land with all speed, to some place where I will never again hear another human voice.

CREON: I would have already done so, but first wished to learn from the gods what I should do. I have sent for a fresh oracle.

OEDIPUS: But the previous instructions were quite clear: the patricide is polluted and must be cast out, or executed.

CREON: Yes, but in time of great need it seems advisable to double check.

OEDIPUS: Would you take such care in regard to a man as horrid as I?

CREON: Yes, and this time you should put faith in the god's pronouncement.

OEDIPUS: In the meantime, I ask that you do right by your sister, who lies within the house: bury her properly. As for me, don't let the city of my father find me living in it tomorrow. Let me go to my mountain, Cithaeron. Mother and father wanted me to die there, so there I will die.

This much I know: neither sickness nor any other random evil will kill me, for I should not already have been saved from death if some strange destiny did not still await me. Well then, let my fate guide me where it wishes.

Don't worry about my two boys, for they are men now and wherever they are will be able to survive. But my two poor girls... Their table was never far from mine, and they always shared in everything I touched. We have never been apart, and I beg you, my lord Creon, please take care of them. If I could only hold them one last time, and cry together...

Enter Antigone and Ismene, the daughters of Oedipus

What is this? Do I hear my darlings crying? I do! Creon takes pity upon me and sends my daughters to me – could it be true?

CREON: It is. I brought them here because I know full well how much you love them and what comfort they bring you.

OEDIPUS: Bless you for doing this: may the gods show you a better path than the one they offered me.

Girls, where are you? Come take my hands – do you see what the hands of your brother have done to your father, who once looked at you with such gleaming eyes? Unknowing, unseeing, I brought you both forth from the very same place I was born.

I weep for you though I cannot look upon your faces. I weep for the bitterness that will be in your lives, and the cruelty of the life you'll now be forced to lead.

What curse is there you haven't inherited? What gatherings will you attend that you won't leave in tears rather than sharing in the pleasure of the event? And when you are of marriageable age, where is the man who will dare take on the disgrace that clings to this family as a dowry? There is no one, my poor children: it is quite certain that you are to die childless and alone.

O Creon, as you are the only father left to these girls, their real parents now perished, do not let them wander, beggars, spinsters, and outcasts. They are your own blood, please remember: take pity on them, and don't let them suffer because of me. Please agree, noble Creon, and touch my hand.

If you were older and wiser, children, I'd offer you advice – but as things are, please just pray, for my sake, that you may make a better life than your father had.

CREON: Enough of these tears, now – it's time to go inside.

OEDIPUS: I'll do so if I must, though it gives me no pleasure.

CREON: Everything that runs its proper course is good.

OEDIPUS: I go inside on one condition.

CREON: Tell me.

OEDIPUS: That you send me from this land.

CREON: You ask a gift only the god can give.

OEDIPUS: But I am hated by the gods!

CREON: Then perhaps you'll get your wish.

OEDIPUS: Do you really think so?

CREON: I am not accustomed to saying things I do not mean.

OEDIPUS: Then lead on.

CREON: Let go of the children and come along...

OEDIPUS: No! Don't take them away from me!

CREON: You just can't help yourself, can you? Your days of trying to control destiny are at an end, Oedipus.

Exit Creon and Oedipus

CHORUS: All who live in our ancestral Thebes, look upon the storm that has buried poor Oedipus. He who knew how to solve the riddle of the Sphinx, a mighty man, whom every citizen used to envy and admire.

It is wise always to look to the end, and make no judgment as to whether a man is favoured in this human race until he has crossed the finish line.

Translated from the Greek by Stephen Russell, PhD
English by Jonathan Allen and Stephen Russell

Chapter 9
Plautus
Pseudolus

The Story: Plautus was a Roman playwright who was famous for his comedies. Many of his comedies remind us of those from Shakespeare, who was deeply influenced by Plautus – and they also remind us of the rather benign twists that we often see on standard television sit-coms.

Pseudolus is the story of a clever slave who tries to help the son of his master marry the young prostitute with whom he has fallen in love. This play, along with Plautus' *Miles Gloriosus* and *Mostellaria*, were the basis for the play and film *A Funny Thing Happened on the Way to the Forum*.

Characters

    Pseudolus, the slave of Simo
    Calidorus, the son of Simo
    Ballio, a pimp
    Simo, an old Athenian
    Callipho, Simo's friend
    Phoenicium (silent)
    Harpax, a soldier's servant
    Charinus, a friend of Calidorus
    Slave Boy, of Ballio
    Cook, of Ballio
    Cook's Helpers
    Simia, the slave of Charinus

Pseudolus

Scene: The play is set in Athens – right outside the houses of Ballio, Simo, and Callipho.

Prologue: If any of you want to stand up and stretch your legs, now would be the best time to do it. A play by Plautus is about to begin.

Enter Calidorus, looking tired and despondent, followed by Pseudolus

PSEUDOLUS: You're very quiet, young master. If I could somehow figure out from your silence what's bothering you, I'd be happy to save us both the trouble – me the trouble of asking you, and you the trouble of having to answer me. But since that's not possible, I'm going to have to ask you a few questions. Master, can you tell me why it is that you've been going around these past few days as if you're half-dead? And why do you keep carrying that tablet with you wherever you go, and covering it with your tears, instead of finding someone that you can use to confide? Come on, master, tell me what the problem is. Let me know the thing I don't know.

CALIDORUS: Oh Pseudolus, I'm the most miserable man in the world!

PSEUDOLUS: Jupiter forbid it!

CALIDORUS: Oh, Jupiter has nothing to do with it, I'm afraid. I'm suffering from the miseries of Venus, not Jupiter.

PSEUDOLUS: But then why don't you just tell me all about it? You used to tell me all about your various problems – I was your chief confidant.

CALIDORUS: And you still are.

PSEUDOLUS: So then tell me what's bothering you. I'll help you in whatever way I can – with money, service, or good advice.

CALIDORUS: Oh, just look at the letter on this tablet – and you can see for yourself the misery that's overtaken me.

PSEUDOLUS: Sure, just hand it here. But...what's this thing here? What does it all mean?

CALIDORUS: What is it?

PSEUDOLUS: All these letters up here, they look like parents, jumping on top of their children, which are the letters down there.

CALIDORUS: Oh, why are you making a joke of this?

PSEUDOLUS: Maybe a Sibyl could make something out of this gibberish – but I don't think that anyone else could decipher it.

CALIDORUS: But why are you so mean to those little letters there? They sit there on that sweet little tablet and were written by that beautiful hand...

PSEUDOLUS: What? I didn't realize that chickens had hands. For surely this is the scratching of a hen or chicken.

CALIDORUS: Oh, you're a moron – either read the letter or give it back to me.

PSEUDOLUS: Ok, ok, I'll read it. Uh-hum...ok, I'm reading now – just give me your soul.

CALIDORUS: But I don't have my soul at the moment.

PSEUDOLUS: Then you'll have to find some from somewhere.

CALIDORUS: No, you won't get it from me. My soul is right there in that tablet - in that wax. It's there and not inside me.

PSEUDOLUS: Oh Calidorus, I can see that you've got a girlfriend!

CALIDORUS: Where? Where is she?

PSEUDOLUS: She's right here, in this wax on the tablet.

CALIDORUS: Ugh – may all the gods and goddesses above...

PSEUDOLUS: ...preserve me and keep me safe.

CALIDORUS: For a moment there you made my heart leap up just like the grass in the summer – but just as quickly as I rose, the very next moment I died.

PSEUDOLUS: Well, then just keep quiet while I finish reading.

CALIDORUS: Then why don't you just read it?

PSEUDOLUS: "Phoenicium to her lover Calidorus...through the messenger of wax and wood and letters...sends her dearest wishes...and wants to have her own dearest wish from you...she wants it with all of her soul...with tears in her eyes...her mind and her soul tremble in distress..."

CALIDORUS: Oh, it's horrible Pseudolus! I don't know where I can find her dearest wish so that I can send it back to her.

PSEUDOLUS: And what's her dearest wish?

CALIDORUS: Money...silver...

PSEUDOLUS: You want to send her something in silver when all that she sends you is something in wood? Man, quite that horrible businessman you are!

CALIDORUS: Just keep reading – you'll soon see why it's so important for me to find some money from somewhere.

PSEUDOLUS: "I have been sold, my dear...my master, the pimp, has sold me to a foreigner, a Macedonian soldier...for two thousand drachmas. The man paid fifteen hundred already before he went away...and so now we are only waiting for the remaining five hundred. The soldier left a kind of token with the pimp here...his likeness that is stamped into the wax with his ring...and when a man arrives with the same seal then I am go be sent with him...the day is set for this too...it's the next Dionysia."

Wait – that's tomorrow!

CALIDORUS: Oh, and now you see why I'm doomed! You need to find a way to help me, Pseudolus!

PSEUDOLUS: Just let me finish the letter...I see there's more here.

CALIDORUS: Yes, please keep reading, and I can imagine that it is her voice that is speaking the words. Please, go on, even though this is a bittersweet potion for me to drink right now.

PSEUDOLUS: "This is the end of all our happy days and hours...our sweet meetings...our talk and games and little jokes...those kisses and all the sweetness...all that cuddling...our bodies so close...the soft lips and the sweet nibbling...the little caressing and squeezing of my breasts...and the sweet delights of love...all of this is now gone, sent out into the winds...it's all thrown away for eternity...if you can't find a way to help me, or if I can't find a way to help you. I've told you everything that I know...so now I am waiting to find out how much you love me...or whether you just pretend to love me. Farewell."

CALIDORUS: It's such a sad, terrible letter, Pseudolus.

PSEUDOLUS: Oh, it's terrible.

CALIDORUS: But doesn't it just make you cry?

PSEUDOLUS: No – I've got eyes that are just like stones...can't make them cry no matter what.

CALIDORUS: How is that?

PSEUDOLUS: Oh, my family is full of dry-eyes.

CALIDORUS: And...are you going to help me?

PSEUDOLUS: But what can I do to help you in this?

CALIDORUS: Oh, why me?

PSEUDOLUS: You can save the "why me's" – that much I can do for you.

CALIDORUS: Oh god – I don't know that I can find a way to borrow that kind of money.

PSEUDOLUS: Ah...why me?

CALIDORUS: And I hardly have a penny of my own!

PSEUDOLUS: Ah...why me?

CALIDORUS: And tomorrow that man is going to take my girl away!

PSEUDOLUS: Ah...why me?

CALIDORUS: Is this the way you are going to help me?

PSEUDOLUS: I only do what I can, sir. I've got a whole pile of "ah...why me's" stored away here in our house – enough to last a lifetime, I'd venture.

CALIDORUS: But I really need your help. Can't you lend me just one drachma – I promise to give it back to you tomorrow.

PSEUDOLUS: My god, I don't think I could come up with a drachma, even if I sold my body. What do you want with the money anyway?

CALIDORUS: I want to buy a rope.

PSEUDOLUS: What for?

CALIDORUS: To hang myself. I've made up my mind that I am going to take my refuge in everlasting darkness before the day ends.

PSEUDOLUS: Wait – then how am I going to get my drachma back? Is that your great idea – to kill yourself and cheat me out of a drachma?

CALIDORUS: It's clear to me that life is now just impossible...if she has been ripped away from me and led off.

PSEUDOLUS: But this is nothing to cry about you silly fellow – you'll survive this.

CALIDORUS: But why shouldn't I cry? I mean, I don't have any money and have no idea where to turn to get any money...

PSEUDOLUS: Hmm...if I read this letter correctly, you're going to have to cry tears made out of silver. But your tears are doing as much good as trying to catch rain with a net. But just don't you worry – I won't abandon my master when he is in love. Somehow or other, I'm going to find a way to find some money for you. I can't yet exactly say where it's coming from yet – I only know that it will come. I can tell by the twitching of my eyebrow.

CALIDORUS: I only wish that your actions would be equal to you words.

PSEUDOLUS: C'mon, you know what kinds of crazy things I am capable of doing once I raise my magic wand!

CALIDORUS: The hope of my entire life now is in your hands.

PSEUDOLUS: Well what if I promised that I would get you two thousand drachmas? Come on then – tell me that I should get you the money, so that I will have to fulfill my promise. C'mon – make the demand...I'm dying to make the promise.

CALIDORUS: Ok – Pseudolus, will you find me two thousand drachmas today?

PSEUDOLUS: Indeed I will! Now don't bother me anymore about it. If I can't find any other victim to give me the money, then I'll have to look to your father and ask him.

CALIDORUS: Oh bless your soul! May you always be mine! But, since I am a proper and dutiful son, I have to say this – why not ask my mother as well?

PSEUDOLUS: You just leave it to me and then you can rest easy on whatever eye you choose.

CALIDORUS: Whichever eye? Don't you mean whatever ear?

PSEUDOLUS: Uhmm...I like to play around with the common expressions a bit. Now nobody can say that he didn't hear word of this and that he wasn't notified. To all the people here in the assembly, all the audience as well, and to all my friends and acquaintances, I hereby announce that today you should all be on your guard against me and that none of you should trust me today!

CALIDORUS: Shh! Please, for heaven's sake – be quiet!

PSEUDOLUS: What's the problem?

CALIDORUS: I just heard the door of Ballio – the pimp – make a sound over there.

PSEUDOLUS: I'd like to hear the sound of his legs – breaking.

CALIDORUS: Ohhh – and here comes the old bugger now. Let's hide back here in the corner.

Enter Ballio, leading various slaves with a whip

BALLIO: Come on then – come on out here then, all of you now – you lazy good-for-nothings. I was a fool to buy you and I am a fool to keep you...not one of you has any idea how to behave properly. I wouldn't get anything out of these people if I didn't use my trusty whip here. I've never seen men who look so much like asses – and with your skin so tanned and calloused that the whip hardly does a thing. If you try to beat them, then you just end up feeling more pain than they do.

But this is the sort of people these wasters of my whip are. They've only got one basic rule in life – whenever you can see a chance, then you just rob, steal, lift, and take anything you can...then run. This is just how they live, and you're left with the result that it would be better to leave wolves in charge of a henhouse than to leave these people in charge of your house.

All the same, when you take a glance at them they don't seem so bad fellows to look at – but it's their work that's horrible. Now, all of you there, just pay attention to me. Listen carefully to me, if you don't turn your attention to me, if you can't get those sleepy expressions off your faces and look alive, then I'll gladly take this whip here and draw some lovely patterns on your body with it – you'll be more colorful than the finest drapes and rugs, that's for sure! Yesterday I told you what I wanted from you, and I told all of you what your place was, but you little devils are so stupid that it looks like you all need a beating to remind you where you stand.

That's just how you all are – tough and dumb, and so much so that I and my friend the whip here can't make much of an impression on you. Just look at these slaves – they're not even paying the slightest attention to me. Oh, I'll show you to ignore me! There! How do you like the feel of that! That's what happens when slaves ignore their masters. Now I want all of you to line up in front of me here. But you there – yes, you. Go get some water for the cook's copper pot. And you over there, with the axe – I am making you head of the chopping division.

SLAVE: Sir, but the axe is really dull.

BALLIO: I don't care at all about that. You fellows are pretty worn down as well – with beatings. But do you think that makes me any less interested in getting you to work? Now you there, it's your job to make this place shine – so go to it. As for you, I want you to put the drapes on the couches. And you over there – go clean the silver and make sure that it's shiny. And so when I get back from the forum, I'd better find all these things swept, mopped, polished, cleaned, and nice and shiny.

It's my birthday today; in fact, I want all of you to help me celebrate it. Hey you there – yes you, boy – go get meat, some bacon, some sweetbread, and then throw some cow's udder into the pot so it can stew. Do you hear me? I plan to entertain some very high-up gentleman, and I want to do it in style, so that they'll think that I have a lot of money. So get inside, the lot of you, and get yourselves busy. I don't want to have any delays when the cook gets here. I'm going to the market, to see what kind of deal I can make with the fish-seller.

So let's go boy. You go first – I want to keep an eye out so that no one steals our money from you.

But wait! There's just something that I forgot to say back at home. Girls, where are you? Come out here right now and listen to me.

Enter several of his prostitutes, including Phoenicium

Now then, my darling girls, listen up. I know that you spend your time in idle luxury, relaxing, and living the easy life – you women with all your wealthy gentlemen callers. Today I'm really going to put you to the test, for I am going to prove which one of you has looking to her own freedom and which one of you is just thinking about her own stomach, or about sleep. Today I'm going to find out who will be a freed-woman and who will be a slave. Make sure that I see a lot of gifts from your lovers come flooding in today. If I don't get enough supplies for the next year on this very day then tomorrow I'll put you out on the streets. It's my birthday today, and you all know it.

So where are they all now? Where are all those boys, those fools, for whom you light up their hearts with love, to whom you give the joy of life, the sweet kisses they desire? Hmmm...where are they? I want to see them standing right in front of this house, holding out massive amounts of presents for me. I mean, why do you think that I gave you so many jewels and clothes and all the things you need? And what have you given back to me yet in return for it? Nothing – except a loss of money. The only passion you really show is for wine. Your stomachs are filled right up with it, while I have nothing.

Ok, the best thing for me to do is to talk to you individually, one by one, to keep any of you from saying that she wasn't informed. Now just pay attention – all of you. I'll start with you, Hedytium. The grain dealers love you – the men who visit you could bring enough grain here to last me for a year. You need to see to it that they bring us all lots and lots of grain – so much that they'll have to change my name from Ballio the pimp to Ballio the grain king.

CALIDORUS (TO PSEUDOLUS): Are you listening to that criminal talk? Have you ever heard such pompousness?

PSEUDOLUS: Yes, he sounds like quite a scumbag – but shh, let's keep watching him to see what happens.

BALLIO: Aeschrodera, now you listen here as well! The men who come to see you are the butchers – they compete with pimps like me, because we're both in the business of giving people what is bad for them, and what they don't want. I want you to get your lover-boy friends the butchers to bring in a room's worth of meat by the end of the day or...I swear I'll stretch you out on a meat hook myself.

CALIDORUS (TO PSEUDOLUS): God, hearing him talk makes me so angry!

PSEUDOLUS: I can't believe that the young men of Athens put up with a fellow like this one here. Where are all of them – where are the young men hiding – those lusty young studs who visit this pimp for his girls? Why don't they just all band together and rid the city of this fellow? But, of course what I just said is foolish – for why would they try to rid the world of the fellow who has enslaved their passions!

CALIDORUS: Oh, please be quiet.

PSEUDOLUS: What's wrong with you?

CALIDORUS: When you talk I can't hear a word that he says.

PSEUDOLUS: Ok...ok...I'll keep quiet.

CALIDORUS: I'd be happier if you actually did so rather than merely say so.

BALLIO: And as for you Xystilis, just listen up. The men who are in love with you deal in oil and they have lots – and I mean lots – in supply. So if I don't have oils brought here in the bagful by tomorrow, then I'll wrap you up in a bag and taken to the whorehouse down the street. You'll be given a bed there, but it won't be to sleep on, if you catch what I am trying to say to you.

Do you catch what I'm telling you? With all those friends of yours just awash in so much oil, have you even done one thing to help your fellow salves here earn a drop of it so they can pretty up their precious heads? Or that I can use in my salad dressing? But I get it – oil isn't your thing...you like the wine. Fair enough, but you'd better just do what I say or you'll really be sorry.

And now, as for you Phoenicium, the darling of the wealthy gentlemen, always so close to buying your freedom, always good at making an agreement, but horrible at seeing it through. You'd better get me lots and lots from your friends today or I'll make sure that your backside is tanned purple. Oh, I'll do it too!

Exit Ballio, leading all of his prostitutes inside his house

CALIDORUS: Oh Pseudolus, did you hear what he just said?

Pseudolus: Of course I did – I'm giving it my full attention.

Calidorus: I have to stop him from putting my sweetheart out on the streets – what do you think I should send him as a bribe?

Pseudolus: Just relax – I'll do the worrying for both of us. This guy is an old friend of mine – we know each other very well. Since today is his birthday, today I'll send him a whole lot of trouble.

Calidorus: But what's the point of that?

Pseudolus: Just you worry about something else – I've got this.

Calidorus: But...but...

Pseudolus: But nothing!

Calidorus: But my heart is in such pain.

Pseudolus: Just act like a man.

Calidorus: I can't.

Pseudolus: You need to try.

Calidorus: But how can I stop feeling this way?

Pseudolus: Just try thinking about something hopeful rather than letting your emotions get the better of you.

Calidorus: Pish posh – what's the good of being in love if you can't act like a fool?

Pseudolus: Oh, good grief.

Calidorus: Oh Pseudolus, please let me act like a fool – please.

Pseudolus: Do as you like – I'll just be somewhere else...see you later...

Calidorus: No wait! Just stay here and I'll do anything you say.

Pseudolus: Now you're thinking.

Enter Ballio, with the boy who is carrying his money

Ballio: Ok, it's time to head off – let's go, boy!

Calidorus (to Pseudolus): Hey – he's leaving! Why don't you call him back?

Pseudolus: You just calm down – I'll do everything just when it's the right time.

Calidorus: But he's going to leave!

Ballio: C'mon there boy – why on earth are you such a slowpoke?

Pseudolus: Hey there, birthday boy...yoo-hoo, birthday boy! I'm talking to you there, birthday boy. Come back here – hey! – look over here. You may be busy, but we want to talk to you.

Ballio: What's this? Who's bothering me when I'm in such a hurry?

Pseudolus: An old friend.

Ballio: An old friend means a dead friend. I need friends for the present.

Pseudolus: Now you're being rude.

Ballio: And you're being a pest!

Calidorus: Stop him, Pseudolus – grab him.

Ballio: Let's go boy! Forward!

Pseudolus: Come on Calidorus, we'll intercept him over here.

Ballio: Go to hell, whoever you are!

Pseudolus: But I want to talk to you.

Ballio: However, I don't want to talk to you – either one of you. C'mon here boy – let's go.

Pseudolus: But aren't I allowed to have a word with you?

Ballio: You're allowed – I just don't want to.

Pseudolus: Not even if it can bring you profit?

Ballio: Can't I just go on my way?

Pseudolus: No...no...not so fast.

Ballio: Let go of me!

Pseudolus 163

CALIDORUS: Ballio, just listen!

BALLIO: If all you have are words, then I'm not listening.

CALIDORUS: But I've always paid you before

BALLIO: But I'm not interested in what you have paid in the past.

CALIDORUS: And I'll definitely pay you when I finally have the money.

BALLIO: So when you do have the money, then – and only then – you can have the goods.

CALIDORUS: Oh no – then all of the money and gifts I gave you were just a waste.

BALLIO: Don't waste your time, young fool. Speeches will do you nothing when you have no assets.

PSEUDOLUS: But at least have a look to see who this gentleman is.

BALLIO: I've known for a long time who he was – but who he is now, well, he can know that for himself. Now boy, let's go!

PSEUDOLUS: But can't you just give us a moment – it'll be profitable for you.

BALLIO: Well that's completely different. You know even if I were in the middle of making a sacrifice to Jupiter almighty, with all of the materials right there with me at the altar, and if I suddenly saw the chance for a profit, I'd completely forget about that sacrifice. I mean, profit is a type of religion, and you can't afford to show disrespect to that god, no matter what.

PSEUDOLUS (ASIDE): Wow – he mocks the very same gods that all men worship.

BALLIO: Hmm...maybe I will talk to you, then, after all. Hello then – a really good day to you, the dirtiest and slimiest slave in town!

PSEUDOLUS: And in turn may the gods give you all that you so duly deserve – in other words, may they help you not one bit.

BALLIO: How are you doing, Calidorus?

CALIDORUS: I'm in complete agony, I'm in love, and I'm broke...

BALLIO: That's very sad – but I can't run my house on feeling sorry for people.

PSEUDOLUS: Yes, of course – we all know what you're interested in. But do you know what we have in mind?

BALLIO: It's pretty easy to make a guess – you want to see me ruined.

PSEUDOLUS: Well, that's true, but that's not the reason that we shouted at you to come back. Now, please just pay attention.

BALLIO: Fine – I'm listening, but please come to the point quickly, because I've got a very busy day in front of me.

PSEUDOLUS: This fellow here, my master Calidorus, feels really sorry and ashamed that he didn't pay you the two thousand drachmas that he promised you for his girl's freedom on the day he promised to pay you.

BALLIO: I imagine he is sorry – but it's so mush easier to be sorry than it is to be angry. He feels ashamed because he hasn't paid, but I feel angry because he hasn't paid.

PSEUDOLUS: Oh, but he will pay it – he will. Just give him a few more days. He's afraid that you're going to sell her because you're angry with him.

BALLIO: But he had the chance to pay me the money long ago, if he really wanted to.

CALIDORUS: But how could I? What if I didn't have the money?

BALLIO: If he's really in love, then he'd have found a way, a loan maybe, to take from a friendly money-lender, with the bit of interest, or maybe you could have just robbed your father.

PSEUDOLUS: Rob his father? You're absolutely evil – I feel sorry for anyone who gets advice from you.

BALLIO: Pimps don't give good advice.

Calidorus: Besides, I don't think I'd be able to rob my father. The old man is way too clever, way too sharp. And yes, even if I could, then my duty as a son would stop me.

Ballio: Of course – so late at night you can then snuggle up to your father, instead of Phoenicium. But since your duty as a son is so important, may I ask if everyone is like your father to you? Isn't there anyone you can ask for a friendly loan?

Calidorus: Well, I don't think the term "friendly loan" even exists these days.

Pseudolus: Come on Ballio – nobody's so foolish as to lend money these days, especially after those nameless banker's made their money, closed their shops, and stole everyone's money. Since then, everyone's careful about loaning money.

Calidorus: Oh, this is horrible. I can't find a penny anywhere. It's so horrible to be dying of two things at once – love and lack of money.

Ballio: Well, maybe you could buy some oil illegally and sell it in the market. I imagine you'd make twenty thousand drachmas in no time at all.

Calidorus: But I can't – the law says that I'm still a minor, so no one will give me credit.

Ballio: I know that law – it's the same one that keeps me from giving you credit.

Pseudolus: Right, credit? Good grief, haven't you already taken enough from him already?

Ballio: A real lover is the man who is prepared to keep on giving forever. He has to pay and pay and pay. When all the money is then gone, then he can give up loving.

Calidorus: Don't you have a heart at all?

Ballio: No – not when you come here with nothing. Your words don't mean anything to me. All the same, I wish you well and I'll be happy to see you up and alive.

Pseudolus: What do you mean? Does he look dead to you or something?

Ballio: Well, if he comes to me with that kind of story, then he's certainly dead to me – that's for certain. Life ends for a lover the moment he has to come to a pimp with such requests. But, my boy, you can come to me any day you like – just be sure that you bring money with you. As to your current lament, it's like you're asking your stepmother for pity.

Pseudolus: What? Were you married to his father?

Ballio: Good god no!

Pseudolus: But just do what we ask of you, Ballio. I promise you, if you're nervous about trusting him, then you can place your trust in me. Just give me three days and I'll be sure to find the money somewhere on land or sea.

Ballio: I'm supposed to trust you?

Pseudolus: Why not?

Ballio: Well, because I'd rather trust a wild dog with a feast of lamb meat than trust you.

Calidorus: I've treated you so well, and this is how you're going to treat me in return?

Ballio: So then what would you have me do? What am I supposed to do?

Calidorus: I just want you to hold onto her for the next six days or so, and please don't sell her and make me, her lover, die of misery.

Ballio: Well, then cheer up – I'll wait six months even, if you like.

Calidorus: Oh, that's amazing. You dear, wonderful man!

Ballio: But there's more – I can give you even better news.

Calidorus: How could the news get even better than this?

Ballio: Because your girl Phoenicium is no longer for sale.

Calidorus: She isn't?

BALLIO: I assure you that she isn't.

CALIDORUS: Oh Pseudolus, go get some offerings, so we can make sacrifices to this Jupiter almighty here. This man is a greater Jove to me than Jove himself.

BALLIO: Oh please, don't do that – just give me a few cutlets of lamb...that will be fine.

CALIDORUS: That's it – go Pseudolus, go get some lambs – don't you hear what our Jupiter here just told us!

PSEUDOLUS: I heard, I heard. I'll go, but it will take me a while – I'll have to run out as far as the city gates, I think.

CALIDORUS: Why so far?

PSEUDOLUS: Because that's the place where I'll find the best killers. And while I'm there I'll get some birch sticks to help make this sacrifice to your Jupiter here a success.

BALLIO: Oh, you can just go to hell.

PSEUDOLUS: Well, that's where the Jupiter of pimps is going.

BALLIO: I bet you'd be happy to see me dead.

PSEUDOLUS: How so?

BALLIO: Because once I'm dead, then there'd be no one more useless than you.

CALIDORUS: What happening here? Tell me, please, are you serious? Are you telling me that my Phoenicium is for sale or not?

BALLIO: Of course not – I sold her long ago!

CALIDORUS: What? How?

BALLIO: How? Just as she is - her clothing isn't included, but all of her bodily organs are included.

CALIDORUS: You've sold my girl?

BALLIO: Yup – for two thousand drachmas.

CALIDORUS: For two thousand drachmas!

BALLIO: Or four payments of five hundred – whatever. I sold her to an officer from Macedonia, and he's already given me fifteen hundred.

CALIDORUS: What is all this that you are saying?

BALLIO: That your girl has been turned into my money.

CALIDORUS: Why did you do that?

BALLIO: Because I could – she was mine, after all.

CALIDORUS: Pseudolus – quick, go bring me a sword!

PSEUDOLUS: What do you want with a sword?

CALIDORUS: To kill this man, and then end my life.

PSEUDOLUS: Why don't you just end your own life? His life will be over soon by starvation anyway.

CALIDORUS: Ballio, please answer me – you shameless liar, didn't you just swear to me that you would sell her to anyone but me?

BALLIO: That's right – I said that.

CALIDORUS: And you made a formal promise.

BALLIO: Yes, the promise was all formal and properly dressed up to boot.

CALIDORUS: And so you've broken your oath – you rascal.

BALLIO: Yes, but I've got money now at home. I may be a rascal pimp, but I now have cash at home. You may be an honest man, and come from an honest family – but you don't have a penny to your name.

CALIDORUS: Pseudolus, please stand on the other side of him, so we can assault him with all kinds of bad names.

PSEUDOLUS: Sure thing – I'll do this as quickly as if I were running to the court to gain my freedom.

CALIDORUS: Give him some really bad insults.

PSEUDOLUS: Oh, I'll insult you Ballio...you evil man.

BALLIO: It's true – I am.

CALIDORUS: Rascal!

BALLIO: That's true as well.

PSEUDOLUS: Scoundrel!

BALLIO: Indeed!

CALIDORUS: Grave robber!

BALLIO: Fair enough.

PSEUDOLUS: Dirt-bag!

BALLIO: I like that one.

CALIDORUS: Deceiver of friends!

BALLIO: That's what I do.

PSEUDOLUS: Parricide!

BALLIO: Ok, now it's your turn Calidorus…

CALIDORUS: Blasphemer!

BALLIO: That's just about right.

PSEUDOLUS: Perjurer! Liar!

BALLIO: Oh you're starting to become boring.

CALIDORUS: Law-breaker!

BALLIO: That's better.

CALIDORUS: Corrupter of youth!

BALLIO: Oh, exactly.

CALIDORUS: Thief!

BALLIO: Boring!

PSEUDOLUS: Criminal!

BALLIO: Lame!

CALIDORUS: Public nuisance!

BALLIO: It's that obvious?

PSEUDOLUS: Imposter!

CALIDORUS: Scum!

PSEUDOLUS: Pimp!

CALIDORUS: Slime!

BALLIO: Wow – the two of you are an amazing choir!

CALIDORUS: You beat your father and mother!

BALLIO: Yes indeed – and I even killed them as well, since it was easier than having to feed them. Do you blame me for it?

PSEUDOLUS: Our words here are doing nothing – it's a complete waste of time.

BALLIO: Isn't there anything else that the two of you would like to add?

CALIDORUS: Is there anything at all that you're ashamed of?

BALLIO: Oh, I'd be rather ashamed of having to admit that I'm a suitor who hasn't a penny to my name, that's for sure. However, even though the two of you have heaped such abuse on me, I can still say this: that officer is supposed to bring the remaining five hundred today – and today is the deadline, according to our agreement – and so if he doesn't pay me, then I'll be forced to do my duty.

CALIDORUS: And what's your duty?

BALLIO: Why, you just bring me the money, young man, and I'll break the agreement that I made with him. My duty is always to follow the money. If I had the time, I'd stay and chat some more, but I'm really busy right now, you see. Just remember, if you don't have any money then it's useless coming to me and looking for pity. My thoughts are clear, and it's up to you to make of them what you will.

CALIDORUS: No, please just wait.

BALLIO: Sorry I've got a lot to do!

Exit Ballio and the slave-boy

PSEUDOLUS: And you'll have a lot more to do soon enough! I've got that fellow, I've got him. I swear, unless all the gods stand against me, then I'll skin him alive and fry him up right in front of us as if he were a fish. Now Calidorus, I need your help.

CALIDORUS: Gladly – at your service, my most helpful sire!

PSEUDOLUS: We need to siege and capture our position before the end of the day. And to do this we're going to need a man who's clever, wise, intelligent, careful, and crafty – someone who can carry out orders and doesn't fall asleep when he's on duty.

CALIDORUS: So then what are you going to do?

PSEUDOLUS: I'll let you know when it's the right time. There's no point in going over it twice – this play is long enough as it is.

CALIDORUS: That's a perfectly reasonable observation.

PSEUDOLUS: So then just you go and get your friend or friends to come here as soon as possible.

CALIDORUS: But I don't know whether I have any friends that I can count on.

PSEUDOLUS: Yes, I know how it is. So then you have another job – make out a list of your friends, and then select the one you can trust the most.

CALIDORUS: I think I can bring someone here soon...

PSEUDOLUS: So then go – by talking you're just wasting time!

Exit Calidorus

Good, so this leaves you here on your own, Pseudolus. What on earth are you going to do now? You talked a good game, but what does it all add up to? As for having any idea of what to do, or some money, I have absolutely no idea where to begin. But just like a poet, who takes his tablets and hunts for what isn't there and then turns his lies into truth, I'll make myself a poet now and try to turn my own lies into truth, to create something out of nothing.

It looks like I'm going to have to invent those two thousand drachmas, since it looks like they don't really exist anywhere on this earth right now. But in order to do that, I'll have to get my speaking skills under good control. And wow, here comes my master Simo right now, walking down the street with his neighbour Callipho. Hmmm...it looks like I'll have to dig the two thousand drachmas out of his coffin if I am going to give anything to my young master. I'll just get out of the way so I can listen to their conversation...

Pseudolus retreats, while Simo and Callipho enter

SIMO: You know, if the people of Athens were looking for a dictator among the good-for-nothing lazy spendthrifts and those who are obsessed with sex, then I don't think they could find a better candidate for the job than my son. My word, the whole city is talking about how he is trying to buy the freedom of his mistress, and how he is desperate to find the money for it. I heard about all of this from others, but I had a suspicion of for quite some time already, even though I didn't let on.

PSEUDOLUS: Hmph...oh, the old man has already figured it all out? This could be a fatal blow to my plan... the scheme may be ruined. So my plan to go looking for cash – through these two fellows – is at an end, and the road is completely cut off. Since he's already on to us, then there's nothing for this pirate to loot.

CALLIPHO: Well, if I could have things my way, I'd hang every last one of those who tell lies, along with the ones who listen to them. Come on, all those stories you hear about your son being in love with a prostitute and wanting to steal money from you – it's altogether likely that they're all a pack of lies. But even if these stories are true, what's the big deal? Really, has he done anything that's so surprising, especially as morals go these days? Is it some new thing for a young man to be in love and to want to buy the freedom of his lady?

PSEUDOLUS: Now that's a wise old gentleman there!

SIMO: It may be quite normal, but I still object to him doing it.

CALLIPHO: But you need to realize that it doesn't matter whether you object. Just like you weren't the same when you were his age! If a father expects his son to be morally perfect than he must have been so himself. But as for you, your sins and extravagances were so numerous that they could be divided up among the whole population of the city here – one for each man. Why is it so surprising if the son takes after his father?

Pseudolus: Ach, mein Gott! How rare it is to see such a clever and sensible individual. That's just the sort of father every son should have.

Simo: Who's talking here? Oh, it's that slave of mine – Pseudolus. He's the little devil who's corrupting my son – he's the lead tempter and tutor in my son's quest for vice. He's the one I'd like to see punished with my whip.

Callipho: But it won't do you any good to make such a display of your anger. It would be much better to approach him in good spirits and then ask whether these rumours are true. When you are in a difficult spot, it's best to be moderate.

Simo: Fair enough – I'll follow your advice on this.

Pseudolus: Whoa, Pseudolus, they're coming closer to you. Better get that speech of yours ready for the old man.

Greetings! First to my master, as it is always proper to do, and any other greetings that are left I send to his good neighbour here.

Simo: Hello there Pseudolus – and what are you doing today?

Pseudolus: Oh...not much...just standing here...as you can see.

Simo: Oh Callipho, look at the way he's standing there – doesn't he look as if he's pretending to be a prince?

Callipho: Well, he does seem to have quite the air of self-confidence – that's for certain.

Pseudolus: It's proper for an honest slave to have the air of a proud man, especially when he is in the presence of his master.

Callipho: Now Pseudolus, there are a few things about which we want to question you. Some things are a bit cloudy for us and we want you to clear them up for us.

Simo: Watch out Callipho – he'll soon make you think you're talking to Socrates rather than Pseudolus.

Pseudolus: Not at all. I'm very aware that you've had a poor opinion of me for some time now. I know that you think I'm very dishonest. It's almost as if you want me to be good-for-nothing and worthless. But I'm fiercely determined, sir, to be good-for-something.

Simo: Then please open up your ears, Pseudolus, and let my words find their intended destination.

Pseudolus: Please, sir, say what you wish – pay no heed to the fact that I am angry with you.

Simo: You, a slave, are angry with me, your master?

Pseudolus: You find that really amazing?

Simo: Well well, from the way you are talking, I guess I should take extra care not to make you angry. No no, I wouldn't want that. It seems that you have in mind to give me a different kind of beating than the one I usually give you.

Callipho: I do say – if you think that he's so dishonest, it seems to me that he's right to resent you.

Simo: Ok ok – let him be angry. I'll just take care that he doesn't do me any harm. Now Pseudolus, please answer a few of my questions.

Pseudolus: Sir, ask me anything you like. You can trust that my response will be like the one that comes from Delphi.

Simo: Good – then I'll hold you to that promise. Do you know anything about my son being in love with some music girl?

Pseudolus: Ja – dass ist richtig.

Simo: And that he's trying to buy her freedom?

Pseudolus: Dass ist auch richtig.

Simo: And are you somehow trying to figure out a way to get two thousand drachmas out of me by some sneaky scheme?

Pseudolus: Me? Take money from you?

Simo: Of course – so that you can give it to my son and he can buy his girlfriend's freedom? Isn't that true? Speak up!

Pseudolus: Auch richtig, Auch richtig!

Callipho: Oh my, he is confessing.

Simo: Isn't that just what I told you Callipho?

Callipho: Yes, I remember.

Simo: The very moment that you heard about all of this, why didn't you come and tell me?

Pseudolus: I'll tell you – because I wasn't going to be the one who continued that disgusting practice of a slave denouncing his master to his other master.

Simo: Callipho, you'd have him taken off and beaten for this, or sent to the mills, wouldn't you?

Callipho: I'm not so sure, Simo. I mean, has anything wrong really been done?

Simo: Absolutely – the greatest wrong.

Pseudolus: Please, don't bother Callipho. I think I have a good sense as to what is happening here. If I made a mistake, then it's my own fault. So please, dear master, give me your attention now and let me tell you why I kept you in total ignorance of your son's affair. I mean – I knew that if I told you I'd be sent to the mill and beaten.

Simo: And did you know that the same would happen to you if you didn't tell?

Pseudolus: Yes, I knew that too.

Simo: Then why wasn't I informed?

Pseudolus: Because it was a choice between two forms of evil – one that was close and one that was far away.

Simo: So what will the two of you do now? You won't get any money out of me, that's to be certain, especially now that I'm aware of what's going on. And I'll send out notices telling people not to loan you two a penny.

Pseudolus: Sir, as long as you are on this earth I'll never go begging anyone else for money, I swear in the name of Jove. But you're the man who'll give it to me – you're the one I'll get it from.

Simo: What? You're going to get it from me?

Pseudolus: Absolutely!

Simo: If I give you anything, may I lose an eye!

Pseudolus: Oh you'll give it to me – I'm only telling you so that you can be on the lookout for me.

Simo: I tell you, if you do somehow manage to get it, then I'll congratulate you for having performed a remarkable feat.

Pseudolus: And I'll perform it indeed!

Simo: And what happens if you fail?

Pseudolus: Oh, then you can beat me. But what if I'm successful?

Simo: Then I swear by the gods that you'll be able to keep what you get, without punishment.

Pseudolus: Please be sure to remember that.

Simo: Do you think that I can't figure out how to look out for myself after I have been warned?

Pseudolus: Oh…I warn you, sir – do look out, do look out. I tell you – nay, I warn you – look out, look out! With those very hands of yours you'll give me all the money today.

Callipho: Heavens! Simo, this man is quite the amazing specimen if he's able to do this.

Pseudolus: Oh I will do it, sir Callipho – and if I don't then you can take me as your slave.

Simo: Well that's quite the friendly offer Pseudolus – I guess you're not my slave now, or so it seems.

Pseudolus: And would the two of you like me to tell you something that would surprise you even more?

Callipho: Yes indeed – I think I could listen to you all day.

Pseudolus: Before I embark on the contest I just mentioned…I'm going to engage in another contest, one that will be remembered in all the ages.

Simo: What contest?

Pseudolus: Just you watch! I'm going to wage a little war on your neighbour there, the pimp Ballio. I'm going to use clever schemes and tricky stratagems in order to remove the music girl that your son is dying for from the clutches of that pimp. And I'll do all of this in style, I may add.

Simo: What on earth?

Pseudolus: And both of these contests will be completed by the end of the day today.

Simo: Well then, if you're going to achieve all of those accomplishments today, then you'll be an even mightier man than the king himself, I dare say. But if you happen to fail, I suppose you won't object to being beaten and thrown to the mill immediately?

Pseudolus: Of course – but not for one day only, but rather put me there for every day! But, if I happen to succeed, will you give me the money to pay the pimp, of your own free will?

Callipho: That seems like a fair request, Simo. Tell him that you will.

Simo: Wait a minute. I'm not so sure about this. How can I be certain that you two reprobates – you and Ballio, I mean – haven't conspired together and made some sneaky arrangement beforehand that will allow you to steal some money from me?

Pseudolus: Sir, do you think that I'd be so daring as to do something like that? My word – I'd have to be the boldest slave alive! Ok ok, master Simo, I'll state it this way – if in any way Ballio and I have been conspiring together to steal money from you, then you can take all the birch pens you can find and write all over me, just as if I were a parchment.

Simo: That sounds fair. Then start your contest as soon as you like.

Pseudolus: Callipho, sir, I'd like to ask you to put yourself at my service for this day, and please put aside any other business that you might otherwise have.

Callipho: I'm afraid that yesterday I already made plans to go out to the farm today.

Pseudolus: But can't you change your tactics, like a good soldier?

Callipho: Fair enough – I'll stay here on your account. I really do want to see these contests of yours, Pseudolus. And if it turns out that Simo here is unwilling to pay the money, then I'll gladly pay it myself.

Simo: Oh, I'm good for the money. My word is my bond.

Pseudolus: Of course you won't default, sir. Because if you did, then you'd never hear the end of it. Come now, both of you, let's get you gentlemen out of the way so that I can start my scheming.

Callipho: Indeed – you're the boss!

Pseudolus: But Callipho, please don't forget that I want you to be right here at home for when I need you.

Callipho: Oh yes – I'll be there.

Exit Callipho into his house

Simo: As for me, Pseudolus, I'm going to the forum, but I'll be back soon enough.

Exit Simo

Pseudolus: I have a suspicion, sir, that you'll be back really soon. As for you people out there – yes, you people in the audience – I think that you are a bit suspicious that I made all these promises to do such amazing deeds merely to keep the lot of you amused while this play rolls forward and that you suspect that I don't have any intention of doing what I said I would.

Well, that's where all of you are wrong. I'm going to keep my word on this – there's no doubt about that. But there's one other thing that I can promise you –

right now I have absolutely no idea how I am going to do this – I just know that I will do it. Anyway, what's an actor for if he can't pull off crazy stunts like these? And if he can't do this kind of thing, then he should get off the stage and make way for those who can.

Hmmm...I'd like to go inside for a bit, if you would all excuse me. I need to gather all my tricks and schemes and mull them over. But I'll be back soon enough – I won't keep you waiting long. In the meantime the flute-player here will help the transition to the next scene.

Exit Pseudolus, to the music of a flute-player

After a few minutes Pseudolus enters again, walking on to the music

PSEUDOLUS: Hallelujah! Everything's coming up just rosy for me – it's all just peachy. There's no reason to have any doubts, and no reason to fear, especially now that this scheme is stored away safely here inside of me. A plan like this can't go to someone who has a weak heart – no, things only go just as you make them go. Just take the job and do it.

And I can already see my forces lined up inside my mind, in double and triple lines of tricks and deceits. I'm ready to meet the enemy head on. And I can tell this to you here – to all of my friends out there in the audience – that through the noble spirit of my ancestors and my own tricky ways I'll easily defeat my enemy and take what is rightfully mine as the spoils of victory. This enemy, mine and yours alike, this Ballio, I will "ballistify" him completely. Just watch me.

That's right, I'm going to lead my forces there, and I'll take him by storm. I'll make the first attack right on Ballio's house here. Once that is accomplished – it will be an easy thing to do, to help out my allies – the next step is to lead my troops against this other house here, the one that belongs to my master Simo. Now this second victory will allow me to load myself up with all kinds of spoils of victory, and we'll all carry away more loot than we can possibly imagine. And my enemies will then know that I was born to defeat them and that I am just who I am. That's just who I am from my birth – I am born noble and it's right and proper for me to do great things and to leave a great name for myself from my deeds.

But who is this I see coming this way? Who is this unknown character who is walking into my midst and carrying a sword? What's he doing here? I need to hide and find out what he's up to...

Enter Harpax, while Pseudolus hides in the background

HARPAX: This appears to be the neighbourhood that he described to me, if my eyes are working properly. Yes, this is the place that my master told me about – he said the pimp lived in the seventh house from the gates of the city, and that's where I am supposed to bring this money and token for the girl. All the same, I really would like someone to give me more precise directions as to where this pimp Ballio lives.

PSEUDOLUS: Oh my, this is just the man I want. This is a new twist, but it also brings with it a new possibility. I'll start by working on the new scheme first, and let all those other ones that I just started sit on the shelf for now. Oh, I'll take care of this arms-bearing soldier in military style, I will!

HARPAX: Hmm...I think I'll knock at this door here and see if anyone's home.

PSEUDOLUS: Whoa! Just wait a minute there, sir, whoever you are. You will please stop that incessant knocking. I've come out here on behalf of all the doors to beg that you stop abusing them.

HARPAX: Are you this Ballio fellow?

PSEUDOLUS: Not really – you might say that I'm his Sub-Ballio.

HARPAX: What does that mean exactly?

PSEUDOLUS: I'm the fellow who takes stuff in and gives stuff out – the supply guy.

HARPAX: You mean the head butler, so to speak?

PSEUDOLUS: No no – I'm the man who gives orders to the head butler.

HARPAX: Are you a slave or a free man?

PSEUDOLUS: At this very moment I'm a slave.

HARPAX: That's what I thought, and it seems to me that you deserve to stay that way.

PSEUDOLUS: It may be worth your while to take a look in the mirror before you say bad things about others.

HARPAX (ASIDE): This fellow is up to trouble, I reckon.

PSEUDOLUS (ASIDE): The gods are on my side today! This fellow will be the base on which I'll commit all my forgeries and fakes today.

HARPAX (ASIDE): What's he saying to himself anyway?

PSEUDOLUS: Now now young man, look here.

HARPAX: Yes, what is it?

PSEUDOLUS: Have you been sent here on behalf of that Macedonian soldier? Are you the slave of the fellow who bought a girl from us here and who paid my master fifteen hundred and still owes him five hundred?

HARPAX: Yes, that's right. But how on earth do you know who I am? The fact is that before today I have never been in Athens and I've certainly never set eyes on you before.

PSEUDOLUS: I just thought that you looked like the kind of fellow who would come from that soldier. For when he departed a while back, today was the day that was fixed as the deadline for getting the final installment of the money to us, and it still hasn't arrived.

HARPAX: Oh no, I have the money right here with me.

PSEUDOLUS: So you have it right there?

HARPAX: I do.

PSEUDOLUS: Then why don't you just give it to me now?

HARPAX: Give it to you?

PSEUDOLUS: Why of course give it to me! I take care of all my master Ballio's business interests. I take in all the money for the house and I make all the necessary payments as well as settle any debts that need to be settled.

HARPAX: That's ok, thanks. I don't think I'll trust you with this money here. I wouldn't do it even if you were the accountant of Jove in heaven.

PSEUDOLUS: Come on, it would be settled this way in a real jiffy.

HARPAX: I'd rather keep it settled right here in this wallet.

PSEUDOLUS: Damn you! Who do you think you are that you can come here and throw accusations about that challenge my integrity and honesty? Do you think that I haven't been trusted with larger sums than that hundreds of times already?

HARPAX: It's completely possible for others to trust you in such a way, but that doesn't mean that I have to trust you in the same way.

PSEUDOLUS: You might as well just shout out that I am trying to cheat you of your money!

HARPAX: Ok, you could say that if you like – and it seems as if that is exactly what I do suspect you are trying to do. What is you name, by the way?

PSEUDOLUS: (aside) The pimp has a slave called Syrus, so that'll do.

My name, sir, is Syrus!

HARPAX: Syrus?

PSEUDOLUS: Yes, that's my name.

HARPAX: Well, all of this talk is just wasting time. If your master is home, whatever your name is, can you just call him out so that I can do the business with him that I was sent here to do?

PSEUDOLUS: Of course – if he were at home, then I would gladly call him outside. But if you'd like to give me the money, then the matter would be even settled more quickly than if you gave it directly to him.

HARPAX: Yes, but don't you understand what I'm telling you? My master sent me this money to use as a payment, not to lose it. I think that what's making you so excited is that you are dreaming about getting your hands on it. I'm not going to trust anyone except Ballio himself.

PSEUDOLUS: But he's not here right now. He's busy right now and is out dealing with a matter at the courthouse.

HARPAX: And I hope that it turns out well for him. So then as soon as I think it will be likely for him to return home, then I'll come back here.

But here's something that you can do, if you are his slave. You can take this letter and give it to him. On the top of it is the token that your master and mine agreed would work as a sign regarding the business about the girl.

PSEUDOLUS: Yes, I know it. He told me that he wanted the girl to be led away by the man who brought the money here to us and also carried a seal that was stamped with his own likeness. We have a copy of it inside the house.

HARPAX: You know the whole situation?

PSEUDOLUS: Why shouldn't I?

HARPAX: So then please give this token to him.

PSEUDOLUS: I'll do that. But what's your name, by the way?

HARPAX: It's Harpax.

PSEUDOLUS: Oh my – then you should run away, and be quick about it, Harpax! You don't like me and, by god, you won't get into this house, you harpy! We'll have none of you harpacity here, let me tell you.

HARPAX: I've earned that name because I'm well known for taking my enemies alive from the field of battle.

PSEUDOLUS: I imagine that it's more likely you received it from stealing pots from people's homes!

HARPAX: Not true at all. But do you know what I'd like you to do, Syrus?

PSEUDOLUS: I'll know when you decide to tell me.

HARPAX: I'm staying at a pub just outside the gates of the city here, the third house down. It's run by an old woman named Chrysis – she's fat and walks with a limp.

PSEUDOLUS: Well, what of it?

HARPAX: Whenever your master gets back, just come there and get me.

PSEUDOLUS: Yes sure – it would be my pleasure.

HARPAX: The journey here has really tired me out, as perhaps you can see, and I really need to rest and get some refreshments.

PSEUDOLUS: That sounds like a very smart and sensible plan. But please take care that I don't have to go hunting for you when I need to bring you back here.

HARPAX: That won't be a problem. I'm just going to have a small lunch and then I'll take a nice nap.

PSEUDOLUS: That's a pleasant thought.

HARPAX: Are we all set, then?

PSEUDOLUS: Oh yes – please go on your way and have your nap.

HARPAX: Indeed I will – see you soon!

Exit Harpax

PSEUDOLUS: Oh Harpax, be sure that they give you plenty of blankets! It will do you well to sweat all of this out of you.

Oh you wonderful gods above! The arrival of that man there just saved the day. I was far far far off the road, not sure where I was going, but this man set me right again in one fell swoop. You know, Fortune herself could not have made a more fortunate appearance than his fortunate arrival when he brought that fortunate letter with him. Why, this is a venerable cornucopia of goodness – everything that I want is stored up inside of it. Just peeing in I can see tricks, schemes, money, and the loving mistress for my young master!

Now's the time to be boastful and stick my chest out. I actually had the whole thing worked out already and set down to the smallest detail, exactly as I wanted them. Things were in their proper place and I knew each step that I wanted to take in getting that girl away from that pimp Ballio. But this is what always happens – the best laid plans of a hundred clever men can often be knocked down by one goddess – lady luck, Fortune. The truth is this – it's only the way that a man uses Fortune that makes men call him wise. Whenever we hear about someone who has had a run of good luck, we call him shrewd and clever, and we laugh at the fool whose situation has come to misery.

But it seems to me that we are all fools, even though we don't realize it, for we are always rushing so fast after one thing or another, as if we have any idea what is good for us and what isn't good for us. We leave behind certainty and look instead for uncertainty. And so keep at, doing the same kind of thing, until death finally creeps up on us.

Anyway – enough of this philosophizing. I do like to blather on, don't I? But, my gods, the lie that I just made up a moment ago, when I said that I was the servant of the pimp – that was worth its weight in gold, I must say. With this letter that I am holding in my hand I'm going to be able to trap three people – my master Simo, the pimp, and the fellow who gave it to me.

Oh, this is lovely! Here's just another thing that I was hoping would happen right about now, for I can see young master Calidorus coming this way right now, and he's bringing someone with him.

Enter Calidorus and Charinus, while Pseudolus hides in the background

Calidorus: There, now I've told all of it to you, the sweet and the bitter alike. You now know all about my love, my sadness, and my need.

Charinus: Yes, it's all quite clear to me. The only thing I want to know is what you need me to do?

Calidorus: I'm not sure yet. Pseudolus told me to find a friend who was willing to help and who had a lot of energy.

Charinus: Then you've done a very good job, since in me you've brought along a friend who wishes you the very best. But who is this Pseudolus? He is new to me.

Calidorus: Oh, he's a sight to behold – he's my chef de mission, so-to-speak. And he said he'd take care of the things I just told you about.

Pseudolus (aside): I must address this fellow in a loud and confident manner.

Calidorus: What's that deep voice I hear?

Pseudolus: Oh oh, dear lord and master, I, your slave Pseudolus, seek a word with you, my lord and king, so that I may give you happiness three times over, three triumphs and three schemes won over three adversaries. The details of this triumph are sealed inside this little document that I have for you here.

Calidorus: Oh Pseudolus – well done!

Charinus: He looks to me more like a villain in a tragedy.

Pseudolus: Sir, come this way, approach me, hold out your hand, and be prepared to take hold of your fortune.

Calidorus: Am I to give you the nickname of "hope" or "victory" right now, Pseudolus?

Pseudolus: Both titles will do nicely.

Charinus: Then I greet you both! But what is it that you have done?

Pseudolus: It's ok…things are fine…there's no reason for worry.

Calidorus: Oh Pseudolus, come on – this is the man I caught.

Pseudolus: You "caught" him?

Calidorus: I mean, this is the man I brought to help us.

PSEUDOLUS: Who is he?

CALIDORUS: His name is Charinus.

PSEUDOLUS: Fantastico! Well then, I'm very charmed to meet him, to be sure!

CHARINUS: Please, if there's anything I can do in this caper, just let me know.

PSEUDOLUS: Thanks very much. You are very kind, Charinus. But we really shouldn't bother you.

CHARINUS: Bother me? What do you mean? This won't bother me at all.

PSEUDOLUS: Ok, just wait a minute then.

CALIDORUS: What's that in your hand?

PSEUDOLUS: This is the letter, and the token, that I just intercepted.

CALIDORUS: Token? What token?

PSEUDOLUS: The one that was just brought here from that soldier. His slave brought it here along with the other five hundred drachmas. He was all set to take your girl away with him, but I just got the best of him with my trickery.

CALIDORUS: How so?

PSEUDOLUS: Come now – we're performing this play for the benefit of these spectators here, and they already know how, since they were here when it happened. I'll tell the two of you later.

CALIDORUS: So what do we do now?

PSEUDOLUS: You're going to take your girl in your arms at the end of the day when she is free and finally with you.

CALIDORUS: I am, really?

PSEUDOLUS: Yes, absolutely – you yourself will do this, as long as this head of mine survives, and as long as the two of you can find me a man in a hurry.

CHARINUS: What kind of man?

PSEUDOLUS: A bad man, a sly one, a clever one – one who, as soon as he understands the basic essentials of a task, he can complete it by means of his own intelligence and through his own ability. Oh, and one who is not too well known around here.

CHARINUS: Is there any problem if he's a slave?

PSEUDOLUS: Actually, I'd much prefer a slave to a free man in this matter.

CHARINUS: I think I can supply the very kind of man you're looking for – a clever and sly fellow whom my father just sent here from Carystus. He hasn't been outside the house since he arrived here and this is his first time in Athens.

PSEUDOLUS: You are a wonderful help. And I'm also going to need five hundred drachmas. But this will only be a loan, mind you, and I'll pay it back to you in full by the end of the day. The father of your friend Calidorus here owes me that much.

CHARINUS: You don't have to go looking for that. I can give it to you.

PSEUDOLUS: Oh you're arrival is absolutely perfect, my friend. And I'll also need a military coat and a sword and a hat.

CHARINUS: I can get you those as well.

PSEUDOLUS: That's amazing! Good work Charinus, you and I will make a wonderful team, I think. But as for this slave that just arrived from Carystus – does he have any sense?

CHARINUS: He's got the sense of a goat, if I am to judge from the smell of his armpits.

PSEUDOLUS: Then it would be good if the fellow wears a long-sleeved coat. But is he a sharp fellow?

CHARINUS: Yes, he's as sharp as concentrated acid.

PSEUDOLUS: And what if we wanted him to act all sweet – can he do that as well?

CHARINUS: No problems. Syrup, raison wine, honey-wine, grape-juice, honey in all kinds of different ways – there is talk that he once set up a whole refreshment stand on his own.

PSEUDOLUS: Wonderful. Well done, sir Charinus – you've bested me at my own game. But what is the name of this slave?

CHARINUS: His name is Simia.

PSEUDOLUS: And can he change directions quickly when he's in a tight spot?

CHARINUS: He can spin faster than a top.

PSEUDOLUS: Pretty clever, is he?

CHARINUS: Yes, but he's paid the price often enough for it through his bad deeds.

PSEUDOLUS: But what is he likely to do if he ever gets caught in the act?

CHARINUS: He's as slippery as an eel – so he'll get away.

PSEUDOLUS: And so he's reliable.

CHARINUS: As reliable as a law.

PSEUDOLUS: Well, to hear you talk, it sounds like he's quite the good fellow.

CHARINUS: Just wait until you meet him. As soon as he sets eyes on you, he'll straightaway tell you what it is that you want from him. But what is your plan anyway?

PSEUDOLUS: It's this. Once I have him all dressed up, then I want him to pretend that he is the slave of that soldier. He's going to bring this letter and token, along with the five hundred drachmas, to the pimp, and he'll take the girl from the pimp as well. There – now you know the entire plot. As for all of the details, I'll have to coach the fellow personally about how he'll be able to bring it off.

CALIDORUS: Come on then, Charinus, we'd better get going then.

PSEUDOLUS: You just bring this fellow of yours to me as soon as you can, and make sure that he's dressed up and all ready for action. Now hurry along!

CALIDORUS: We'll be ready before you are!

Exit Calidorus and Charinus

PSEUDOLUS: Get a move on, both of you! Well then, all of this finally sets my mind at ease. Any moment of doubt or uncertainty that I had has been removed. I can lead in all of my forces now, since all of the omens are in their rightful places. I'm feeling confident that I'll be able to finish off my challengers in this contest.

And so the next thing for me to do is to get to the forum myself so that I can prepare this Simia, and give him all of the necessary instructions for his task. He can't make any slip-ups here, but he'll have to pull this little caper off like an expert trickster. And, under my command, we'll soon take down the village of Pimpville in this contest!

Exit Pseudolus

After a few moments, a Slave Boy enters from the house of Ballio

BOY: When the gods make a boy the slave in a house that belongs to a pimp, and when they make him an ugly boy in addition to that, then as far as I can understand the situation, they've really made his life a bit of a miserable mess. That's the sort of slavery that I've found here, where all the troubles and miseries of every kind are placed on my shoulders. I can't find anyone who will take the slightest interest in me. So, since no one shows any affection in me, therefore I don't see the point in making myself look nice and presentable.

And now today is the birthday of this pimp here, so he's been threatening each and every one of us, from the youngest to the oldest, that whichever one of us didn't get him a wonderful birthday present, then that fellow would die tomorrow after being tortured in a most brutal way. Oh my, I don't have any idea what I can do now, looking at the situation that I am in. I'd love to be able to do what the others are doing, but I don't have any money, so I can't match the things that are done by those who have money or resources. So unless I can figure out a way to send the pimp a present today, by tomorrow I'll be in a whole mess of trouble.

That will be so horrible – why me? I'm still so afraid of my master and what he might do to me. I might be able to handle this, if someone could put something in my hand to make it worth my while. But it looks like I'll have to bite my tongue now, since I see the master coming home now and bringing a cook with him.

Enter Ballio, his Cook, and the Cook's Helpers

BALLIO: They call that place there Cooks' Market, but it seems to me that it should be called Crooks' Market. If I'd spent my whole life looking for a worse rascal than this cook that I've found right here, then I don't think I could do it. I couldn't find one who is more yacky, more boastful, more stupid, and more useless.

I can't figure out why Pluto haven't called him yet to hell, unless the god left him here so that he can make dinners for the dead bodies. Well, he's certainly the man who can please the dead customers – that's for sure.

COOK: If that's what you think of me, then why on earth did you hire me?

BALLIO: It was due to necessity. There was no one else. But why were you sitting there in the market – why were you the only one who still hadn't been hired?

COOK: Here's the reason. If it looks like I am a bad cook, the fault isn't mine, but rather it due to other people's meanness.

BALLIO: How do you reason that one out?

COOK: I'll tell you. When people come to hire themselves a cook, no one looks for the best and the most expensive. They only want to find the cheapest. That's why I was sitting along in the market today. Those cheap people only want to pay a measly drachma for a cook. Me, I'm not going to work for anyone unless they are willing two pay me at least two drachmas.

I'm better than those ordinary cooks, who season their plates with all kinds of condiments, treating your guests just as if they were all cattle, filling them up with all sorts of garbage to fatten them up. They give them cabbage, beets, spinach, and for flavour they add fennel, coriander, garlic, parsley, and horrible mustard – the kind of stuff that stings the eyes of the people who have to prepare it.

When these cooks come to prepare your meals, they don't use seasonings, but screech owls that go inside of your guests and peck the insides right out of them. And this explains why the people around here live such short lives – because they fill their bellies full of garbage like this. These are the kinds of things it's repulsive even to mention, let alone eat. In this region men eat the kinds of plants that animals won't touch.

BALLIO: Then what is it that you use? Do you have some heavenly seasonings that allow you alone to give people longer lives, since you find fault with everyone else's cooking?

COOK: Yes – that's absolutely right. Anyone who eats the food that I have made will live to be two hundred years old. You see, when I add a sprinkle of crinnelhogwobble in the pot, or even some ris-matazz, frizzle-frazzle, or even some oohyeah, the meal immediately heats up all on its own in no time at all. But those are the seasonings that I use for seafood – for land animals I use grigorgranga, rightonteria, and ineedadrinkia.

BALLIO: Oh! I pray that one day soon Jupiter will strike you for your spices and for all the lies you are telling!

COOK: But I still haven't finished.

BALLIO: Ok, then finish, and get this over with.

COOK: When all of the pots and pans are heated up, I open all of them – and the smell from all of them flies toward the heavens with its outstretched arms.

BALLIO: So the smell of the food has outstretched arms?

COOK: Oops, I made a mistake.

BALLIO: How so?

Cook: I meant to say that it has outstretched feet. And this is the odor that Jupiter has every day for his own dinner.

Ballio: And what if nobody hires you – what happens to Jupiter's dinner then?

Cook: Then he goes to bed without any supper at all.

Ballio: Oh you can just go to hell – do you think that I'm going to pay you two drachmas for this nonsense?

Cook: I realize that my cooking is rather expensive, but I assure you that I'll make you forget the price once you see my work.

Ballio: You mean your work is stealing from your clients?

Cook: Come on now – do you really imagine that there's a cook around who doesn't have the claws of an eagle?

Ballio: And do you expect to be allowed to go anywhere without having your claws tied up and kept safe from trouble? Hey there boy – yes, you over there – I want you to go inside quickly and make sure that everything we own is cleared out of the way of this fellow here. And I want your eyes to never leave his eyes. Wherever he happens to look I want you to look in the same spot. If he wanders about, then you wander about with him. If his hand goes out for something, I want your hand to go out right beside his. If he happens to pick up anything that belongs to him, you can let him have it – but if it belongs to us, then you just grip it tightly on the other side. If he moves, you move too; if he stands still, you do the same; if he kneels down, you kneel down. And every one of his underlings here will have someone to watch them as well.

Cook: Now now – you really don't need to worry.

Ballio: Why don't I have to worry when you are coming into my house to do whatever you want?

Cook: But just you wait until you see what kind of great mixture I can make for you with my pot! Why, it'll be just like Medea when she cooked up old Pelias and made him young again, as they say, from his old bones to fresh young blood, with all of her potions and magic – and that's just what I'll do for you.

Ballio: Potions? Does that mean that you are some kind of poisoner as well?

Cook: Not at all – I am the kind of fellow who saves people.

Ballio: Really? So how much would you charge me to teach me that one trick you just mentioned?

Cook: Which one?

Ballio: The one that allows me to protect my things from your stealing hands.

Cook: It'll cost you two drachmas, if you trust me. If not, then it'll cost you at least a hundred. But tell me, sir, are you giving this party today for friends or enemies?

Ballio: I'm giving this party for my friends, of course.

Cook: But why don't you invite your enemies instead? I'm going to be serving them all such a delicious feast, everything is going to be so finely and wonderfully seasoned, that everyone will be so overwhelmed by the first taste that they'll end up eating their fingers off.

Ballio: Then please, before you serve a single bite of this food to my guests, you and your helpers should have a taste of it, so that you can all eat off your own fingers – that will keep you from stealing my things.

Cook: I think you really don't believe what I'm telling you right now.

Ballio: Oh do shut up – you're really starting to tire me out. There's my house right there. Quickly – go on inside and start preparing my dinner. Go on!

Cook's Helper: It's time for all of you to go in and sit down at the table now. The dinner is ready right now and the longer it sits there, the more chances are that it's going to go bad.

Exit the Cook and the Cook's Helpers

BALLIO: What a snarky little fellow! He's already got quite the tongue on him – and he's probably a thief too, just like his master the cook. I'm not sure what I should be on the guard against most – I've got these crooks working in my house and my neighbour over there – Simo, the father of Calidorus – told me when I just bumped into him at the forum that I should watch out for his slave Pseudolus, since he is up to no good. He said the Pseudolus was full of all kinds of schemes to steal that girl away from me today, and that he promised Simo that he would use some form of trickery to remove Phoenicium from my house. So I'm just going to go in and tell all of my people to be on the lookout of Pseudolus and not to trust a word he says.

Exit Ballio

After a pause, enter Pseudolus

PSEUDOLUS (TALKING TO SOMEONE WHO IS BEHIND HIM): If the everlasting gods ever wanted to help any men, they certainly want me and Calidorus to succeed and the pimp to die, otherwise they would never have produced such a clever fellow as you to be my assistant in this scheme.

Wait! But where is this fellow now, anyway? Have I lost my mind, talking to myself like this? Oh gods, I think the fellow has just made a fool out of me. The two of us so clever, but I can be such a bad lookout at times. Oh no, if this character has given me the slip, then this will be the end of me and there'll be no chance that I can carry off my plans today.

Ah there – here he comes! And look at him – he's sauntering this way with the kind of strut that suggests he's cock of the walk.

Enter Simia, in a military costume

Hey there, I was looking all over for you, and I was starting to worry that maybe you took a run for it.

SIMIA: Well, it wouldn't have been the first time for me, I can tell you.

PSEUDOLUS: Where were you?

SIMIA: Exactly where I wanted to be.

PSEUDOLUS: Yes, I know that.

SIMIA: If you know that, then why did you even ask?

PSEUDOLUS: Ok – what I want to do right now is give you some advice.

SIMIA: You shouldn't advise me, since it looks like you're the one who really needs advice.

PSEUDOLUS: You seem to be getting a bit too snooty with me, buddy.

SIMIA: Snooty, me? I am supposed to be snooty, aren't I? Am I an officer or what? It's all just a part of the method acting.

PSEUDOLUS: Ok, that's fine – but I just want to go forward with the job we've got to do.

SIMIA: Do you see me doing anything else?

PSEUDOLUS: Then...c'mon, move quickly.

SIMIA: Oh no, the pace for me is to walk leisurely.

PSEUDOLUS: But now is the best time for us – while that other fellow is asleep at the inn, this would be the time to get in there first.

SIMIA: Oh, why are you in such a hurry? Relax, man – don't worry a bit. In fact, I rather hope that this other soldier shows up as well and he tries to present himself as a representative of the officer. Ha! He'll never beat me at playing Harpax. You don't have to worry – I'll take care of everything so that it just works out peachy. With my tricks, I'll give this strange military fellow the scare of his life, and he'll end up denying that he is himself, but instead he'll say that I am him.

PSEUDOLUS: How can you do that?

SIMIA: Man, you're killing me with all these questions.

PSEUDOLUS: That's fine, sorry – there's a good fellow, now.

SIMIA: See, you don't have to teach me what I'm already good at. In fact, I bet that I'll be able to teach you a few things about lying and deceiving.

PSEUDOLUS: Then may Jupiter bless you for it!

SIMIA: Oh, he does, he does. But how do I look? Is this all right?

PSEUDOLUS: It looks perfect.

SIMIA: Good then.

PSEUDOLUS: I hope that the immortal gods give you everything you could want to have.

(aside) I won't say everything you deserve, since that would be less than nothing. I'm positive that I've never seen a better crook than this one here.

SIMIA: Were you speaking to me?

PSEUDOLUS: Ummm...no. But I can't tell you about all the good things I'll do for you if you can only do a good job in this and give it your fullest and most serious attention.

SIMIA: Can you just shut up then? It makes a thoughtful soldier like me forget everything that he has to know when he is constantly harassed not to forget those very things that he already knows. I've got it all – it's all fine, stored right here in my heart. The plan and my tactics are all worked out.

PSEUDOLUS: Good boy!

SIMIA: Hmph...I don't think either of us are "good boys."

PSEUDOLUS: But, just be careful that there are no mistakes...

SIMIA: Oh just shut up!

PSEUDOLUS: I swear by the gods...

SIMIA: ...who must hate you after all the lies you have told....

PSEUDOLUS: ...I swear, Simia, that I've never seen such a clever liar as you – I hold you in such esteem. I love you, I am in awe of you, I respect you.

SIMIA: Oh now, I'm a master at handing out that kind of garbage, so don't try such nonsense on me.

PSEUDOLUS: Oh, just to think about the wonderful present that I'll have for you if you pull this off – if you make it a success.

SIMIA: Oh...this is so tedious.

PSEUDOLUS: I'll give you such wonderful food, wines, perfumes, and all kinds nice little drinks with fancy things in them. Oh, and there'll be a wonderful little girl for you to have all to yourself, so you can kiss and kiss and kiss her again.

SIMIA: That does sound rather nice.

PSEUDOLUS: Oh, you'll be really happy with all of this – if you bring it off.

SIMIA: I tell you, if I don't succeed, then the hangman can fit me for a noose. So let's just get going – which house belongs to the pimp?

PSEUDOLUS: It's the third door along here.

SIMIA: Shh! Watch out – and be quiet. A door is starting to open in that house.

PSEUDOLUS: Maybe the house is feeling ill.

SIMIA: What?

PSEUDOLUS: It's going to vomit out our pimp right here in front of us.

Enter Ballio, from the house, while Pseudolus and Simia hide in the background

SIMIA: So is that the fellow there, this pimp?

PSEUDOLUS: Yes, that's him.

SIMIA: He doesn't look very impressive – kind of pathetic, actually. I mean, look at how he walks – it seems like he is moving sideways, just like a crab, rather than like a normal person would walk.

BALLIO: Hmm...perhaps that cook isn't so dishonest, after all – for a cook, anyway. He hasn't stolen a thing so far...except for a ladle and a cup.

PSEUDOLUS: Psst...Simia, here's your chance. Go, do it now, while I wait here.

SIMIA: Indeed it is – showtime.

PSEUDOLUS: Go on then, and be careful what you do and say…I'll keep back here in the shadows, so that I can lay an ambush.

SIMIA (STEPPING FORWARD): Now then, I'm sure that I must have counted correctly. This is the sixth street over from the gate of the city, and this one here must be the lane I'm supposed to enter, but I can't rightly remember how many houses down I'm supposed to go…

BALLIO: What's this? Who's this fellow over there in the military coat? Where's he from? Who's he looking for? Hmm…he looks like a stranger to these parts, since he's no one I've ever seen before.

SIMIA: Oh, there's someone over there who undoubtedly can help me out with my problem.

BALLIO: He's headed this way. I wonder where on earth this guy is coming from.

SIMIA: Hey there, you over there! Yes, you with goat-beard…can you tell me something?

BALLIO: Well now, and not even a "hello" or "good day" first?

SIMIA: Sorry, but I don't have any of those to spare.

BALLIO: Then you won't get anything from me either. Chew on that.

PSEUDOLUS (ASIDE): This is a horrible way to start.

SIMIA: Do you know anyone here in this town? Hey, I'm asking you a question!

BALLIO: Yes, I know someone…me.

SIMIA: Then you're doing quite well, I suppose. They say that only one in ten people actually knows himself.

PSEUDOLUS: Oh good, I'm saved – he's starting to use philosophy.

SIMIA: I'm looking for a man around here – quite the bad little man. He's a law-breaker, and shameless, untrustworthy, and doesn't respect the gods.

BALLIO: That sounds like it could be me, since I often answer to all those names. But I'd prefer to hear a name first. What the proper name of this fellow?

SIMIA: His name is Ballio, the pimp.

BALLIO: Ha! I knew it. Well then, young man, I'm the man you're looking for.

SIMIA: You're Ballio?

BALLIO: Indeed I am.

SIMIA: But those clothes of yours make you look rather like a burglar.

BALLIO: Yes, and if you ran into me in the dark, you wouldn't be able to catch hold of me.

SIMIA: Good. My master wanted me to bring to you his cordial greetings. Oh, yes, and here's the letter. Please take it – he told me that I was to give this to you.

BALLIO: What's the name of the fellow that sent you then?

PSEUDOLUS: Oh-oh…now we're in a mess. He doesn't know the name – we're doomed.

BALLIO: Come on, tell me the name of the man who sent you.

SIMIA: I think you had better look at the mark on the letter first, then you can tell me the man's name yourself. I want to know if you really are this Ballio whom you claim to be.

BALLIO: Just give me the letter here then.

SIMIA: Good – take it and see if you can identify the mark.

BALLIO: Oh yes indeed, that's the mark of Polymachaeroplagides – that's his image, no question. Yes, I know him. Hey, young man, the name of the man is Polymachaeroplagides.

SIMIA: Good – I can see I did the right thing in giving you the letter, now that you thankfully spat out the right name of…Polymachaeroplagides.

BALLIO: And what's your master doing right now?

SIMIA: Oh, exactly what you would expect a brave and courageous soldier to be doing. But I'm going to have to ask you to hurry and read this letter all the way through – that's all you have to do – and then take this money from me, so that I can take the girl to my master. I'm supposed to be back a Sicyon today or I'll lose my head tomorrow. My master, you see, is very strict about his orders.

BALLIO: I know, I've met him.

SIMIA: Then please, read the letter without wasting any more time.

BALLIO: I will, I will – just be quiet and let me. "From Captain Polymachaeroplagides to the pimp Ballio, a letter sealed with the likeness and markings that have been agreed upon by us both." Ok, that's the seal that I just saw on the front of the letter.

"The person bringing this letter to you is my assistant, Harpax." That's you, right? You're this Harpax fellow?

SIMIA: That's me indeed.

BALLIO: "He's carrying this letter. I want you to take the money from him, and send the woman back with him when he leaves. It is appropriate to add comments of good wishes at the end of a letter, and I would have done so if I thought you were worthy of them."

SIMIA: So, what about it then?

BALLIO: Hmph...just give me the damn money, will you, and you can take the girl.

SIMIA: Then what are we waiting for – here you go!

BALLIO: Come on inside, we'll get the girl.

SIMIA: Right behind you!

Exit Ballio and Simia into the house

PSEUDOLUS: What a clever fellow that Simia is, if ever I've seen one! Man, the fellow's so good that he's even got me worried that he'll do to me just what he did to Ballio there. I'd be sorry if he did that, let me tell you, because I think I'm starting to like the fellow.

Anyway, it looks like now I've got three things to be worried about. First, I still have a nagging fear that my ally in there could desert me at any moment and make an agreement with my enemy. Second, I fear that my master Simo might come back from the forum at any moment now and catch the crooks – I mean, catch us – with all of the loot that we've seized. Finally, I'm a bit nervous that the real Harpax might show up here again before this other Harpax can make his escape with the girl.

Oh damn it, they are taking such a long time! My heart is beating a mile a minute and feels like it could fly out of my body at any moment...if he doesn't bring the girl I don't know what...wait, the door is opening – it looks like victory! I've defeated the guards! Ha ha.

Enter Simia with Phoenicium

SIMIA: There there, don't cry. You don't understand what's going on Phoenicium, but you'll soon have a better idea when you get to see who you're having dinner with. I'm not taking you to that Macedonian thug who has caused all those tears of yours. No, you're going to see your beloved Calidorus and it won't be long before you are with him and hugging the man you want to hug.

PSEUDOLUS: What on earth kept you inside for so long? My heart was pounding away in my chest to the point of bursting because of all the stress and worry.

SIMIA: Keep quiet, fool! You're criticizing my conduct here and now, while we are still very much in the thick of enemy territory? Wouldn't the better idea be to get out of here fast?

PSEUDOLUS: Yes, you're right, even though it comes from a bad man, you're right. Let's get out of here – straight to the cup of victory!

Exit Pseudolus, Simia, and Phoenicium

After a moment, enter Ballio

BALLIO: Well that's that – now I feel relieved since that soldier fellow took that girl safely away with him. Ha! Just let devil Pseudolus come here now and try to use trickery so that he can steal her away from me. I'd rather swear a thousand oaths or be charged with perjury than to be made the fool at the expense of that fellow so that others can laugh at me.

I think I'll be able to get quite the laugh at his expense once I see him. But I imagine that he is on his way to the treadmill now, where he should be. I'd like to see my neighbour Simo here as well, so he can share all the fun with me.

Enter Simo

SIMO: I wonder how my Ulysses is going – that Pseudolus, I mean – while he is attempting to steal the goddess from the temple.

BALLIO: Hello, dear Simo. Come here, let me shake your hand, you lucky man.

SIMO: Why? What's happened?

BALLIO: There's nothing left to fear.

SIMO: What do you mean? Has Pseudolus already been here to see you?

BALLIO: No.

SIMO: Then why are you so happy?

BALLIO: You're money is now safe – that two thousand drachmas that Pseudolus bet he would get out of you. Well, you're money's safe.

SIMO: My heavens, I wish that were true.

BALLIO: Well, if somehow he gets possession of that girl today and gives her over to your son, then you can get the two thousand drachmas from me if you like. Go ahead, make me promise it – please. I want you to feel completely secure that your money is all safe. I'll even give you a woman yourself, if you like.

SIMO: Fine, there doesn't seem to be any risk, as far as I can see, in accepting your terms. So, you promise to give me two thousand drachmas?

BALLIO: I'll give you two thousand, yes.

SIMO: It looks like I'm doing rather well with this arrangement. But what's this promise all about? Why should I no longer be afraid of him? I want to know what's been happening.

BALLIO: He will never, and can never, get that girl away from me. You remember that I told you that she had been sold to this soldier from Macedonia?

SIMO: Yes, I recall that.

BALLIO: Well, the slave of that soldier just brought me the final part of the payment along with his sealed token...

SIMO: Which was what?

BALLIO: A letter that confirmed he was who he claimed to be. And this slave of the Macedonian just took the girl away with him, no more than ten minutes ago.

SIMO: You're telling me on your honour?

BALLIO: And where am I supposed to find honour?

SIMO: And you're quite positive that our friend Pseudolus hasn't played some massive trick on you?

BALLIO: Oh no – the letter and the token are absolutely legitimate. He just took the girl away to Sicyon. It's all fine – I swear.

SIMO: Well then! Now we can make Pseudolus a resident of the mills as soon as possible! I'm sure he's earned his one-way ticket there.

But what's this? Who's that fellow with the military coat coming this way?

BALLIO: I've no idea. But let's just watch where he's headed and see what he's looking for...

Enter Harpax

HARPAX (TO HIMSELF, THE OTHERS CAN'T HEAR HIM): I tell you, any slave is useless if he doesn't pay attention to his orders, and he's doubly worthless if he can't do what he's told without having to be reminded. What's more, those slaves who act like they are free the moment they escape the sight of their masters, and then they take up all kinds of silliness and shenanigans – they're going to remain slaves an awfully long time, behaving that way. They don't have one good quality, except for their persistence in evil.

I don't approve of spending time with or talking to lazy good-for-nothings like that, and I try to avoid them whenever I can. Myself, I do exactly what I'm told, and I imagine that my master is still around even when he happens to be away. I think it's better to fear him when he's away, so that you don't have to fear him when he is present.

Anyway, I've got this job to finish. I listened to my instructions and I stayed at that inn, just waiting for that Syrus fellow to show up, the one I gave my letter and token. He said that he'd come get me when the pimp came home. But since he didn't come to get me and didn't call me, I've taken it upon myself to come back here on my own to see what's going on. I'm not going to let that fellow make a fool out of me, that's for sure.

It looks like the best thing to do would be to knock at the door and call someone outside. I want that pimp to take my money and give me the girl so that I can bring her back with me...

BALLIO: Hey, Simo, listen here.

SIMO: What's up?

BALLIO: This one's mine.

SIMO: What do you mean, yours?

BALLIO: I mean he's there for my taking, ready to be caught in my net. He's looking for a girl, obviously, and it looks like he has money. Oh, just wait until I get ahold of him!

SIMO: So you're going to take him in one fell swoop?

BALLIO: Exactly. You have to take them when they're ready for the taking – when they're fresh and hot. Good men only bring me poverty – I need the bad men to survive. Honest men have their purpose, but I need worthless men for my business to be successful.

SIMO: And in turn the gods will give you exactly what you deserve.

HARPAX: Well then, here it is – I'll just knock on this door to see if Ballio's home yet.

BALLIO: Psst...Simo, it looks like Venus is being quite kind to me, always sending me these spendthrifts, good-timers, eaters, drinkers, and pornographers. These people are very different from your type, since you are the kind of person who doesn't allow yourself to have a good time and so doesn't like it when others enjoy themselves.

HARPAX: Hello, is anyone in there?

BALLIO: Do you see, Simo? He's coming straight to my home and net. I'll rid him of his money soon enough – I think my omens are looking good.

HARPAX: Hey in there - will someone open up!

BALLIO (COMING FORWARD): Hello there, you in the coat – what do you want?

HARPAX: I'm looking for the fellow who owns this house – the pimp named Ballio.

BALLIO: Well then young man, whoever you are, you don't need to look any more.

HARPAX: Why is that?

BALLIO: Because you are here and Ballio is here and you are looking at him.

HARPAX (TO SIMO): Are you Ballio?

SIMO: Don't start thinking that I'm the pimp now, young man, unless you want me to hit you with my stick here. This fellow here is the pimp you want. He's Ballio.

BALLIO: That's right – this fellow here is a genteeel-man....la-dee-da. But, my dear Simo, even though you are a fine upstanding gentleman, I still know about all the debt you've racked up in the forum and how at times you can't find a dime unless a pimp like me will loan you something.

HARPAX: Hey there – if you're this Ballio, then why don't you just talk directly to me?

BALLIO: Oh but I am, sir. How can I help you?

HARPAX: I have some money here for you – here, take it.

BALLIO: My hand has been out a long time already, just waiting for it, in fact.

HARPAX: Here you go then. That's five hundred drachmas counted out in good solid currency. I was told to bring this to you by my master Polymachaeroplagides, who said that once I gave you this money I was then to bring back the girl Phoenicium with me.

BALLIO: So your master sent you?

HARPAX: Yes, that's right.

BALLIO: You mean the soldier?

HARPAX: Exactly.

BALLIO: The one from Macedonia?

HARPAX: Indeed, that's the one.

BALLIO: So you were sent to me by Polymachaeroplagides.

HARPAX: Once again – yes.

BALLIO: And he told you to give me this money here?

HARPAX: He did – if you are Ballio the pimp, that is.

BALLIO: And you're supposed to get a girl in return from me?

HARPAX: That's what I was told.

BALLIO: And he said that her name was Phoenicium?

HARPAX: You remember her, I can see.

BALLIO: Just wait a moment, please – I'll be right back. (He moves toward Simo.)

HARPAX: Don't take too long. I'm in a bit of a hurry, and you can see that it's getting quite late already.

BALLIO: Yes, I see. I just want to talk to my friend over here for a bit....so just wait for a minute and I'll be back...

(To Simo) Now then, Simo, what happens now? I've caught this fellow in my net, haven't I? This guy with the money is trapped, isn't he?

SIMO: How do you mean?

BALLIO: You mean that you can't see what's happening here?

SIMO: Not really, no.

BALLIO: Your slave Pseudolus has paid this fellow here to pretend that he's the messenger from the Macedonian officer.

SIMO: And did this fellow over there already give you the money?

BALLIO: I have it all right here – can't you see?

SIMO: Then don't forget to let me have half the winnings – we should share in the profits.

BALLIO: Oh I don't care – you can have the whole lot of it.

HARPAX: Hey here – how long are you going to keep me waiting?

BALLIO: Oh, I'll be just one more moment....Psst, Simo, what do you think we should do?

SIMO: Maybe we can have some fun with this imposter, and we can keep playing him until he realizes that he's been caught.

BALLIO: Sounds good – please come with me then. Well then, so you're the slave that belongs to this soldier, eh?

HARPAX: Yes – as I already told you.

BALLIO: And how much did he pay to acquire you?

HARPAX: It cost him the price of his courage and victory in battle. I was the one who commanded the forces where I came from.

BALLIO: What's that? So he stormed the prison where he found you then?

HARPAX: If you keep talking to me like that, then you should be prepared to hear abuse in return.

BALLIO: How many days did it take you to get here from Sicyon?

HARPAX: One and a half days.

BALLIO: That's a quick job!

SIMO: Well, you can see that he's quite a strong young man. Just look at those legs of his! I bet those are the kind that would have to wear really large prison chains.

BALLIO: And I suppose that you slept in a nice bed when you were a boy – right?

HARPAX: Yes, sure – that's normal.

BALLIO: And...you know...did you have a nice time in the bed...just as young men like to do?

SIMO: Of course he did!

HARPAX: What the hell is this? Are the two of you both crazy?

BALLIO: And I suppose that you spend many a night with your officer, when he was out on the night watch, just like good friends, with his sword in your scabbard, so-to-speak...

HARPAX: Oh to hell with you!

BALLIO: I imagine that you're going there yourself – in due time, maybe by the end of the day.

HARPAX: Just send the girl out to me, or give me back my money.

BALLIO: Just wait a second.

HARPAX: Why? What on earth are you doing?

BALLIO: I just wanted to touch your coat. Hmmm...tell me – how much did it cost you to rent this for the day?

HARPAX: What do you mean?

SIMO: And how much did it cost to borrow this sword of yours?

HARPAX: These two need a good thrashing, I think.

BALLIO: And what about your hat?

HARPAX: Hey – let go of that!

BALLIO: What did the hat's owner charge you so that you could borrow it today?

HARPAX: What owner? What on earth are you talking about? Everything that I have is mine – I paid for it all with my own money.

BALLIO: The money that you keep close to your waist, no doubt – right?

HARPAX: I think the two of you are really looking for a beat-down.

BALLIO: Oh relax – just calm down. But do tell me this one thing – how much are you earning today? How much is Pseudolus paying you?

HARPAX: Pseudolus? Who's that?

BALLIO: That's the name of your instructor – the one who put you up to this game of trying to get the girl out of my house with your trickery here.

HARPAX: What Pseudolus? And what trickery are you talking about? I've never met any person who goes by that name.

BALLIO: Really? Then why don't you just beat it out of here then! We're not giving any handouts to criminals and thieves today. So you can just go tell Pseudolus that what he sent you for has already left, with another man – that is, another Harpax got here first.

HARPAX: Another Harpax? But I'm the real Harpax!

BALLIO: Yeah, so you claim. You only dream that you could be the real Harpax. You see, Simo, this guy's a crook plain and simple.

HARPAX: Enough of this! I gave you the money, right in front of this door here, just a few moments ago when

I arrived, and earlier today I gave your servant a letter that had the token sealed inside it – and that token was the image of my master.

BALLIO: Uh...what's that? You gave a letter to a slave of mine? What slave was that?

HARPAX: I gave it to Syrus.

BALLIO: Oh-no, but wait...maybe this imposter here is being a bit too clever and just over-playing his part. That rascal Pseudolus had it all worked out – he gave this devil the money, exactly the same that was owed to me. No, I won't believe you, for that letter was brought to me earlier today in person by the real Harpax himself.

HARPAX: Damn it all, my name is Harpax – I am the real Harpax! The soldier from Macedonia is my master. I'm not pretending to be anyone I'm not, nor am I trying to cheat you. As for this Pseudolus, I've never heard the name before.

SIMO: Well then, pimp, it seems unlikely that you'll ever get that girl back now.

BALLIO: Oh heavens – this is all just getting worse and worse. I'm starting to become more and more afraid, the more I hear this fellow here talk. When he mentioned the name Syrus, it rather shocked me and sent a chill up my heart, because I suddenly had the thought that Pseudolus might have been pretending to be Syrus.

Ok then, my good fellow, what did that guy look like, the one you gave the token to earlier today?

HARPAX: He had red hair, a fat belly, thick legs, dark skin, a big head, sharp eyes, a red face, and these really huge feet.

BALLIO: Oh no, you've destroyed me by telling me about his large feet! That was Pseudolus. It's over. Simo, I'm done for, ruined.

HARPAX: Wait a minute – I can't have you dying before I get my money back from you. I mean the whole two thousand drachmas.

SIMO: Yes, and I'm getting two thousand as well.

BALLIO: And you're going to take from me what I just threw out there as a joke?

SIMO: Bad men deserve to lose their bets and their fortunes.

BALLIO: Then at the very least hand over Pseudolus to me.

SIMO: I'm going to let you have Pseudolus? What did he do? Didn't I warn you over a hundred times to watch out for him?

BALLIO: He's completely ruined me.

SIMO: But he's only robbed me of two thousand drachmas.

BALLIO: What am I going to do now?

HARPAX: Well, you can give me my money, then maybe you can go and hang yourself.

BALLIO: Oh go to hell! Hmph...come on then, follow me to the forum and I'll give you your money.

HARPAX: Oh, I'll follow indeed.

SIMO: But what about me?

BALLIO: I'll settle my debts with foreigners today, and tomorrow I'll take care of local business. It looks like Pseudolus landed me with a death sentence today, when he found that imposter to come see me today and take the girl.

Ok Harpax, you can follow me now. And as for all of you – yes, you out there in the audience – don't expect to see me coming home by this street. In the future, and under the circumstances, I plan to use the back alleys.

HARPAX: If you could only walk as fast as you talk, then you'd be in town already by now.

BALLIO: Today was my birthday. I think it will be known as my death day from now on.

Exit Ballio and Harpax

SIMO: Well well, it looks like I got the better of old Ballio, and my slave scored quite the victory over his enemy as well. Now I think what I'll do is prepare a reception for Pseudolus. No, it won't be the kind of reception that you may have seen in other comedies – the ones with whips and chains.

No, I'm going to go right in the house now and get the two thousand drachmas that I promised I'd give him if he managed to win. I'll bring it out and put it right into his hands before he even asks for it. I swear, he must be the cleverest, trickiest, and most skillful creature alive. The trick that Ulysses pulled off in order to take Troy is nothing compared to what Pseudolus can do.

Yes – I'll just go in, get the money, and I'll surprise him when he arrives.

Exit Simo into the house

After a moment, enter Pseudolus, stumbling and drunk

Pseudolus: What's this all about? Feet…what are you doing? Is this…the way to act? You going…to stand or…not? Or do you….want…someone to find me lying here…on the ground…and carry me off? I tell you…you feet…you'll be in a whole mess of problems if…you let me fall down. You'll have to reckon with…me. Let's…keep going then. Listen to…my orders…do this today.

The real problem with wine…you see…is that it catches you by the feet – like a tricky wrestler. O my heavens, I'm just having the best drunk ever, I am I am. It was the bestest of parties…yes, sir…yes, sir…such wonderful food there…everyone so friendly and happy…such elegance…it was if it were for the gods. I mean this…there's no use talking around it, is there?…all these things are the reason we…love being alive…when everything makes you smile…everything looks charming…it feels like we are the closest to the gods.

And…when a lover is holding the girl he loves…with their lips and tongues held together…two of them are one…each of them pressed tight…breast to breast…heart to heart…or one pale hand of the girl…she lifts the cup…and gives a drink to her boy…no angry glances…no boredom…an no one to…to ruin their joy…instead there are flowers everywhere…

perfumes and fragrances…lots of wonderful stuff everywhere….lots of drink and food everywhere…no one to ask me anything…so sweet.

Ooh yeah, this is how the young master Calidorus and I spent the day…celebrating my great victory over the enemies. I left the others back there…they're still drinking…and making love…everyone's got a girl…even one for me too…everyone soooo happy. The moment I stood up, they all asked me to dance…so I did some little moves…like this here…pretty good, eh what? I think…I've been a pretty good student…of Greek dancing. I had my coat wrapped around me…and I gave a few steps…like this here…just having a ball. Then they all screamed for more…so I did it all once again…and I started again…like this…to be a bit different. I was just about to go back…to my girl…so I could get me some loving…then when I went spinning around and…pop…I fell. So that was the end of the show…and when I was wrestling with myself to get up…I ruined my coat in the process.

Oh gods, I gave them such fun with my accident, though…they gave me another cup afterward…and I drank it all down…then they gave me a new coat and I took off the old one. So I came over here…to get some fresh air. Now I'm coming from my young master to my senior master…to remind him of his agreement.

Hey in there! Someone in there tell Simo that I am here!

Enter Simo, carrying a bag of money out of sight

Simo: Well, if that doesn't sound like the well-known villain himself! Hello? What the devil is this? What's this all about?

Pseudolus: It's your loyal servant…Pseudolus…wearing the garlands…of victory.

Simo: Just look at him – free and easy as a bird. And take a look at the way he's standing – it looks like he's awfully comfortable and relaxed in my presence, isn't he? I wonder how I should act toward him – should

I be harsh or kind? But this money here tells me that I can't be rough with him – if I'm ever going to use him in the future, that is.

Pseudolus: Greetings...sir...from this rascal to you, the gentleman.

Simo: Very kind of you, Pseudolus.

Pseudolus: [Burp!]

Simo: Oh yuck! Damn you Pseudolus – please get some distance from me.

Pseudolus: Why...all this...pushing me around?

Simo: What are you trying to do, with all of this burping and belching in my face?

Pseudolus: Oh...that's ok, my sweetie...just put your arms around me...and hold me up so that...I don't drop. Don't you see that I'm soaked...and smashed?

Simo: How do you get the nerve, Pseudolus, to get so drunk in the middle of the day and go wandering through the streets, drunk out of your mind and wearing flowers in your hair? Where do you get the nerve?

Pseudolus: But...it's real real nice...

Simo: Yes, you like it, don't you? But can you just stop breathing and belching in my face, please.

Pseudolus: But I've got a really lovely belch, Simo, so don't be put off by my belching.

Simo: You devil – I think that you're capable of gulping down an entire vineyard – no, four vineyards – in less than an hour.

Pseudolus: But let's make it a winter hour – the hours are shorter then.

Simo: You may be right there. Anyway, where have you just come from? From what port are you sailing that well-sodden vessel of yours?

Pseudolus: Your son and I...have just been out drinking and fornicating...but, Simo, let me tell you, we did it! I got one past old Ballio! I did what I said I would do – I kept my promise.

Simo: You're a real scoundrel, Pseudolus.

Pseudolus: Blame that girl...she's got her freedom now, and she's over there somewhere...with your son...on a couch.

Simo: Oh, I know all about it already, and how you did it as well.

Pseudolus: Well then...why are you so slow in giving me the money?

Simo: I admit it – this money is yours by right. Here you go – take it.

Pseudolus: So you're giving me the money after all, even...after you said you'd never give it to me. So come on then, help me put it on my shoulder and follow me as I strut about to celebrate my victory.

Simo: What – I'm supposed to put it on your shoulder for you?

Pseudolus: Oh...you will...I know that...you will.

Simo: What am I going to do with this devil? The nerve – taking my money and then going the extra step to laugh and mock me as well!

Pseudolus: I am the champion, my friends, I kept on fighting...to the end....

Simo: Ok, just turn your shoulder then, so that I can load you up.

Pseudolus: Here's my shoulder.

Simo: I never thought that it would come to me acting as your servant. Oh, what am I going to do?

Pseudolus: Oh, stop you're crying and complaining.

Simo: But think of how much I'm suffering!

Pseudolus: Just think of how much I'd be suffering if you weren't suffering!

Simo: What? Can you do this, Pseudolus? Can you take all of this money here from your own master?

Pseudolus: Oh yes – with the greatest satisfaction and pleasure.

Simo: Oh, just let me keep some part of the money, please – can you find it in your heart to let me keep a bit of it?

Pseudolus: No – I won't agree to that. You're not calling me greedy, are you? If you try that tactic you won't get a thing from me. I mean, how much mercy would you have shown me – and my back! – if I hadn't been successful today?

Simo: Ok, fine. But I'll have my chance to get even with you soon enough, I suppose.

Pseudolus: That's fine, threats are all right – I can take them.

Simo: Ok then, just shove off you – I'm leaving now.

Pseudolus: But wait! Come back, please.

Simo: Come back? Why would I do that?

Pseudolus: Please...just come back here. It's ok – I won't do anything to fool with you.

Simo: Ok – I'm back.

Pseudolus: You are coming with me now. We're going to go to the place where the booze is flowing.

Simo: I'm supposed to go drinking...with you?

Pseudolus: Now just do what...I tell you to do. Orders are orders. If you do as you're told, I'll see to it that you get half...maybe even more...of this money here.

Simo: I'll do it. I'll go – take me wherever you like.

Pseudolus: So you're not really angry with either me or your son about this at all – are you, Simo?

Simo: Not at all – not in the least bit.

Pseudolus: Then let's go – please, come with me.

Simo: I follow your lead. But shouldn't we invite the audience along with us?

Pseudolus: Good gods no! These people out there never think of inviting me along anywhere, so I'm certainly not going to invite them. But if all of you out there want to show your appreciation to this troupe and this play, then I'll invite you here again... to another performance tomorrow!

Exit Pseudolus and Simo

Translated from the Latin by Stephen Russell, PhD

Chapter 10
Euripides
The Cyclops

The Story: *The Cyclops* is known as a "satyr play." After a day in which one tragic poet presented his trilogy of plays, usually all of which were based on the same theme or narrative, there would then be a short satyr play at the end of the day that would take a scene from that trilogy and poke fun at it. Satyrs are half-goat, half-human creatures who like to drink and fornicate – and who are closely associated with the god of wine, Dionysus. Their leader is Silenus, and the characters in these plays often wore large phallic-like appendages to emphasize that it was a farce. Euripides' play *The Cyclops*, a reworking of the scene from *The Odyssey* in which Odysseus meets the Cyclops Polyphemus, is the only surviving satyr play that we have, so most of our ideas on how these plays functioned stem from this play.

One small note: this play is not a tragedy. Rather, it's a coarse and often vulgar comedy. So do feel free to laugh while you read. I hope that I have translated this play in a way that does justice to its comic intent.

Characters

Silenus, the father of the satyrs
Chorus, of satyrs (who have been captured by the Cyclops)
Odysseus
Polyphemus, the Cyclops
Odysseus' crew (silent)

Scene: in front of the cave that belongs to the Cyclops Polyphemus

Enter Silenus from the cave

SILENUS: O Dionysius, the labours and agonies that I have had because of you have been numberless – the one that I have now as well as the ones I had when I was young and had a stronger body. The first labour that comes to mind is the one when you were a child and Hera drove you mad and you went off and left behind your mountain nymphs and your nurses – and I had to go after you to find you. The second time was the battle with the earthborn Giants and I took my position and made my stand at your right side, protecting you with my shield, and I struck Enceladus with my spear right in the centre of his breastplate, and I killed him dead! Hmmm... let me think...did I really do this, or did I dream it all up? Am I telling another lie right now? No, by Zeus, I'm not, Dionysus, for I even shared the spoils with you later.

But now I am suffering from a labour that is so much greater than those other ones. This third one is a doozy, for when Hera stirred up those Tuscan pirates against you so that she could have you sold as a slave to some far off country, I heard all about it and so I got into my ship with my sons and then set out to find you.

I stood there, right at the front of the ship, and I myself steered the boat while my sons rowed along and made the grey sea turn white when they moved their oars – all the while we kept our eyes on the look-out for you, my lord.

But when we were going around Cape Malea, a wind from the east suddenly hit the ship and we were pushed toward this crag of land next to Mt. Aetna. It's here that the one-eyed sons of Poseidon, those man-eating Cyclopes, live in their caves that are so far off from the rest of the world.

One of these Cyclopes – his name is Polyphemus – has caught us and we are kept here as slaves in his house. So instead of drinking wine and eating, doing the kinds of things you world approve of, O Dionysus, we now have to take care of the flocks in this for this godless one-eyed Cyclops.

And so my sons, since they are young, are taking care of the sheep out on the hillsides, while I have been told to stay here and do the housework. I sweep, fetch the water, and cook the thankless meals for this damn Cyclops. And now, my lord Dionysus, please excuse me for a moment, because I have to give the house a quick sweep right now with this rake so that my master, that one-eye, and his sheep can come home to find a clean cave....uhh....I mean, a clean house.

Enter the Chorus (of satyrs), driving sheep in ahead of them

But now I can see my sons coming this way with the flocks. My boys, what's this? You look like you now have the same rhythm and beat to your step as you did when you went partying with Dionysus to Althea's house, dancing all the while to the music from the lyre.

CHORUS (TO A WANDERING RAM): And where do you think you're going,

O you son of a noble family of goats –
Don't you realize that this road leads
To the crags and cliffs?
Isn't it rather this way that's the best path
To reach the gentle breezes and the meadows?
There at the mouth of the cave there's some food
And the wave of a river to drink,
And all of your bleating children
Are sheltered there in their bed.
C'mon now, shoo shoo! This way here!
Come on now over here to feed
On the slopes of your pleasant and dewy home.
Do I have to throw a rock at you?
On with you, this way here,
You horny old head of the household!
You're supposed to be the protector and guardian
Of the Cyclops' sheepfold, for all the while
That he is out wandering in the wilderness.
(to a ewe)
And that goes for you as well,
Time to get those mammaries of yours home!
It's about time for you to get in that cave
And nurse your young'uns!
Those little bleaters of yours
Have slept all day and really miss their mommy.
Come on! Get on in – time to give up
The crags of Aetna and get on inside
This nice big pen of yours.
O, but there's no Dionysus here,
No wine, no dancing, no waving the wand
In our Bacchic worship, no mighty beating of drums,
No fresh drops of wine.
And I can't join the nymphs on Mt, Nysa
And sing drinking songs to Aphrodite,
Like when we chased after the goddess of love so swiftly
In the old days, me and my girlfriends,
Those Bacchants who were so fast
On their white feet.
O dear lord Dionysus,
Where are you right now
Without us, your companions,
Where are you shaking your golden hair?
I was once your happy servant,
But I now am a slave to this one-eyed Cyclops;

I'm a slave in exile,
And I have to wear these crappy rags for clothes,
This damn goatskin,
And I miss your friendship and company,
O dear lord Dionysus.

SILENUS: Shhh! Be quiet, boys! Take the animals and get inside the cave quickly!

CHORUS LEADER: You heard him! Let's do what he says. But first, father, what's the rush? What's wrong?

SILENUS: I can see a ship down there on the beach. And it's Greek! And the sailors are headed right now toward our cave with the person who must be their leader. On top of their heads and around their necks they're carrying empty containers and sacks, so they must be after food – and some of them are carrying pails for water.

O strangers – whoever you are – what shitty luck you have!

But who on earth can they be? They surely have no idea what our master Polyphemus is like, or that this ground here is unfriendly to visitors and guests, or that their rotten luck has taken them to the land of the Cyclopes, who make meals out of human flesh.

Now all of you just be quiet while I try to find out why they have come to this rocky area around Sicily and Mt. Aetna.

Enter Odysseus and members of his crew

ODYSSEUS: Hey there! Hello! Strangers, do you think you might be able to show me where I can find a stream with freshwater? Our thirst is killing us. And do you know of anyone who might sell some supplies to some needy sailors?

But what's this? It looks like I've just marched into a festival for Dionysus – or his city even! For I didn't realize that you were a group of satyrs gathered at the front of the cave here. I should pay my respects to the oldest first, since he's no doubt the man in charge. Hello there, my dear man!

SILENUS: And a big hello to you in return, stranger. But please tell me your name and country, if you don't mind.

ODYSSEUS: I am Odysseus, from Ithaca – the lord of Cephallene.

SILENUS: Oh, I've heard of you – you're that famous liar, the bastard son of Sisyphus.

ODYSSEUS: Yeah, that's right – but you might want to keep the abuse to yourself.

SILENUS: And from what port did you set out so that you'd come here to Sicily?

ODYSSEUS: My crew and I came from Troy and the war that happened there.

SILENUS: What? You couldn't figure out a way to get home?

ODYSSEUS: Well, the winds and the storm blew us here.

SILENUS: Damn – that's the same thing that happened to me.

ODYSSEUS: You were also forced to come here against your will?

SILENUS: Oh yes – we were in the midst of chasing the pirates who had carried off Dionysus.

ODYSSEUS: Then what is this place here? And who lives here?

SILENUS: This is Mount Aetna – the highest peak in all of Sicily.

ODYSSEUS: But where are the walls, and the streets, and the towers, and all the other marks of civilization?

SILENUS: This isn't a city, dude – no people live in these rocks.

ODYSSEUS: But what is it that lives in this land – wild animals?

SILENUS: That's easy – the Cyclopes live here, and they have these caves here, not houses.

Odysseus: But who is in charge of them here? Who is their ruler? Or is there some form of democracy here?

Silenus: They have no use for that kind of stuff. They're savages and live alone – there's nobody in charge.

Odysseus: But how do they survive? Do they plow the field and sow the grain of Demeter?

Silenus: They live entirely on milk, cheese, and the flesh of sheep.

Odysseus: Do they have any of the drink of Dionysus – the wine that comes from the vine?

Silenus: Hell no! That's why this land that they inhabit never has any dances or any fun at all.

Odysseus: Are they friendly toward strangers here?

Silenus: Oh, they say that the meat from the flesh of strangers makes a lovely dinner.

Odysseus: What? Are you telling me that they eat human flesh here?

Silenus: Yup – everyone who comes here has been eaten up so far.

Odysseus: And this Cyclops of yours, where is he right now? In his house over there?

Silenus: Nope – he's taken his dogs and gone off to hunt wild dogs on the side of Mount Aetna.

Odysseus: So what do we have to do if we want to get out of here?

Silenus: I have no idea, Odysseus – but I'll do anything that I can to help you.

Odysseus: Ok, maybe you can sell us some bread – we don't have any left.

Silenus: I already told you – there's nothing to eat here except for meat.

Odysseus: Well, meat is ok – that's a good way to get rid of hunger.

Silenus: Oh – and we also have cheese and milk, of course.

Odysseus: So bring it all out then – the customer should get a chance to see what he is buying.

Silenus: But how much money or gold are you going to give me in return?

Odysseus: I don't really have a lot of money or gold... but I do carry the drink of Dionysus – wine.

Silenus: No fucking way! Thank the gods - that's what we've been dreaming about for so long now.

Odysseus: Yes, the son of the god, Maron, gave this wine to me.

Silenus: You mean the boy that I once raised in my very arms?

Odysseus: Absolutely – the son of Dionysus.

Silenus: And....is the wine still on your ship...or do you happen to have it with you right now?

Odysseus: I have some in this wineskin here, old man – take a look.

Silenus: That thing there? Psh! That wouldn't even amount to one mouthful for me.

Odysseus: I promise you – you won't be able to drink this wineskin dry.

Silenus: What is this? Does this wineskin produce its own wine?

Odysseus: Yep – for every gulp you take the wineskin gives two.

Silenus: Wow! What a lovely fountain you have there. I am in love!

Odysseus: Would you like to have a little taste of it first without water?

Silenus: That seems fair – the buyer should get a chance to sample the merchandise, after all.

Odysseus: Check this out – I even have a cup to go with the wineskin.

Silenus: Quick, pour some of it in there. I want to remember what it feels like to drink.

Odysseus: There you go!

Silenus: Oh god, what a beautiful wine!

Odysseus: How can you already know that? But I haven't even given it to you yet...

Silenus: My dear boy, I can smell it!

Odysseus: Fair enough – then it's time for you to take it and drink it. Now your praises won't be just words.

Silenus: Ahhhh...ohhhh...damn - Dionysus is asking me to dance...boom bam..la la la...sh'mone motherfucker!

Odysseus: Doesn't it go down your throat nicely?

Silenus: Oh yeah – all the waaaay down to the – burp – I mean, to the tips of my toes.

Odysseus: But we'll also give you some money in addition to this wine.

Silenus: Screw the money, friend – just keep pouring the wine!

Odysseus: Ok – then you bring out some of that cheese, or a lamb or two.

Silenus: No problems – right away. I don't give a fig for my master. I'd do anything to drink down a full cup of that heavenly wine. I'd give you the entire flock of all the Cyclopes for it, and then when I am good and drunk, I'd go take a run from the highest cliffs and leap into the sea. Wheee! Any man who doesn't like to drink is a fool and has no dick. Hmmm....yeah, that's right, in fact when you're drunk that's the best way to make our peckers stand on end, and it helps us when we are trying to grab a handful of titties, and browse our hands over the soft and wet areas while we stroke her pussy. And of course it also leads us to dance and forget our cares.

And so why shouldn't I want to drink this down all the way so that I can forget about this stupid Cyclops here and his one-eye? To hell with him...

Exit Silenus into the cave

Chorus Leader: Hey, look here, Odysseus – we need to have a little chat with you.

Odysseus: Sure, of course – you're all my friends and I am your friend.

Chorus Leader: Did you really capture Troy and then take Helen as your prisoner?

Odysseus: Yup, and then we sacked and looted the whole house that belonged to Priam and his sons.

Chorus Leader: Well...and after you caught and took Helen as your captive...did all of you then take turns fucking her? I mean, she likes to bang a lot of men – right? That hot little traitor! She saw the tight pants on Paris' legs, and the golden necklaces that he wore, and she went all horny for him. And she left behind that poor little man, that Menelaus.

Oh I wish that the female race ceased to exist – except when it is sucking on my cock, that is!

Enter Silenus from the cave

Silenus: Ok look right here, my lord and master Odysseus – here are all the flocks of lambs that now belong to you – and all the children of those lambs thrown in for good measure. And here's a shitload of cheeses – all the kinds that I could dig up, all made from the best curdled milk we have here.

Go ahead – take them. Take them quickly, please, and get away from the cave as soon as you can, but not before you give me my part of the bargain – that sweet drunk that is the vine of Dionysus...

Oh crap – here come the Cyclops now...what are we going to do?

Odysseus: It looks like the jig is up for us, then. Is there anywhere we can flee or hide?

Silenus: Hmmm...you could go inside the cave – nobody would see you there.

Odysseus: That sounds like it could be a dangerous plan – just like walking straight into the spider's web.

Silenus: It'll be fine – there's all kinds of places to hide in that cave.

Odysseus: I can't bring myself to do that. The whole of Troy would groan so loudly if it were to hear that I, Odysseus, ran away and fled from just one man when I stood my ground there so often, holding my shield in my hand, fighting off that endless number of Trojans.

No – if I am going to die, I'm going to die nobly. Or, more preferably, if I live on, I'll do so with self-respect and my reputation still intact.

Enter the Cyclops

Cyclops: Hey, what the hell is going on here? Why are you all acting so lazy? And what's up with all of this uproar? Do you think that it's some kind of Bacchic holiday? But, I hate to tell you, you're Dionysus ain't here – none his bronze clingers nor any of his rattling clangers are here either.

More to the point – how are my newborn lambs doing in the cave? Have they rushed back to their mothers to get a suck at the tits? And what about the milk? Have you turned it into cheese yet and filled the baskets with this freshly made cheese?

Well, what do you have to say in response? Answer me, damn it, or I'm going to have to hit someone in the head with my club and beat the crap out of all of you until you beg me to stop through your tears. Look at me, not down there, when I am talking to you.

Chorus Leader: There – we're looking up at you as if you were Zeus himself. In fact I can even see a bit of your brother Orion in you.

Cyclops: Is my dinner ready for me to eat, or what?

Chorus Leader: It is – ready and waiting for you. You only have to gobble it up.

Cyclops: And are the mixing bowls all filled with milk?

Chorus Leader: There's enough there that you could drink a whole vat of it, if you want.

Cyclops: Is it cow's milk or sheep's milk – or is it some mixture of both?

Chorus Leader: It's whatever you want – just as long as you don't swallow me.

Cyclops: No, you'd be the last person I'd swallow. You'd be the death of me – dancing around inside of my belly with those dance steps of yours.

Hey, what's all that going on over there at the entrance to my cave? Have some pirates or thieves come here? Who are all those people? I see lambs and sheep from my cave that are tied up and bound, and my buckets of cheese are all over the place – and the old man there looks as if someone beat him around the head, look at all those red marks that cover his face. His face is all red!

Silenus: Oh...oh...poor me. I've got such a horrible fever from having been beaten up!

Cyclops: By whom? Who's the one that's been beating you about the head, old man?

Silenus: Oh, it was these men right here, because I wouldn't let them take your property for his crew.

Cyclops: Don't they know that I am a god and that my ancestors are gods?

Silenus: Well, I told their leader here, but they just went on stealing your stuff anyway, and what's even worse, they started in on the cheese, even though I tried to stop him, and then they began to take your sheep off to their ship.

And then – get this – he said that they were going to chain you down with a three-foot collar, and then squeeze you so tightly that the shit would come streaming out of your one eye, and then they'd cover your back with lashes from the whip. Then they are going to tie you up in chains and throw you on their boat, so that they can sail away with you and sell you to be a slave to someone who needs help moving rocks and shit like that.

Cyclops: Hmmm...is that right? Ok – you over there, you little satyr, go and sharpen my knife – and make it snappy. And then set a big bunch of sticks in the pit and light a fire.

I'm going to kill this leader fellow at once – him and the rest of his crew – and I'll stuff myself from the boiled, or maybe fried, meat of their flesh. It will be so tender that I won't even need to carve it.

Sweet – I'm completely fed up with mountain food anyway. I've had enough lions and deer lately, and it's been way too long since I've had a real good taste of human flesh. Mmmm...

Silenus: Well said, master – it's good to have a change in diet. And it has been quite some time since we've had visitors here at the cave.

Odysseus: But Cyclops, please let your visitors speak. We came here from our ship hoping that we could buy some food. And this guy over here, once he had something to drink, sold us all these sheep and all this cheese in return for a cup of wine. He was just as willing to sell it as we were willing to buy it.

I mean, everything he just told you was a lie. You can see that he is trying to sell all your stuff behind your back.

Silenus: Me, steal? Lie? Why, how dare you, sir! Damn you to hell!

Odysseus: Sure – you can damn me all you like if I am lying, which I'm not.

Silenus: I swear, O Cyclops, I swear in the name of your father Poseidon, in the name of great Triton and Nereus, in the name of Calypso and the daughters of Nereus, in the name of the holy waves in the sea and every type of fish that swims in them...I swear, dear master, dear Cyclops, O sweet little Cyclops, that I wasn't trying to sell your stuff to these strangers. And if I am telling a lie, then you can kill my children for it, as dear as they are to me!

Chorus Leader: What the fuck? And may you die as well then! I even saw you selling all of this stuff here to the stranger. And if I am lying, then you can kill my father, as dear as he is to me! But you shouldn't blame these strangers here.

Cyclops: Hmm...I think that you, child, you're the one who's lying, and that your father is the honest one here. I'd put more trust in him and his honesty than I would in king Minos himself, the judge in Hades.

But I do want to ask you strangers a question. Where have you come from? What's your country? And tell me in what city you grew up.

Odysseus: We're from Ithaca. After we finished sacking Troy, we set sail to go home and we ended up here on your island, Cyclops. The winds blew us here off course.

Cyclops: So are you the people who went to destroy Troy because that slut Helen was stolen from Greece?

Odysseus: Yes, we are those people, and that's what we did. And that terrible deed is now done – thankfully.

Cyclops: The lot of you should be ashamed of yourselves. I mean, really – going to war against the Trojans for the sake of one woman?

Odysseus: But a god was the real reason for it! You really shouldn't blame any mortals for this.

All the same, O noble son of the sea god Poseidon, we beg of you and ask you as free men: please, don't kill me who have come to your cave, your home, as friends. Any meal that you make out of us would be a sin against the gods.

For, my lord, it is we Greeks who protected your father Poseidon and kept him safe within the walls of his temples throughout every part of Greece. We're the ones who kept his sacred harbour in Taenarus safe and unharmed, and we did the same for Cape Malea. The rocky peak of Sunium, which is filled with silver and sacred to the goddess Athena, and the sanctuaries of Geraestus – all of them are safe thanks to us.

We didn't allow the great disgrace of allowing Greek possessions to fall into the hands of the Trojans. And now you too even play a role in all of these events – for where we are right now, here in Sicily under this volcano Aetna, you are living in a part of Greece in this very spot.

Well, anyway, even if you don't agree with what I just said, we have this law in the human world that says that shipwrecked sailors are supposed to receive food and protection. They're supposed to receive hospitality...and clothing...and that you're supposed to treat us nicely. And, above all, this rule says that you are not – and I repeat NOT – supposed to chop us up into little bits and then roast us over the fire on sticks before you put us in your belly.

The land of Priam – that Troy from which we came – has brought enough tragedy and sadness to Greece, since its plains and rivers have soaked up the blood of all those thousands who were killed in the war. Wives have been made widows, mothers have lost their sons, and old men have had their hair turn grey, going to the grave childless. If you are thinking of cooking up and eating some of the few Greek who remain from that war, in that unholy meal of yours, then where will anyone in Greece turn for help and safety?

Listen to me, Cyclops – change your plan, give it up. Forget this hunger and this horrible plan and choose to do what is right instead. For many people end up suffering in the end when they try to achieve profit by doing evil deeds.

Silenus: I want to give you a little piece of advice here, Cyclops – eat every bit of this man's flesh and don't leave anything untouched. What's more, if you have a good chew on his tongue, then you'll become very clever and eloquent, just like he is.

Cyclops: O little man, little Greek man, it's money that is the god to wise and clever men – the rest is just bullshit and fine-sounding words. I don't care in the slightest about my father's caves along the coast. Why did you think that I would? Why did you even mention them? And I'm not afraid of Zeus' thunder either, stranger – for I don't really think that he is more powerful than I am.

I've never given a thought to Zeus before, and I won't care about him in the future – and I'll tell you why. When Zeus sends down his rain from above, I get my shelter from the rain in this here cave and I have a feast on lamb or some wild animal. I fill my belly till I'm stuffed, then I stretch and wash down the meal with a vat full of milk. And then I turn the vat over and drum on it and make a noise in here that's loud enough to rival Zeus' thunder. And if that noise isn't enough, I add farts to increase the volume.

And when the wind from Thrace comes down here and brings us snow, I cover and wrap my body in the skins of beasts, then I build and light a huge fire – and so I don't have to pay any attention to the snow.

The earth itself brings forth the grass that feeds my flock, and it does so whether it wants to or not. And I sacrifice these animals to no god other than me. I certainly don't sacrifice them to the other gods – no, they are dedicated to my belly alone, the greatest of all the gods. To eat and drink your fill, and to do this each and every day – this is Zeus in the eyes of intelligent men. As for all those little men who pass laws and make everyone's life complicated – fuck 'em. I'm going to go right on doing what I've always been doing – pleasing myself. And that means that I am going to eat you all up.

But, to be fair, I will give you some presents that people typically offer their guests. I'll give you fire to warm you up, salt to put all over your body, and water from my father, along with a bronze pot he once gave me. Of course, when the water in that bronze pot reaches the boiling point, it will cook you up really nicely.

So now, I want all of you little Greek men to go inside and stand around the altar of the god who rules that cave in there – and you are going to provide some nice entertainment for me in addition to a fine meal.

Odysseus: Good god – I've gotten out of so many tight spots in Troy, and so many on the high seas as well, only to wind up washed ashore on the coast of this heartless and godless thing!

O Pallas Athena, divine daughter of Zeus – please now, now is the time to help me, if ever there was a time! For right now I've encountered greater trouble than any I ever met when I was at Troy – this is the type of danger from which there is no escape.

And you, O Zeus, protector of guests and strangers, you who live and rule among the bright stars in the heavens – please look down on my problems and help me! For if you don't look after me now, then you can't be Zeus – but you must rather be some worthless god instead.

The Cyclops pushes Odysseus and his crew forward into the cave

CHORUS:

O Cyclops, open your huge jaws and vast mouth!
Your dinner is ready –
The limbs of your guests,
Whether they are boiled, roasted, or even broiled,
Are ready for you to chew and devour
As you sit back and relax
Dressed in your old goatskin.
Just don't ask me to dine with you!
You can have that feast all to yourself –
I'll just keep my distance from this cave,
As far away as I can be
From the Cyclops on Aetna;
This disgusting glutton
Who stuffs himself on the flesh
Of his guests.
So savage, such a stranger to mercy,
This one who cooks on his fire
The stranger who have asked for his help,
And who boils them all up
And then scoffs them down,
While his evil mouth chomps on human meat
Plucked from the burning coals of the fire.

Enter Odysseus from the cave

ODYSSEUS: O Zeus, how can I even begin to say what I just saw in that cave? It was all so terrible, so incredible – the kind of stuff you only hear about in stories. It's the stuff of myths – do real men act this way?

CHORUS LEADER: What happened, Odysseus? Did that godless Cyclops really eat up all of your crew?

ODYSSEUS: Not all, but he picked up two of them, the ones who had the fattest bodies – and he weighed them in his hands.

CHORUS LEADER: That's so horrible – how could you stand to watch it all?

ODYSSEUS: As soon as we went inside this rocky cavern, he first spent his time with the fire, making sure that it blazed up to a great height, and so he tossed huge logs from a mighty oak tree on top of the fire. It was enough oak to load three wagons. And after the fire was going strong, he then put his bronze kettle on top of the fire to get the water up to boil.

Right next to the fire he spread out a bed of pine and fir branches on the ground. After he finished milking the cows and the sheep, he filled this huge mixing bowl right to the brim with milk – it probably contained maybe five hundred litres. And then he set right next to it this huge wooden cup that must have been four feet wide and six feet deep. Then he got all the cookware ready that he needed to make a feast, and when that sick and disgusting cook had everything that he needed, he then snatched up two of my men.

When he took hold of the first one he quickly cut his throat over the bowl, then he grabbed the second one by his foot and smashed his head against a rock until his gory brains were all over the place. Next, he cut them up with a sharp blade and he roasted them on top of the fire while he put their arms and legs in the pot to boil. I was standing right next to the Cyclops while he did this – oh, why me? – and tears were pouring down my cheeks while I watched him do these horrible things. The other members of my crew were off hiding, huddled up just like birds in the corners of the caves, all of their faces were white as ghosts.

But then he leaned back, feeling a bit bloated after that awful meal he had just made of my two crew-members, and so he let out the most god-awful belch that I have ever heard. It smelled something terrible, let me tell you. At that very moment, some god sent an amazing idea to me. I filled a cup with this wine that Maron gave me and then I set the wine before while I said these words to him: "O Cyclops, son of the sea-god Poseidon, come, take a swig of this divine drink that the grapes of Greece offer you here – this joyful drink, this wine from Dionysus!"

He was completely stuffed with that repulsive meal, but he took the drink into his hand and then drained it all in one quick gulp. He was overwhelmed by this, then he raised his hands in appreciation and said: "Wowza! Dear friend, you're the best – my bestest friend...my pal all right. You've given me this awesome drink and it, uh, it puts, uh, it's just great to drink this after such a good meal!"

I saw that this drink was giving him pleasure, and that he was quickly becoming drunk, so I gave him another drink right-away, since I knew that the wine would soon make him completely shit-faced and that this would be his ruin, for I would be able to pay him back.

Then – what an amazing sight! – he started to sing... he was becoming sooo drunk...and I was giving him one drink after the other and this started to make his belly all warm. So he's sitting in there right now, drunkenly singing away while my crew is in there crying in fear – you can hear the echo of his singing even out here.

So I've just taken the chance to sneak out here because I wanted to ask you whether you want to help me out and finally be free of this monster so you can go and live again in the halls of Dionysus along with his nymphs and Naiads. Your father already agreed to this when I asked him in the cave, but he's really a weakling, and, just like the Cyclops there, I can also see that he's already a bit gone on the sauce. I mean, he's holding that cup so tightly in his hand you'd think he were glued to it. But all of you are still young, and so I think I can trust you with this. So come on, follow me and you can save yourselves. This way you'll be able to get back to your old friend Dionysus – who is sooo very different from this Cyclops here.

Chorus Leader: O my dear friend – if only we can finally see the day when we can escape from this godless Cyclops. It's been so long now that this cock of mine has been a bachelor, with no place to rest its head.

Odysseus: Listen to what I have in mind that will set you free. I'm planning quite the punishment for this disgusting beast.

Chorus Leader: Go ahead – tell me. I'd rather hear this plan of yours than all the harps in Asia.

Odysseus: He is so happy with this drink from Dionysus that he wants to go visit his brothers and party with them.

Chorus Leader: I think I catch your meaning. You're going to lay an ambush on him in the woods and then you'll cut his throat or push him off some cliff or something like that.

Odysseus: What? No, nothing like that at all. I had something that involves a bit more trickery.

Chorus Leader: What's your plan then? We've already heard a great deal about your cleverness.

Odysseus: Well, to start I'm going to stop him in his attempt to go out and party with his friends by telling him that he should be careful not to give any of the other Cyclopes this wine, but that he should instead keep it all for himself and enjoy all the pleasures that it brings all by himself.

But he'll eventually fall asleep, as happens soon after any drinking binge, and then I'll take my sword and use it to sharpen up the trunk of an olive tree that is sitting in there. I'll make it all pointy on one end and then I'll stick it in the coals of the fire to make it really really hot. Then, when it's almost to the point of burning, I'll lift it up on high and then drive the thing right through that one eye of the Cyclops. It will melt his eye and he'll be turned blind.

So just like a carpenter plays so comfortably with his tools, with his hammer and nails, that's how easily I'll force this burning log into that monster's eye – and I'll blind him once and for all time.

Chorus Leader: That's fucking amazing! This plan of yours leaves me so excited that I want to jizz.

Odysseus: And after I stab him in the eye, then I'll take your father and all of you, set the lot of you on my ship, and we'll high-tail it out of here, sailing away from this land as fast as we can.

Chorus Leader: Do you think that there might be a way for me to help out in blinding this Cyclops? I mean, it's just like pouring a libation to the gods – everyone gets to help out in some way. Perhaps I can help drive the stake through his eye? Dude, I really want to take part in this.

Odysseus: Yeah, of course – you are all going to have to take a part in this – the log is huge and we'll all need to lift the thing together.

Chorus Leader: I could happily try to lift the weight of a hundred wagons if it would mean that we're giving that Cyclops a horrible death! Let's just burn the ugly bugger's eye as if we're burning a wasps' nest!

Odysseus: Then just shush now! You all know the plan, and so when I say the word, you have to do what your master here tells you to do. That's me. There's no chance that I am going to save myself and leave my men in there alone and trapped inside. It would be easy for me to escape alone, of course, since I have just managed to come out of the cave now. But it just isn't right to save myself alone and completely abandon my crew.

Exit Odysseus back into the cave

Chorus: Come on, everyone, who is going to stand first here, and who will stand second in line? Let's all get ready to put our hands on that burning log, the one we're going to shove right into the eye of the Cyclops and destroy his sight.

Wait! Shhh…be quiet!

I think I can see the Cyclops. Yes, here he comes, all liquored up and singing some drunken song. He's staggering his way out of his rocky cave, that home of his. Good grief – what a horrible voice he has!

C'mon then, let's teach him a little bit about how a good party song should sound, then after we give him this lesson in culture, we'll poke his damn eye out!

Enter the Cyclops from the cave, propped up by Silenus

Odysseus follows behind them

    Happy is the man who can shout
    The Bacchic song – whoo-hoo!
    Off to the party,
    For him the wine keeps flowing,
    His arms are wrapped around
    His bestest of friends!
    And waiting for him, that lucky stud,
    On his bed at home
    Is the hot young body
    Of his slutty mistress
    With her shining hair
    And oiled-up body –
    The man shouts,
    "Who can get this door for me?"

Cyclops: I said goddamn! I am so freaking ripped right now – I love all this messing around that comes with drinking too much wine. I'm like a boat, and stuffed all the way up to the top deck – but the top deck is my belly, and I'm filled with wine – and I'm drunk – real real drunk! Bwa-ha-ha-ha!

But all of this good booze has….it has…what? Wait…it has made me remember…it has remembered me. Hmmm…where was I? Oh, yes, I need to share this wine with my bothers…no, my brothers. I need to go find the other Cyclo…Cyclo…Cylco-dobolops…you know, all the other one-eyes like me, and then we can party all together.

Come here, my little friend, hand me the wineskin.

Chorus:

    With the beautiful glance
    From his lovely eye
    The dapper Cyclops comes out
    Comes out from his house,
    As handsome as a groom,
    As handsome as a lover-boy,
    A tender young nymph waits for this groom,
    She waits there in the cave;
    She's burning, she's in heat,
    And soon will give him the crown,
    To celebrate you,
    As the king of fuck-town!

Odysseus: Hey Cyclops, listen here for a second. I'm really good friends with this Dionysus – you know this Dionysus that you are and have been drinking.

Cyclops: Who is this...this Dionysus? Is he worshipped as a god?

Odysseus: Oh yes – he is the greatest joy that mortal men have in their lives.

Cyclops (burps): Well, he makes a damn good burp, I tell you that!

Odysseus: That's exactly the way he is – he doesn't do any harm to anyone.

Cyclops: Wait – but how can a god live in this eensie-weensie little wineskin?

Odysseus: Oh, he's just fine wherever you put him.

Cyclops: But it's not right for a god to cover himself in skins.

Odysseus: What's the problem, if you're getting pleasure from him? Do you have some problem with the wine-skin?

Cyclops: The wineskin is shit – but I really love this wine.

Odysseus: So why don't you just stay here and get drunk, Cyclops. Just relax and enjoy yourself.

Cyclops: You mean I shouldn't go and give some of this to my brothers?

Odysseus: Yes – just keep it to yourself. You'll bring more honour to yourself that way.

Cyclops: But...if I gave it to my friends I'd be more useful...I'd be more liked...

Odysseus: Yes, but booze and parties always end in fights and fisticuffs.

Cyclops: Yes, I may be drunk...but...no one's going to lay a hand on me, mister!

Odysseus: That's right, my friend – it's best to stay at home when you've had too much to drink.

Cyclops: But whoever drinks and doesn't party is a dolt, a fool.

Odysseus: On the contrary – whoever stays at home when he is drunk is smart and wise.

Cyclops: Silenus? What do you think we should do? Should we stay here at home?

Silenus: Yes, I'd stay – what do we need with more drinkers, Cyclops?

Odysseus: And, anyway, the ground here is so soft, so perfect for resting, with all of the flowers, so good for sleeping...

Silenus: There there....isn't it nice to have a nice drink when the sun is so hot outside? Why don't you just lie down...yes, set yourself down and stretch out on the grass.

The Cyclops lies down and Silenus sneakily puts the mixing bowl behind him

Cyclops: There – all down now. Wait – why did you put the bowl behind my head?

Silenus: I just don't want anyone to tip it over.

Cyclops: You little bugger! You were planning to filch my booze! Put it back here, in the middle between us, where I can keep my eye on it.

Hey stranger, I never did get your name.

Odysseus: My name – it's No-body. But how are you going to thank me for this wine that I gave you?

Cyclops: Thank you?...oh...I know, I'll eat you last of all your crew...yes, eat you last.

Silenus: Excellent idea, Cyclops – that's a well-deserved present for your guest!

Silenus quickly sneaks some wine

Cyclops: What? What's that? You're drinking my wine when I'm not looking!

Silenus: No...not at all – the wine just kissed me, that's all. It said I have beautiful eyes.

CYCLOPS: You just had better be careful – you may love the wine, but it doesn't mean that she loves you...

SILENUS: That's not true at all. In the name of Zeus, this wine here has fallen head-over-heels for my good looks.

CYCLOPS: Hmmph...pour me a cup of it, but just pour it – and give it to me when you are done.

SILENUS: But is this the right mixture? Let me have a little taste to check...

Silenus takes a quick drink

CYCLOPS: You little bugger – give me the damn drink! I want my booze!

SILENUS: Just a second – by the gods, I won't give it to you before I see you wearing this crown of flowers here...and I have another taste.

Silenus offers the Cyclops a wreathe of flowers while he drains his cup dry

CYCLOPS: This wine-pourer of mine is a little thief!

SILENUS: That may be true, but this wine is sooo sweet. Ooh here comes another drinkie for you, Mr. Cyclops! Now, you just wipe your mouth before I give you another.

CYCLOPS: There – I've wiped it all up. My mouth and my beard are clean now. More wine! More!

SILENUS: Just settle yourself down on your elbow there – that's it, gently – and take a good long drink...just as you see me drinking – and now you don't see me.

Silenus drains the cup, his face hidden as he empties it out

CYCLOPS: Hey – what are you doing there?

SILENUS: Just having a good guzzle of wine.

CYCLOPS: Stranger, I want you to be my wine-pourer. You take the flask there.

ODYSSEUS: Well, the wine will feel at home in my hand, that's for sure.

CYCLOPS: Come on then – gimme gimme!

ODYSSEUS: I'm pouring it out right now – just you take it easy, friend. Relax.

CYCLOPS: Relax? That's not easy to do when you're drunk, you know.

ODYSSEUS: Here – here's a cup for you. Take it and drink it all down – every last drop of it. The drunk and his bottle must reach their end together.

CYCLOPS: Oh sweetness – the vine that produced this must be a wizard, a genius even!

ODYSSEUS: And if you keep drinking after such a big meal, and keep at it with the sauce till you fill up your belly, then you'll soon sleep as sweetly as a baby. But if you don't drink it all, then Dionysus will get you! He'll make your throat all dry and make you feel icky all over.

CYCLOPS: Whoa – hey-o...I feel like my head is swimming. I've never felt so much pleasure before. Ooh...ahh...the earth and the sky - they are all twirling around my head, mixed up together like a... what'dyacallit?

Hey – I can see – where? – oh, there it is again...it's the throne of Zeus...and there's the whole group of the holy gods. Heellooo there gods!

Do you...do you think I should try to give the gods some little kissies?

The Chorus dance around him, pretending to be ghosts or gods

Ooh...the Graces there...they have the hots for me – I think they're making the moves on me. No – I can't fuck you tonight. With my Ganymede here...well, he'll be plenty good enough for me if I take him off to the sack. He'll bring me a great sleep – a magnificent honour to fuck him. Sorry about this, my Graces – but I like boys more than girls, for some reason...

The Cyclops grabs Silenus, mistaking him for Ganymede

SILENUS: What is this, Cyclops? Am I supposed to be Zeus' little boy Ganymede?

CYCLOPS: Damn right you are! And I'm Zeus – you're the boy I stole from Dardanus!

Silenus: Oh crap – I'm done for, my children. Horrible. Unspeakable things are going to happen to me.

Cyclops: What's this? Are you going to be so snooty to your lover just because he's drunk?

Silenus: Fuck me – the wine that I have to drink now is going to be pretty bitter.

Exit the Cyclops into the cave, dragging his lover Ganymede/Silenus

Odysseus: Come here, quick, you children of Dionysus, you sons of nobility. Our mark is inside the cave right now. In a few minutes he'll puke out his disgusting meal of human flesh – that's what drinking does. And in the cave, just inside the long hallway, our poking-stick, that log of oak, is all ready on the flame and it's started to give out smoke.

There's nothing really left to do other than poke out this Cyclops' eye. But all of you will have to prove that you are men.

Chorus Leader: Oh, but our wills are like rocks or stones inside! But let's go into the cave before my father gets raped...or eaten. Everything is ready to rock and roll on our side.

Odysseus: O lord Hephaestus, ruler of the land of Aetna here, please help us burn out the eye of this neighbour of yours. Let's all be rid of him for once and all.

And you, O Sleep, the child of dark Night, please come here with all your might and help us attack this beast that is so hated by the gods!

After all of our amazing and glorious deeds that we performed at Troy, please don't let Odysseus – me – and his crew be killed by a thing who has no respect for gods or men. If he does kill us, then we'll all just have to make Chance into a goddess, and to rank her even higher than all other ones.

Exit Odysseus into the cave

Chorus:

A bitter wrench is about to grab
The neck of this beast
Who likes to eat his own visitors;
Fire is about to destroy that one shining eye of his;
Our poking-stick, so large and daunting,
Already is waiting, its tip burning hot
And sitting and resting in the coals.

Oh come on you wine! Do your thing!
Help us rip out the eye of this lunatic Cyclops;
Make sure that he'll forever
Regret the day that he drank you down!
For myself, all I want to do is to see Dionysus
Wearing his ivy,
And to leave far behind this cave of the Cyclops –
Will I ever see such pleasure and joy again?

Enter Odysseus from the cave

Odysseus: Be quiet, will you, shhh! Be quiet you little animals, for heaven's sake – just keep it down. I don't want to hear any one of you even breathe, or clear his throat, or even blink for that matter. He's asleep now and we can't let this monster wake up, for then we won't be able to burn out his eye with our fire-stick.

Cyclops: Ok – we're keeping quiet. No sound will escape these lips.

Odysseus: Good – then let's all get to work. You're all going to go inside and grab hold of the end of our fire-log. Its pointy end is now red-hot.

Chorus Leader: You should tell us what roles you'd like each of us to play in this. Who's going to be the first one to lift this burning piece of wood? Let us know how we all can take part in this adventure, so we can all burn out his eye together and share in whatever fate has in store for us.

One member of the Chorus: But here where we're standing, over here by the cave's door...it's a bit too far away for us to lift the log and reach his eye.

Another member of the Chorus: And all of a sudden I'm finding it hard to walk.

One member of the Chorus: The same for us too! We can't walk either. Just while we were standing here we suddenly sprained our ankles and legs. Oww!

Odysseus: So you sprained your ankles just by standing there, doing nothing?

Another member of the Chorus: And my eyes are all full of dust and ash, and I can hardly see straight.

Odysseus: It looks like these helpers of mine are worthless cowards.

Chorus Leader: Hey now, just because I'm worried about my back and my spine, and I really don't want to see my teeth lying on the ground – is that supposed to mean that I'm a coward?

But I know a spell and song from Orpheus that's so amazing it will make our weapon stand up all on its own and then fly into the skull of old one-eye there and set him on fire.

Odysseus: I knew from the very start that this is the type of people you were, and now it even becomes clearer. It's necessary for me to make use of my friends in this caper. So if you don't have the strength and daring to help me, at least you can cheer on my men so that your words of support will give them courage.

Exit Odysseus into the cave

Chorus Leader: I'll do this, and he can let his soldiers take all of the risks for us. We'll be the cheerleaders from the sidelines. Let the Cyclops burn!

Chorus:
> Hey hey, ho ho
> That one-eyed Cyclops has got to go!
> Do it, boys, go to it!
> Push it in hard,
> Burn out the eye of that monster
> Who eats his guests!
> Burn him down, light him on fire –
> That shepherd of Mt. Aetna.
> Twist it in, turn it then, but watch out,
> For in pain he might do some harm to you!

Enter the Cyclops from the cave, with blood streaming from his eye

Cyclops: Ahhhhh! Ohhhh! My eye! My eye! It's been burned – there's nothing left.

Chorus Leader: What a lovely tune – please keep singing that for us, Cyclops.

Cyclops: What? Ohhhh! Fuck....ohhhh! I've been assaulted – they've destroyed me! But you'll never be able to get away from me, you dirty pile of scum that did this to me. I'm just going to stand here in the doorway to the cave and block the entrance with my hands and arms.

Chorus Leader: Why are you shouting like that, Cyclops?

Cyclops: I'm ruined.

Chorus Leader: Well you do look rather shitty, that's for sure.

Cyclops: I feel like shit.

Chorus Leader: Did you get so drunk that you ended up falling into the hot coals?

Cyclops: No-body destroyed me.

Chorus Leader: Good, then nobody's hurt you at all.

Cyclops: No – No-body blinded me...No-body stabbed me in the eye!

Chorus Leader: So then you're not blind at all.

Cyclops: I'm as blind as you, it seems!

Chorus Leader: And how is it that nobody could make you blind?

Cyclops: You are making fun of me. But where is this No-body? Where's No-body?

Chorus Leader: That's easy – nobody is nowhere, Cyclops.

Cyclops: I'm talking about the damn stranger – you know what I mean. He's the one who did this to me. He got me so drunk and then did this to me. What a horrible guest!

Chorus Leader: Well, wine is very dangerous and tricky – it creates all kinds of problems when you try to wrestle with it.

Cyclops: Just tell me this, please – have they already escaped or are they still inside the cave?

Chorus Leader: They're actually over there, keeping quite quiet – under the cover of that cliff.

Cyclops: Where? To which side of me? To my left or to my right?

Chorus Leader: Uhhh...to your right. Yes, to your right side.

The Cyclops moves away from the entrance and heads to the right

Odysseus, his crew, and Silenus, sneak silently out of the cave

Cyclops: Where?

Chorus Leader: Right there – a little bit more...do you have them?

Cyclops: Ahhh...crap! No – I don't have them, but I think I've done some more damage to my head!

Chorus Leader: And it looks like they've just given you the slip as well.

Cyclops: What? But didn't you say they were this way here?

Chorus Leader: No I mean this way here?

Cyclops: Dammit – what way are you pointing?

Chorus Leader: Just turn to your left, now turn to your right, now left again – there they are on your right!

Cyclops: Assholes – you're making fun of me, tricking me while I am in misery.

Chorus Leader: Ok – I won't trick you anymore. He's right there in front of you now.

Cyclops: Where are you then, you little bastard who did this to me?

Odysseus: Oh, I'm at a safe distance from you – where I can keep the body of Odysseus safe from any harm.

Cyclops: What? Odysseus? This is a new name that you are using.

Odysseus: But this name is the very one that my father gave me – Odysseus. And it looks like it was your destiny to be punished for that ungodly meal you made out of my crew. It would have been wrong of me to raze Troy to the ground and not get my revenge on you for what you just did to two of my men.

Cyclops: Oh my – the ancient prophecy has been fulfilled! It said that one day a man named Odysseus would come from Troy and blind me. But the prophecy also said that you, in turn, would be punished for doing this to me – that you would have to wander over the seas for many years.

Odysseus: Whatever, buddy. I really don't care what you have to say – this thing is over here. As for me, I'm going to head down to my boat on the shore. Then we'll take the ship and sail for home over this Sicilian Sea.

Exit Odysseus and his crew

Cyclops: Oh no you don't! I'm going to break off a piece of this here rock and crush you and your crew beneath it. I may be blind, but I'll be able to reach the top of the mountain quickly through the tunnel in my cave.

Exit the Cyclops into the cave

Chorus: And as for us, we'll join with Odysseus and his crew. And we'll always take our orders from sweet delicious Dionysus!

Exit the Chorus and Silenus

ranslated from the Greek by Stephen Russell, PhD

Chapter 11
Publius Annius Florus
On Spartactus

Epitome 2.8

The Story: There are three significant accounts of the runaway slave Spartacus who roamed around Italy in 73-71 BC. Plutarch and Appian wrote the first two accounts. The third is here, by Florus, in his *Epitome*, which he wanted to serve as an addition to Livy's history of Rome.

I don't know how to describe the war that was caused and led by Spartacus. For slaves acted as soldiers, the officers in this conflict were gladiators (men of the lowliest class and led by the worst kind of men) – and all of this meant that Rome became the subject of mockery while she suffered many horrible defeats.

Spartacus, Crixus, and Oenomaus broke out of the gladiatorial school of Lentulus with thirty or perhaps more gladiators and then escaped from Capua. Then they summoned other slaves to join their campaign, and they quickly collected more than 10,000 followers. These men, who had been originally content just to have escaped, soon began to long for revenge as well.

The first position that attracted them (a suitable one for such ravenous monsters) was Mt. Vesuvius. When they were besieged there by Clodius Glabrus, they responded by sliding down ropes made out of vine-twigs through a passage in the hollow of the mountain down into its very depths, and then they escaped from the mountain through a hidden exit, after which they seized the camp of the general in a surprise attack that was completely unexpected.

They then attacked other camps, that of Varenius and afterward that of Thoranus; and they roamed over the whole of Campania. Not satisfied with merely plundering country houses and villages, they then attacked to Nola, Nuceria, Thurii and Metapontum with savage destruction.

With fresh supporters arriving each day, they soon had the appearance of a regular army. They made for themselves crude shields of branches and the skins of animals, and swords and other weapons by melting down the iron in the slave-prisons. To ensure that they had everything that a proper army should have, they obtained a cavalry by breaking in herds of horses they encountered, and his men took to Spartacus the insignia captured from the Roman generals. And this man accepted these honours – the man nor who was once a Thracian mercenary, had then become a Roman soldier, and from a soldier became a deserter, then a robber and bandit, and finally, thanks to his strength, a gladiator.

He also gave his officers who died in battle funerals like those of Roman generals, and ordered that his Roman captives to fight at funeral games of his officers, just as if he were trying to wipe out all his past dishonor by having become a giver of gladiatorial shows instead of a gladiator.

Next he actually attacked generals of consular rank, and thus he defeated the army of Lentulus in the Apennines and destroyed the camp of Gaius Cassius at Mutina. Elated by these victories, he then even thought about marching on Rome itself – which would have been a major disgrace to us.

At last a combined effort was made, supported by all the resources of the empire, against this gladiator, and Licinius Crassus vindicated the honor of Rome. Our enemies (I am ashamed to give them this title) were beaten and forced to flee by Crassus and so took refuge in the furthest parts of Italy. Here they were cut off in the angle of Bruttium and were preparing to escape to Sicily, but they were unable to obtain ships – so they tried to cross the swift waters of the straits on rafts made out of beams and barrels bound together with branches.

Failing in this attempt, they finally ventured forth and met a death worthy of men, fighting to the death as was fitting for those who were commanded by a gladiator. Spartacus himself fell as a general would, fighting most bravely in the front ranks of his troops.

Translated from the Latin by Stephen Russell, PhD
English version by Stephen Russell and Laura Holtebrinck

Chapter 12
Apollodorus

PERSEUS AND BELLEROPHON

The Story: Perseus is a child of Zeus and is one of the most famous heroes in Greek mythology. He is an ancestor of the hero Heracles.

[2.3.1] Bellerophon, the son of Glaucus, who was the son of Sisyphus, accidentally killed his brother Deliades (or according to some, Peiren, or as others say, Alcimenes) and so came to Proetus to be purified. And Proetus' wife Stheneboea fell in love with him and let him know that she wanted to have an affair. When Bellerophon rejected her advances, she told Proetus that Bellerophon had been trying to seduce her. Proetus believed his wife and so he gave Bellerophon a letter to take to Iobates, in which it was written that Iobates was to kill Bellerophon when he arrived with the letter.

When Iobates read the letter, he told him that it contained orders for Bellerophon to kill the Chimaera, believing that he would be destroyed by the monster, for it was more than a match for many man, let alone just one. It had the front of a lion, the tail of a dragon, and its third head, the one in the middle, was that of a goat, through which it breathed fire. And it devastated the countryside and destroyed the cattle; for it was a single creature with the power of three beasts. It is also said that this Chimaera was raised by Amisodarus, and Homer also agrees with that – and Hesiod says that it was the offspring by Typhon on Echidna, as Hesiod relates.

[2.3.2] So Bellerophon got on his winged horse Pegasus, the offspring of Medusa and Poseidon, and soared up high until he could shoot down the Chimaera with his arrows from above. After that contest Iobates ordered him to fight the Solymi, and when he had finished that task also, he ordered him to combat the Amazons. And when Bellerophon had killed them as well, Iobates picked out the supposed bravest young men of the Lycians and told them to lay a trap for Bellerophon and then kill him. But when Bellerophon killed all of these young men, Iobates, greatly admiring his strength, finally showed him the letter and begged him to stay with him; moreover, he gave him his daughter Philonoe in marriage and left his kingdom to Bellerophon when he died.

[2.4.1] When Acrisius asked the oracle how he could get male children, the god said that his daughter would give birth to a son who would kill him. Fearing this would happen, Acrisius built a bronze chamber under ground and he kept his daughter Danae there with a guard in front. However, she was seduced, some say by Proetus, which provided the reason for the quarrel between the two brothers; but others say that Zeus had intercourse with her in the shape of a shower of gold that poured through the roof into Danae's lap. When Acrisius afterwards learned that she had given birth to a child, Perseus, he refused to believe that she had been seduced by Zeus, and so he locked his daughter and the child in a chest and then threw it out into the sea. The chest was washed ashore on Seriphos, and Dictys found it there, released the mother and child, and he raised the boy.

[2.4.2] Polydectes, the brother of Dictys, was then the king of Seriphos and he fell in love with Danae, but could not get close to her because Perseus was now a grown man. So he called together his friends, including

Perseus, under the pretext of collecting contributions towards a wedding gift that would allow him to marry Hippodamia, the daughter of Oenomaus. Now Perseus declared that he would get anything, even the Gorgon's head, so Polydectes asked the others to give him horses - but he did not take horses from Perseus, instead telling him to bring the Gorgon's head.

So under the guidance of Hermes and Athena Perseus made his way to the daughters of Phorcus – Enyo, Pephredo, and Dino. Phorcus had them with Ceto, and they were sisters of the Gorgons, and they were old women from their birth. The three women had only a single eye and a single tooth between them, and they passed them to one other in turns. Perseus got possession of the eye and the tooth, and when they asked for them back, he said he would give them back if they would show him the way to the nymphs. Now these nymphs had winged sandals and the kibisis, which they say was a type of wallet.

They had also the cap of Hades. When the daughters of Phorcis showed him the way to the nymphs, he returned the tooth and the eye to them, and coming to the nymphs got what he wanted. So he slung the wallet (kibisis) over his shoulder, fitted the sandals to his ankles, and put the cap on his head. When he was wearing this cap he could see whomever he pleased, but he himself was not seen by others.

After having also received an adamantine sickle from Hermes, he then flew to the Ocean and caught the Gorgons while they were asleep. They were Stheno, Euryale, and Medusa. Now only Medusa alone was mortal; for that reason Perseus was sent to fetch her head. The Gorgons had heads with scaly serpents twined about them, and they had great tusks like those of swine, and they had bronze hands and golden wings, with which they flew; and they turned to stone everyone who looked at them. So Perseus stood over them as they slept, and while Athena guided his hand and he looked with averted gaze on his bronze shield, in which he beheld the image of the Gorgon, he cut her head off. When her head was cut off, from the Gorgon sprang out the winged horse Pegasus and Chrysaor, the father of Geryon. Medusa had conceived these previously with Poseidon.

[2.4.3] So Perseus put Medusa's head in the wallet (kibisis) and then left. The Gorgons woke up from their sleep while he was leaving and they pursued Perseus, but they could not see him because of the cap, which made him hidden from their view.

Flying past Ethiopia, where Cepheus was king, he saw the king's daughter Andromeda set out in chains as prey for a sea monster. For Cassiopeia, the wife of Cepheus, claimed that she rivals the Nereids (sea-nymphs) in beauty and boasted that she was better than all of them. The Nereids became very angry with this, and Poseidon, who shared their anger, sent a flood and a monster to cause havoc in the land. But the prophet Ammon predicted that they would be saved from this disaster if they gave Cassiopeia's daughter Andromeda as a prey to the monster. Cepheus was forced by the Ethiopians to do this, and so he tied his daughter to a rock.

When Perseus saw Andromeda, he fell in love with her and promised Cepheus that he would kill the monster if the king would let him marry the rescued girl. The king agreed and the two of them swore oaths to bind their agreement. Then Perseus challenged the monster, killed it, and freed Andromeda. However, Phineus, who was a brother of Cepheus, and to whom Andromeda had first been promised in marriage, plotted against Perseus; but Perseus discovered the plot, and by showing the Gorgon's head he turned Phineus and his fellow conspirators immediately into stone.

And having come to Seriphos he found that his mother and Dictys had taken refuge at the altars to escape the violence of Polydectes. So Perseus entered the palace, where Polydectes had gathered his friends, and with his own face turned away he showed them the Gorgon's head. And everyone who looked at it were turned to stone, each in the same spot and position that he happened to have been at the time. Perseus then appointed Dictys as king of Seriphos, after which he gave back the sandals, the wallet (kibisis), and the cap to Hermes - but he gave the Gorgon's head to Athena. Hermes brought former items back to the nymphs and Athena placed the Gorgon's head in the middle of her shield. But there are some who say that Medusa was beheaded because that's what Athena wanted – for they say the Gorgon had once claimed to rival the goddess in beauty.

[2.4.4] Perseus hurried off with Danae and Andromeda to Argos to see Acrisius. But when Acrisius heard about this he was afraid of what the oracle had predicted and so he left Argos and left for the land of Pelasgians. Now Teutamides, the king of Larissa, was holding athletic games in honour of his dead father, and Perseus came to compete. He took part in the pentathlon, but in throwing the discus he struck Acrisius on the foot and killed him instantly.

Thinking that the oracle had been fulfilled, he buried Acrisius outside the city and, because he was ashamed to return to Argos to claim the inheritance of the one he had killed, he went to Megapenthes, the son of Proetus, and arranged to exchange kingdoms with him, giving him Argos. So Megapenthes became king of the Argives, and Perseus became king of Tiryns – and Perseus also fortified Midea and Mycenae.

[2.4.5] Perseus had the following sons with Andromeda: before they arrived in Greece they had Perses, whom they left behind with Cepheus (and from whom it is believed that the kings of Persia are descended); and in Mycenae they later had Alcaeus, Sthenelus, Heleus, Mestor, and Electryon. They also had a daughter, Gorgophone, who married Perieres.

Alcaeus had a son, Amphitryon, and a daughter, Anaxo, with Astydamia, the daughter of Pelops – but some say he had these children with Laonome, the daughter of Gouneus, while others say that he had them with Hipponome, the daughter of Menoeceus. Mestor had Hippothoe with Lysidice, the daughter of Pelops. Hippothoe was eventually carried off by Poseidon, who brought her to the Echinadian Islands, where he had intercourse with her and she bore Taphius. This Taphius colonized Taphos and called the people Teleboans, because he had travelled so far from his native land. And Taphius had a son, Pterelaus, whom Poseidon made immortal by planting a golden hair in his head. And to Pterelaus had six sons: Chromius, Tyrannus, Antiochus, Chersidamas, Mestor, and Everes.

Electryon married Anaxo, the daughter of Alcaeus, and they had one daughter, Alcmena, and nine sons: Stratobates, Gorgophonus, Phylonomus, Celaineus, Amphimachus, Lysinomus, Chirimachus, Anactor, and Archelaus. And Electryon also had an illegitimate son, Licymnius, with the Phrygian woman Midea.

Sthenelus had two daughters, Alcyone and Medusa, with Nicippe, the daughter of Pelops. And he afterwards had a son, Eurystheus, who also ruled over Mycenae. For when Hercules was about to be born, Zeus declared to the gods that the descendant of Perseus who was just about to be born would rule over Mycenae, so Hera became jealous and persuaded the Ilithyias to slow down Alcmena's delivery, and likewise arranged that Eurystheus, the son of Sthenelus, would be born early – at the seven month mark.

[2.4.6] When Electryon was ruling over Mycenae, the sons of Pterelaus came there with some Taphians and claimed the kingdom that belonged to Mestor, their maternal grandfather; but when Electryon ignored their claim, they drove away his cattle. When the sons of Electryon tried to retrieve the cattle, they challenged and killed one other. Of the sons of Electryon only Licymnius survived, who was still young; and of the sons of Pterelaus only Everes survived, who was guarding the ships. The Taphians who managed to escape sailed away, taking with them the cattle they had stolen, and they gave them to Polyxenus, the king of the Eleans; but Amphitryon bought them back from Polyxenus and brought them to Mycenae.

Wanting to avenge the deaths of his sons, Electryon was preparing to wage war against the Teleboans, but first he entrusted his kingdom to Amphitryon. He also entrusted his daughter Alcmene to him, making Amphityon promise that she would remain a virgin until he returned. However, as he was bringing his cows back, one of them charged forward, and Amphitryon threw the club at them that he was holding in his hands. But the club rebounded from the cow's horns and struck Electryon on the head and killed him. Thus Sthenelus used this as a pretext to banish Amphitryon from the whole of Argos, while he himself took control of the throne of Mycenae and Tiryns; and as for the city of Midea, he called for the sons of Pelops, Atreus and Thyestes, and entrusted it to them.

Translated from the Greek by Stephen Russell, PhD

Hyginus

THE STORY OF HERCULES

The Story: Hercules, or Heracles (in Greek), is probably the best-known and most famous hero in Greek and Roman mythology. His adventures are numerous and they defy a simple rational order. The Latin mythographer Hyginus, who wrote in the 4th or 5th century AD, provides a brief overview of some of this hero's more *herculean* exploits.

29 – Alcmene

When Amphitryon was away fighting in the war against Oechalia, Alcmene welcomed Jupiter in her bedroom thinking that the god was her husband. He entered her room and told her what he had done in Oechalia, so she went to bed with him because she believed that he was her husband. He enjoyed his time with her so much that he took away one day and joined together two nights, so that Alcmene wondered why that night was so long.

Later when she heard that her victorious husband was at hand, she showed no concern because she thought she had already seen her husband. When Amphitryon came into the palace, and saw that she wasn't very concerned, he began to wonder and complain that she didn't welcome him when he arrived. Alcmene answered: "You already came and slept with me, and told me what you had done in Oechalia." When she had told him everything, Amphitryon realized that some god must have assumed his form, and from that day onward he did not sleep with her. But she gave birth to Hercules from the love she shared with Jupiter.

30 – The Twelve Labours Imposed on Hercules by Eurystheus

When Hercules was a newborn, he strangled with his own two hands the two snakes that Juno had sent – and from this act it was discovered that Hercules was the first born.

1. He killed the Nemean Lion, which was an invulnerable monster. Luna (the Moon) had nourished this lion in a cave that had two openings, and after he killed it he took its skin to wear as a type of protective covering.

2. He killed the nine-headed Lernaean Hydra at the spring of Lerna. This monster was the offspring of Typhon, and was so poisonous that it killed men with her breath, and if anyone passed by when she was sleeping, it would breathe on the traveller's tracks and he would die in the most excruciating way imaginable. With the guidance from Minerva (Athena), he killed the Hydra, then disemboweled her and dipped his arrows in its poisoned blood. And so whatever he later hit with his arrows did not escape death. This would also be the reason for his own death later on in Phrygia.

3. He killed the Erymanthian Boar.

4. In Arcadia, he captured the wild stag with golden horns and brought it back alive to show Eurystheus.

5. On the island of Mars (Ares) with his arrows he killed the Stymphalian Birds, which shoot their own feathers out as arrows.

6. In one day he cleaned out all the cattle dung from the stables of King Augeas. Jupiter gave him a great deal of help with this. He diverted a river into the stables and this washed away all the dung.

7. From the island of Crete he brought back alive to Mycenae the bull with which Pasiphae slept.

8. He killed Diomede, the King of Thrace, along with the slave Abderus and Diomede's four horses that fed on human flesh. The names of the horses were Podargus, Lampon, Xanthus, and Dinus.

9. He killed the Amazon Hippolyte, who was the daughter of Mars (Ares) and Queen Otrera. Then he took from her the belt of the Amazon queen; then he gave his prisoner Antiope to Theseus.

10. He killed the three-bodied Geryon, the son of Chrysaor, with a single spear.

11. He killed the huge serpent, Typhon's son, which had the task of guarding the golden apples of the Hesperides near Mount Atlas. After he did this he brought the apples to King Eurystheus.

12. He brought the dog Cerberus, also born from Typhon, from the lower world for the king Eurystheus to see.

31 – Hercules' Other Labours

In Libya he killed Antaeus, the son of Earth. This man compelled visitors to wrestle with him, and when they were exhausted he would kill them. Hercules in turn wrestled him and killed him.

In Egypt he killed Busiris, whose custom it was to sacrifice his guests. When Hercules heard of this customary practice, he allowed himself to be led to the altar dressed in the sacrificial headdress, but when Busiris was about to invoke the gods, with his club Hercules killed both him and his attendants at the sacrifice.

He killed Cygnus, the son of Mars (Ares), conquering him by force of arms. When Mars arrived there, and wanted to fight Hercules because of his fallen son, Jupiter hurled a thunderbolt between them and in this way separated them.

At Troy he killed the sea-monster that was about to devour Hesione. He killed Laomedon, Hesione's father, with arrows because he did not hand over his daughter to him as he had agreed. He killed the bright eagle that was eating out the heart of Prometheus with arrows.

He killed Lycus, the son of Neptune, because he was planning to kill his wife Megara, the daughter of Creon, and their sons Therimachus and Ophites.

The River Achelous used to change himself into all sorts of shapes. When he fought with Hercules to win Deianira in marriage, he turned himself into a bull. Hercules broke off one his horns, presenting it to the Hesperides (or the Nymphs), and the goddesses filled it with fruits and called it Cornucopia.

He killed Neleus and his ten sons for refusing to cleanse him or purify him at the time when he had just killed his wife Megara, daughter of Creon, along with his sons Therimachus and Ophites.

Hercules killed Eurytus because he wanted to marry his daughter Iole but he refused to let him marry her.

He killed the centaur Nessus because he tried to rape Deianira.

He killed the Centaur Eurytion because he wanted to marry Deianira, the daughter of Dexamenus, his fiancée.

32 – Megara

When Hercules had been sent off by King Euystheus to get the three-headed dog Cerberus, Lycus, the son of Neptune, was left with the thought that Hercules had died on the journey. So Lycus planned to kill Hercules' wife Megara, daughter of Creon, and his sons Therimachus and Ophites, and then seize control of the kingdom. Hercules, however, arrived back on the scene and killed Lycus. Later, when Juno (Hera) sent Hercules into a fit of madness, he killed Megara and his sons.

When he came to his senses, he begged Apollo to give him an oracular reply on how to cleanse himself of this crime. Because Apollo was unwilling, Hercules became angry and carried off the tripod from Apollo's altar. Jupiter later ordered him to return it and also told Apollo to give him an answer, even though the god was unwilling. Because of this offence Hercules was given over by Mercury (Hermes) as a slave to Queen Omphale.

33 – Centaurs

When Hercules came to the court of King Dexamenus and was warmly welcomed there, he violated Dexamenus' daughter Deianira, but promised that he would marry her. After Hercules left, the Centaur Eurytion, son of Ixion and Nubis, also asked for Deianira as a wife. Her father, fearing violence from the Centaur if he refused, promised her to him. On the appointed day the Centaur came with his brothers to the wedding. Hercules intervened, killed the Centaur, and led his fiancée home.

Likewise at another wedding, when Pirithous was marrying Hippodamia, the daughter of Adrastus, drunken Centaurs tried to carry off the wives of the Lapiths. The Centaurs killed many Lapiths, but many Centaurs were killed by the Lapiths in turn.

34 – Nessus

Deianira asked the Centaur Nessus, the son of Ixion and Nubis, to carry her across the Evenus River. He picked her up but while he was carrying her, in the middle of the river he tried to rape her. When Hercules arrived there, and Deianira called him for help, he filled Nessus with his arrows. As he lay dying, Nessus, knowing how poisonous the arrows were, since they had been dipped in the poison of the Lernaean Hydra, drew out some of his blood and then gave it to Deianira, telling her that it was a love-charm. If she ever wanted to prevent her husband from leaving her, the Centaur said, she should smear his garments with this blood. Deianira believed him and so kept the vial of his blood carefully preserved.

35 - Iole

When Hercules sought to marry Iole, the daughter of Eurytus, and was refused, he then attacked and destroyed Oechalia. In order to make Iole beg for him, he threatened to kill her parents right in front of her. But she had a resolute mind and so suffered to see them murdered before her very eyes. When he had killed them all, he took Iole as captive and sent her ahead of him to Deianira.

36 – Deianira

When Hercules' wife Deianira, daughter of Oeneus, saw Iole, who was a girl of remarkable beauty, arrive as a captive, she feared that the girl would steal her husband. So she remembered the instructions Nessus had given her, and she sent a servant named Lichas to bring Hercules a robe that was dipped in the blood from the Centaur.

A little bit of the blood fell to the earth, and when the sun touched it, it began to burn. When Deianira saw this, she knew that Nessus had lied to her, and so she sent another man to stop the one to whom she had just given the robe. But it was too late – for Hercules had already put it on, and it immediately burst into flames. He threw himself into a river to put out the blaze, but even greater flames burst forth. When he tried to take the garment off his own flesh came off with it. Then Hercules sent Lichas, the one who brought the garment, whirling round and round, and threw him into the sea. At the place where Lichas fell a rock appeared that is now called Lichas.

Then it is said that Philoctetes, the son of Poeas, built a pyre for Hercules on Mount Oeta, who then mounted it and became immortal. For this service Hercules gave Philoctetes his bow and arrows. As for Deianira, because of what happened to Hercules, she killed herself.

Translated from the Latin by Stephen Russell, PhD

Apollodorus

THE RETURN OF ODYSSEUS

The Story: After the fall of Troy, Odysseus took 10 long years to arrive back home to his island of Ithaca. Homer talks about this journey in *The Odyssey*. In this mythographical account, Apollodorus mentions many of the same stories that appear in *The Odyssey*, but he also adds some other strands to Odysseus' myth that either take place on the same journey homeward or after he has arrived back in Ithaca.

Epitome book 7

[7.1] Some people say that Odysseus wandered near to Libya, while others say that he travelled closer to Sicily, and still others say that he sailed around the Ocean or the Tyrrhenian Sea.

[7.2] After he departed from Troy and went out to sea, he soon reached Ismarus, a city that belong to the Cicones, and he captured this city in war, and pillaged it, sparing Maron alone, who was priest of Apollo. When those Cicones who lived in the mainland heard what was happening, they came in arms to fight against him, and he was forced to retreat back to the sea and then fled after having lost six men from each of his ships.

[7.3] He landed in the country of the Lotus-eaters, and so sent some of his men to learn who lived there, but they tasted the lotus and remained where they were; for in that land there grew a sweet fruit called the lotus, which caused whoever tasted it to forget everything. When Odysseus learned about this, he held the rest of his men back and dragged those who had tasted the lotus by force to the ships. And he set sail for the land of the Cyclopes and approached its shore.

[7.4] Leaving the rest of his ships on the neighbouring island, he approached the land of the Cyclopes with only a single ship, and landed with twelve companions. Near the sea there was a cave that he entered, and he brought with him the skin of wine that Maron had given him. This cave belonged to Polyphemus, who was a son of Poseidon and the nymph Thoosa; he was a huge and wild cannibal, and he had one eye on his forehead.

[7.5] And they lit a fire and sacrificed some of the young goats, and then they feasted. But the Cyclops came back and, after he had driven in his flocks, he put a huge stone in front of the door. When he saw the men he ate some of them.

[7.6] But Odysseus gave him some of Maron's wine to drink. He drank it down and asked for another, and when he had drunk the second, he asked Odysseus for his name; and when Odysseus said that he was called Nobody, Polyphemus said that he would eat Nobody last and the others first, and that was the token of friendship which he promised to give him in return for the wine. And overcome by drunkenness from the wine, he then fell asleep.

[7.7] Odysseus found a club lying there in the cave, and with the help of four comrades he sharpened it, and then, after heating it in the fire, he blinded the Cyclops with it. And when Polyphemus cried out to the other neighbouring Cyclopes for help, they came and asked who was hurting him, and when he said "Nobody," they thought that he meant that he was being hurt by nobody, and so they went home.

[7.8] When the flocks wanted to go out to their usual pasture, he opened up the cave, but he stood in the doorway and with his hands spread out he felt the sheep as they went past beneath his legs. But Odysseus tied three rams together, and slipping himself under the largest of the three, he hid under its belly and made his way out along with the sheep. Then, after he untied his comrades from the sheep to which they had been tied, he led the animals to his ship. As he was sailing away he shouted out to the Cyclops that his name was Odysseus and that he had managed to escape from his hands.

[7.9] Now the Cyclops had been warned by a soothsayer that he would be blinded by Odysseus; and when he learned his name, he tore away rocks from the ground and hurled them into the sea, and the ship barely escaped the onslaught of the rocks. From that time onward Poseidon was angry with Odysseus.

[7.10] Going out onto the sea with all his ships, he then came to the island of Aeolia, where the king was Aeolus. He was appointed by Zeus to be the keeper of the winds, with the power to both calm them and send them forth. He welcomed Odysseus and entertained him, and then he gave him an ox-hide bag in which he had placed the winds. After learning which winds he'd need to use on his voyage, Odysseus tied up the bag tightly to the boat. Odysseus used the appropriate winds and had a successful voyage. But when he was very close to Ithaca and could already see the smoke rising from the main town, he fell asleep.

[7.11] But his comrades, thought that he was carrying gold in the bag, so they untied it and let the winds go free. They were thus swept away by the winds and were driven back again along the path they had just sailed. When they came once again to Aeolus, Odysseus asked him for another favourable wind; but Aeolus drove him off the island, saying that he could not save him when the gods were obviously against him.

[7.12] So he sailed on and came to the land of the Laistrygonians, where he placed his own ship the furthest away. Now the Laistrygonians were cannibals, and their king was Antiphates. Odysseus wanted to learn about the people who lived there, so he sent some men to investigate. And the king's daughter met them and led them back to her father.

[7.13] Her father quickly grabbed one of them and devoured him; but the rest of Odysseus' crew fled, and so the man pursued them, shouting and calling together the rest of the Laistrygonians. They all hurriedly ran to the sea, and by throwing stones they were able to break up the boats - and then they ate the men. Odysseus cut the cable of his ship and turned quickly out to sea; but the rest of his ships were destroyed and their crews were all killed.

[7.14] With the only one ship that he had left, Odysseus came to shore at the island of Aeaea. This island was the home of Circe, who was the daughter of the Sun and Perse, and a sister of Aeetes; she was skilled in all kinds of magic and enchantments. Odysseus divided his crew into two groups, but he himself remained by the ship, in accordance with the lot that he drew, while Eurylochus and twenty-two of his crewmembers went to meet Circe.

[7.15] At Circe's invitation every one of them entered her house except for Eurylochus; and to all of them she gave a cup that she had filled with cheese, honey, barley, and wine – and she mixed some form of enchantment drug into this. And when they had drunk the mixture, she touched them with a wand and changed their shapes – she turned some of them into wolves, others into pigs, and she made some donkeys, and others lions.

[7.16] Eurylochus saw everything that had happened and ran back to Odysseus so that he could tell him what he witnessed. And then Odysseus went to Circe with a magical plant that he had received from Hermes. He threw this plant into Circe's magical potions that she gave him after he entered her house, with the result that he was the only member of his crew who was not transformed into an animal after drinking from her mixture. Then he took out his sword and would have killed her, but she calmed his anger and returned his crew to their original forms. And after she had made a promise to him that she would not cause any harm, Odysseus went to bed with her, and she bore him a son, who was called Telegonus.

[7.17] Odysseus stayed there for a year, and then he sailed out onto the ocean, where he first made sacrifices to the souls of the dead in Hades – consulting the soothsay Tiresias, as Circe had advised him to do, and meeting with the souls of both heroes and heroines. He also saw his mother Anticleia and Elpenor, who had died from a fall off Circe's roof.

[7.18] He then returned back to the island of Circe, and she sent him on his way again. He went out onto the sea and sailed past the island of the Sirens. The Sirens were named Pisinoe, Aglaope, and Thelxiepia; they were the daughters of Achelous and Melpomene, who was one of the Muses. One of them played the lyre, another sang, and another played the flute, and by these means they were able to persuade passing mariners to long to stay with them.

[7.19] These Sirens had the shapes of birds from their thighs downward. When he was sailing by them, Odysseus wanted to hear their song, so he followed Circe's advice and plugged the ears of his comrades with wax, but ordered that he himself would be tied to the mast. When the Sirens were singing in his ears and persuading him to remain there with them, he begged his crew to untie him, but they bound him up even tighter, and this is how he managed to sail by them. Now there was a prophecy that said that the Sirens would die themselves whenever a ship would pass them and escape their song – so they died.

[7.20] And after that Odysseus came to a point where he had two choices to travel. On one side there were the Clashing Rocks, and on the other side there were two huge cliffs, and in one of them lived Scylla, the daughter of Crataeiis and Trienos or Phorcos; Scylla had the face and breast of a woman, but from her edges she had six heads and twelve feet – all of which were those of dogs.

[7.21] And on the other cliff was Charybdis, who drew up the water and vomited it out again three times a day. Listening to Circe's advice, he avoided the passage near to the Clashing Rocks, and he sailed next to the cliff where Scylla lived – where he stood fully armed and ready at the front of the boat. Scylla appeared, as expected, and she snatched up six of his crew and devoured them.

[7.22] And from there he went to Thrinacia, an island that belonged to Helios the Sun, where his cattle were grazing. Odysseus and his men were stranded there due to lack of wind. But when his crew slaughtered some of the cattle and ate them because they had no food, the Sun reported this to Zeus, and when Odysseus finally set sail once again, Zeus struck his ship with a thunderbolt.

[7.23] And when the ship broke up, Odysseus clung onto the mast and drifted toward Charybdis. But when Charybdis sucked down the mast, he grabbed ahold of an overhanging wild fig tree and waited there; and when he saw the mast shoot up again out of Charybdis, he threw himself onto it, and he was carried across the wide sea to the island of Ogygia.

[7.24] He was received there by Calypso, the daughter of Atlas, and she went to bed with him and bore him a son, Latinus. He stayed with her for five years, and then he made a raft and sailed away. But on the high sea the raft was broken in pieces because of Poseidon's anger, and Odysseus was washed up naked onto the shore of the Phaiacians.

[7.25] Now Nausikaa, the daughter of king Alkinous, was washing the family's clothes, and when Odysseus begged her for protection, she brought him to her father Alkinous. She welcomed Odysseus as a guest, then gave him gifts and sent him off to his native land with an escort. But Poseidon was angry with the Phaiacians, and he turned that ship to stone and surrounded the city with a mountain.

[7.26] And when Odysseus arrived in his native land he found that his entire house had been ruined. The suitors believed he was dead and were therefore courting his wife Penelope. From Doulichion fifty-seven suitors came:

[7.27] Amphinomus, Thoas, Demoptolemus, Amphimachus, Euryalus, Paralus, Evenorides, Clytius, Agenor, Eurypylus, Pylaimenes, Acamas, Thersilochus, Hagius, Clymenus, Philodemus, Meneptolemus, Damastor, Bias, Telmius, Polyidus, Astylochus, Schedius, Antigonus, Marpsius, Iphidamas, Argeius, Glaucus, Calydoneus, Echion, Lamas, Andraimon, Agerochus, Medon, Agrius, Promus, Ctesius, Acarnan, Cycnus, Pseras, Hellanicus, Periphron, Megasthenes, Thrasymedes, Ormenius, Diopithes, Mecisteus, Antimachus, Ptolemaius, Lestorides, Nicomachus, Polypoites, and Ceraus.

[7.28] And from Same twenty-three suitors came: Agelaos, Peisandros, Elatus, Ctesippus, Hippodochus, Eurystratus, Archemolus, Ithacus, Peisenor, Hyperenor, Pheroites, Antisthenes, Cerberus, Perimedes, Cynnus, Thriasus, Eteoneus, Clytius, Prothous, Lycaithus, Eumelus, Itanus, Lyammus.

[7.29] And from Zacynthos came forty-four suitors: Eurylochus, Laomedes, Molebus, Phrenius, Indius, Minis, Leiocritus, Pronomus, Nisas, Daemon, Archestratus, Hippomachus, Euryalus, Periallus, Evenorides, Clytius, Agenor, Polybus, Polydorus, Thadytius, Stratius, Phrenius, Indius, Daesenor, Laomedon, Laodicus, Halius, Magnes, Oloitrochus, Barthas, Theophron, Nissaius, Alcarops, Periclymenus, Antenor, Pellas, Celtus, Periphus, Ormenus, Polybus, and Andromedes.

[7.30] And from Ithaca itself there were twelve suitors: Antinous, Pronous, Leiodes, Eurynomus, Amphimachus, Amphialos, Promachus, Amphimedon, Aristratus, Helenus, Doulichieus, and Ctesippus.

[7.31] All these men had made the journey to the palace and consumed the herds that belonged to Odysseus at their feasts. And Penelope was forced to make a promise that she would agree to marry when she finished the shroud for Laertes, and she wove it for three years, weaving it by day and undoing it by night. In this way Penelope deceived the suitors, until they finally found out what she had been doing.

[7.32] And when Odysseus learned about what things were like at his home, he went to his servant Eumaeus disguised as a beggar. He revealed himself to Telemachus and went with him to the city. When they were on their way into the city the goatherd Melanthius, a mere servant, met them and mocked them. When they entered the palace Odysseus begged for food from the suitors and he found a beggar there named Irus so he wrestled with him. He revealed his identity to Eumaeus and Philoitius, and along with them and Telemachus he laid a plot against the suitors.

[7.33] Penelope brought the bow of Odysseus to the suitors, which he had once received from Iphitus many years ago. And she told them that she would marry whichever man it was who could bend and string the bow. When none of the suitors could do this, Odysseus took it and shot down the suitors – along with the help of Eumaeus, Philoitius, and Telemachus. He also killed Melanthius, and the handmaids who slept with the suitors – and then he revealed who he was to both his wife and his father.

[7.34] And after making sacrifices to Hades, and Persephone, and Tiresias, Odysseus made the journey on foot through Epirus, and came to the land of the Thesprotians, where he made a sacrifice to Poseidon, as the soothsayer Tiresias had advised him to do. But Callidice, who was at that time queen of the Thesprotians, urged him to stay and offered him the chance to be her king and husband.

[7.35] And she slept with him and produced a son with him – Polypoites. After he married Callidice, Odysseus ruled over the Thesprotians as their king and he defeated in battle the neighbouring peoples who attacked them. But when Callidice died he handed the kingdom over to his son and returned to Ithaca, and he discovered that Penelope had given birth to another son for him – Poliporthes.

[7.36] When Telegonus learned from Circe that he was the son of Odysseus, he sailed out in search of him. And when he arrived at the island of Ithaca, he stole some of the cattle for himself, and when Odysseus came out to fight for them, Telegonus wounded him with the spear that he held in his hands, which was tipped with the needle of a stingray, and Odysseus died from the wound.

[7.37] But when Telegonus discovered whom he had killed, he bitterly lamented, and he brought the corpse and Penelope back to Circe, and there he married Penelope. And Circe sent both of them away to the Islands of the Blest.

[7.38] But some say that Penelope was seduced by Antinous and was therefore sent away by Odysseus to her father Icarius, and that when she came to Mantinea in Arcadia she gave birth to Pan, whose father was Hermes.

[7.39] But others say that she was killed by Odysseus himself, for they say that she was seduced by Amphinomus.

[7.40] And there are some who say that Odysseus, after the relatives of the suitors he had killed made accusations against him, brought the matter to the judgment of Neoptolemus, who was the king of the islands off Epirus. And they say that Neoptolemus, thinking that he would get possession of Cephallenia once Odysseus was out of the way, thus condemned him to exile. They add that Odysseus went to Thoas, the son of Andraimon, in Aetolia, and when he was there he married the daughter of Thoas – and Odysseus died there in his old age, leaving behind a son that he had by her – Leontophonus.

Translated from the Greek by Stephen Russell, PhD

Chapter 13
Virgil

The Fall of Troy

The Story: Book 2 of Virgil's *Aeneid* provides the most extensive extant account of the fall of Troy that we have in ancient literature. The Trojan hero Aeneas recalls the destruction of his once great city, and how he was forced to flee from the ruins along with his family so that he might find another home for the fire of Troy.

The Aeneid, Book 2

Everyone fell silent, and they kept their intent gaze on him; then father Aeneas spoke thus from his raised couch:

"O queen, the pain you are asking me to describe is too much for words. You want me to recall how the Greeks defeated the lamentable kingdom of Troy – the horrific sights that I myself saw and the ones in which I played a great part. What man from the troops of Achilles, what man from the forces of Dolops, or what soldier from battle-hardened Ulysses could hold back the tears in telling such things? But now the dew-filled night is hurrying away in the sky and the falling stars are trying to persuade us to go to sleep. However, if your desire to know of our disaster is so great, and to briefly hear about the final struggle of Troy, even though my mind shudders to remember these things – and, in fact, it shudders and recoils in grief – nevertheless, I'll begin.

"Broken in war and pushed back by fate, the leaders of the Greeks, since so many years had passed by already, managed with the help of Pallas Athena to build a wooden horse as big as a mountain, and they weave it together with planks made from fir trees. They act as if it's an offering to help them get a safe return – this is the story that is spread. But here, within its dark shadows, they secretly enclose the soldiers who are chosen the best for such a mission and they fill up the belly of the horse with armed men.

"Tenedos is an island that is visible from Troy and is well-known by its reputation – it was very wealthy while Priam's kingdom was still strong, but now it's only a bay and an unsafe place for ships to make anchor. We thought that they had left with the wind and were headed back for Greece. So the entire land of Troy frees itself from its long sorrow. We open up the gates; it becomes a joy to go out and look at the former Greek camp, the stations they deserted and the shores they left behind. Here is where the troops of Dolops made camp; this is where cruel Achilles slept; and over here is where they used to face us in battle.

"Some of us are amazed at what the maiden Minerva left us – that gift of death – and they go out to marvel at the massive size of the horse. And Thymoetes is the first one to urge us to bring it inside our walls and place it within our citadel. Either he did this out of treachery or the doomed fate of Troy was already heading in that direction. But Capys, and people whose minds had better and wiser opinions, suggested that we hurl this horse – this trick from the Greek – headlong into the sea. They said that this gift is not to be trusted, and that maybe we should light it up with blames placed underneath, or maybe we can stab at and examine its belly for secret hiding places. The crowd is wavering and is torn into different opinions on what to do.

"Then, first there before everyone, and with a great crowd following behind him, Laocoön rushes down from the heights of the citadel in a raging hurry, and he shouts to us from a distance: 'My poor countrymen – what is this insanity? Do you actually believe that the enemy has sailed away? Do you think that the gifts from the Greeks are free from treachery? Is Ulysses known for this kind of behaviour? Either some Greeks lie hidden inside of the frame of this horse, or this thing has built as an engine of war to be used against our walls, to spy against our homes and to come down to the city from above. Whatever this thing is, I fear Greeks when they bear gifts.'

"When he said this Laocoön then hurls his mighty spear with great force into the side of the beast and the curved frame of its belly. The spear stood there shaking, and the insides of the beast resounded as if the cavity were hollow – and it sent forth a moan. And if both the fates of the gods and our minds had not been perverse, then he would have forced us to violate the Greek hiding place with our spears, and Troy would now still be standing and you, lofty city of Priam, you would still remain!

"But look – meanwhile some Trojan shepherds were shouting with a great clamour and dragging toward the king a young man whose hands were tied behind his back. To make this very event take place and to open up Troy to the Greeks he deliberately put himself out there to be found even though he was a stranger to us. He must have been confident in his spirit to meet one of two ends: either to tell his tricky lies or to meet a sure death. From everywhere young Trojan men came running in, all eager to see this stranger, and many of them take turns in mocking the captive. But please, now you will hear about the duplicity of the Greeks and from a single crime you'll learn about everything...

"For while he stood amid the crowd of people who were gazing back at him, the stranger was confused, without arms, and he threw his eyes at the crowds of Trojans. He said: 'O god, what land will accept me now, what sea will take me in now? Or what fate finally waits for me now... poor miserable me? I don't have any place at all among the Grecks, and the Trojans as well, they run about and they call wildly for vengeance and my blood.' At his scream our hatred ceased, our anger was put in check and our desire for violence was changed. We asked him to say from what blood and family he came, and what news he might have. We say that he should bear in mind that he's our prisoner and that he should behave as a prisoner.

"And finally the man set aside his fear and speaks these words: 'Surely king,' he says, 'whatever happens I will tell you the whole truth – and I won't deny to you that I was born a Greek. I'll own up to that right from the start – even if Fortune has decided that Sinon is going to spend his days in misery, in her menacing spite she won't be able to call him false and a liar. If by some chance speaking you happened to have heard the name of Palimedes, the son of Belus, and the glory of his fame. The Palasgians killed this Palamedes, who was innocent, because someone gave false evidence, through the lies of witnesses, and because he was opposed to the war. But they mourn him now that he is bereft of light. Well, I was sent along when I was very young to serve in his company of troops, because my father, although he was poor, was a relative of this Palamedes. While he stood safe in his princely power and was a powerful voice inside the councils of the kings, we also had a great name and certain renown. But when this man passed from the world above through the deceitfulness of tricky Odysseus – the story is well known – then I started to drag my ruined life through darkness and sorrow. I was angry in my heart about what had happened to my innocent and fallen friend.

"'Nor did I keep quiet in my anger, but whenever there was a chance, if I could ever return to my native Argos in triumph, I swore openly that I would enact vengeance on behalf of my friend, and these words of mine awoke fierce hatred against me. This for me was the first appearance of evil; from this point Ulysses would always cook up new charges against me and terrify me with them; from this point he would constantly spread dark rumours against me in the crowd and he'd try to say that he was a witness as he'd encourage others to take up arms against me. He wouldn't even rest until he could use Calchas as his tool...but why am I bothering to pointlessly recount this miserable tale? Or why should I cause you any delay? If you think that all Greeks are equal, and if this is enough for you to hear that – then take your vengeance against me at once! That's exactly what the fellow from Ithaca – Ulysses, I mean – would want, and it's something that the sons of Atreus would pay you a great reward for doing!'

"Indeed this caused us all the more to ask him about what had happened, since we were strangers to Pelasgian trickery. So shaking still he continues with his story and he speaks from his false heart:

"'For a long time the Greeks often wanted to leave Troy' he says. 'They wanted to make a retreat, because they were tired out from the long war. And how I wish that they had only done so! Often only a fierce storm on the sea would stop them and the wind would frighten them from making an attempt to leave. Moreover, even when this horse was ready, a structure made from beams of maple, storm clouds still thundered throughout the sky. We were confused, so we send Eurypylus to ask the oracle of Apollo, and from that shrine he brings back these dark and gloomy words: "With the blood of a slain virgin, Greeks, you paid respects to the winds, when you first came to these Trojan coasts. With blood you must win your return and gain our favour with a Greek life." When these words came to the ears of the crowd, their spirits were amazed, and a cold chill ran through the depths of their bones. For which person is fate preparing this doom? What person is Apollo claiming as victim? At this point the Ithacan – that conniving Ulysses – drags the prophet Calchas out with a huge commotion, places him into the middle of the crowd, and demands to know what it is that the gods want. And many people had already predicted that I was the target of this rat's cruel plan and they silently saw what was about to happen.

"'For ten days the prophet was silent in his tent, unwilling to accuse anyone with his own mouth and send them to sure death. Reluctantly, forced onward by the shouts of Ulysses, he finally holds to the agreed plan and he breaks his voice and points me out for the sacrificial altar. Everyone approves of this; and what each man feared for himself he bore with patience when that fate turned to the ruin of someone else.

"'And now the horrible day was at hand – they were preparing the sacred rites for me so that I could be sacrificed. The salted meal was made and the sacrificial ribbons were placed around my head. I admit it, I snatched myself from death – I broke free of my bonds and I lay hidden all night among the muddy reeds of a nearby marsh, waiting and hoping for them to set sail, and wondering whether they would do so. And now, now I have no hope at all of ever seeing my ancient homeland, or my sweet children, or the father whom I miss so dearly. Perhaps the Greeks will punish my family for my flight, and that their death will wash away this guilt of mine. But I beg of you, in the name of the gods above, the powers that know truth, in the name of any form of honesty and trust that may still exist untainted among men, please pity me in my great suffering. Please pity a soul who is suffering things he doesn't deserve to suffer!'

"He was crying, and so we grant him his life and even began to feel sorry for him. Priam himself spoke first and orders that his tight chains and bonds be removed and then he said these words in kindness: 'Whoever you are, from now on you can forget about the Greeks you have lost. You will be one of us. But now please give me full and truthful answers to me when I ask you these questions – what was the reason that they built that huge monster of a horse? Who came up with the idea? What is the purpose of it? Does it have some religious significance? Is it a machine of war in some way?'

"Priam's questions ended. And the other one, who was trained in the art of Pelasgian lies, lifted his hands that we had just released from chains to the sky, and he said: 'I call upon you to be my witness, you eternal fires up in the heavens and your imperial majesty. I call upon the sacrificial altars and the swords that I managed to escape. I call upon the sacred ribbons of the gods that I wore as a sacrificial victim. I call upon all of you and I ask you to allow me to break my sacred oath of allegiance to the Greeks. I ask that it be right for me to justly hate them now and to bring all of their secrets out into the open. I am no longer held by any of the laws of my homeland. But you, Troy, if I can keep you safe, then you must keep your word and save me, if what I tell you is true and pays you a great return.

"'All the hopes of the Greeks and their faith since the beginning of the war always rested on the help of Pallas Athena. But from that time that unholy Diomedes and Ulysses, the schemer behind every crime, took it upon themselves and dared to rip the fateful Palladium, the image and statue of the goddess, from the sacred place in its temple outside of Troy, killing the guards who protected it on the heights of the citadel. Then they lifted up the sacred image and dared with their bloody hands to touch the sacred headbands of the virgin goddess. From that time onward the hopes of the Greeks turned to nothing and thus disappeared – their strength was broken and the mind of the goddess was against them.

"'Then Athena gave clear signs of her disapproval by sending portents and omens that were not to be doubted. The statue had scarcely been placed within the Greek camp, when from its opened eyes there blazed forth fire, and a salt-like sweat was streaming over its limbs, and three times – it's amazing to say! – the goddess herself jumped forth from the ground with her shield and brandishing her trembling spear.

"'Immediately Calchas says that they have to flee across the sea, and he gave the prophecy that the Greeks would never be able to take Troy until they first seek new omens back at Argos – and that they have to bring back that image of the goddess with them, which they have taken away with them across the sea in their curved ships. So now they are sailing back to Greece with the wind – but they are doing so in order to get more arms and help from the gods. And then soon they plan to cross the ocean again and be back here when you no longer expect them. That's how Calchas interprets the omens.

"'And they have set up this image here, this horse, as a way to atone for what they did to the goddess Athena's statue that they ripped from the Palladium, for the insult to her divinity, to expiate the sin they committed against her. So Calchas told them to build a huge structure with interweaving timbers that reaches to the sky – and to build it so high that it cannot be taken through the gates or through the walls of the city, so it wouldn't be able to protect the people if they take it in with their ancient sense of piety and faith. For if any of your hands violate this offering to Minerva [Athena], then complete destruction – and may the gods turn this prophecy on Calchas instead! – will fall upon Priam's empire and the Trojans. But if your hands are somehow able to lift it and bring it inside the city, then Asia will advance to the mighty walls of Greece, and this would be the doom that would await our Greek descendants!'

"These were the traps and the deceptions that Sinon laid for us – and we believed all of it. All of his lies and false tears were able to overwhelm and defeat us – a people who neither Diomedes, nor Achilles, nor ten long years of war, nor a thousand ships could defeat.

"But here there came another omen, greater and more frightening by far, falls upon my poor people, and it confuses the minds of them because they didn't foresee what it meant. Laocoön, who was the chosen priest of Neptune [Poseidon], was sacrificing a huge bull at the holy altars. And what happens then? Look! Suddenly over the peaceful waters from Tenedos – I shudder to recall this – two huge serpents are with their endless coils are leaning their breasts into the sea and making their way side by side to our shore. Their breasts rise among the waves, and their blood-red crests tower high above the waters – the rest of their bodies plough the sea behind them and their huge backs curl up in immeasurable folds. A huge sound is made throughout the foaming and salty sea, and now they have reached the fields of Troy, and with their blazing eyes covered over with blood and fire, they were licking their hissing mouths with their flickering tongues.

"We turn pale at the sight and flee. But they make a steady course right for Laocoön. First each serpent embraces the small bodies of his two sons and entwines them both, eating at their poor limbs with their huge bites. Then they seize him as well, when he comes running up to help his children and carrying a weapon – they take him and they wrap him up in their many folds. And now they encircle his waist twice, twice they wrapped themselves around his throat with their scaly bodies – and they tower above his head with their lofty necks.

"All the while Laocoön is struggling with his hands to break himself free of their coils, and his priestly clothing is covered in gory blood and black venom. And at the same time he is constantly shouting horrible cries to the heavens, just like the bellowing that a wounded bull makes when it is shaking an ill-placed axe from its neck and it tires to flee the sacrificial altar. But the two snakes then escape, gliding away to the highest temples of the city and they head directly for the citadel of fierce Athena, where they can seek shelter under her feet and under the circle of her shield.

"At that moment a strange new fear creeps through the shuddering hearts of everyone there, and they agree that Laocoön has paid the just penalty for his crime – because with his spear he had violate the sacred timbers when he threw that accursed spear into its back. And everyone shouts that the image, the horse, should be led into the city where it should be worshipped and placed in front of the sacred image of the goddess.

"And so we open up the walls and lay bare the buildings of our city. Everyone puts themselves to the task – and under the feet of the horse they place gliding wheels, and around its neck they stretch forth rope made from hemp. This is how the machine designed by Fate climbed our walls, its belly fat with hidden arms. Around it boys and unmarried girls run around and sing sacred hymns and they played and rejoiced to take their turn at touching the rope with their hands. Upward the horse moves, and the threatening thing glides right into the heart of the city.

"O my country! O Troy – home of the gods! O walls of the Trojans, so famous in war! Four times when it was at the very threshold of our wall it stood still, and four times from its belly the arms made a sound. Nevertheless we press on without thinking, blind with rage, and we set the cursed monster in our holy citadel. At that moment even Cassandra opened her mouth to predict the future doom, but by order of the god she was not ever to be believed by the Trojans. We unfortunate people, for whom that day was our last, we spend it decorating the shrines of the gods throughout the city with festal wreathes and flowers.

"Meanwhile the sky is turning and night comes rushing forth from Ocean, wrapping up all the earth and the sky and the treachery of the Greeks in its shade. Throughout the city the Trojans lie spread out in silence, and sleep embraces their tired limbs. And now the Greek enemy, their fleet gathered together was leaving from Tenedos, sailing in battle array amid the friendly silence of the quiet moon. They are looking for the well-known shores, when the royal ship raised forth its signal flame – and then Sinon, who was saved by the cruel fates of the gods, sneakily opens the pine bolts and releases those Greeks who were trapped inside the horse's belly. Once the horse is opened up they are now returned to the air, and from its hollow wood the grateful Greeks come rushing out: the captains Thessandrus and Sthenelus, and horrible Ulysses, sliding down a rope that had been lowered, and Acamas and Thoas and Neoptolemus, from the family of Peleus and the son of Achilles, and Machaon who came out first, and Menelaus, and Epeos, the man who designed this trick. They move around and swarm the city that is buried deeply in sleep and wine. They kill the guards, and when the gates are opened they welcome in all of their comrades and they join their own units as they planned.

"It was the time when the first sleep, the most pleasing gift from the gods, begins to creep over wearied mortals. In the middle of sleep – look! – Hector appears to be at hand before my very eyes and he was streaming with tears. He seemed as he once did when he was torn by the chariot, black with bloody dust and leather straps piercing though his swollen feet. Oh god, why me – what a sight he was! How different he was, how much changed from that Hector who returned with the spoils of Achilles or the one who threw Trojan fires all over the Greek ships. He was wearing a filthy beard, hair that was hardened with blood, and bearing those wounds, those many wounds, that he received around the walls of his homeland. On my own accord I seemed to start crying myself, and I call the man, and I force out these sad words: 'O light of Troy, best hope of the Trojans, what long delay has kept you? Hector, so long awaited by us, from what shores do you come? After so many deaths of your people, after so many sufferings of your people and city, we weary ones finally see you now! What is the shameful reason that has disfigured your once serene face? Why do I see these wounds?'

"But he says nothing, nor does he pay heed to my empty questions. But leading forth a heavy sigh from the depths of his heart, he says: 'Ahh, flee, escape, son of the goddess – tear yourself from these flames! The enemy hold our walls. Troy is falling from its lofty peak. You have given enough to your fatherland and Priam. If Troy could have been defended by anyone's right hand, it would have been defended by mine. To you Troy entrusts her sacred things and household gods – take them to share your fate. Seek a mighty city for them that you can finally establish after you have wandered over the sea.' So much he said to me, and from the innermost sanctuary in his hands he brings forth the great goddess Vesta, with her sacred ribbons, and the eternal flame of Troy.

"Meanwhile on every side the city is in confusion and despair, and more and more, although the house of my father Anchises was remote and stands in the back and is covered with trees, the sounds become clearer and the horrors of battle get closer and closer. I shake the sleep from myself and I quickly go up to the very height of the roof and stand there with my ears listening intently. It sounds just like when a flame falls on a field of grain from a furious south wind, or just like a mountain river that destroys the fields with its rushing torrent – it ruins the growing crops, all the work of oxen, and it drags down the forests. All the while the shepherd listens, not knowing, dumbfounded, taking in the sound from the highest rock but not knowing what it is. I was that shepherd.

"But then in a moment the truth becomes clear and the duplicity of the Greeks is made evident. Soon the great house of Deiphobus lies in ruins, with the god of fire towering above it. Soon his neighbour Ucalegon is on fire – and the broad straits of Sigeum reflect the flames. Then there is the shouting of men and the sound of trumpets, and so out of my mind I grab for my arms. There is little purpose for arms, but my heart is yearning to gather a force for war and to rush forward with my comrades to the citadel. Frenzy and anger are driving my mind forward headlong, and suddenly it seems like a beautiful thing to die in arms.

"But look now – there's Panthus escaping from the Greek swords. Panthus, the son of Othrys and priest of Apollo on the citadel, carrying in his own hand the sacred things, the defeated gods as he drags along his little grandchild and in a frenzy he makes his way to my doors. 'Where is the greatest crisis Panthus? What citadel should we seize?' I had scarcely said these things, when with a groan he answers these words: 'The last day and the final hour has come to Troy. We were Trojans, but no more. Troy and the glory of Troy was great – but no more. An angry Jupiter has carried off everything to Argos – the Greeks are the masters in our burning city. That high-standing horse pours forth armed men in the middle of our walls and Sinon, the victor, arrogantly spreads flames around. Some men are standing at the wide-open gates, as many thousands as ever came here from Greece. Others have raised weapons and are blocking the narrow streets. A battle-line of steel has been made, with its blade unsheathed, and it is prepared to die. The first guards of the gates are barely able to attempt to fight back, but they seem to be fighting blindly against the enemy.'

"These were the words from Panthus, the son of Othrys, and by divine will I am driven into the flames and the fighting, where the dark Fury of war, where the din of battle and the shouts reaching up to the stars were calling me. I came across old comrades in the moonlight and they gathered with me – Rhipeus and Epytus, mighty in arms, and Hypanis and Dymas, and young Coroebus, the son of Mygdon. In just those days it happened that he came to Troy because he was burning in love for Cassandra, and as a son-in-law he was bringing help to Priam and the Trojans. Oh, that unlucky fellow – he didn't listen to the warnings of his bride in her prophetic frenzy.

"When I saw everyone in such close ranks and ready for battle, I addressed them with these words: 'Young men, the bravest of soldiers and yet this is all in vain. If it is your desire to follow me as I dare to fight to the end, and this final battle, you see how things stand for us. All the gods on whom this empire stood strong have now departed – their shrines and altars have been abandoned. You are rushing in to help a burning city. Then let us die and hurry into the midst of the battle! There is one salvation for the defeated – that there is no hope of salvation.'

"Thus a certain amount of madness was added to their spirits with these words. And from that moment, just like ravaging wolves on a dark and misty night, which have been driven out of their lairs by a ravenous hunger that gives them no rest and pushes them blindly forth, leaving their young behind with their throats all dry – just like those wolves we pass through the enemy and their swords – on our way to meet a sure death. And we make our way to the heart of the city, with the black night and its sheltering darkness hovers all around us. Who could talk about the horrors of that night? Who could speak of the slaughter? Who could cry enough tears to match the pains and sufferings? The ancient city falls – it had ruled an empire for many years. Lifeless corpses lie strewn about in heaps throughout the streets, and throughout homes and the sacred thresholds of the gods. But it's not just Trojans alone who pay the penalty with their blood: sometimes courage returns to their hearts of the defeated and the conquering Greeks fall dead. Everywhere around us there is cruel pain, everywhere there is panic and everywhere is the image of death.

"The first Greek to come up against us was Androgeos, who met us and had a large group of Greeks with him. He didn't realize who we were – he thought we were his allies, in fact – so he called out to us with these friendly words: 'Hurry up, men! What is the reason for your delay and sluggishness? Other people are sacking and lighting Pergamum on fire – and are you fellows arriving just now from the ships?' That was what he said and suddenly, when he didn't receive a reply that was convincing, he realized that he had fallen into the midst of the enemy. He looked stunned and drew back his checked foot along with his voice. He was just like a man who has crushed a serpent that he didn't see while going through the rough thorn-bushes, and in a sudden fright he moves back when the snake rises up in its anger and puffs out its dark and swelling neck. That was just how Androgeos was, recoiling in terror at the sight of us – and moving back from us. We make a charge at them and surround them with a thick wall of weapons, and due to their ignorance of their surroundings they became frightened, so we take them and kill them as we catch them.

"Fortune was kind to us in our first effort, and here we are, happy and excited with our success, and so Coroebus, his spirits rising, says: "O comrades, friends, let's take the first road of safety that Fortune first offers to us, and let's do what she approves. Let's change our shields and put on Greek insignias from the ones that are here. Whether this is wrong and deceptive or courageous, what does it matter when you are dealing with an enemy? Our dead enemies right here will give us our weapons.' Saying this, he then puts on the crested helmet of Androgeos, and his shield with beautiful bronze, and he places the Greek sword to his side. Rhipeus does this, and so does Dymas, and all the young men were happy to do this – each man arms himself with the newly won spoils.

"And so we move on, mixed up among the Greeks, and with hardly a god protecting us, and through the blind night we fight many battles, and we send many Greeks to Hades. Some of them flee back to their ships, and some hurry back to the safe shores; some of them also climb back into the horse again because of their great fear, and they try to hide in its familiar womb.

"But no! It's wrong for men to put faith in things when the gods are unwilling. Look! Here comes Priam's daughter, the young girl Cassandra – she is being dragged, with her hair streaming all over the place, dragged from the temple and shrines of Minerva, pointlessly stretching her blazing eyes to the heaven. She had to use her eyes, because chains encircled her tender wrists. Coroebus, his soul set on fire by this, could not bear the sight of his Cassandra in chains, and so he threw himself in the middle of the group, onward toward death. All of us follow him and we rush in with our arms at the ready.

"At this point from the high peak of the temple above we are overwhelmed by the weapons of our own people, and a most tragic slaughter happens due to the appearance of our Greek arms and the confusion regarding our Greek crests. Then the Greeks themselves, with a shout of anger about the girl we just stole back from them, they gather together and attack us. Ajax fights the most fiercely, and the two sons of Atreus, and the entire army of Dolops. The scene is just like when a hurricane bursts forth and diverse winds clash against one another – the west and south and east winds, the last one proud of his eastern steeds. The forests groan as well and Nereus, with foam all around him, is savage with his trident and he makes the sea roar from its lowest depths.

"There even appear those whom through the dark night and its shadows we had earlier chased off by means of our trickery and had driven to other parts of the city. They first recognize that our shields and that our weapons are deceptive, and then they note that our speech has a different tone to it. Immediately they overwhelmed us with their numbers, and Coroebus is killed by the right hand of Peneleus right next to the altar of the warrior goddess. And Rhipeus falls as well – the most just and honest man of all the Trojans. He was also the greatest protector of what is right – but the gods had another plan in mind for him. Hypanis and Dymas die, cut down by their fellow Trojans. And as for you, Panthus, you found that neither your goodness nor your priestly garments of Apollo could cover you as you slid to your death. I call as witness the ashes of Troy and the funeral flame of my people – I call on you to witness that in your downfall I did not avoid weapons or battles and that if the fates had decided that I should have died at the hands of the Greeks, then I would have earned it that night.

"From that point we are torn away, Iphitus and Pelias along with me – Iphitus is now old with many years, and Pelias is slow-footed because of a wound from Odysseus. Straightaway we are called by all the noise to palace of Priam.

"Here indeed a mighty battle is taking place, just as if there were no wars anywhere else, as if no-one else were dying throughout the city. In this place we see the unstoppable god of war, Mars, and Greeks rushing toward the roof, and the gateway besieged with a tortoise-shell of shields. Ladders cling to the walls and men struggle to climb them under the very doorposts. With their left hands they hold up protecting shields against the spears, and with their right hands they tied to grasp hold of the top of the walls. For their part the Trojans are tearing down their towers and the roofs of all their buildings. With these things as weapons and missiles, for they sense that the end is near, they are preparing to defend themselves up to the very moment of death. And they send rolling down onto the enemy the golden rafters and the finely decorated ceilings of their ancestors. Other Trojans have gone down to the ground and with their drawn swords they are blocking the gates from inside, and they stand shoulder to shoulder ready to fight. Our spirits are moved to bring help to the palace of the king, and to relieve our men there with our assistance, and to add a fresh force to the defeated.

"There was an entrance and secret doors, and a passage that ran from house to house under Priam's palace, and there was a gate left behind at the back, through which, while the empire still stood, poor Andromache often was accustomed to take herself unaccompanied to see Hector's parents, taking her son Astyanax with her to visit his grandparents. I slip in through this door, and I climb to the highest part of the roof, where the luckless Trojans were throwing their missiles in vain. A tower stood on the edge, rising toward the heavens from the rooftop, from which point all of Troy could be seen – this is where we used to go and view the Greek ships and their camps. We gather around this tower and, just where its topmost levels offered the weakest joints, we ripped it from its lofty perch and thrust it forward at the enemy. And with that sudden fall it brings a thunderous destruction, and it crashes down upon a great number of Greeks. But others, even more Greeks, still come onward, and there's no letup in the hail of rocks and the missiles of every kind do not cease.

"Just before the entrance of the palace and the front gate is Pyrrhus, the son of Achilles, was proudly dancing about, flashing forth with the bronze light of his weapons. He looked just like a snake that has fed on poisonous plants and kept hidden the entire winter in the cold earth, but now it suddenly emerges into the daylight, with its skin cast off, is once again renewed. Glistening in its youth, with its breast lifted upward the snake coils along its slithering back, and towers toward the sun and flicks its three-forked tongue out of its mouth. Pyrrhus looked just like that snake.

"And with him are huge Periphas and Automedon, his armour-bearer and the man who drove the horses of Achilles. With him as well are all the young men from Scyros, who are approaching the palace and they throw flames onto the roof. As their leader Pyrrhus himself grabs hold of a battle-axe and with it he smashes through the hard stone of the gateway, tearing the bronze-plates hinges from their doors. Then he cut a panel out of the mighty timber of the door, and he made a gaping hole, a window into the palace with a wide view. The house inside is now before their eyes and its long halls are made bare. The inner chambers of Priam and the kings of old are open to view, and the people inside see armed men standing on the very threshold.

"But inside the house there was confusion, shouting, and moaning – and deep in the heart of the hollow chambers the house rang with the cries of women. Their cries reach as far as the golden stars. Then through the huge palace frightened mothers wander and they fix themselves to the doorposts, embracing them and kissing them. But Pyrrhus presses on with the power and strength of his father. No bars nor any guards themselves are strong enough to stop him. The gate is tottering under the repeated blows from the battering ram, and the doors, wrenched away from their sockets, finally fall forward. An opening is made with force. The Greeks come storming through inside, and they kill the guards and they fill the wide halls with their soldiers. No foaming river, when it breaks its barriers, has overflowed and with its torrent overwhelmed the resisting banks – no overflowing river has had as much fury as those Greeks that night – even greater than that river that rushes furiously down upon the fields in a great wave, and all the cattle and their pens are swept all over the plains.

"I myself saw Neopteolemus [Pyrrhus], mad for the slaughter, and the twin sons of Atreus on the threshold. I saw Hecuba and her hundred daughters, and I saw Priam polluting with his own blood the altars and fires that he himself had sanctified. Those fifty famous bedrooms, the great hope of offspring, the doors that stood proud with spoils and barbaric gold – they fall. The Greeks now control everything that isn't destroyed by fire.

"Perhaps you may also ask what happened to Priam. When he saw that his city had been captured and had fallen, that the gates of the palace had been wrenched off and that the enemy was in the very heart of his home, the old man pointlessly put on his long-unused armour on his aged and trembling shoulders, he takes hold of his useless sword and made his way to the thick of the enemy to meet his death. In the middle of the palace under an open sky there was a large altar and near to it was an old laurel tree that leaned over it and embraced the household gods with its shade. Right at this spot, around the altar here, Hecuba and her daughters huddled together in vain, just like doves who were driven down in a black storm, and they sat there with their arms around the statues of the gods.

"When she saw Priam equipped and ready with the arms of his youth, she said: 'My poor husband, why are you armed like this? This is madness? Where are you rushing? It's too late to make an armed defence, for any kind of help like that – it would be too late even if my Hector himself were here. Please, come here. This altar will be a protection for all of us, or you will die with us.' With those words she took the old man toward her and she found him a place at the altar.

"But look! Suddenly there was one of his sons, Polites. He was trying to escape the murderous Pyrrhus, and so he fled, wounded, through the armed enemies and down the long halls. And Pyrrhus presses on right after him, eager to strike, pushing him with his spear and at any moment on the point of catching him. Polites finally came in front of the eyes of his parents, fell down right in front of them, and died with his blood pouring out in front of them.

"Death was now everywhere around Priam, but he didn't hold back, nor did he spare his voice and anger. He shouted out: 'If there is any righteous power in heaven that cares about acts such as these, I pray that the gods will repay you properly for this crime and that they will give you the reward that you deserve! You made me watch my own son's murder, right before my eyes, defacing me and defiling me with death. You're not the son of Achilles! You are a liar – he didn't treat his enemy Priam like this. No, he respected the rights of a suppliant – he gave me back the death-pale body of Hector so that I could bury it, and then he let me return to my kingdom.'

"And after he said these things the old man threw his weak and harmless spear. It was quickly pushed away by the clanging bronze shield and it hung uselessly from the raised centerpiece. Pyrrhus said to him: 'So then go, you just then go to my father as my messenger, and you tell him all this – especially this terrible thing that I have done and how I've disgraced him. Go ahead. Now you die!' And then he dragged Priam, who was trembling and slipping in the pool of his own son's blood, right up to the altar. He wound one hand in Priam's hair and the other one he raised his shining sword and buried it deep into Priam's side as far as the hilt.

"Priam's destiny finished like this. This was the fated end for him – to see Troy all in flames and its citadel destroyed. This man who had been the proud ruler of so many peoples and lands in Asia. His great body lies there, decapitated, on the shore – the head hacked off from the shoulders, a corpse without a name.

"It was then for the first time that I understood the horror that was all around me. I stood there amazed, stunned, and suddenly there rose into my mind the image of my own father, as I looked down upon the king, who was his equal in age and was breathing out his last due to that cruel wound. There also came into my mind the image of my wife Creusa, who I had left behind, the thought of my house that was about to be destroyed and plundered, and the fate of my young son Iulus. I look back and I scan the forces of men who are fighting around me. Everyone exhausted, they have all either left me and thrown their bodies from the roof to the ground or they dropped their suffering bodies into the flames.

"And now I was left alone, I caught sight of the daughter of Tyndareus, Helen, keeping watch at the doors of the temple of Vesta, where she was staying quietly and hiding. The bright fire gives me light as I wander around and I cast my eyes here and there over the scene. She, this Helen, fearing the anger that the Trojans would have against her because of the overthrow of Troy, fearing the anger of the Greeks, and fearing the anger of Menelaus, the husband she had abandoned – she, this woman who was sent to be a Fury and the undoing of both her homeland and ours, had hid herself away and was crouching, this miserable creature, right by the altars.

"A fire blazed up in my heart – I start to feel an angry desire to avenge my ruined country and to make her pay the penalty for her crimes. I said these words: 'So this woman will still live to set eyes on Sparta and her native Greece once again, and she's going to have a parade as a queen in the triumph she has won? Is she going to see her husband and her home, her parents and children, served by a train of Trojan servants and Trojan slaves? Did Troy die by the sword for the sake of this woman? For her sake did Troy burn up in flames? For her was the Trojan shore so often soaked in blood? No! Although there's no real fame worth remembering that can be won by punishing a woman, and such a victory doesn't deserve any praise – all the same, I am going to win praise wiping out this evil and for exacting a punishment against her that she so richly deserves! I'll also take such pleasure in feeding the flames of vengeance that are in my heart, and I'll satisfy the ashes of my people.'

"I was throwing out such things and I was rushing forward in a furious mind, when my loving mother [Venus], never before so clear in front of my eyes, offered herself for me to see, in pure radiance and gleaming through the darkness of the night. She revealed herself as a goddess just as the gods in heaven see her, and she caught me by the hand stopped me, and she spoke these words with her rosy lips: 'My son, what is this anger that could be so strong to stir up this wild fury within you? Why this rage? Where is all the love that you used to have for me? Won't you go to first consider where you have left your father Anchises, who is old and crippled with age, and whether your wife Creusa and your son Ascanius are still alive? The entire Greek army is prowling around them and they would have been carried off by the flames or slashed by the enemy swords if my loving care were not there to protect them.'

"She continued: 'My son – it's not the hated beauty of that Spartan woman Helen that is responsible, nor is it Paris that is to blame. Rather, it's the gods, the unrelenting and cruel gods that are to blame – they are the ones who are overturning the wealth of Troy and making it fall headlong from its lofty position. Take a look around you – I am going to tear away all the cloud that encircles and covers you and is obscuring your mortal vision. You are my son and so you shouldn't be afraid to do what I command. So look out now – here where you see the shattered piles and the rocks that have been torn away from rocks and waves of smoke mixed with dust, Neptune [Poseidon] is shaking the walls and the foundations of the city with his great trident, and he is tearing up the entire city from its base. Here also you can see Juno, the most cruel of all, who is the first to seize the Scaean gates at the front of Troy, and she is standing there with her sword at the ready and she furiously calls in enemy reinforcements from their ships.'

"And still my mother spoke: 'Now look even at the highest towers of Troy. Turn your head there and you'll even see that Pallas Athena is already sitting on the very top of your citadel, gleaming out from her storm cloud and fierce with her Gorgon-shield. It's my father Zeus himself who is giving courage to the Greeks and making them strong. He himself is stirring up the gods against Trojan arms. You have to escape, my son – you have to put an end to your struggle here and flee quickly. I will never leave you..and I'll put you down safely right now beside the entrance to your father's door.' Thus spoke my mother, and then she covered herself up in the thick shades of night. And there before my eyes I finally saw the dreadful vision that she mentioned – all the gods in their might, acting together as enemies of Troy.

"At that moment it seemed to me that the whole of Troy was sinking into the flames and that Neptune's city of Troy was being overturned from its very base. It looked just like an old ash tree that is high in the mountains, that farmers have been hacking away at with blow upon blow of their double-edged axes, trying very hard to bring it down. Again and again, the tree threatens to fall, it shakes from its trembling foliage and the head of the tree nods forward until if finally little by little it is overcome by its wounds, so it gives out one last groan and then it breaks, spreading its ruin all along the ridge. At that moment Troy reminded me of that tree. So I quickly go down and, with the god leading me, I make my way through the enemy and the flames. Weapons make way for me and the flames drew back for me.

"And now, when I had arrived at the door of my father's house, my ancient house as well, my first wish was to take my father to the high mountains so I was searching for him. But he refuses to go on living and endure exile now that Troy has been laid low. He cried to me: 'You – you and people like you who are young and have fresh blood, and whose strength stands solid in its native vigour, you people must attempt to flee...But as for me, if the gods above had wanted me to lead a longer life, they would have protected this home for me. I've already seen of this city and survived its capture, and that was more than enough for me. Therefore you can say goodbye to my body that will lie here; say your goodbyes and then you can depart. I'm going to find death with my hand, just like a soldier would do. The enemy won't take any pity on me, but will seek my spoils. I can bear the lack of a burial. I've long been hated by the gods and have lingered in this life for a long time, ever since the father of the gods and the king of men breathed on me with the winds of his bolt and touched me with his fire.'

"So my father persisted, saying and recalling such things, and he could not be moved from his spot. But opposite him we were all spread out in tears – my wife Creusa, and Ascanius, and the whole house – all of us begging my father that he not bring destruction down on us along with him, and saying that when fate is bringing destruction already, he shouldn't wish to add more weight to its blows. He still refuses, clings to his purpose, and remains in his seat. So again I rush in to bear arms and in my complete misery I hope for death. For what plan was open to me now? What fate was now out there for us? 'Did you think, father, that I would be able to run away and just leave you here? Did such an unspeakable thing fall from a father's lips? If the gods above make the decree that nothing in this city is to survive, and if your mind is fixed on this and it's your pleasure to throw yourself and those you love into the city of Troy that is about to die, for the gate lies open for those very deaths. And very soon Pyrrhus will be here, all covered in the blood of Priam – that man who slaughters a son before the eyes of his father, and the father who is at the altar. Was this the reason, dear mother, that you took me here amid weapons and fires, so that I might see the enemy in the heart of my home, and that I might see Ascanius and my father and Creusa next to here – that I might see them slaughtered, with their blood all mixed together? Arms men, bring in the arms! The final light is calling the defeated. Give me back to the Greeks. Let me go back and rejoin the battle. Never on this day will we all die unavenged!'

"So once again I strap on my sword and I press my left arm to my shield, fitting it on, and I was bringing myself quickly out of the house. But look – right on the threshold my wife was grasping my feet and clinging to me and she was stretching forth little Iulus to his father. She said: 'If you are going away to die, then take us with you to share your fate. But if from your previous experiences you place some hope in the arms that you've put on, then first protect this house. To whom are you going to abandon little Iulus, to whom with you abandon your father, and what about me, once called your wife?'

"Crying such things she filled the entire house with her pain. When suddenly a miracle appeared, that was wondrous to tell. For between the hands and faces of the sad parents – look! – from the top of the head of Iulus, a small ray of light seemed to pour out from him and the flames seemed to lick around soft hair and feed off his forehead without causing him any harm. We were trembling with fear and we hurried to shake out his burning hair and put out this holy fire with water. But my father Anchises was happy and lifted his eyes to the stars and he stretched forth his palms to the sky and raised his voice: 'O almighty Jupiter, if you are moved at all by any prayers, please look to us – this is all we ask – and if we deserve it through our piety, then give us help, o Father, and confirm this omen!'

"The old man had barely spoken when with a sudden bang there was thunder on our left and a star fell from the sky, from the heavens, through the darkness and drawing a fiery tail with its great torch of light. We watch it glide over the highest roofs of the houses and bury itself, still shining bright, in the woods of Mount Ida, leaving its path marked out behind it – a broad stretch of light, and the whole place all around smelled of sulphur.

"At this sight my father was at last convinced and he lifts himself to his feet and he addresses the gods and prays to this holy star. 'Now there is no delay. I follow and, wherever you lead, I am there. O gods of my fathers, save my house, save my grandson! This sign is yours, and Troy stands in your mighty hands, in your will. Yes, my son, I yield and I don't refuse to go with you and be your companion.'

"He stopped there, and now through the wall of the city the fire is heard more clearly, and the fiery heat rolls closer. 'Come then, dear father, place yourself on my neck. On my shoulders I'll carry you – this task won't weigh me down a bit. However things may turn out, we two will have one common danger, and there will be one salvation for the both of us. Let small Iulus come along with me, and let my wife follow behind closely. As for you, household servants, turn your minds to what I say. As you leave the city there is a mound and an ancient temple of lonesome Ceres, with an old cypress tree nearby, which was preserved for many years through the reverence of our fathers. We're all going to go to that one spot from our various directions. You, father, take in your arms the sacred things and the gods of our fatherland. As for me, since I am fresh from battle having left such recent bloodshed, it would be wrong of me to touch these things until I can wash myself with some running water.'

"I said these things and over my broad shoulders and lowered neck I place the covering of a skin from the golden lion, and I bend down to take up the weight of my father. Little Iulus clasps himself to my left hand and he follows his father with his unequal footsteps. Behind that my wife follows. We carry on through the shadows and, even though no shower of missiles nor any Greeks massing in opposition could so recently frighten me, I am now scared by every breeze and startled by every sound, since I am so nervous and fearing for the lives of my companions and my fate.

"And now I was getting close to the gates, and I seemed to have avoided everyone on the way out, when suddenly crowding around my ears the sound of marching feet is heard and my father is looking through the darkness and shouts: 'Son, flee, my son flee! They are getting close to us! I can see their glowing shields and their shining bronze.' Here in my terrible confusion some terrible and unfriendly god – I don't know which one – tripped up my mind. For while I was moving down the secret paths and leave behind the streets that I know so well – o no! – my wife Creusa has been ripped away from me by some miserable fate. Did she stop? Did she wander away from the road or did she sit down due to exhaustion?

"I don't know what happened. But she wasn't returned to my eyes, nor did I take a look back for my lost love, nor did I even have a thought about her, until we arrived at the mound and the sacred home of ancient Ceres. Here at last, when everyone was gathered, she alone was missing, and she was not with her child and her husband. I was so upset – what man or god did I not reproach in my frenzy? What crueler sight did I see in the overturned city? I entrust Ascanius and my father Anchises and the Trojan gods to my friends and I hide them all in a hollow cave. Then I myself seek the city again and put on my shining arms. I am determined to renew every disaster and risk, and I plan to retrace the whole way back into the city and once again to expose my head to great dangers.

"At first I seek once again the walls and the dark thresholds of the gates, through which I left the city. I take note of and follow the footprints that I can see, and I search through the dark night with a careful eye. Everywhere terror fills my heart, and the silence itself scares me. Then I turn myself toward the house, if by chance she had somehow perhaps made her way back there. But the Greeks had all rushed in and were filling up the entire house – and the devouring fire was being pushed toward the roof by the wind. The flames tower above, and the heat travels toward the sky.

"I go forward and once again I see the citadel and the house of Priam. And now in the empty front halls of the sanctuary of Juno both Phoenix and hard-hearted Ulysses were chosen to guard over and protect the loot. Here from everywhere were all the Trojan treasures – torn away from burning shrines, tables of the gods, bowls made of solid gold, and all kinds of plundered clothing... all of this is heaped up in a pile. And young boys and frightened woman stand around there in a long line.

"I even dared to throw out my voice through the shadows and I filled the streets with my shouts, and sadly moaning again and again I called Creusa's name over and over – all to no avail. But as I was rushing around the buildings of the city in my frenzied search, the sad phantom and ghost of Creusa herself rose before my eyes, but an image that was larger than she was in life. I was stopped in my tracks; my hair stood out on end; my voice stuck in my throat. Then she spoke to me thus to help ease me of my cares. She said these words: 'O dear husband, why are you so ready to give yourself over to such mad bouts of frantic grief? These things don't happen without the approval of the gods. That you can take away Creusa from here as your companion is not possible – the king of Olympus above does not allow it. Your fate is a long exile, and you must cover a vast stretch of sea. And you'll eventually come to the land of Hesperia, where the Lydian Tiber flows with a smooth advance through rich fields of farmers. When you get there you'll have happy days, kingship and a royal wife. Wipe away the tears for your beloved Creusa. I'll never get to see the proud homes of the Myrmidons or the Dolopians, and I'll never go to be a slave of Greek women – I, who am a Trojan woman and the wife of the son of divine Venus... But the great mother of the gods keeps me here on these shores. And now farewell, and protect the common love of our child.'

"When she said these things, she left me crying and wanting to tell her so much more, and then she fades away into thin air. Three times I tried to throw my arms around her neck; three times her phantom image fled my arms, clasped in vain – she fled me just like a light breeze and as light a dream in flight. Then at last, when the night ended, I went back to my companions.

"And here I discovered that a huge number of new companions had gathered, mothers and men, an army brought together for exile – but a pitiable crowd. They came in from all directions, ready to follow me with all their hearts and resources to whichever land on the sea I would want to lead them. And now Lucifer (the Daystar) was rising above the top peaks of Mount Ida and was leading in the day. The Greeks were guarding the gates, it was all blocked up, nor was there any hope of rescue. I yielded and, taking up my father, I left for the hills."

Translated from the Latin by Stephen Russell, PhD
English text by Stephen Russell and Laura Holtebrinck